Women's Identities at **War**

Women's Identities at

GENDER, MOTHERHOOD, AND POLITICS IN BRITAIN AND FRANCE DURING THE FIRST WORLD WAR Susan R. Grayzel

THE UNIVERSITY OF NORTH CAROLINA PRESS

CHAPEL HILL AND LONDON

Manufactured in the United States of America
Set in Monotype Garamond and Gill types by Tseng Information Systems
The paper in this book meets the guidelines for permanence and durability of
the Committee on Production Guidelines for Book Longevity of the Council
on Library Resources.
Library of Congress Cataloging-in-Publication Data
Grayzel, Susan R.
Women's identities at war : gender, motherhood, and politics in Britain and
France during the First World War / by Susan R. Grayzel.
  p. cm.
Includes bibliographical references and index.

1. World War, 1914–1918 — Women — Great Britain.   2. World War, 1914–1918 —
Women — France.   3. Women — Identity.   4. Women — Great Britain — History —
20th century.   5. Women — France — History — 20th century.   I. Title.
D810.W7G665   1999
940.53′082 — dc21   98-47607
                CIP

03 02 01 00 99   5 4 3 2 1

Some material in Chapters 3, 4, and 6 previously appeared in somewhat different
form in the following articles:

"The Enemy Within: The Problem of British Women's Sexuality during the
First World War." In *Women and War in the 20th Century: Enlisted with or without Consent,*
ed. Nicole Dombrowski (New York: Garland Press, forthcoming). Used with
permission of the editor and Garland Press.

"Mothers, Marraines and Prostitutes: Morale and Morality in First World
War France," *International History Review* 19, no. 1 (Feb. 1997). Used with
permission of the editors.

" 'The Mothers of Our Soldiers' Children': Motherhood, Immorality, and the War
Baby Scandal, 1914–1918." In *Maternal Instincts: Motherhood and Sexuality in Britain,
1875–1925,* ed. Claudia Nelson and Ann Sumner Holmes (Houndsmills, Hampshire:
Macmillan, 1997). Used by the permission of Macmillan Press.

" 'The Outward and Visible Sign of Her Patriotism': Women, Uniforms, and
National Service during the First World War," *20th Century British History* 8, no. 2
(1997). Used by the permission of Oxford University Press.

ISBN-13: 978-0-8078-2482-5 (cloth : alk. paper)
ISBN-13: 978-0-8078-4810-4 (pbk. : alk. paper)

FOR MY FAMILY

CONTENTS

ILLUSTRATIONS

ACKNOWLEDGMENTS

This book is the culmination of my attempts to answer questions that I have been pondering since I was an undergraduate, although not in any way a definitive answer to them. In that sense, it owes its existence to historical circumstances (the creation of Greenham Common and the revival of the feminist peace movement in the 1980s, for instance, which sparked a series of ongoing personal, political, and intellectual interests) and to the generosity of many individuals.

I want first to thank the following institutions for the support that enabled this work. I am most indebted to the University of California at Berkeley, its graduate division, and especially its department of history for funding the bulk of the original research. And at later stages, the Andrew J. Mellon Foundation gave me the gift of a year for writing and revision; a Bernadotte E. Schmitt Grant from the American Historical Association allowed for follow-up research; and the University of Mississippi helped to insure its completion. Funds from the University of Mississippi's Ventress Order subsidized the cost of the illustrations. I am grateful to all.

I am delighted that I can finally thank Joe Boone, Judy Coffin, and Deb Nord for their teaching and their support that led me to decide to enter graduate school and that I can acknowledge my long-standing debt to Susan Pedersen; from the time that she, as a graduate student, advised my senior thesis, she has both taught me and shown me how to be a historian.

Beyond its financial support, Berkeley provided a wondrous environment for an apprentice historian, and I am grateful for all I learned from my inspiring teachers and fellow graduate students. Most especially, I thank Tom Laqueur, who has tolerated my ongoing need for advice by reading many drafts with patience, good humor, and astonishing critical insight. I also owe a great deal to Susanna Barrows, who actively encouraged my journey across the English Channel and shared her knowledge of France and the Third Republic with me, and to Mary

Ryan, for her example and for teaching me how to think about gender and women's history across national boundaries. And only Sue Schweik herself knows how much her powers of critical analysis definitively shaped the discussions of gender and the literature of war that follow.

I am grateful to the staffs of all the many archives, institutions, and libraries where I conducted research, but I must single out those at the interlibrary loan office of the J. D. Williams Library at the University of Mississippi; at the Hoover Institution Library at Stanford University; at the Archives de la Préfecture de Police, the Bibliothèque Marguerite Durand, Institut Français d'Histoire Sociale, and the Salle des Périodiques at the Bibliothèque Nationale; at the Public Record Office; at the Fawcett Library, especially David Doughan; and above all at the Imperial War Museum, especially Nick Hewitt, Michael Moody, Catherine Moriarty, and Mary Wilkinson.

I am also profoundly appreciative of the many scholars who offered advice and often more direct assistance at the various stages and on various drafts and pieces of this project, most particularly: Stéphane Audoin-Rouzeau, Lisa Cody, Deborah Cohen, Alice Conklin, Nicole Dombrowski, Jean Gallagher, Nicky Gullace, Ruth Harris, Ann Sumner Holmes, Chris Johnson, Susan Kent, David Kuchta, Sheryl Kroen, Donna Landry, Philippa Levine, Laurie McLary, Laura Mayhall, Claudia Nelson, Maura O'Connor, Julian Putkowski, Lou Roberts, Lynn Sharp, Len Smith, Regina Sweeney, Sandra VanBurkleo, Jessica Weiss, Julie Wheelwright, Jay Winter, Angela Woollacott, and members of writing groups at the University of California at Berkeley, the University of Michigan, and the University of Mississippi. I am especially grateful to Laura Downs and William Irvine for their astute comments at a critical stage, and to Sonya Rose, for her insights and encouragement. For their interest and aid in transforming this project into a book, my thanks to the staff at the University of North Carolina Press, especially, Lewis Bateman, Mary Caviness, Mary Laur, and the two readers for the Press.

I also want to thank my supportive colleagues in the department of history at the University of Mississippi, and the students I have taught here, at the University of Michigan at Ann Arbor, and the University of California at Berkeley for reminding me why I am writing this book and making me think harder about how my work fits into the broad trajectory of modern European history.

Over the course of nearly a decade, I have spent many months in London and Paris and thus have accumulated significant debts there, particularly to Clare Collins, Andrea Fellows, Violaine Lecuyer, Etta Logan, Daniel Mollenhauer, and Hannah Davis Taieb for making my time in Europe so much easier and more enjoyable. I also want to say a long overdue thank you to the following community of friends for their perspective and encouragement: Jessica Beels, Branwen Gregory, Karen Heath, Roo Hooke, Lisa Hunter, Muriel McClendon, Anne Nesbet, Marcia Yonemoto, Liz Young, and Simone Davis.

This book is dedicated to my family so that I can properly acknowledge the immense support of my brothers, Jon and David, as well as my parents, Arthur and Estherann Grayzel. I am more grateful to them than they could ever know for instilling in me a love of learning and giving me the freedom to pursue it. Above all it is for the family I live with: for Sarah Grayzel-Ward, for teaching me a final lesson about motherhood's cultural construction and its daily labor and joys, and finally, for Joe Ward, colleague and true partner, whom I thank deeply for the countless times he brought his considerable skills to the reading of this manuscript and for the other myriad ways in which he returned the favor of helping get this book into print.

BRIEF CHRONOLOGY OF
THE FIRST WORLD WAR

1914
June
   Assassination of Archduke Franz Ferdinand and wife, Sophie,
      in Sarajevo.
July
   Austria-Hungary declares war on Serbia.
   French Socialist leader Jean Jaurès is assassinated.
August
   Declarations of war from Russia, Germany, France, and Britain—
      war begins; German invasion of Belgium and France.
   Women's Volunteer Reserve and Women's Defence Relief Corps
      (among other women's service organizations) set up in Britain.
   Patriotic appeal is made to French women from largest French
      women's organizations.
   First German air raid on Paris.
September
   Battle of the Marne—halts German offensive and leads to stalemate
      and the start of trench warfare by late fall.
December
   First German air raids in Britain.

1915
January
   First official reports of German violations of human rights in
      occupied France are published; launches debate over the
      children of rape in France, which lasts through May.
   Clara Zetkin appeals to socialist women across Europe to end
      the war.

March

Zetkin's appeal leads to antiwar conference of socialist women
in Berne.

April

Gas used for first time by Germany on western front.

Second battle of Ypres–German offensive.

Battle of Gallipoli begins.

The International Women's Peace Congress meets at The Hague,
with no French women attending. The largest French women's
organizations instead issue their own address to women of
neutral nations. The Hague Conference creates the Women's
International League.

May

Lusitania sinks.

Coalition government established in Britain.

Bryce Report issued after investigation into alleged German
atrocities in Belgium (U.K.).

July

First *permissions* (leaves) granted to French soldiers.

August

National register set up for men and women between fifteen and
twenty-five (U.K.).

September

Battle of Loos.

1916

January

Conscription arrives in Britain via First Military Service Bill.

February

Battle of Verdun begins (very heavy French casualties, lasts through
December).

April

Easter Rising in Ireland (U.K.).

Deportation of young women and other civilians for forced labor
(France).

May

Conscription expanded to include married men (U.K.).

Battle of Jutland.

July
> Start of the battle of the Somme, with very high casualties (lasts through November).

December
> Prime Minister Asquith replaced by Lloyd George (U.K.).

1917

February
> Revolution begins in Russia after strikes and mutinies.

March
> Wave of strikes hits France.
>
> Women's Army Auxiliary Corps created.

April
> United States enters the war.
>
> Third Military Service Bill extends conscription up to age fifty and to Ireland for the first time.
>
> French offensive at Chemin des Dames begins, followed by the first French army mutinies.

May
> More strikes in France, especially of women workers.
>
> Mutinies in French army (also in June).

June
> First U.S. troops reach France.

July
> Third battle of Ypres, or Passchendaele, an unsuccessful and costly British offensive, begins and lasts through November.

October
> Second phase of Russian Revolution leads to Bolshevik takeover.
>
> Execution of Mata Hari for espionage.

November
> Georges Clemenceau assumes position of prime minister of France.
>
> Women's Royal Naval Service created.
>
> Arrest of Hélène Brion for treason.

December
> Armistice signed between Russia and Germany.

1918

January

    Women's vote debated and passes Parliament, enfranchising most women over thirty (U.K.).

March

    German offensive on the Somme, at first successful; leads to the shelling of Paris (March–August).

    Trial of Hélène Brion.

    WAAC cleared of scandal by Commission of Enquiry.

    Treaty of Brest-Litovsk takes Russia formally out of the war.

April

    U.S. troops enter war on western front.

July

    Allied counteroffensive begins.

August

    Last German air attacks in England.

November

    Armistice signed on the 11th.

December

    Demobilization of British army begins.

    First general election in U.K. in which most women over thirty vote.

1919

February

    Debates over the vote for women begin in the Chamber of Deputies (France).

May

    Chamber votes to approve women's suffrage (France) (the measure will stall in the Senate, which will not debate the issue until November 1922, when it is voted down).

June

    Treaty of Versailles signed.

1920

July

    Creation of law to repress abortion and outlaw advertising for contraception (France).

November

    Unveiling of the Tomb of the Unknown Warrior in London and of the Unknown Soldier in Paris.

Women's Identities at **War**

Introduction

WOMEN'S IDENTITIES
AND MODERN WAR

> It is enough, if not too much, to say that there was a great and
> dreadful war in Europe, and that nightmare and chaos and the
> abomination of desolation held sway for four horrid years. . . . Men
> and Women acted blindly, according to their kind. . . . They went
> to the war, they stayed at home . . . they got rich, they got poor,
> they died, were maimed, medalled, frost-bitten, tortured, impris-
> oned, bored, embittered, enthusiastic, cheerful, hopeless, patient,
> or matter-of-fact, according to circumstances and temperament.
> —Rose Macaulay

In her 1923 novel *Told by an Idiot,* Rose Macaulay offers as neat a summation of the First World War as anyone, and a useful reminder that any
generalizations about the war and its affects on any category of social
beings, such as women, are dangerous things to make. In the current
state of historiography on gender and particularly women, it may be
just as dangerous to employ terms such as "women" and "identity."
Still, while acknowledging that "women" are culturally constructed
and that the myriad circumstances of war affected each individual in
unique ways, this book will, nevertheless, argue that the First World
War does constitute an important arena for studying collectively the

book located in specific historiographical moment

largest group of adult noncombatants' efforts to make sense of their gender and national identities at a pivotal moment of the modern era.[1]

As a starting point, here is a piece of wartime fiction. In "The Shirker," a 1915 story by popular British romance novelist Berta Ruck, a man and a woman confront each other across the dinner table. She questions why he is "afraid to face the trenches" and soon denounces him as a "shirker." In response, the man undermines his accuser simply by asking, "Are you a soldier's mother?" When the woman admits to being no one's mother, the man—an engineer working for the government—points to her greater failing: "[Germany's] women haven't refused to fill the cradle year after year—bringing up six and seven boys to be soldiers," and he triumphantly concludes the story by crying out, "It's you that are the shirker!"[2]

This exchange illustrates one powerful set of ways in which appropriate feminine behavior was defined along, perhaps, the most traditional of lines, despite the modernizing context of the First World War. Contrasted with soldiering, the dominant, gender-specific role that was explicitly denied to them, women evaded their duty not by refusing to fight, but by refusing to produce future fighters. Since it offered them a status equivalent to the soldier, motherhood provided a means by which to target and unify *all* women, to make them feel that they, too, had an essential part to play in supporting the war.

What follows will focus on the contested nature of women's loyalty to their nations and to themselves, but it will continually find that debates about women became debates about mothers. While motherhood formed the basis for no coherent, natural politics—both pacifists and patriots alike spoke for and with the voice of mothers—it became a primary way to talk about women during the war since it allowed for appeals to women across region, ethnicity, class, and even nation. By linking women with mothers and men with soldiers, wartime rhetoric stressed the "naturalness" of these normative categories, thus conveniently eclipsing other kinds of masculinity and femininity.

World War I was the first European (and ultimately global) war of the modern era to demand the full participation of both combatants and noncombatants. While this may not have been obvious in August 1914, by the time the armistice was signed on 11 November 1918, tens of millions of men and women had been mobilized to support the war effort, with millions killed or injured directly or indirectly in the participant countries. The war presented women with new opportunities for education, employment, and national service. Yet the responses of

European societies to the war's innovations and its devastating costs were as conservative as they were forward-looking.

This book analyzes the role of the war in determining the meaning of gender and of gender in determining the meaning of the war from the earliest days of the conflict through its immediate aftermath. It uncovers the multiplicity of voices in Britain and France that sought to define just what women's contributions should be during this first modern, total war. Rather than completely undermining specific assumptions about gender in each nation, the war, from its outset, paradoxically both expanded the range of possibilities for women and curtailed them by, among other things, heightening the emphasis on motherhood as women's primary patriotic role and the core of their national identity.[3]

Motherhood, defined by various wartime figures as women's fundamental contribution to the state, provided a subject onto which a range of other issues and problems—from women's work to their morality—were transposed. This meant that the maintenance of gender order in society via an appropriate maternity became a fundamental tactic of the war. Commentators continually reminded women that what happened at "home" was pivotal to what happened in the theater of war. Further, while many voices proclaimed the dawn of a new age for women, they also celebrated women's accomplishments as workers, military adjuncts, and stalwart supporters of national efforts in the most conventional of terms. In particular, voices across the political spectrum lamented what they saw as one of the war's greatest costs: the potential loss of women's childbearing capacities.

As an exercise in comparative French and British history, this book studies two of the most significant participant nations in order to chart more effectively the resilience of Western gender systems despite the upheavals wrought by the war. Looking carefully at Britain and France allows us to see both specific national patterns and structures and the striking commonalities in terms of their maintenance of older varieties of femininity. For despite differing traditions of everything from tolerance for dissent to the strength of their respective women's movements, to the initial structures of their military, to the wartime distinction between being occupied in part by an invading army or not, I have been struck by how similarly these two nations defined the broader issues raised about women and gender during the war.

While an ever-growing literature on gender and war has focused largely on national studies, by looking at these two nations in tandem we can begin to distinguish what impact the war had on gender across national boundaries. Britain and France endured the full extent of the war together, allied in defense of rhetorically similar goals. They provide an important and useful setting for the analysis of how truly limited were any transformations for western European women's gender identities over the entire course of the war years.

For example, the sources that illustrate women's political struggles during and immediately after the war reveal crucial differences between the French and British states and their respective "feminist" movements. British feminists assembled and safeguarded the records of their organizations, and their archives as well as the publications of the feminist and mainstream press have largely been preserved.[4] In France, where feminists also created important archival collections, many of the richest accounts of their activities are found not in organizational minutes but in the archives of the Prefect of Police and the Sûreté, in police reports on meetings that were neither illegal nor, in most cases, places for the expression of ideas that threatened the war effort. What this might suggest about a more "liberal" British state and a more "centralized" French state is, of course, complicated by the existence of strictures like wartime Britain's Defence of the Realm Regulations that stifled civilian expression, mobility, and behavior.

There are, of course, other key distinctions. Britain had a predominantly Protestant populace, versus France's predominantly Catholic one; Britain was the much larger imperial power and more concerned with the quality of its population, while France, since its defeat in the Franco-Prussian War and the rising strength of its more populous rival Germany, was a state obsessed with its falling birthrate and with the quantity of its population. Nonetheless, the language of wartime politicians, activists, journalists, writers, and producers of popular culture on both sides of the channel resonates with one another. Both sides emphasized women's central importance as either threats to or supporters of men and morality. More significantly, in each nation women were portrayed as necessary to a postwar recovery built on creating and sustaining stable population growth; indeed, expressions of anxiety about women's behavior in relationship to reproduction seem only to have become more similar in both countries over the course of the war.[5] Given both nations' increasing wartime concern with population growth, many viewed women as problematic participants in the national effort in both states and instead insisted on motherhood as defining the national duty and identity of all women. Much of this book will investigate where, when, and why different emphases were placed on French and British wartime motherhood, but it will also repeatedly uncover how, even in seemingly unrelated public debates, motherhood could be used to call upon women regardless of their nationality.

This war took place on so massive a scale that it would appear to have altered society and culture so profoundly that it marks one of the formative moments of the twentieth century or, indeed, the end of the long nineteenth century. From the political changes associated with new government policies to the emergence of surrealist art and modernist literature, the First World War has been viewed as marking a violent transition from one era to the next. Starting with Paul Fussell, who argued that something as fundamental as "modern memory" came into being with the war, some scholars have tried to demonstrate that many new cultural practices and important government policies directly emerged from this war, while others have stressed continuities with the prewar era but noted the war hastened the spread of these practices and policies.[6]

The enfranchisement of many of Europe's women in the war's aftermath has also led historians to focus on the influence of the war on women's lives and gender relations. Yet, this study suggests that one should be cautious about drawing conclusions about a British state more open to granting women the full rights of citizens than France's; both French and British feminists during the war believed that popular opinion had been won over to women's suffrage, whether by virtue of their services to or their sacrifices for the state. However, wartime evidence from these two western European allies indicates that even as many public voices praised women's heroism and service—their newfound "citizenship" or "civic mindedness"—they feared that women's supposedly new attitudes to work and life also posed a threat to the maintenance of the social order that had to be contained.

Recent national studies by Susan Kent on Britain and Mary Louise Roberts on France have analyzed the "reconstruction" of gender after the war. By implicitly assuming that the war itself so fundamentally challenged the meaning of gender roles in each country that they needed to be reworked in the interwar period, they have deemphasized continuities between the war and postwar years and between the experiences of civilians and combatants.[7] In contrast, a detailed examination of the war years themselves uncovers the specific ways in which the effects of the war were not transformative for women because of how some of the most traditional elements of the gender system became implicated in the maintenance of the war from the beginning.

In addition to the works by Roberts and Kent, recent comparative studies by Susan Pedersen and Laura Lee Downs have explored two significant twentieth-century phenomena that evolved from this war: the welfare state and gender-specific divisions of labor. Both of these books demonstrate the importance of the comparative study of transnational events. In her exploration of family policy and the origins of the welfare state from 1914 to 1945, Pedersen shows how Britain and France evolved two different strategies for the common problem of how to support families. Downs uses French and British case studies to explore the development of what was a decisively transnational phenomenon between 1914 and 1939, the way the workplace reflected assumptions about women's inequality.[8] Taken together, these books show that because of the similarities and differences in each nation's attitudes toward women, the family, feminism, and the polity, comparisons between Britain and France yield a deeper understanding of the causes and meanings of political and cultural changes both in these individual nations and across Europe.

Building upon these insights, this book focuses on a number of ways in which gender became a locus of evolving public debate in arenas beyond remunerative work and public policy during the war years themselves. The chapters that follow will explain why women's wartime experiences and the cultural representations, political debates, and social expectations they inspired would seem to have called into question the very meaning of gender yet ultimately reinforced fundamental aspects of women's gender identity, by continually maintaining the power of categories such as "mother." They will complicate and contextualize a specifically modern struggle over "gender" identity, the cultural set of beliefs constructing "women," in terms of both femininity and the "female" body.[9] Some historiography about women and the First World War has emphasized either the war's breaking down of old barriers or its destruction of the prewar feminist movement. In these scenarios, the war either benefits or hinders women's struggles for equality. A large portion of this literature has also documented the specific activities assumed by women during the war, like nursing or munitions work.[10]

I am not interested in returning to debates about whether the war was "good" or "bad" for women. I want instead to uncover a more complex wartime gender terrain, one that includes a strong feminist presence and new forms of sexual subjectivity that were circumscribed by older assumptions, by internal and external restrictions on changing the meaning of gender for women. A transnational study reveals that women's experiences and understandings of the war were not just defined within each nation or in terms of specific occupations but were created in tandem with a wide range of cultural ideas about gender. If some women in Britain joined the armed forces and certain French women ran villages in occupied France, these steps toward occupying new public and civic spaces did not mean that they were spared the grief, dislocation, and even guilt caused by massive death tolls. Nor were they immune from the heightened anxiety about national survival in terms of population. Whatever they did, they were always "women," usually regarded as potential or actual mothers. As such, they had performed crucial cultural, ideological, and emotional work to preserve and empower the nation.[11]

Even though Britain and France began the war with very different sorts of armed forces, by the middle of the war, conscription existed in both nations, with military service providing the core of masculine identity. However, whatever assumptions have been brought to the traditional study of war as involving two separate and gendered spheres of "home front" and "front line," contemporaries viewed women as being central and active participants in societies mobilized for the first modern, total war. There was a continuum between these spheres as the war was constantly brought "home" to women. While the First World War created the concept of the "home front," it never stabilized the boundaries separating war from home. This occurred partly because the rise of mass culture provided new means of conveying experiences of war, despite censorship, to a large and avid audience. Changes in education in the late nineteenth century had produced populations across Europe, certainly in Britain and France, that were more literate and formed a national audience — of civilians as well as soldiers — for posters, cheap newspapers, and all the other artifacts of popular culture.[12]

Some scholars have focused on the variety of literary responses to the war as heralding the birth of new, modern forms of literature. The soldier-author, in particular, has come to represent an innovative form of subjectivity, one whose ironic tone and authority rely on claims of "authenticity" rooted in personal, even bodily, experience.[13] Above all, the seemingly unknowable bodily pain of warfare became the basis for denial of women's claims to speak authentically of war. Yet one counterpart to the soldier — the mother — remained his gender-specific equivalent, as childbirth provided her with another type of embodied, authentic, pain-ridden and even life-risking experience. The upheavals of the war enhanced the centrality of motherhood for constructing women's gender identity, despite the war's arriving at a moment of heightened feminist activism that helped challenge such assumptions.[14]

Rather than seeing women's identities imposed from above, solely for economic or ideological reasons, I want to insist that attention be paid to how cultural understandings about gender determined politics. If policy changes could direct the terms of specific wartime debates about women, cultural forces could both undermine and support these social mandates. As a work engaged with cultural history, this study closely examines how knowledge about women was produced. It draws on a range of texts—including novels, newspapers, posters, and cartoons—to explore the ways in which women's functions were debated and their desires expressed, and to analyze the discourse on gender, women, and war that subsequently emerged. However, it is also concerned with political changes, the material conditions that shaped women's lives, and questions of women's agency in response to the cultural cues that they received. This study therefore utilizes, for example, the records of criminal court cases as well as legislative debates. By examining the interaction between social policy and cultural media across national borders, it aims to offer a more complicated and multicausal understanding of what was happening to contemporary understandings of gender during the war.

Chapter 1 sets the cultural parameters for the war by exploring contemporary efforts to define its geography and, in particular, by revealing the instability of the divide between home front and war front. By comparing the work of such well-known male combatant authors as Henri Barbusse with a range of women writers, it reveals the creation of a shared, national war experience and the importance of women's emotional work. It further suggests, through such evidence as the testimonials about the treatment of women in occupied France and a London infanticide case attributed to "air raid shock," that the war also materially blurred the boundaries between the fronts, helping to erode the crucial divide between combatant and noncombatant.

Chapters 2, 3, and 4 reveal intense wartime concern with the bodies, particularly the reproductive functions, of women. Chapter 2 looks closely at the maternal body as a site of battle and at the vanishing line between the fronts by analyzing the representation of atrocities against women in French and British propaganda. As the British were shown the fates of "women murdered and worse" in Belgium, French civilians debated whether French women had the right to kill "a child of a boche rape." Imaginative literature in both Britain and France provided a potent way to rouse national indignation against Germany and national sympathy for war's female victims, as this chapter demonstrates how concern with rape evolved into concern with attacks on motherhood and the potentially compromised "racial" future of the nation. Chapter 3 then turns to social policy and women's labor, documenting the importance of motherhood in debates over soldiers' illegitimate offspring and in wartime anxiety about the conflicting needs to employ women in new occupations and to promote population growth. Chapter 4 continues the analysis of the wartime discourse concerning the female body by examining debates positing women's nonprocreative sexuality as a threat to both the social order and the war effort. By interpreting images of women as carriers of disease and disorder, the chapter compares French and British strategies for coping with the problems arising from "new" forms of sexual subjectivity. Despite the two nations' similar ways of defining this problem, the chapter reveals their widely divergent methods for resolving it, with Britain, contrary to expectations, instituting a much more widespread system of regulating women's bodies.

Chapters 5 and 6 analyze women's more overtly political activities: pacifist dissent, patriotic service, and struggles for political rights. They examine attempts to negotiate the contradictions between gender and national identities. Chapter 5 focuses on dissent through a case study of the treason charges leveled against French feminist Hélène Brion, who made her trial into a debate over the role of women in war. Her case provides a forum for discussing government concern with women's support for the war in the context of broader feminist pacifism in Britain and France. Chapter 6 then complicates debates about women's political rights and the limits and meanings of citizenship in the modernizing context of the First World War. After analyzing British women's struggles to obtain the emblems of national service, it compares French and British public discussions, particularly legislative debates, concerning women's civic responsibilities and political rights, especially voting, and explores the limitations imposed by a rhetoric that stressed service and sacrifice in explicitly gendered terms as women's most important contributions to the nation.

Finally, the book concludes with a brief chapter that begins to assess the war's legacy for women's gender and national identities. Taking as its focus the use of women as the chief mourners in national and local ceremonies of commemoration, it demonstrates that the grieving mother became a potent vehicle for the expression of collective memory and sorrow. The representation of feminine images on war memorials themselves also indicates that the cultural means through which wartime experiences were conveyed served to emphasize the interdependence of the fronts.

The scale of the First World War increased the importance of noncombatants, and particularly women, in the affairs of nations at war. The disruptions it caused were highly contentious, and the following discussions of wartime literature, rape, the social policing of mothers, sexual disorder, pacifism and dissent, civic participation, and mourning will illuminate interconnections across geographical and gender boundaries. They will demonstrate how motherhood served as an anchor for stabilizing gender during this total war and how the resiliency of the gender system shaped how the war was defined and experienced.

Defining the
Geography of War

CONFIGURING THE

BOUNDARIES BETWEEN

THE FRONTS

Redefining War Literature and the Fronts

The term "home front" entered into common English usage during
the First World War, intensifying the identification of the battle or war
front as intrinsically masculine and the home front as exclusively feminine.[1] This association of men with the front lines and women with the
home, of course, has a history as old as war itself. Yet, as the innovation of applying the adjectives "home" or "domestic" to the military
term "front" would suggest, the First World War involved civilians in
a way not found in any previous modern European war.

Despite the separation implied by this new language, the boundaries
erected between home and war fronts were often porous. The presumed
stability of such divisions was further challenged by the presence of
women in the invaded regions of France or women serving in the battle
zone as nurses, ambulance drivers, doctors, and, eventually, members
of the British armed forces. It was also complicated by the vast number
of male noncombatants. However, the idea of separate fronts helped
to maintain the status quo of gender identities and enabled the reinter-
pretation of popular assumptions about the appropriate roles of men
and women during the war without threatening the social order.

There were various ways in which the fronts could be crossed—

through letters, newspaper accounts, and, by the middle of 1915, the literal presence of men on leave at home and of women serving in the combat zone. Literature also proved one of the most important media for transgressing these borders and conveying, despite censorship, a diverse set of responses to the war to a broad audience of men and women. As recent studies by James Smith Allen and Joseph McAleer have shown, the populations of France and Britain during the Great War contained more readers than ever before. Allen finds that literacy was "nearly universal" in France by the end of the nineteenth century, and it had increased dramatically among women. He argues that as French audiences diversified, gradually comprising broader age groups, non-Parisians, and more social classes, "women shared to a greater extent in the world of print."[2] McAleer's study of popular reading in twentieth-century Britain draws on evidence from publishing practices to explore the rise of "lower-middle/working-class" culture, particularly its literary forms. According to McAleer, by the war's end, women "presented a large and captive market ready to be exploited by advertisers and by publishers dispensing romance and adventure." In particular, the commercialization of fiction made separating popular and mass fiction more difficult; works by romantic novelists, like Ruby M. Ayres, were meant to be both popular and "for mass consumption." McAleer provides more information about reading habits during the Second World War, yet his study of changes in publishing practices and readers' reactions to popular and mass literature suggests that British audiences during the First World War saw reading as "a popular leisure activity." Although wartime fiction generally reflected some prevalent attitudes and concerns—endorsing marriage, motherhood, and a patriotic outlook—it was also subject to the whims of the reading public. Readers' opinions and reading habits influenced sales and hence publishers' actions.[3]

This chapter draws on a variety of predominately literary accounts by British and French women and some men about their lives during wartime to analyze the cultural work of maintaining barriers between war and home.[4] While some of these texts posed specific critiques of the war and its gender arrangements, others documented the "emotional work" of patriotic, moral support that women provided to soldiers in battle.[5] The cultural reshaping of ideas about the nature of authenticity and experience that have been associated with this war depended, in part, on concrete changes in the ways in which the war was fought.

While the experience of French women under occupation challenged the division between home front and war front, the emergence of air warfare—and the air raid in particular—further blurred these boundaries, such that the crucial divide between combatant and noncombatant began to erode. Although recent scholarly attention has been paid to wartime culture and those writing from the perspective of the "home front," this chapter offers a transnational interrogation of the production of these distinctions. In order to uncover how men and women constituted their gendered identities in the context of war and imagined the circumstances of their wartime worlds, the following analysis of wartime culture examines works both produced and circulated only *during* the war, focusing on public attempts by both men and women to show the war "as it was."[6]

A Separate Experience of "War"?

In its most influential literary accounts, the First World War has been represented as a war fought heroically by men in arms who, in many cases, misled by leaders, became the ultimate victims of politicians and civilians. Yet even in the most canonical of war texts, those written by men literally scarred by battle, the gendered divides separating these combatants from civilians were both maintained *and* bridged.

Henri Barbusse has long been seen as one of the archetypal male war writers and lauded for conveying an eyewitness experience of war. In 1916, Barbusse completed *Le feu,* or, as it is known in English, *Under Fire,* during the six months in which he recovered from battle wounds.[7] Given the elevated status accorded the soldier-writer during this war, Barbusse's war service and injuries increased the novel's credibility, and *Le feu* went on to win the Prix Goncourt. First appearing as a serial in *L'Oeuvre,* it was published in full at the end of 1916 and was available in translation in England by July 1917, where, according to Samuel Hynes, it became the most widely read war novel in 1917 and 1918.[8] The British might have been encouraged to read it by reviews proclaiming that Barbusse provides "a series of extraordinarily vivid and pointed actualities which out-Zola Zola in their horror and their poignancy," or that he offered a "very full, vivacious picture of the French soldier as he appears in his various types."[9] Barbusse set out to tell "the story of a squad," the daily lives of ordinary French men at war. While its ultimate message, like that of more famous postwar novels like Remarque's *All Quiet On The Western Front,* can be read as antiwar, its more immediate concern is to present the heroism of the simple foot soldier, the French *poilu*—the equivalent of the British "Tommy."[10]

The plot of Barbusse's work, like that of Remarque's, ignores great scenes of heroic valor and focuses instead on the details of trench warfare. Barbusse begins and ends with abstract visions, but, in between, he introduces a cast of characters including not only naive youths but also fathers, workers, and men deeply connected to their homes. Barbusse also demonstrates that as their wounds are inflicted and their deaths and the circumstances of war take place, they form a cohesive whole united by common experiences of sacrifice and suffering.

Yet the women connected with them and with the nation are also embedded in his account of these soldiers' lives. First, women and men cross the borders between the battle lines and home in the letters that flew back and forth between soldiers and their lovers, wives, and mothers during the war in both actual fact and literary representation. The importance of such correspondence within the novel to the lives of the male characters cannot be overestimated. Here Barbusse introduces a scene of soldiers' letter-writing:

> A sentimental gentleness seems to have overspread little Eudore, who is . . . lost in meditation, pencil in hand, eyes on paper. . . . He has gone home.
>
> In this time of letter-writing, the men reveal the most and the best that they ever were. . . .
>
> Through their outer crust of coarseness and concealment, other hearts venture upon murmured memories . . . women and their gentleness around the shaded lustre of the lamp. (39)

In this description, the writing of letters not only reveals the combatant's "most and best" but also involves geographic mobility: "going home" to "women and their gentleness." Throughout the novel, men receive letters from home as reminders of their domestic lives and ties. A short while after the men are described writing home, a member of the company receives a letter from his mother: " 'When you get my letter,' he spells out, 'no doubt you will be in the cold and mud, deprived of everything, my poor Eugène—' He laughs: 'It's been ten days since she put that down for me, and she's clean off it. . . . We've had hard times, but we're all right now' " (82–83). The temporariness of their being "all right" underscored both maternal fears and the way in which the voicing of fears was assigned to absent women. Relative to most of the women whose presence is felt in the novel, these men will inevitably be "deprived of everything," but Biquet's laughing response to this letter showed the importance of being able to reassure those at home, and letters, in this text and others, could both alienate soldiers and civilians and link them.

Barbusse provided other examples of the continual reminders of the women back home, insisting on the naturalness of this geographic displacement and of its importance for the fighting man. Starting with a number of joking references to the popular phrase "Pourvu que les civils tiennent" (32)—which suggested that the war would be won only "if the civilians hold out"— civilians are quickly feminized.[11] The civilians encountered on brief respites from frontline duty are invariably women (67–68). Men reveal their connection to women at home by making little trinkets for them (39), or by carrying their photos as talismans into battle (55). Not only are images circulated but so are tales of time spent with women on leave, details about food eaten and kisses exchanged (99–106). Women are thus filtered through the war zone as a kind of sustenance, and going home, the ultimate object of desire, means returning someplace allegedly untouched by war.

Yet, in another account of a visit home, the soldier Poterloo finds German soldiers quartered in his house, and things "naturally" associated with home and battle front change places to a disturbing degree. Barbusse, through Poterloo's story, demonstrated that women at home could also be a potentially demoralizing element in soldiers' lives. Poterloo recounts a clandestine visit to see his wife and child in the occupied zone. Sneaking into Lens, he walks by the window where she is staying and finds her with Germans the family has been forced to house:

> I saw her plainly. . . . She was smiling. She was contented. . . . Not a forced smile, not a debtor's smile, *non,* a real smile that came from *her.* . . .
>
> Do you catch on? She was smiling, my wife, my Clotilde, at *this* time in the war! Have we only got to be away for a time for us not to count any more? You take your hook from home to go to the war, and everything seems finished with; and they worry for a while that you're gone, but bit by bit you become as if you didn't exist, they can do without you to be as happy as they were before, and to smile . . . my Clotilde, mine, who at that chance moment when I saw her, whatever you may say, was getting on damned well without me!

. . . Tell me, shouldn't I have had good reason to jump into the room, fetch her a couple of swipes.

. . . I know all right I was getting violent, I was getting out of control.

. . . She can't prevent herself from being well off, and contented, and letting her self go, when she's a good fire . . . and company, whether I'm there or not. (157)

Poterloo justifies the violence of his response by locating his wife's behavior in terms of its context, at "this time in the war," and in terms of its authenticity, "not a forced smile." The betrayal, however, seems to come from the very act of "smiling" itself, an idea he repeats throughout the account. The smile indicates her "being as happy" as before, her not only surviving but possibly flourishing, and provides the basis for the great fear of being forgotten. The importance of his need to have her *not* "getting on damned well without me" indicates the way in which changes in gender arrangements caused by the war threatened the war itself. Her smile haunts him even when he rejoins his squad as it unsettles his notions of himself as provider and protector, even though, ostensibly, he continues to perform both functions as a soldier. Further, the incident showed soldiers' dependence on women to provide that essential quality of remembering and keeping alive their absent man.[12]

Siegfried Sassoon, another canonical war writer who addressed both home and war fronts, also exemplifies the combatant-author whose words help to define the imagination of Britain's experience of war. Sassoon was also influenced by Barbusse, as the epigraph for his volume of poems *Counter-Attack* (1918) reveals: "In the desolate respite of that morning, the men who had been pinched by fatigue, whipped by the rain, [and] shaken up by thunder all night . . . remembered how much it [war] had developed in them and around them all the worst instincts without exception; wickedness to the point of sadism, egoism to the point of savagery, the need to enjoy to the point of madness."[13] In two wartime collections of poems—*The Old Huntsman* (1917) and *Counter-Attack*—Sassoon attempted to show the experience of war directly and, like Barbusse, provided references to the fighting man's domestic ties and his treatment by civilians. A review of his first book of poetry drew careful attention to poems such as "The Hero":

What Mr. Sassoon has felt to be the most sordid and horrible experiences in the world he makes us feel to be so in a measure which no other poet of the war has achieved. As these jaunty matter-of-fact statements succeed each other such loathing, such hatred accumulates behind them that we say to ourselves, "Yes, this is going on; and we are sitting here watching it," with a new shock of surprise, with an uneasy desire to leave our place in the audience, which is a tribute to Mr. Sassoon's power as a realist.[14]

Given such praise for Sassoon's "realism," how do civilians feature in his poetry? In "A Working Party," Sassoon demonstrated the ordinariness of the man who "three hours ago blundered up the trench":

> He was a young man with a meagre wife
> And two small children in a Midland town;
> He showed their photographs to all his mates
> And they considered him a decent chap.[15]

His undifferentiated "decency" is thus shown by his possessing and sharing pictures of his wife and children. Now, "he must be carried back, a jolting lump/[b]eyond all need of tenderness and care." The exploding shells have taken him beyond the world of such a family life, however figuratively it might have been carried into battle. In "Dreamers," Sassoon again wrote of how, despite being sworn to "action," soldiers were tied to the domestic, because they "think of firelit homes, clean beds, and wives."[16]

When ostensibly speaking more directly to an audience of civilian women in "The Glory of Women," Sassoon listed their faults:

> You worship decorations; you believe
> That chivalry redeems the war's disgrace.
> You make us shells. You listen with delight,
> By tales of dirt and danger fondly thrilled.
> You crown our distant ardours while we fight,
> And mourn our laurelled memories when we're killed.
> You can't believe that British troops "retire"
> When hell's last horror breaks them, and they run,
> Trampling the terrible corpses—blind with blood.[17]

Women, according to this litany, provide the basic machinery of war. They make "shells" and, more significantly, they provide the necessary moral support. Indeed they demand that men be glorious heroes—by believing the lies told of the glory of war and by worshiping "decorations," "chivalry," and "tales of dirt and danger." In short, they misread all the signs that true soldiers know to be false, choosing to crown "our distant ardours," unwilling to see "the terrible corpses." Again, among their other tasks of emotional work, which Sassoon simultaneously acknowledged and condemned, listening, remembering, and, most importantly, mourning are all construed as women's wartime activities. Mourning was the most problematic, since it remained the primary task that women "must" do, but one they failed to perform correctly. Sassoon here, too, as in "The Hero," ironically used the naive mother as the absolute counterpart to the soldier, as the speaker informs the "German mother dreaming by the fire" that her son's "face is trodden deeper in the mud." Moving beyond national boundaries, Sassoon attacked all women—although showing more sympathy for the German mother than the British one—for not sufficiently understanding, and thus continuing, war.

The bitterness of Sassoon's attack on women specifically emerges when one contrasts "The Glory of Women" with "Remorse," a poem that speaks of fathers. Here, the soldier-subject describes the nightmare of an attack, watching the Germans run while "Our chaps were sticking 'em like pigs." Reflecting on "things in war one dare not tell," he pities the "poor fathers sitting safe at home," reading "of dying heroes and their deathless deeds."[18] These fathers are not faulted for their ignorance nor portrayed as rejoicing in the glories of war as the women at home are.

Both Henri Barbusse and Siegfried Sassoon fought in the trenches of the First World War, suffered wounds, and lived to write about themselves, both as soldiers while battles raged around them and as veterans in the aftermath of the war. Their status as combatant-authors gave special legitimacy to the truth-claims each made about war as lived and embodied experiences. The visions they preserved of war have been seen as portraits of actions and thoughts that by their very nature and context excluded women and the feminine. Yet feminine and domestic concerns crept into their works in complex and important ways. Representations of femininity—either the unsettling sexualized blade of Sassoon's bayonet that "glitters naked, cold and fair" in "The Kiss" or the descriptions of letters and photos of wives and mothers that soldiers carried—easily entered the battle zone.[19] Women possessed the power to assist war or demoralize soldiers, as seen in Poterloo's encounter with his wife and Sassoon's attacks on women's "glory." The presence of women in the most male of texts illustrates how certain visions of femininity could be integrated into the experience of the battlefield.

Writing the War Back Home in Britain

Fiction by noncombatant British writers, ranging from May Sinclair to H. G. Wells, reminded their British readers of wartime costs and domestic devastation.[20] Commenting on such phenomena as Zeppelin raids and the significant presence of Belgian refugees as well as describing the losses inflicted by war, these novels documented a nation torn apart despite its seeming distance from battle lines. British women novelists like Sinclair and Rose Macaulay demonstrated how fully the war was brought home to their female characters, but in ways that only served to underscore their characters' feelings of helplessness and inadequacy. The pain of being excluded from the presumably real business of war, from fighting itself, interestingly enough leads to opposite choices regarding the war as depicted in their work.

When May Sinclair describes the outbreak of war in *The Tree of Heaven* (1917), Dorothea, the younger of her two female protagonists, feels the ravages of war through empathy. She envisions that the Belgians' "towns and villages flamed and smoked behind them" as they "felt German bayonets at their backs. . . . And there were terrible things. . . . Women and girls idiotic with outrage and grief."[21] Although Sinclair muted the graphic violence of war, and she herself had witnessed the western front, the harm experienced by civilians permeated this scene. If Sinclair did not write about mud, rats, and the thunder of guns, her readers were given smoking villages and towns, the "feel" of "German bayonets." In *The Tree of Heaven,* in response to the experience of the Belgian refugees, Dorothea wants only to escape the shame of being a noncombatant:

> And as Dorothea drove her car-loads of refugees day after day in perfect safety, she sickened with impatience and disgust. Safety was hard and bitter to her. Her hidden self . . . wanted to go where the guns sounded and the shells burst, and the villages flamed and smoked; to go . . . where the refugees had gone, so that her nerves and flesh should know and feel their suffering and their danger. She was not feeling anything now except the shame of her immunity. (301)

Recognizing that being English is the only thing that protects her, Dorothea longs to go to Flanders, in order both to help and to face the situation head on. Staying in England causes her to feel that the "war makes it detestable to be a woman" (303).

However, she becomes engaged to Frank, the man she has just realized she loves, on the eve of his departure for battle. In an effort to overcome her helplessness, she decides to volunteer as an ambulance driver but changes her mind after her fiancé convinces her not to. He acknowledges her desire "to tackle the hardest and most dangerous job. Naturally." However, he explains: "You can't expect us to fight so comfy, and to be killed so comfy, if we know our womenkind are being pounded to bits in the ground we've just cleared." As Dorothea points out, "I was thinking of those Belgian women, and the babies—and England; so safe . . .," he persuades her by saying: "You can do more for them by staying. . . . I'm asking you to take the hardest job, really" (313–14).

This exchange suggests both the actual dangers awaiting women who assisted in the battle zone and the limits to their aid. Knowing the woman he loves is safe and waiting for his return becomes far more important to the soldier than the work provided by women as comrades in arms. This insistence on women remaining feminine by not taking on masculine roles, in particular by not entering the so-called war zone, occurred in numerous wartime stories and novels by both men and women.[22] Sinclair seems to endorse this view here, even as Frank, in departing, reminds Dorothea that "it's *your* War, too—it's the biggest fight for freedom"(315). Yet these very words suggest that Dorothea's role, like that of all women, was secondary. In the end, Sinclair indicates that staying home may be "the hardest job" but one women must accept for the successful outcome of the war.

Rose Macaulay's *Non-Combatants and Others* (1916) presents a similar dilemma facing her main character, Alix Sandomir, who literally becomes sick from the war and experiences her sense of exclusion as more painful than anything else.[23] In a novel that attempts to locate noncombatants in relation to war, Macaulay offers a series of gender-specific war experiences. The novel begins with Alix staying with her cousin's family, where the two daughters Dorothy and Margot perform an endless variety of female war work in a world of specifically feminine duty. Beyond this, there is the world of traditional femininity exemplified by Evie, the daughter in the house in which Alix also stays. Finally, Alix's mother, Daphne Sandomir, represents an alternative conception of women's duty by vigorously pursuing peace activities. Aside from these female role models, Alix has the examples of her brother, a writer who detests war; his friend Reverend West, excluded from fighting on religious grounds; and the man she realizes she loves, Basil, an artist whose art has become a casualty of war. Yet the only place Alix can locate herself is as a "noncombatant," painfully cut off from everything. Macaulay, through Alix, like Sinclair, through Dorothea, demonstrates how this intense pain of not being able to participate leads on the one hand to pacifism and on the other to unqualified support for the war. The problem for each woman writer and character comes from her knowing what the war is really about and yet remaining unable to be in the midst of it.

Women also confronted old truths or new inventions caused by war such as the innovation—at least in medical terminology—of shell shock. Women were well aware of men with wounded minds as much as bodies, and such victims were not solely the province of male combatant-authors. Macaulay provides a vivid instance of this phenomena, and the entire plot of Rebecca West's *The Return of the Soldier* centers around the severity of shell shock. When soldiers came home on leave, women were not necessarily spared their nightmares, unconscious speech, and other stories they were not meant to hear.[24]

Women's representations of wartime life included what continue to be seen as the real elements of war—soldiers, violence, refugees, shell shock, and death. The front line, particularly in France, could not remain the exclusive property of male soldier-writers. Many works, of which those I have discussed are but a few examples, reflect fervent attempts to convey what women were denied the right to speak of: a war not measured by the knitting of socks but by detached bits of dead bodies. Despite the prevalence of attacks, such as Sassoon's, on those who will "never know / the hell where youth and laughter go," women were not as sheltered as Sassoon would have had his readers believe— nor did they necessarily want to be sheltered—from the "hell" into which their men descended.[25]

Nor were women the only ones troubled by their sense of exclusion from the blood and muck of war. H. G. Wells's best-selling *Mr. Britling Sees It Through* (1916) provided the perspective of those male noncombatants too old to fight while simultaneously documenting the transformation of Britain at war. The protagonist, Mr. Britling, represents a kind of idealized, English intellectual gentleman who is also curiously feminized as a mourning parent, having lost a best-loved son to the war. And as a review in *The Times Literary Supplement* noted, "One faculty which the last two years have sharpened to the last perfection . . . is the power of recognizing a mean or vulgar touch on the subject of the war. It can be said absolutely that Mr. Wells' book is not this, nor ever within sight of it." Despite its imperfections and its uncertain claim to being "great novel," it was "a proud achievement." [26]

Wells's novel deals almost exclusively with civilian life in Britain, starting with a long prewar portrayal of life in Essex. Yet in the novel's accounts of military action and reports of Belgian refugees, the war is brought decisively home. Like the women authors just discussed, Wells used a variety of means to portray the war: presenting rumors of outrage and atrocities, reports from refugees fleeing to Britain, the presence of troops training locally, and the letters sent to Mr. Britling from his soldier son, Hugh.

Hugh Britling's letters describe the boredom of trench warfare: "[T]he trenches have disappointed me. They are the scene of tiresome domesticity." Yet he also reveals its dangers: "The shell knocked me over and didn't hurt me a bit. . . . When I got up on my knees I saw Jewell lying about six yards off—and his legs were all smashed about . . . Pulped!" [27] Subplots involving a woman sending a man off to war, a young mother coping with a missing husband, and Mr. Britling's loss of his son vividly represent the range of grief and frustration experienced by both men and women at home. In the end, his son's death prompts Mr. Britling to a long discourse on the meaning of war and the prospects of peace, and he laments that "all the world was losing its sons." As he reflects on his son's death and the death of a young German family friend, Britling concludes, even while holding Germany responsible for the war, that his generation must "make ourselves watchers and guardians of the order of the world. . . . If only for the love of our dead." [28]

When Wells's book was translated and published in France as *M. Britling commence à voir clair,* some critics viewed Wells as accurately capturing the spirit of his nation and conveying a valuable lesson to Britain's ally. Gaston Rageot, in a lengthy piece in the *Revue Hebdomadaire,* wrote that Wells had managed to explain the "complicated" motivation of the young English who fell during the war. Unlike French men who died to defend their country, the representative of young England, Hugh Britling, doesn't "hate" Germany and sees the "absurdity" and "folly" of war yet is willing to make the "absolute sacrifice." Wells, through the story of the Britlings, enabled his readers to comprehend, according to Rageot, "the entire history of his homeland at war." [29] As Barbusse had done for the French combatant, Wells provided an image for the British noncombatant that transcended national borders while simultaneously conveying a specific national experience.

Like similar efforts to portray the war in light of home conditions in France and Britain, *Mr. Britling Sees It Through* conveyed the connections between the fronts. War came home in the fiction of noncombatants. As the works discussed here have all demonstrated, neither front could remain the exclusive province of one sex or the other. And as we will see, even fiction with much less serious intentions showed the omnipresence of war in domestic life.

Reading the Wartime Romance

"And I knew you would [make good]. That's why I kept on writing so faithfully. It is not much a woman can do at home in wartime, and half of us are eating our hearts out because all we can do, in comparison seems so feeble and futile."

"Feeble and Futile!" repeated Ronnie; "you're the levers! There would be no fighting in the trenches, believe me, if there were no women at home. They mean everything! They and all they stand for, are the *raison d'être* of the war."[30]

Thus goes a typical exchange in Annie Swan's *The Woman's Part* (1916), a novel illustrating the experiences of young Scottish lovers caught in the grip of war where, as *The Times Literary Supplement* put it, "everything goes well with everybody after temporary tribulations."[31] Amidst the embraces and the heartache, Swan delivers a message that has everything to do with the maintenance of morale at home, with telling women that the work of support that they performed was truly the raison d'être of war. Such subtexts can be found in a number of women's romance novels written and published during the 1914–18 war in both Britain and France. These novels provided more than a distraction for women experiencing enormous social, political, and emotional upheaval; they also served a didactic purpose of explaining and interpreting women's wartime roles. Some of these roles were far from new. Being supportive sweethearts and mothers clearly took precedence over new opportunities for economic independence or even wartime service. Yet these novels grappled with the tensions faced by predominantly bourgeois heroines who wanted to, and often did, take active parts in aiding the war effort even as they coped with unfamiliar tensions and suffering caused by the separation from, and often the loss of, those they loved.[32]

Women writers of popular fiction also insisted on their works' authenticity and topicality by trying to depict the war "accurately." Although often couched in overly sentimental language, their descriptions of battles attempted to portray a war filled as much with death as with heroism. Ruby Ayres's popular romance novel *Richard Chatterton, V.C.* (1915) depicted its hero watching waves of dead men fall back around him, witnessing "shambles of dead bodies and great yawning holes."[33] Only moments before a detailed battle scene, Ayres describes the heroine, Chatterton's beloved Sonia, thinking of

> . . . a picture she had seen recently in an illustrated paper of a crowd of laughing "Tommies" snugly ensconced in a trench, smoking their pipes and boiling tea in billy-cans.
>
> Underneath the picture had been written the legend that " 'Tommy' is always cheerful and smiling, even though the German trenches are scarcely a hundred yard away." (263)

As Sonia turns her thoughts to Chatterton, "for the first time a small, troubled doubt crept into her mind as to whether that picture had been a true representation" (263). In these two passages, Ayres not only outlined the essence of battlefield experience—death expected and received and evident everywhere—but she also pointed to the ways in which such experience was masked for civilian consumption. In doing so, she also ironized the so-called home front. By juxtaposing the battle scenes with the sanitized depiction of the Tommy in the trench, Ayres implicitly claimed that she would be delivering a portrait of the hero at war more honestly than illustrated papers would.

The Times Literary Supplement's view of such novels in wartime seems evident from the following review of *Richard Chatterton:*

> For an unambitious novelist the lines on which a war novel of the sentimental kind should run are quite simple. There must be a "well-to-do" slacker who is too much bored to enlist. His fiancée discards him in consequence and takes up with another fellow. The slacker enlists, gets the V.C. and is badly wounded. Then the two essentials are that he should hear a false report that she has married the other fellow, and she should hear a false report that he is dead. Of course, there can only be one ending; but a little spice may be added "to taste" before the happy finale in the form of a pretty nurse who . . . loves the V.C. All this is to be found in *Richard Chatterton, V.C.* And the best that can be said for it is that the writing of it (though a good deal padded) is not quite so trite and obvious as the plot.[34]

Although dismissive of such works, this review pointed to an important and repeated aspect of the British women's romance novel: the encouragement of women as crucial for men's participation in the war. From the character of the ne'er-do-well Ronnie in Annie S. Swan's *The Woman's Part*, to Chatterton in *Richard Chatterton, V.C.,* to a variety of young men in Berta Ruck's collection of short stories, *Khaki and Kisses* (1915), men who might be potential "shirkers" are spurred to action in hopes of winning the women they love.[35] Such fiction thus helped to tell women how they were supposed to act under the new circumstances of this total war. They were meant to be supportive and inspirational, performing roles with such humility as to render themselves invisible, as demonstrated in this exchange that closes *The Long Lane to Happiness,* Ayres's sequel to *Richard Chatterton:*

> "How perfectly absurd! Why, it's you they're all so excited about! Just as if I counted at all—except as a little person who is very proud to be your happy wife."
>
> "The best part of me, Sonia! If it hadn't been for you, nothing of all this would ever have happened; I might still have been rotting about London, doing nothing."[36]

True happiness at the novel's end comes from the knowledge that Sonia has inspired the heroism that has saved Richard from being a "rotter."

Berta Ruck's full-length wartime romance novel, *The Courtship of Rosamond Fayre* (1915), explored the pain of a virtuous young woman like Rosamond who loves a man she believes to be both engaged to someone else and a shirker, "for no one likes to have to associate with 'wasters' in time of War!"[37] Initially, she tries to lose herself in doing independent recruiting work, handing out leaflets to likely young men in the streets of London (295–99). Only when the man Rosamond loves appears in khaki—"as if he'd been born in it" (361)—at the end of the novel can they eventually confess their love for one another, and she can revel, especially after he returns wounded from the front, in being "a hero's wife" (371). Among other messages, Ruck informed her female readers that true love would only come from a man in uniform and that a partially disabled hero was better than any noncombatant "waster."

In Victoria Cross's *Evelyn Hastings* (1917), another wartime romance set in an unspecified war, a young wife's love is so all-encompassing that from home she knows the instance that her husband is wounded, although she confesses when he proposes that she loves the flag more than him. Through her prayers, she is even able to visit her beloved Cecil, alone and abandoned with his injuries, and thus has the strength to reject the news that he is dead. Indeed, she is able to predict the exact day and time when he does return to her. Again, the power of her faith is seen, quite literally, as sustaining her man at war.[38]

The emotional work of loving the correct man so as to prompt him to correct actions was a constant refrain in wartime romance novels, and one not limited to British texts. Living in an invaded country, French women writers showed the omnipresence of war in their lives by portraying the tensions faced by middle-class heroines who actively aided the war effort, even when their labor consisted of "emotional work," the vital sustaining of *bon morale*. One early French war novel, *La veillée des armes* (1915), by popular author Marcelle Tinayre, was praised by André Beaunier for creating a heroine who, in her patriotism and love, "resembled France a little." It was also lauded by Alice Berthet in the feminist periodical *La Française* for showing the "power of current intense emotions . . . an inestimable value for the future." Berthet also quoted approvingly Tinayre's statements regarding women's patriotism, which was "not of the same nature of that of men" because it was rooted not in "the brutality of instinct" but in love of "the hearth, the husband, the child." Berthet further praised the vivid descriptions of the women who learned how to give their men to the nation in the hours preceding mobilization in August 1914.[39]

La veillée des armes, as Tinayre explained in her preface, attempted to reflect the transformation of Paris, its men, and particularly its women from 31 July to 2 August 1914.[40] Focusing on one devoted couple, Simone and François Davesnes, Tinayre widened her lens to include all the inhabitants of their ordinary street and to document their reactions to the unfolding of contemporary events from the trial of Madame Caillaux, to the assassination of Jean Jaurès, to the newspaper headlines proclaiming the actual mobilization for war. Tracing the evolution of her heroine into a patriotic model of stoicism, Tinayre illustrates the agony produced by, and the importance of, women's support for the war. Even as one of her working-class characters, the news agent Mme. Anselme, dies from anxiety and sorrow over the mobilization of her only son, Tinayre offers a heroine who, through her tears, can say: "I let you leave, I give you to France."[41] Beyond the specific granting of her husband to the nation, Simone, in her beauty and devotion, also serves as a raison d'être for the war. A young man who dines with the Davesnes the night before his departure, reflecting on Simone's blond hair, "intelligent eyes, shaded blue and gray as the Seine beneath the changing sky of Paris," and imagining "this woman grazed by the enemy," realizes "that to defend her, it would be joyous to die" (258). If women thus provided a necessary spur to action, were the things worth defending, they also had a more specific role to play, without complaint, to "give to the *Patrie* [fatherland] the flesh of their flesh. . . . [A]ll the mothers, of all nations, . . . had children in pain, nursed them in their fatigue, fed, . . . raised, during twenty years, the beautiful young men promised to death" (203–4).

Showing the entire city weeping beneath a thunderstorm on the eve of its men's departure, Tinayre revealed the specific, parallel task of women. Painting a portrait of the city, Tinayre described a world where men had dominated the events of the day, but "during that supreme night that commenced, they [men] were going to live as lovers, as spouses, by all the forces of flesh and heart. Night gave them to woman" (264). What the night gives to women, women in turn give to the nation: "[I]n all the houses of innumerable cities, men and women loved one another, drunk on tears and caresses, during that stormy night. . . . [L]ove prepared its revenge. The course of life, on the verge of being broken off in so many places, remade elsewhere the sacred fabric of the future. Of these good-byes, a whole people would be born, and the future France would sprout from the flanks of mothers" (276). Even as women fight back their tears at the Parisian train stations and the women of the street comment that other mothers would envy Madame Anselme her premature death, the future of the nation is being preserved by the emotional and reproductive labor of the mothers of France.

Lucie Delarue-Mardrus, evoking a civilian world not restricted to real or potential mothers, self-consciously addressed the difficulty of dealing with women's lives during war by calling her 1916 novel *Un roman civil en 1914*.[42] On one level, offering a modern and undeniably war-specific courtship plot, *Un roman civil* tells the classic story of two antagonistic personalities—a dedicated physician, Francis Malavent, and his able nursing assistant, Elisabeth Clèves—who gradually come to see that they love each other. Praised in the *Mercure de France* for the "alert plume" and even comic touch of its author, *Un roman civil* was recognized as a story that revealed, through its subtle details, the effects of the war on its characters.[43] The story is set in motion by the war, which comes upon the sleepy country setting of August 1914. Lacking Tinayre's painstaking details of the events leading up to its arrival, Delarue-Mardrus announced the war's entrance in a passage that echoed other contemporaneous responses to the war, seeing it immediately as an earth-shattering rebuke to the established order and highlighting the extent to which its very presence in a domesticated atmosphere of "tangos and parties," of thoughts of "science ... progress ... pleasure and frivolity," challenged the *entire* community as a race that no longer possessed heroes (34). Yet the immediate responses seem strikingly gendered as Elisabeth faints to the ground while Jean, Francis's younger brother, acclaims the news.

The reaction of the community, not just the family, also showed readers a world both altered by war and maintaining traditional notions of gender despite the arrival of war: "All the boys sang, all the families wept. The humble, everyday [train] station became, like probably all the stations in France at the same hour, heroic" (54–55). Through the character of Francis, Delarue-Mardrus also conveyed shock at the occurrence of war in "our modern, civilized" era (63–65). Yet the voicing of doubts, as in much of wartime literature, only served to strengthen the ultimate espousal of the main characters' patriotism; love of country and belief in its justified war aims inevitably overcame the civilians' understandable antipathy to war. For the male characters, and in particular for the character of Francis in this novel, war is rejuvenating (65). For women, as we have already seen, patriotism is explicitly rendered as different because they cannot fight. Instead, the women of the community gather together to learn from Francis how to care for the wounded—"all demanding one sole thing: to serve" (74).

Yet the service rendered by middle-class women extends beyond caring for men. In one crucial exchange, overheard by Francis, Elisabeth chides the female cook for complaining: "You ought to be ashamed, when you have seven brothers in uniform, to make your voice heard. Women have nothing to do but keep silent while their men fight. It's not, in this moment, the women's turn to cry out. It's men who are suffering, and they sing. You, one asks nothing of you but that you be quiet, and you're going to be quiet!" (90).[44] At such moments the didacticism of the novel became clear. Through these words of criticism and through the model of Elisabeth, who bravely refuses to flee when news of the invasion of France is heard (100), the silent, supporting heroine, who aspires only to be worthy of the men who fight for her, was offered to the reader as a universal norm. These "norms" were meant to erase class differences among women—like the parallels created for soldiers in male war texts—and can be seen both implicitly in Elisabeth's words above and explicitly in the following passage: "Irreconcilably disparate, these small and large volunteers, united by kind, unified in their dress, formed the feminine will of the country. Thus each of these women, to do her French woman's duty, came forth from her egoism, . . . from her caste" (129–30). Here traditional feminine qualities of selflessness suggest a natural transcendence of differences among women, yet Elisabeth, the bourgeois heroine, must also tell a working-class servant how to behave, suggesting that class distinctions were not so neatly erased.

Despite the important roles played by women who appeal directly for male action, war intrudes uneasily upon the civilian world of the novel. After laughing with joy at a French victory, women readers could witness, along with Francis and Elisabeth, the horrors of the wounded (152). Such scenes, as they appeared in wartime popular fiction, served two distinct purposes. They allowed a presumably civilian audience to examine their own relationships to the soldiers, the wounded, the monstrous costs of war that they themselves were concurrently witnessing; like Francis, the audience could vicariously curse war, having likewise witnessed its devastation. At the same time, depictions of suffering, by their very presentation in the plot of such fictions, became contained and rendered explicable. The arrival of the wounded soldiers mostly served to provoke a mutual sympathy between the two protagonists: "Around the beds of the wounded, a sort of unspoken camaraderie, made with comprehending looks and smiles of approval, sometimes brought Francis and Miss Clèves nearer together" (185). The war thus might be seen as a convenient backdrop for the inevitable love story between nurse and doctor, yet the concept of "camaraderie" itself—in this case between men and women—carried with it an association with the troops and the key ingredient of military morale.

However, before leaving Francis and Elisabeth to each other—although never explicitly—Delarue-Mardrus throws in a few additional twists of the plot to suggest the strength of both her heroine and of the women of France. In a remarkable scene, Elisabeth herself denounces marriage and expresses a desire to be free and alone. Elisabeth then explains that her fainting on the day war broke out was not due to feminine fear but because "the country passed before me. I couldn't stand it. I fell. I was jealous" (223). Here is an example of women's painful sense of exclusion shaping their responses to war, including anger as well as the desire to be of use. From a love story contained within the bounds of war, women could learn a variety of morale-boosting lessons—that their services as nurses were vital, that young soldiers would gladly kill for them, that they could inspire public and private heroism, and, most profoundly, that they perhaps ultimately could hold the key to France's life or death.[45]

If *Un roman civil* showed the importance of the devoted and dedicated young nurse and *La veillée des armes* the power of wifely and motherly support, other texts illuminated wartime innovations in women's roles. Jeanne Landre's *L'école des marraines* (1917) explored the diverse responses of a group of women fulfilling the newly created and uniquely French position of the *marraine de guerre* (commonly known as *marraine,* or godmother), a woman who adopted and faithfully wrote to a soldier—who was known as her *"filleul"* or "godson"—at the front.

In January 1915, in a gesture of support to soldiers who either lacked a family to send them letters or packages or were cut off from their families in the occupied areas of France, the "Famille du Soldat"—a charitable organization to allow such men to be "adopted" by a *marraine de guerre*—was created. The *marraine de guerre* represented a new opportunity for women to exercise traditional functions of moral support, while it quickly came to be seen as providing the alluring possibility of violating norms for contact between men and women and for female conduct.[46] Given the relative anonymity of letters, *marraines* quickly became constructed not as the maternal figures that the term "godmother" would imply, but as potential objects of sexual fantasy and even fulfillment. The *marraine* prompted varying reactions (some of which will be discussed in Chapter 4). For example, in reviewing Landre's novel, the critic Rachilde launched an attack on the *marraines*.[47] If, by acting as a *marraine de guerre,* Rachilde asserted, the French woman had given "her heart, her heart knew reasons that reason did not know and acted under the influence of reckless fantasy."[48]

L'école des marraines begins with an introduction to the wartime world of Parisian women, who are all focused on how they may best support France in its hour of need. The cover of the novel and subsequent advertisements for it used an illustration of a mustachioed soldier in uniform embracing a fashionably dressed woman in a train station to display its focus on love during wartime.[49] Once again, love was shown as ennobling as the novel began with the following description of French women: "Following the example of men who totally gave of themselves, women made it a point of honor to give the best of themselves to their homeland" (8).

After establishing her general tone regarding these women, who were caught on the outside of the great campaigns and not allowed

The cover illustration from Jeanne Landre's L'école des marraines *(1917).*
Courtesy of the Bibliothèque Nationale.

to fight but only to be fought for, Landre introduces her protagonist Claude Brevin, a young, female artist. Claude is a bit cynical, smart, not untalented but without the suffering that would render her a "great" artist (10–11). Landre then describes a typical group of women, all *marraines,* who are busily knitting for their soldiers. Claude alone stands outside of this group, wondering at their energy: "Where are they going, where are they running to? Towards what imprudence, what adventure? They can come, our heroes, these ladies are ready!" (14).

Beyond her mocking tone, Landre ensured that her readers understood that more than superficial interest in soldiers transforms the lives of these women. Claude reflects on the anxiety of her friend Yvonne who has not heard from her beloved in four days and then moves from her specific plight to the national one: "She thought of other young, anguished spouses, of anxious mothers, of fiancées who dared no longer wait, of departed comrades, already mown down for the most part, and she did not understand why some women could still be amused by everything, by nothing, like they had been in an era when the country was not in danger" (17). Here the standard criticism of women found in male-authored texts appears neatly voiced by the main protagonist of a women's war novel.[50] Yet the difference in perspective also seems evident. Landre, like many other women who wrote of war, criticized women who—implicitly, unlike men—had the choice to escape the ultimate sacrifice of war, who could still be amused and glad to be alive. However, the cost of such a choice also manifests itself in the intense grief and sense of exclusion felt by unattached women whom Claude represents. True patriot that she is, Claude's thoughts are with the soldiers in the trenches, with "the poor sons of France," and she mourns because she lacks someone to cry over (20).

As a counterpoint to Claude Brevin's single purity, Landre provides the character of Lucienne Loche, married but not in danger of losing a great love to war. Lucienne, not deeply in love with her husband, who is not at the front, decides, after reflecting on her jealousy of the stoicism of the truly bereaved "Françaises," to adopt for herself "a 'godson' who will be in danger. I need to be afraid for someone. Translate: I need to love someone" (47). Subsequently, Yvonne persuades Claude to become the "epistolary comrade" of Réné Gerville, her husband's best friend. The contrast thus established between the two types of *marraines,* Claude and Lucienne, must have been apparent to contemporary women readers. Lucienne wants adventure and love and becomes the *marraine* of a man who does not even pen his own letters but like in the plot of Rostand's *Cyrano,* copies them from the letters written by a fellow soldier to his fiancée. The novel thus presents the figure of the *marraine* as embodying a potential for hypocrisy, adultery, and deceit. However, in the end, the idea of the perfect lover as perfect comrade emerges in the casting of the *marraine* as an "epistolary comrade."

Claude, too, initially objects to becoming a *marraine,* although she is persuaded when Yvonne informs her that her *filleul* suffers from "neurasthenia" and needs a "moral" lift.[51] Quickly, however, she finds herself waiting for her daily letter from the soldier, to whom "a *marraine* has given back his moral equilibrium and his good humor" (91). Initially reluctant, Claude and Réné fall deeply in love, which transforms both of them. For Claude, life is altered by having "a godson at the front" (95). She soon realizes that everywhere she turns she meets women who are *marraines,* who give the simple explanation: "[L]ike everyone, am I not a patriot?" (100). Simply being a *marraine* makes a woman a "female patriot," but Claude, unlike Lucienne, truly loves her "godson." While Landre provides a comic subplot involving Lucienne, she clearly presents Claude, who loves and loses Réné from a distance, as a heroine, and a model. Although Réné has died for France, Claude knows: "He was, for her, victory, he was her reason to wish to grow old. They knew each other so well, and without ever having seen each other. All seems strange to vulgar individuals, all is possible for others" (312–13). Landre thus at one moment celebrates this epistolary love, acknowledges the potential criticism of such a relationship, and neatly refutes it by suggesting that love sight unseen would seem "strange" only to the "vulgar" individual. The idea that such an intense love — unconsummated even by sight — could regenerate not only the soldier fighting for France but also the woman at home might have inspired readers to enter into these kinds of relationships or merely to accept those of others. Clichéd though the words of parting in the novel may seem, they may have provided an important space for actual grief to be assuaged, for the female readers of such novels to identify and cope with their own senses of loss.

Nevertheless, Landre places the final word on the *marraine* in the mouth of one of the more cynical denizens of the Paris scene: Trik, a cartoonist, who declares the *marraine* "a necessary object of war, . . . indispensable like a tooth-brush" (317). After pointing out the benefits and pitfalls of this new arrangement between men and women, he concludes that it is, on the whole, a good thing. Despite a subplot chronicling the loss of a beloved to war, the novel ends almost on an upbeat: romance continues, relations between men and women continue, life continues. Delivering that message in a time of war might have been the popular novel's most significant contribution to morale. Jeanne Landre may have peopled her novel with familiar types in unfamiliar, war-specific roles, but her focus remained on the experience of women. War may have been the central preoccupation of her characters, but she did not attempt to show her readers anything further than its potentially ennobling qualities.

In contrast, Ernesta Stern's 1916 novel *Le baptême du courage* tried to portray war from the perspective of a "sophisticated" man who goes off to fight for France.[52] His understanding of the war contained many of the platitudes about male reactions to the war. The protagonist says, "I wanted to be one of the actors in the largest drama. . . . I felt suddenly born in me a need of destruction and of murder" (41). Yet Stern's hero also acknowledges the importance of women and, particularly, the role of his mother on the eve of his departure, who acts with appropriate heroic stoicism: "I knew for certain that her patriotic faith would give her the strength to support the trial that I had inflicted on her" (54). Stern has her hero see in an instant "the universal sorrow which strangles all hearts . . . all my anguished heart went to them [the women of France] in a large rush of pity and love. At that supreme minute, I shared their distress, I understood their profound desolation" (57). This vision of the soldier-to-be's sympathy culminates as he glimpses those left behind and senses that "they would be the greatest victims of the war. We who leave, we will soon be transported into new surroundings, we will have the superb comfort of action and the grandiose spectacles that await us. However many sufferings and deprivations lie in wait for us, we will never know the long and powerful martyrdom of waiting in empty and abandoned hearths" (64). Beyond this explicit tribute to the suffering women of France, the novel provided another example, when the hero finds himself lost and isolated at the front before the battle of the Marne. He awakes from a feverish dream to find himself sleeping on a cadaver, "but horror is succeeded by another sentiment, because he [the corpse] has carried just to his lips a photo which he gave his final kiss. Piously, I kissed it and looked at it: It was a young woman who held a baby in her arms" (101). He then finds his company and goes bravely forth to battle.

This incident suggests a variety of ways in which women played unique roles during wartime. Women were, as in male war texts like *Le feu,* present in battle itself, as the last thoughts of dying soldiers, as the impetus for heroic action, and for literal and spiritual regeneration. And it is not accidental that the photo found on the dead soldier is that of a mother. As the last image—indeed a sacred image—pressed to the lips of the injured and dying, women, particularly as mothers, offer the comfort necessary to give faith and strength to those who continue to fight. As a female-authored text, this novel called attention to the roles of women. It may well be that Stern portrays women as they wanted to see themselves, as stoic sources of comfort, seen and acknowledged as both contributing to and suffering from the war as much as men.

More importantly, this female author speaking through a male character contradicts the message delivered by Elisabeth in *Un roman civil*. In that novel, the main character chastised a woman who dared to complain, by suggesting that it was not "women's turn to cry" because "it's the men who are suffering." Yet, in this novel, a male perspective acknowledges the pain of being left behind, of not being able to participate, which other novels' characters, such as Claude in *L'école des marraines,* echo. Claude's wonderment at women "amusing themselves" during the war is criticism of women's enjoyment, not their suffering during wartime. Thus, both tears and laughter become violations of the ultimate virtue of stoic support, and all of these novels portray the acceptance of loss as praiseworthy, even necessary. For women excluded from the main business of war, allegedly shielded from the instinct for "destruction and murder," these narratives provided cues about how to negotiate a different relationship with patriotism and the war. These authors also provided competing strategies for coping with the problem of being noncombatant, raising the question of whether it was worse to fight or to look on helplessly while those you love must go to a war. While the war was continually brought home, it was also portrayed as somewhere men go off to, showing a complex understanding of the boundaries of the war.

Comparing French women's writings with those of their British counterparts reveals both the transnational and the culturally specific ways in which women's roles during the war were constructed. Both French and British female writers explored the need for women to work in nontraditional roles as much as their obligation to fulfill their destinies as potential if not actual mothers. Yet, British romance novels from the early war years focus more directly on the idea of love as an instigator of appropriate masculinity. In the works of Ruby Ayres and Berta Ruck, women's love redeems the "shirker," or the redemption becomes possible only when the woman realizes the man she loves is indeed a khaki-clad hero. French women had no such need to encourage enlistment at the onset, since French men were already subject to conscription and France had been invaded. However, French novelists did explore new relations between men and women as well as newly invented roles and, in a very real sense, war work for women, like that of the *marraine,* which potentially violated certain prewar standards for bourgeois feminine behavior. If there was room in these tales for flighty lovers and serious ones, for devoted nurses and stoic mothers, for a diversity of messages about what women could do, these stories continued to emphasize women's intimate, transformative connections to war.

Resisting War and Its Gender Arrangements

One indication of the assumption that wartime literature would support the war effort can be found in a novel by a British woman that was banned under the Defense of the Realm Regulations in 1918. The London magistrate who heard the case against Rose Allatini and her publisher, C. W. Daniel, found the novel *Despised and Rejected* guilty of delivering a pacifist message and thus violating the regulation against the wartime production of material deemed likely to affect the recruitment and conduct of the military. Although the case surrounding *Despised and Rejected* has received some attention from critics Samuel Hynes and Claire Tylee for its messages about homosexuality, gender, and pacifism, I want to look at this book's depictions of wartime family gender roles in order to investigate its stereotypes of masculinity and femininity.[53]

Despised and Rejected, like several of Allatini's other wartime novels, begins with a male and female character and the possibility of a love story.[54] The protagonists, Dennis Blackwood, a young composer, and Antoinette de Courcy, however, are far from conventional. She leaves the opening setting of the novel infatuated with another woman, and Dennis, while initially smitten with Antoinette, ends up falling in love with Alan, a young man he encounters on a walking tour in Cornwall. Knowing that he is "abnormal—perverted—against nature," however, Dennis flees from this encounter and returns home. At this moment, war descends upon the community of Eastwold, rousing it to action and making Dennis stand out as an anomaly for refusing immediately to enlist. Escaping from tensions at home, Dennis goes to London, takes up with Antoinette, who falls in love with him, and then runs into Alan. Alan and Dennis finally confess their love for one another, just before Alan is taken into custody as a conscientious objector. At the novel's end, Alan and Dennis are both in jail for their beliefs and Antoinette is left isolated and directionless.

Accounts of the trial against *Despised and Rejected* make much of the fact that the book's pacifism rather than its tolerant portrayal of gays and lesbians, also considered shocking in 1918, led to the initial prosecution of the book. The linkage here between the idea of loving one's fellow man quite literally and refusing to take the life of any man illustrates how profoundly heterosexuality, virility, and masculinity could be caught up in wartime definitions of gender. After all, the book's heroine also has homosexual longings and masculine qualities and ends up opposing the war, but ultimately her femininity is not at risk, at least not publicly.

In contrast to much of the literature considered in this chapter, Allatini never depicted the graphic horrors of battle and only referred to them in order to illustrate that what Germans inflict on the English, the English inflict on them in return. However, she went out of her way to stress the sufferings—using the term "atrocities"—experienced by the conscientious objectors in prison. In the novel, Antoinette tries to tell Doreen Blackwood, Dennis's sister that "[t]hey do queer things to the C.O.s in prison—forcing food through tubes up their noses if they won't eat, putting them in chains and painful irons. . . . The officials . . . can vent their spite upon them as they please, giving them ghastly punishments that may injure them for life."[55] She also points to their bravery in being willing to lay down their lives or their freedom for their principles, implying that this takes as much courage as blindly going off to kill others: "You can't call a man who's ready to go to prison for his convictions a weakling or a coward" (301). In her accounts of both the townspeople of Eastwold and the dissidents and pacifists who frequent a teashop in London, Allatini showed the costs of war in terms of limbs and lives lost at home and abroad, trying not to compare sufferings, but to argue for justice. And in promoting the heroism of two gay men who refuse to fight, she challenged some of the very premises underlying wartime appeals to and constructions of masculinity.

Allatini is ultimately less successful in challenging gender roles and norms within the family. From the novel's outset, she emphasizes the special relationship between Mrs. Blackwood and her son. Making no allowances for the family having sent one son to the front, Eastwold's criticism of Dennis gets back to Mrs. Blackwood. She "half-uneasily" tells Dennis that people think he should go, and he responds, "Do you think I ought to, Mother?" (152). When she tries to evade answering by pointing out that his father wishes him to go, he persists—"And you, Mother?"—until she confesses: " 'I know it's very wrong of me,' she murmured, as if apologising to the wrathful spirits of her husband . . . and the rest of the community, apologising for being a mother first, and a 'woman of England' afterwards." And Dennis concludes the conversation by asking, "Wrong that you should want me not to go out and kill people whose mothers love them every bit as much as you love me?" (152). Here, maternity—the virtue women exemplify in all kinds of war literature—becomes redefined as "selfish" and produces enormous internal conflict. Further, the opinion of the mother, while it might not entirely shape Dennis's actions, does matter; she may well be held responsible for her son's failure to enlist. In the context of *Despised and Rejected,* a mother's endorsement of her son's refusal to fight became a virtue, a redeeming feature of Mrs. Blackwood's apolitical conservatism. However, read from another perspective, it reinforced traditional gender categories within the family, especially maternal culpability for what children, and in this case, sons, do, especially in response to war.

The decision to ban this novel, as well as the censorship of a variety of other texts, illustrates the important ideological work of wartime literature and the potential harm that the government thought could be done to civilian as well as to military morale by such fictional works. The failure of Allatini to adhere to gender and patriotic norms also makes clear that other women's novels examined in this chapter could be seen as serving the important, national functions of reinforcing these norms. Yet this text still shares with the other examples previously discussed one salient feature: a kind of selective realism that portrays some behaviors as being so natural to men and women during wartime as to require no interpretation. The most critical transgressions in Allatini's world are not those against heterosexuality, but those encompassing gender violations with more overtly political stances—men refusing to fight and women refusing to be good mothers and send their sons to battle. Once again, women's imaginative responses to the war offered fragmented and conflicting options, which themselves challenged more official efforts to enforce the overarchingly appropriate response of the sacrificing, stoic, and patriotic mother.[56]

Crossing Boundaries:
Women under Fire and the Limits of Divided Fronts

The fictional texts considered thus far interpreted the war in ways that, to varying degrees, both reinforced and challenged the "stable" separation between war front and home front, men and women. The themes of such fictions were powerfully echoed in nonfiction. One vivid means by which women themselves presented the specter of war for women at home came through accounts of their experiences of the effects of modern war, whether found in the occupied zones of France or under attack from aerial bombardment in Britain. Several French memoirs by women detailing their lives under occupation were quickly translated and published in Britain. Articles and propaganda began to focus attention on how the technological innovations of this modern war could now target innocent civilians. In all of these texts, the border dividing the fronts all but vanished.

In her preface to the English edition of Marguerite Yerta's *Les six femmes et l'invasion,* Mrs. Humphry Ward claimed that "this little book gives a very graphic and interesting account by an eye-witness . . . of life in the occupied provinces of France under the daily pressure of the German invasion. There are many repulsive and odious incidents recorded here . . . but, mercifully, few 'atrocities' such as those which make of the French Governmental Reports, or that of the Bryce Commission, tales of horror and infamy that time will never wash out."[57] *The Times Literary Supplement* also noted that these women "were on the whole fortunate. Their lives were never threatened; while their honour lived under a perpetual threat, it was only once (if we read the story right) in critical danger."[58] In France, the book's "fine observation" was acclaimed as providing a "precious document for History."[59] Here was a woman's account, meant to be a true rendering of German barbarism and the horrors of war. Like Barbusse's work, it appeared in French and was quickly translated. It thus allows for a careful comparison of not only the differences between the obviously censored French and seemingly uncensored English versions but also the differing messages delivered by tales of German brutality in the context of French and British reactions to women in the "zones" of war. For if *The Times Literary Supplement* used the book as a warning to those "English labouring people in town and country [who] might be heard to say, 'We shouldn't be worse off than we are if the Germans did come,'" reviews in other periodicals such as the *Athenaeum* reminded its readers of the book's "treatment of domestic difficulties, compared with which our much-bemoaned privations are indeed but trifles."[60] Moreover, the *Daily News* hailed the work as being "one of the most vivid and 'real' books that have appeared about invaded France."[61]

Les six femmes et l'invasion starts out in a prewar idyll and quickly introduces the innocent women who will be left to fend for themselves at the war's onset. As the title suggests, six women—the author, her mother-in-law, and her four young, unmarried sisters-in-law—share a house in the neighborhood of Laon when war breaks out. Like other accounts of the start of the war in France, the hour of departure finds stoic men and weeping women. These tears merely foreshadow what awaits the women. At the outset, however, the women witness the floods of refugees, without realizing that they could be among them. Here the first of the significant differences between the French and English versions of the book appear. In the English version, Yerta criticizes those who "profited by the woes of others, filched from the rich" as well as those who "were harsh to the fugitives."[62] All such criticisms of French behavior were censored in the original.[63]

With the refugees come tales of "the nameless deeds, the monstrous crimes committed by the Germans. Their stories left us half-credulous, and if terror seized our souls, it was a far-off, unselfish terror."[64] Uncertain whether to leave or not, the women delay making a decision and thus find themselves witnessing the invasion, trapped in the occupied territories.[65] Bit by bit, Yerta documents life under the invasion, a life of demands from self-righteous Germans and requisitions of needed food, and—although she reports no direct physical violence—the townspeople, and especially the women, live in a constant state of fear.

Beyond depicting their isolation and the petty tyrannies inflicted upon them, Yerta provides a few specific incidents where their plight as women comes to the fore. The first occurs shortly after the invasion when Marguerite, the narrator, is forcibly stopped:

[A] soldier I hardly saw in the night muttered something I did not understand about money—five francs. I tried to break loose . . . and answered that we were no shopkeepers . . .

"If you are busy," he said, "another lady would do."

In the dim light of a glimmering window, I caught sight of . . . [the] perfect brute. He looked so strong, his voice was so peculiar that I suddenly understood the meaning of his words. Frightened, I shook my arm to get it free, set off running and got so quickly out of sight he might have believed I had been swallowed up by the night.[66]

The women are able to escape being treated as prostitutes, although one of their constant complaints concerns their nocturnal fear of what the Germans might do.

Part of the Germans' treatment of women, as interpreted by the writer, derived from their arrogance, that "they had a double right to the favour of all women and girls, being at once lords and conquerors," and the women, unfortunately, gain the reputation of inhabiting "the house of the pretty girls."[67] And Yerta recalls what this entailed:

> [A]t nightfall . . . they would come back . . . [making] a frightful uproar, shouting, calling after us. . . . If from upstairs we asked what they wanted, they answered with threats, insults, and invitations to come down. . . .
>
> It was the reign of terror. . . . And you do not understand the meaning of this, you who have not rushed to your light to blow it out for fear its pale glimmer would betray your presence . . . —you who have not realised that you are a woman and weak, and that a dozen brutes will seek more than your life if they succeed in their design. . . . [A]nd if the horrors that have overwhelmed other places have been spared us, at least we have felt their envenomed breath.[68]

Yerta shows how effectively fear controlled these women's lives; yet, terrified though they were, these women never had to face the consequences of an attack whose aim was "more" than their lives.

They do hear about sexual assaults, although "compared with the crimes committed in Belgium and in Lorraine, the misdeeds we shall mention are but little things."[69] According to Yerta, once the Germans had "settled themselves upon us," there ceased to be widespread accounts of rape, although "here and there evil deeds were still spoken of."[70] Yerta even suggests that in some cases, the victims' "imprudence" caused the attacks, since women who had spent their lives in this quiet, kind countryside did not understand that "one was perpetually surrounded by brutes." However, she strongly implies that the "systematic" and "collective" nature of the attacks at the start of the war had changed to "violences that despite being moral were no less terrible."[71]

Here the French version's discussion of rape and sexual violence against women ends, and a long passage of blank space marked "censored" follows. In the English version, however, Yerta explains the meaning of these "moral" yet "terrible" acts, that some desperate mothers "accepted dishonour" so that their children could have "bread and soup" and that "others could not withstand the troubles and vexations that lay in store for good women." Although the women in Yerta's family are horrified when they learn that not all women were blameless when it came to sexual encounters between German soldiers and French women, Yerta notes that sadly "women of the lowest class" and both male and female "traitors" could always be found.[72] Like the censoring of Yerta's earlier accounts of French civilians who did not aid refugees, any suggestions that French women willingly slept with Germans, even for the sake of feeding their children, were removed from the version published in Paris. The terror induced by the Germans and hearsay about German rapes and all manner of German misdeeds were all uncensored—even though such evidence might have dampened morale even as it inspired thoughts of revenge. However, the hint that any French man or woman would willingly consort with the German army, whether through individual weakness or their children's deprivation, could not be presented. The censorship of Yerta's work in France suggests the importance of media control of images that constructed a national enemy and mobilized popular support. While the degree to which censorship of wartime material was effective is open to question, the concern with having control over the kinds of information available about women on the front lines of war comes across clearly.

In April of 1916, women (and men) in occupied France were subjected to more specific actions than those recounted by Yerta: random deportations and forced labor. A postwar history of the occupation of France describes these deportations, which were "impossible to resist," as evoking "horror" and "astonishment" throughout France.[73] At a demonstration protesting these actions, Cécile Brunschvicg, the general secretary of the Union Française pour le Suffrage des Femmes (USFS), read an appeal from French women to those of all countries— "allied, neutral or enemy"—asking for their aid on behalf of "our sisters, victims of force."[74] Details of these deportations were also conveyed to a wartime audience on both sides of the channel in narrative form as well. First, the French government issued its own appeal to the governments of neutral powers, and this document was translated into English in 1916 and published as *The Deportation of Women and Girls from Lille*. Here, these actions were put in the following context: "Not content with subjecting our people in the North to every kind of oppression[,] the Germans have recently treated them in the most iniquitous way."[75] The bishop of Lille, in documents attached to this account, pointed out the special "moral" dangers of the deportations: "the promiscuity which inevitably accompanies removals *en masse,* involving mixture of the sexes, or . . . persons of very unequal moral standing" (16). Others also denounced the mingling of "modest girls and prostitutes" (18).

Another prominent account of the German occupation of France, *En esclavage,* was also quickly translated into English and published as the more sensationalist *Slave to the Huns.* In this work, Henriette Celarié describes the fate of two young women under German occupation and provides even more detailed evidence of the sufferings of women near the battle lines. A review of *En esclavage* in France repeatedly stressed that the Germans' actions were those of "barbarians" who made women suffer not only bodily but "also tortured them in their souls and in their hearts."[76]

Celarié's account follows the tribulations of two "deportées," Yvonne X. and Marie X., who are removed from their families, placed in "cattle cars," taken to small villages, and forced to labor for the Germans. Emphasizing the youth, gentility, and religious scruples of Yvonne and Marie allows Celarié to render their treatment by the Germans even more shocking. Ten soldiers with drawn bayonets are required to separate Marie from her sobbing mother as young women in particular are taken during holy week from Lille to the occupied countryside.[77] German justification for these particular deportations claimed that these women were needed to help work the fields to insure that the civilian population be fed. It soon becomes apparent, according to this account, that they are working directly for the Germans and that their labor is not so much necessary as useful to demoralize the civilian population.[78]

Aside from descriptions of hunger, rat-infested henhouses and shacks, and harsh agricultural work, the specific plight of these bourgeois young women *as* women is repeatedly and graphically emphasized.[79] Unlike the six women in Yerta's account, the subjects of this testament are torn away from their families and must find new types of support and friendship with their fellow captives. Similarly, however, their greatest terror and anguish comes from the sexual threat posed by armed German men. This threat takes both indirect and direct forms. Both Yvonne and Marie report ongoing fears of sexual attack, especially at night, since they are so vulnerable. They are also indignant because the Germans have rounded up both prostitutes and honest women, without distinguishing between them. The Germans have even claimed that all deportees are prostitutes, and the local population believes at first that this is the case. Furious at being surrounded by these "filles publiques" (public girls or prostitutes), Yvonne suggests that this is worse than "physical deprivation." Meanwhile, they hear stories about the plight that deported women in other villages are experiencing, such as the case of a hundred women in a nearby village who are lodged in a granary and forced into prostitution: "Each evening . . . the soldiers call for the women that they desire for the night: 'Charlotte Z., 3 tablets of chocolate . . . Louise G. one mark and a tablet.'"[80]

According to their testimony, Yvonne and Marie themselves escape being victims of direct sexual attacks or forced prostitution. However, almost as shameful to them, they are subjected to gynecological exams by the German authorities. Both witnesses describe in great detail women "pale with shame" and "trembling with anger" at being "treated like 'filles publiques.'" Marie recounts how women who refused such an examination were sent to prison or forcibly undressed by police officers and examined in front of them. Yvonne personally avoids the horror of being examined, but her companions cry out against "the monsters," especially when they are told they are now *good for everything!* The full meaning of being "good for everything" is explained as a "fact" known to these women and not to others in France: "When a woman was possessed by a German, if a child is born, the son is sent to Germany, seed of a soldier, the daughter is left to her mother."[81]

Their plight is even more sensationalized in the British edition of the book. It begins with a publisher's note indicating that "the main reason for issuing this book is that British readers may understand what German occupation of a country may involve. This appears all the more necessary now that we find . . . that English girls are willing to be on terms of amity with enemy prisoners." The very language of the British translation suggests the nefarious nature of the Germans' actions; the first chapter, which describes the deportation of Easter Monday 1916, is entitled "The Maiden Tribute," a clear reference to the famous 1885 exposé of the white slave trade in Britain, and it also refers to the deportation as "rape."[82] Elsewhere certain phrases plainly printed in the French edition are italicized in the English: for instance, the accusation that "*the Germans were not driven by necessity to deport women for land labour*" and the explanation of what happens to children born to women "*possessed*" by Germans.[83] Both English and French versions end with a specific plea to women, and to mothers in particular: "How would you feel if these things had happened to your own daughter?"[84]

The treatment of these women under occupation belies the distinction allegedly maintained between the feminized *arrière* (home front) and the war front. These women are captives of the Germans, forced to live under their watchful eyes, to perform forced agricultural and domestic labor, and to live with constant physical and emotional privations. While the women in these accounts are not subject to death, they are subject to potential violation, impregnation and literal invasions of their bodily integrity in the form of forced medical exams, all at the hands of the German army. Without suggesting equivalencies between soldiers and women under occupation, their direct encounters with the enemy's military demonstrate something far from a protected experience of war. And the war's direct affects were not restricted to those living in occupied France.

Technological change also made women at home targets of war in both Britain and France. The adoption of such new weapons as tanks, machine guns, chemical gases, and fighter planes changed the nature of warfare during World War I, the latter in particular further accounting for the breakdown of meaningful distinctions between home front and front line. Not only was the scale on which technology and these new tools of war were put to use new, but so were the ways in which these tools increased the death tolls. Zeppelin and airplane raids beyond the battle lines attacked targets miles from the war zone in England and helped *literally* to bring the war home to noncombatants and to women in particular. From the start, such novel methods of warfare were viewed as altering the consensus over what was a legitimate war target. Even humorists responded as early as 1914 to airborne attacks on the British coastline by urging the "shameless huns" to "fight our men and ships and guns" and "[n]ot womenfolk and watering places."[85] A more serious 1916 account put it this way:

> In visiting the scenes of the disasters caused by German bombs, in listening to the vivid stories of those who escaped with slight injuries or those who by miracle were absolutely unhurt in the midst of devastation, one waits in vain for descriptions of the hysterical woman, the woman who shrieked with fear or the woman who fainted. There are no such descriptions because there were no such women.

The most extraordinary feature of each of the recent raids has been the calm with which they were faced by the inmates of those little cottages which were destroyed or just escaped destruction by a happy chance.

And in most of these suburban homes there were only women and children.[86]

Even as air warfare brought the devastation of the front line to those allegedly shielded, it expanded the boundaries of heroism. As the writer observed, those ironically both left behind and under attack were "only women and children," and yet they demonstrated the "calm" heroism of combatants. They were not, contrary to gendered expectations, "hysterical" or "fainting." References to the role reversals precipitated by the bombing of civilians in places on the British coast, like Scarborough, appeared in articles urging the full utilization of women's industry: "When Scarborough was bombarded a member of a volunteer force never stopped his flight till he had reached the safety of London. His wife and children were left alone to cope with the dangers of the situation. They were, as householders, well quit of one coward, but they would have been more strengthened had they shared in such counsel as produced the National Guard, the special constables, and other volunteers."[87] This anecdote contained a double message — shaming men of the "volunteer" (not regular) forces for their potential or actual cowardice and pointing to the quiet bravery, and possible, if not necessary, contributions of women.

Official propaganda emphasized the extent to which civilians far from the trenches became casualties of war. The British government's Parliamentary Recruiting Committee issued a poster that defined the brutality of Germans, who had shown their true nature "by murdering defenceless women and children at Scarborough."[88] Another poster pictured a little girl standing before a bombed-out home, while the text asked "Men of Britain! Will You Stand This? 78 Women & Children were killed and 228 Women & Children were wounded by German Raiders."[89] Clearly the threat to homes, women, and children was meant to encourage enlistment, even as it illustrated how close the battle lines had come to a zone meant to be safe and protected.

The terror induced by air raids even became the rationale for a mother's killing her child. Testifying at the Crown's case against Elizabeth Huntley, who was accused of decapitating her daughter, Margaret Wells claimed: "I have known Mrs. Huntley since childhood. She was a

Parliamentary Recruiting Committee poster issued after the Scarborough Air Raids. Courtesy of the Imperial War Museum.

jolly hearted woman until the air raids."[90] Mary Freeman, the sister of the accused, provided additional evidence of her sister's state of mind: "She has complained of her head and was treated by Dr. Holland . . . for air raid shock—She used to shake a lot during the raids—she has not had delusions but was very nervous. . . . Did not sleep well and was depressed."[91] Huntley's doctor elaborated that "she was much up-set by the air raid and had a nervous breakdown. . . . I wanted to get her out of London for a change—she told me her children worried her as in the air raids her children screamed."[92] Later testimony revealed that Mrs. Huntley had fallen and injured her head during one of the air raids, which had caused her to be intensely afraid of them, and the medical officer's report from Holloway Prison concluded that she was "insane" and "unfit to plead to the Indictment."[93]

It is difficult to ascertain whether—like the medical condition known as shell shock, which itself came into being during the war— "air raid shock" could result in such a total breakdown in a woman who, by all accounts, was a devoted and loving mother and yield such horrendous consequences. Did Mrs. Huntley fear that she was going to be killed in her home during an air raid, or did the fear-induced insomnia and injuries caused by repeated air raids trigger her "insanity"? Was she in any way akin to those on the battlefields who suffered from similar war or fear-induced mental anguish but who had less objectionable targets for their outbursts? While these questions are impossible to answer, it does seem evident that for her sister, neighbors, and those who examined her, her having experienced air raids and their terror came up as a *plausible* explanation for her actions. Under these circumstances—and it is also hard to know to what extent Elizabeth Huntley was unique, and whether "air raid shock" became a convincing excuse for infanticide—the blurring of the line indicating who exactly was under fire seems fully accomplished.

In a war where military-induced death could reach those in English—and French—cities as well as French battlefields, the actual women affected by combat were not merely those who, as in the case of the six women in Yerta's account, found themselves unfortunately in the path of armies.[94] The rapid adoption of new military techniques meant that the lines between the war and home fronts were tangibly crossed, and such changes then demanded new ideological justifications. French women came face-to-face with the German army, and British (and French) women were the targets of German aerial attacks. While there are obvious differences between the plights of the young women of Lille and the women of Scarborough, their respective injuries demonstrate that in Britain as well as France women were truly in the line of fire.

Conclusion

This chapter began with canonical soldier-authored literature and ended with discussions of women literally under occupation and under fire. Yet, the literary works that shaped how wartime readers might have imagined the war as much as the air raid illustrate the permeability of the boundary between the allegedly safe and feminized home front and what were presumed to be the brutal facts of the masculine front line. While this chapter has focused largely on fictional crossings, the presence of women under occupation and in the so-called war zone and the presence of soldiers on leave suggest that the boundary between these zones was continually collapsing.

Stories about women refugees or women in the war zones suggest some of the complexities of the wartime situation of women in both France and Britain. Called upon to be active participants in a war effort that required the support of the total population, women involved themselves in a large number of voluntary and paid kinds of war work. Despite these active roles, which granted women a good deal of agency during the war, public discourse also continued to emphasize women's unique and more traditional roles as mothers, wives, and sweethearts—sources of emotional and moral support. The ultimate figure of public interest and anxiety remained the fighting man, and, since women were excluded from the unquestionably necessary and basic task of soldiering, their claims to agency and active participation in the war were, as will continue to be seen, fraught with tension.

Male and female French and British writers ranging from Henri Barbusse and Marcelle Tinayre to H. G. Wells and Rose Allatini tried to show the war "as it was." In so doing, even combatant writers like Barbusse and Sassoon demonstrated the importance of women and their domestic concerns for the continuance of the war, even in the trenches. Others like May Sinclair and Lucie Delarue-Mardrus illustrated how the vivid evidence of refugees and wounded men placed in the so-called home front allowed for no one to escape the knowledge of what the war entailed. As the First World War raged around them, regardless of their geographic position, imagining the war and sharing their tales of war, even wartime love stories, enabled the men and women of war-torn Britain and France to transcend the gender-bound categories—to bridge the gap between divided fronts—in which they had been placed.

The Maternal Body
as Battlefield

RAPE, GENDER, AND
NATIONAL IDENTITY

Rape, Motherhood, and Nationalism

The divide between the home front and war front was transgressed during the war, and among the most obvious embodiments of such transgressions were the war's direct physical attacks on women, acts that were both widely publicized and often sensationalized in both Britain and France. The practice of using the enemy's potential for brutal, and particularly sexual, attacks on a nation's women to mobilize men to arms has a long history. So too does the actual rape of women in warfare. Unsurprisingly, then, allegations of the violent brutalization of women by the German army became a potent recruiting device and rallying cry for the Allies.[1] Yet in this context, the rape of women portrayed as a rape of *mothers* helped to solidify national support—in both France and Britain—against a racialized German enemy, while affirming the centrality of motherhood as a primary source of women's agency and patriotism. In Britain, where there were never such direct threats, propaganda utilizing accounts of atrocities committed against women proved a useful recruiting tool.[2] Even in France, where recruitment was a moot point and the invasion had already virtually silenced opposition to the war, propaganda concerning the German treatment of Belgian and French women further contributed to popular indignation and to making the war a sacred, national cause.

Recent scholarship has also highlighted, as Ruth Harris puts it, "the way the actual victimization of women was transformed into a representation of a violated, but innocent, female nation resisting the assaults of a brutal male assailant."[3] While used metaphorically to speak of invasion—such as the "rape" of neutral Belgium—rape also surfaced in stories about the abuse of civilians that were spread through posters, newspapers, and literature by both men and women. Government-sponsored investigations also sought to document rapes and atrocities by interviewing survivors of German attacks. The conclusions of these inquiries, which provided devastating accounts of the treatment of women and children, were also widely publicized in newspapers.[4] Taken together, such accounts constructed the battle between Germany and the Allies as a struggle between brute force and Prussian militarism, on one side, and reason, the rule of law, and the benefits of French and British civilization, on the other.

Thus, the representation of wartime atrocities bolstered an understanding of gender that aimed to preserve traditional notions of female and male behavior as well as the divide between the sexes exemplified by the home front/war front split. The manipulation of accounts of wartime rape became a powerful way to call upon men to act as *men,* defending women, home, and family as passive, moral domains in need of male protection.[5] It further contributed to the maintenance of the family as a male-headed one, even though many would now be led by women for the war's duration.

Debates in France quickly focused on the problem posed by the infants of rape-impregnated women, infants marked by their German paternity. Suggestions about legalizing abortion for those women raped and impregnated by Germans opened up fissures in French political and intellectual life, raising questions that cut to the heart of what constituted "French" identity. Resistance to the idea of legalizing abortion or tolerating infanticide in such cases hinged not only on questions of preexisting anxiety about depopulation or general morality, but also on whether or not a woman could prove that she had been raped by actual Germans and was not just looking to erase evidence of her own sexual misbehavior. Moreover, the arguments against abortion hinged on the idea that a mother's French "blood" would make her children French and thus offered a version of nationality rooted not in a child being born on French soil, but to a French *mother*.[6] The propaganda value of rape and popular interest in atrocities resided in the notion that the nation's pure women—particularly their wombs—had to be protected from a brutal enemy. One of the primary concerns in the tales of atrocities against women used in propaganda thus centered on motherhood and women's reproductive control over their own fertility, and how these connected to national honor.

In social policy debates, state-sponsored propaganda, and imaginative literature, the consequences of rape were linked to motherhood. Arguments about the impact of rape on the national future coalesced around both the need to maintain the integrity of a nation ("race") and the conflicting desire to preserve an elevated status for the mother, whatever the social consequences. Despite the different national situations of French and British women, representations of wartime rape in both countries supported an understanding of gender that placed motherhood at the heart of civilization and emphasized women's primary status as passive victims of the war. As attacks on women were transformed into attacks on the maternal body, the "essential" and "private" role of mothers became central to the deeply nationalist political purposes to which the accounts of rape were put. As this chapter will demonstrate, by offering the first comparative analysis of these issues, in both France and Britain, fiction was powerfully used to illustrate the plight of rape-impregnated mothers, demonstrating that even this kind of motherhood offered women their fundamental chance for both agency and service to the nation.

French Responses to "Children of Rape"

In her history of French women during the First World War, Françoise Thébaud states that "some women were raped during the invasion, more rarely during the occupation; certain of them were killed in resisting." Without providing any additional information, Thébaud quickly turns to the 1915 debates over the "fruits" of these violations, a subject that has also been pursued in a book-length study of "the children of the enemy" by Stéphane Audoin-Rouzeau.[7] Thus, recent historiography has mirrored the wartime situation, where the topic of the rape of French women in the occupied territories during the German invasion became subsumed in a national debate about what to do with the infants of "boche rape."

The debate even acquired its own wartime history in Georges Docquois's *La chair innocente: L'enfant du viol boche.* Docquois noted that some initially had been skeptical about stories of rape, to the point of lightly retelling humorous anecdotes about these violations. However, "today, a parallel skepticism would be outrageous, inhuman, even more than inhuman, imbecile," for the "question of boche rape" has made even indifferent individuals face these issues with their whole hearts and spirits.[8] Thus, the situation caused by German sexual attacks was alleged to have brought a widespread change in the understanding of rape during the war.

Although he had strong partisan views, Docquois proved to be an avid chronicler of the debates, drawing on newspaper and journal articles to lead his readers "day by day" through discussions about the *viol boche.* He began his account on 7 January 1915, when the Parisian newspaper *Le Matin* noted that a Belgian curé had given a speech stating, "In the name of the God of vengeance who condemns and the God of mercy who absolves, you do not have to perpetuate the abomination of which you were the innocent and sainted victims." The curé, without referring to abortion directly, indicated that "impure blood" would "corrupt the treasure of our veins" and that he absolved women who aborted pregnancies due to rape.[9] Astonished by this sermon, Docquois solicited reactions from various figures, including Paul Bourget, Maurice Barrès, and feminists like Marguerite Durand and Jeanne Schmahl.

The most forceful impetus for the debate over the children of rape that began in January 1915 was the appearance of the first official report of the Commission Instituée en Vue de Constater les Actes Commis par l'Ennemi en Violation du Droit des Gens. While the commission's initial report was issued on 17 December 1914, its findings appeared in the *Journal Officiel* and were disseminated in major Parisian newspapers on 8 January 1915. Thus the front pages of Parisian dailies like *Le Matin, L'Éclair, L'Écho de Paris,* and *Le Figaro* reprinted the commission's conclusions with headlines highlighting the Germans' "savagery and ferocity" and articles reporting the numerous women who "were victims of odious attacks."[10] *Le Matin,* in reprinting the official report "in extenso," declared it "a historic document . . . [that] France has the right to know all in its entirety."[11] Thus the published accounts of the report did not spare readers the details of women raped under the eyes of their husbands or in front of their children; of the rape of eleven year olds; of multiple rapes; and of the rape and murder of mothers and their daughters.[12] The circulation of such stories provided the framework for what Docquois recorded, the growing resonance of debates over the fates of these victims in public forums.

On 19 January, the militant *La Bataille Syndicaliste,* under the heading "Should One Kill the Child of the Barbarian?" pondered the question of abortion. Docquois recounted that in a personal encounter the following day, a wounded man informed him that one of his comrades in the trenches—who had left behind his wife, his fifteen-year-old orphaned niece, and his maid—received a letter stating: "My friend, we are all three pregnant. Do you want us to die?"[13] By the second week of February, Georges Montorgueil was reporting in *L'Éclair* that the minister of the interior, Louis Malvy, had offered full government support for such women and noting the irony that the children who nursed "with the milk of hate" could become "the ones to avenge their outraged mothers."[14]

Moreover, as the public debates that followed further revealed, the appearance of such news was in keeping with the instructions given to censors. According to circulars issued on 22 March and 30 September 1915, newspaper articles dealing with "women victims of violence on the part of Germans" could not advocate anything "the law qualified as a crime"—specifically implying abortion. The appearance, however, of discussions of "philosophical" or "moral" questions raised by such acts of violence was permissible.[15]

Short stories appearing in various major newspapers offered a means by which the possible outcomes for the children of rape could be debated. Through imaginative literature, closely akin to parables, authors offered their opinions on what should be done with these raped mothers and their children. Léon Frapie's "Les Réprouvés" told the story of a young man who sought to redeem his own poverty-stricken parentage by marrying a woman whom he knew to be impregnated as a result of German rape. By raising a child "in total opposition to his author," Frapie suggested that the man would "save" himself and the woman.[16] Within the space of two weeks, *Le Journal* offered two different stories on these issues. One, "La menteuse," focused on a woman who as she is about to die invents an affair with a French man in order to persuade her mother to raise her child. The other, "L'horrible secret," illustrated the dilemma faced by a young, devoted wife, who fears herself pregnant because of rape and must decide what to tell her soldier husband.[17] Realizing that his hearing the truth about her attack would destroy their lives—after he tells her that when a friend of his heard of his wife's rape he killed himself—the wife decides instead to follow the advice of her neighbor and physician by seducing her husband. She thus keeps herself as well as her spouse ignorant of whether the child will be a product of a German rape or a French marriage. The story concludes with the husband's smiling realization that his wife "does not want to lose the occasion [of his leave] to prepare a future defender of the *patrie*."

These tales reduced the issues involved in the case of rape-impregnated women to fairly simplified situations in which choices were clear-cut, but the social policy aspects of the debate became more complicated when the issue moved into the political sphere after 18 February. On that date, Louis Martin, the left-wing senator from the Var, proposed legislation in the Senate that would have "provisionally suspended" all punishments for abortion in French territories occupied by Germany during the war.[18] There were at least three different responses to Martin's proposal. In general, they broke down into support for the possibility of abortion, support for abandonment of the child after birth to be raised by the state (the stance of Minister of the Interior Malvy and Director of Public Assistance Brisac), and the belief—despite the horror of the situation—in the triumph of maternal love and French maternal blood over all. The debate, now centering on abortion, not rape, took to the pages of journals and newspapers, ranging from the feminist periodical *La Française* to *L'Écho de Paris,* which printed the opinion of archnationalist Maurice Barrès. Two special issues of the *Revue* (the former *Revue des Revues*) published a variety of answers to the question: "The child of crime, should he be born?"[19] In these special forums, in articles appearing in the general and medical presses, and in reactions to the queries of writers like Docquois, men and women offered variations on the responses described above.

Meanwhile, official measures to have the children raised by the state were, at least theoretically, being put into action. A confidential June circular regarding refugees specified how such women impregnated by Germans could arrange for the births of these children and if they chose, abandon them to the state.[20] And in the regular report on the general situation of the Department of the Seine, the prefect documented the special provisions made for *femmes violentées* coming from the invaded regions. According to a circular of the Ministry of the Interior, such women were allowed to abandon these children to public care in the capital.[21] In the section of this lengthy report on "Assistance," the prefect noted that steps had been taken to give aid "in a fashion at once the most complete and the most discreet to the unhappy women and young girls" forcibly impregnated by Germans in the invaded territory. Commenting that it was in the interest of the race to avoid abortion, which, "under the blow of truly natural but unreflected emotion," a small part of the public at this "moment envisioned as legitimate," the prefect detailed the measures to be taken to aid those who could not keep and raise these children. Women would be assisted, their deliveries would be kept secret, and the children would become *pupilles* (wards) of the Service of Assisted Children—where they would be prevented from ever discovering their origins or being maltreated as a result of them. The mothers would have the combined resources of the Department of the Seine, Public Assistance of the City of Paris, the departmental inspectorate of assisted children, and the prefect of police at their disposal. In addition, the prefect stated that the special measures undertaken for women violated by the enemy and their children would include the "repatriation" of women to the areas from which they had fled in order to give birth in Parisian hospitals.[22] The report provided no details on how many women took advantage of this preferential treatment or if the number of births of non-Parisian women or the number of abandoned children increased, but it is clear that government policy at the height of the debates of 1915 deliberately sought—in the name of the "race"—to avoid abortion and promote the well-being of these alleged mothers and babies.

Like politicians, influential women debated the fate of rape-impregnated women from the invaded regions. The feminist periodical *La Française* ran a series of articles throughout January and February, with a discussion continuing into May 1915, concerning the "little undesirables." Jane Misme, the paper's editor, emphasized that the blood of these children would be 50 percent French and, "how, in the name of the *patrie,* the family, feminine dignity, pity . . . could a country, a mother, a family reject children born in this country, of this indigenous mother?"[23] A wide range of views, however, were found in the pages of *La Française:* some women, like Mlle. Marguerite André, suggested that "abortion ought to be the rule," while others, like Mme. Laborie, vice president of the French midwives association, warned of the dangers of abortion and cautioned that whatever its origin, the child was a human being.[24]

The overarching perspective of Misme, however, remained clear as she cited letters from soldiers and public figures supporting *La Française*'s stance that mothers should raise their children, whatever their paternity. Indeed, when a distributor of the journal informed

Misme that she could not deliver the issues of *La Française* concerning the debate over the children of rape to a girl's *école supérieure,* Misme responded that these girls were at an age when "the feminine being formed herself physically for maternity. Is this not the hour to begin to make them conscious of all . . . [the] sorrow and duty of the feminine condition?" [25] In a letter to Docquois, Misme argued that the mother was a "saint," the child was "sacred," and that mothers had a duty to their children, just as society and the family had a duty to these women and their offspring. [26] According to this assimilationist argument even the children of rape could be made "French."

Another feminist perspective, delivered to Docquois in 1915 from Jeanne Schmahl, took a different view. "When brute force excluded the possibility of [maternal] choice, of consent," Schmahl argued, "then, the right of the woman becomes absolute. The violation of her person confers on her, unquestionably, the right to decide in what measure she will support the results and consequences of imposed maternity." [27] Here a common split in feminist theory and practice emerged, between those who valorized women's difference, particularly arguing for maternity's preeminence, and those who argued for equal rights, insisting on women being granted the same rights as any liberal individual. Either a woman had control over her body or she was always a mother, first and foremost. [28]

Several other female writers who entered the debate insisted that the choice be left to women but were certain of the outcome: that maternal love or instinct would triumph over all. For Colette, "the unhappy violated [women] did not need to be counseled or guided." [29] She believed that, if left alone, a woman would accept her child once it was born. Other writers, such as Lucie Delarue-Mardrus, insisted that "the women themselves with their heart[s] must find a solution" but that the child produced under these conditions "would be a good *Français,* exclusively French, because of having been born of a French woman, nourished by French milk." Colette Yver not only championed the birth of these children who would be "naturally" loved by their mothers but further pointed out—in response to arguments against racial mixing— that "among the best of us are [those] who have, to some degree, German blood." [30]

These words point to an important element of these discussions, always implicit, and only sometimes explicit: the eugenic problems of Franco-German children as being of a "mixed race." The eugenic aspect of the debate emerged most strongly in the discussions among scientists and physicians. Professor Adolphe Pinard, a prominent obstetrician, leading pronatalist propagandist, and influential writer on maternity, affirmed, in the name of all medical persons, his opposition to abortion and to all methods that would restrict births. Still, even Pinard conceded that, for the infants conceived of German rape, abandonment was the only solution. In contrast, two members of the Scientific Academy—Professors Delage and Henneguy—recognized the "legitimacy of abortion." Henneguy, in particular, argued that "abortion is a crime, but killing an enemy on the field of battle is a glorious act; preventing the birth of a product of a criminal attack is not only licit but even necessary."[31] Because the danger to the French nation-as-race came primarily from the taint of specifically German blood, one French doctor viewed abortion as a way to "déteutoniser."[32]

Celebrated poet and anti-alcohol campaigner Jean Finot offered one of the clearest expositions of a pro-abortion stance based on eugenics. He argued for the elimination of these children "pure and simple . . . even against the desire of the mother who wishes to conserve such a fruit." He explained his adamancy on the subject by using a story he had read—he could no longer remember where—about the exploration of Central Africa:

> [A] European wife of one of the first colonialists who installed himself in Central Africa, was, one fine day, captured by some gorillas. . . . [T]he unhappy woman had [then] to submit, during the long sojourn, to the forced gallantries of her ferocious ravishers. . . .
>
> Finally, by miracle . . . she made her escape and rejoined her husband. In what state, great god, I leave it to you to imagine.
>
> The assiduous passions of these messieurs the gorillas had had the result you guess. . . .
>
> It goes without saying that neither the husband nor the wife hesitated to get rid immediately of a being whose origin was so peculiar!
>
> In reading [of] Boche rapes in Belgium, in the north and east of France, in Poland and everywhere they have passed, this story returned to me.
>
> The German race is truly the race of gorillas, who, because they have stolen the Fire (of Civilisation), imagine they can maintain themselves and be equal to men.[33]

For Finot, the Germans' actions called for "torrents of blood and fire," not the conservation of their offspring. By so racializing the Germans, by reducing them to animals—to gorillas and in this context clearly to colonial men—who thought themselves human, this story powerfully demonstrated why some people believed that the intermingling of German "blood" with that of any other nation would result only in an aberration of nature.[34]

Paul Rabier also persuasively argued for the legitimacy of abortion in such cases in a 1915 pamphlet titled *La loi du mâle: A propos de l'enfant du barbare*.[35] For Rabier, the circumstances of these conceptions as the result of rapes, which involved "repulsion, violence, [and] struggle," would naturally cause women to "hate" the father and feel "indifference if not aversion for the child." Even worse, for some women, pregnancy could not even be traced to one "enemy" but only to a "collective." Under these conditions "maternal love, however beautiful, [could] neither be born nor developed." In such a situation, abortion was "for the species, the most desirable solution, a[s well as] for the innocent child who will not be a pariah and for the mother." Attacking those who denounced abortions, he argued that, in this context, abortion became but another fact of war, no different than a bullet or bayonet wound to a German—and moreover, more charitable to the child than abandonment. In response to those who urged that married or engaged women keep and raise the child—whose "errors" would be corrected by his French parents—Rabier also insisted that paternity, in contrast to his definition of maternity as "natural, profound, [and] generous," was merely "social, superficial," and rooted in "pride."[36]

In his conclusion, Rabier confirmed his belief that abortion was the best solution, but he did offer an alternative, which had an intriguing imperialist perspective. He suggested that if women carried these creatures to term, they should be raised in France by wet nurses for three years and then sent to the colonies to become *français d'outre-mer*. The experience of being "colonialists" would "amend their Teuton blood," and they would be able to create tranquil lives, free from "all bad memories." Thus would the metropolis and motherland remain free of contamination until, bit by bit, these children would be naturalized into French culture. As for the problem of abortion and its effect on women, Rabier was confident that, in the words of Dumas, "motherhood is the patriotism of women" and that French women would continue to prove themselves "good patriots."[37]

As for other responses, the *Journal du Droit International* summed up several official actions, starting with three resolutions passed on the subject by the Ligue Nationale des Femmes Françaises at a conference held in April 1915. The first of these insisted that the violated woman was free to accept or reject a child born from a brutal assault; the second demanded that these women be entitled to reparations for their moral and physical suffering; and the last urged that in cases where mothers decided to raise these children themselves, they should be given an annual pension from the state.[38] The *Journal du Droit*'s 1916 overview also provided one of the rare glimpses of German responses to this issue. An article appearing in *Le Figaro* in February of 1916—later cited by the *Journal du Droit*—quoted an *ordre du jour* from a German general: "[I]n the interest of the mothers, I give orders that with their consent, the children could be sent to Germany, where they will be raised. For a son, the mother would receive 150 marks and 100 marks for a daughter." The statement also declared that no support would be given to women who kept these infants and warned that any infanticides would be judged by a court-martial. This report was also mentioned in *La Depêche,* which described the German offer as buying children "like beasts."[39] Since German acknowledgment of the existence of French women who might have been impregnated by German soldiers cannot be verified, it is difficult to evaluate how factual or widespread was the offer to pay women for these children.

The prominent 1917 infanticide case of Joséphine Barthélemy focused abstract discussions about the German impregnation of French women.[40] Joséphine Barthélemy was a twenty year old from Lorraine who spent six months in prison awaiting her trial and was prosecuted for infanticide before the Court of Assizes of the Seine and acquitted on 23 January 1917.[41] Barthélemy claimed to have been raped by a German in November of 1915, while she was working as a servant at the German Red Cross hospital in Chambly. She later fled the region and took refuge with a married sister, never telling the sister what had befallen her. No one detected her pregnancy. Then, in the middle of an August night, Joséphine gave birth to a child, who she claimed never cried and who was later found dead.[42]

During Barthélemy's trial, her lawyer, Maître Loewel, portrayed her crime as "a legitimate act."[43] In his final pleas, Loewel pointed out: "[T]here is not a soul among you whom sorrow has not touched and who has not cried over the death of a dear being fallen on the field of honor. . . . I ask if Joséphine Barthélemy is guilty for not having let live the child of those who killed your sons, and in answer, I call upon your hearts as fathers and as Frenchmen!" He reminded the jury that they already knew what the Germans had done, they could "read and re-read . . . the official recitation of German atrocities," and described the harsh reality that had confronted Joséphine, who for sixteen months had lived "an infernal existence, working morning and evening for the invader, dying of fatigue and hunger." Outlining the long set of sufferings that had befallen Barthélemy, Loewel further asserted that she was being punished for the fact that as "an ignorant peasant woman" without resources she could not do what other women freely did and have an abortion. He went on to counter questions that her maternal instinct should have prevailed by declaring that the only instinct directing her was that of hate, for the enemy, for the child that would be a continual reminder of her outrage. Suggesting that women like Barthélemy were "legion," Loewel insisted that she was a "martyr," not guilty but herself a "victim" who "refused a life that she had not agreed to create," a life born of a "race of barbarians."[44]

Although Joséphine Barthélemy herself said little at her trial, such emotive arguments may have persuaded the jury, even though it had been established that she had not told anyone of her original attack and that the act of infanticide seemed premeditated.[45] Several newspapers used the word *hébétée* (dazed) to characterize the appearance of this "large" or "strong" young woman at her trial.[46] As one newspaper noted, when asked to recount the crime against her, Barthélemy could move her lips but "pronounce but a few intelligible words."[47] Her silence, despite the questions asked of her and the efforts of her lawyer, suggested to the prosecution and some commentators that her allegations could not be proved. Moreover, several commentators also observed that both German and French men were at Chambly, the site of the crime.[48] Barthélemy's sole reported comment was: "I did not want to have a child born of Boche." While this seemed a compelling enough reason to some, to the most ardent believers in the sanctity of all life, even that conceived in rape, it was inadequate.

While her defense won her an eventual acquittal, one met with bravos and loud applause, according to newspaper accounts, for a number of public figures her trial raised the disturbing specter of further legitimizing infanticide. Marguerite de Witt-Schlumberger, the feminist leader of the Union Française pour le Suffrage des Femmes, claimed to feel no enthusiasm for the triumphant acquittal, however much she pitied this young victim of horrible attacks, because "the little being that she brought into the world was as innocent as she, and she did not have the right to kill it." The prominent obstetrician Professor Pinard also protested the acquittal, avowing the sanctity of human life, whatever its origins.[49]

Perhaps the harshest reaction to Barthélemy's acquittal appeared in a long article by Dr. Gustave Drouineau in the *Revue Philanthropique*. Drouineau called upon the public to decide if it were "possible to introduce into our juridical customs the right that follows the proclamations of the jury of the Seine, that is to say: the woman [as] mistress of her maternity." Recognizing the special case of victims of German outrages, Drouineau nonetheless insisted on the broader implications of this question: Why should a mother who conceived because of rape be more "the mistress of her maternity" than an ordinary woman? It was "illogical and inadmissible," he continued, to think that "nine seconds of paternity counted more than nine months of maternity." He noted that ample public aid was available to women such as Barthélemy and that raising a child in ignorance of his origins, among an "honest peasant family," would eradicate all taint of Boche ancestry. Most importantly, Drouineau insisted that the acquittal of Barthélemy, if taken as a precedent, would be an absolute disaster for France. Citing familiar arguments about the profound danger posed to the nation by the falling birthrate, Drouineau demanded that the error of the Barthélemy jury be the first and last of its kind.[50]

Despite a consensus, shared by Drouineau, about her unintelligence, all of the discussions about Barthélemy remained vague on the question of whether she was a victim of rape or had manipulated public sentiment as an excuse for getting rid of an unwanted child.[51] Her very act of infanticide and public avowal that she did not want the baby because it was "Boche," were enough for some to suspect her motives. A truly innocent woman, they argued, would hide her shame and keep the child. Others publicly voiced their fear that other *filles-mères* caught in the act of "suppressing their children, would say, like Joséphine Barthélemy: "Bah! It's nothing but a Boche."[52] Insisting that French blood and, in particular, the ultimately powerful maternal blood, would make the child "French," partisans in the debates over the permissibility of abortion or tolerance of infanticide challenged the power of the paternal inheritance of nationality established in the civil code while simultaneously ignoring general questions of sexual violence against women, focusing not on their plight but on the future of the nation.

Thus, the question of what to do with the products of German rape divided French commentators onto two sides, one stressing the potent taint of German ancestry and the other the sanctity of French maternal blood. Neither the feminist nor medical communities were able to reach consensus on these points. Strong differences of opinion could be found among intellectual figures like Colette, Delarue-Mardrus, and Finot. If some argued that women had the right to decide what to do with their enforced pregnancies—and the acquittal of Joséphine Barthélemy could point to the power of this rhetoric—others insisted that maternity was a state matter, not an individual one, especially during this national crisis. These debates provided the forum for the struggle over the primacy of blood strains and revealed French wartime attitudes toward questions of gender and a racialized nationalism.[53] They also reemphasized that for women motherhood was synonymous with patriotism.

The Rape of Mothers in British Propaganda

The question of rape and its consequences was also powerfully developed in British propaganda. Between August 1914 and the onset of conscription in 1916, the British Parliamentary Recruiting Committee (PRC) produced a series of posters designed to persuade able-bodied men to volunteer for His Majesty's armed forces.[54] As several historians have demonstrated, the posters partially directed their message to women in hopes that they would act as agents of moral suasion.[55] One early PRC poster asked the "Women of Britain" a series of questions, beginning with: "You have read what the Germans have done in Belgium. Have you thought what they would do if they invaded this Country? Do you realise that the safety of your home and children depends on our getting more men *NOW?*"[56] Implicit in such messages was the idea that the fate of Belgian women was common knowledge and that both empathy with the victims of rape and the threat of their own possible rape would convince women to send their men to war.

In one poster, titled "The Hun and the Home," the idyllic British countryside was contrasted with ruined buildings of the war-torn continent, while the text beneath compared "Our mothers and wives safe" with "THEIR women . . . murdered and worse."[57] Posters showing Belgian victims made clear the fate, considered worse than murder, befalling women. One large poster, with the caption "Remember Belgium," depicted a German officer clutching a bayonet dripping with blood standing on a young woman whose breast lies exposed and whose body is crushed beneath the German's huge boot. The text beside this image claimed to be taken from a British officer's letter appearing in *The Times* in December of 1914 and reads, in part:

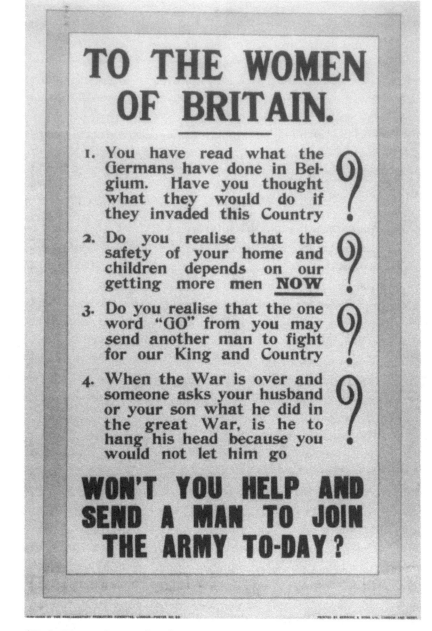

"To the Women of Britain," Parliamentary Recruiting Committee poster.
Courtesy of the Imperial War Museum.

I am in a small village . . . and can see the horrible cruelty of the Germans to the inhabitants. We have got three girls in the trenches with us, who came to us for protection. One had no clothes on, having been outraged by the Germans. . . . Another poor girl has just come in, having had both her breasts cut off. Luckily I caught the Uhlan officer in the act, and with a rifle at 300 yards killed him. And now she is with us, but, poor girl, I am afraid she will die. She is very pretty, and only about 19, and only has her skirt on.

To drive the message home, the very bottom of the poster asks the viewer: "Should You Stand by While Such Things Go On? Our Brave Soldiers at the Front Need Your Help."[58] The effect of the visual imagery and the tales of horror suggested a natural and vast gulf between the honorable British officer and the abusive German. This certainly echoed French propaganda.[59]

The circulation of tales of horror and depravity as a way of signaling inherent, even racial, differences between Germans and Allies received strong support from official quarters. In Britain, a committee of inquiry, led by Lord Bryce—a man thought to be impeccably honest—was created to evaluate the reports of "outrages."[60] In a manner akin to the propaganda discussed above and to the documentation of French government accounts, the Bryce report presented testimony showing "how women were publicly raped in the market place of the city, five young German officers assisting." Other women victims were described as having had their breasts cut off, and accounts depicted fleeing women with "children falling out of their mothers' arms."[61]

A closer examination of the kind of evidence presented in the report demonstrates that while the Bryce committee focused on crimes against women in general, it reported numerous attacks on women who were mothers, which implied the full horror of the German assault. The appendix of the report included examples of a woman raped in her ninth month of pregnancy as well as of rapes resulting in impregnation.[62] The repeated image of the cutting off of breasts highlighted the vulnerability of a female appendage clearly linked to a woman's maternal functions, and the description of children falling bleeding from their mothers' arms also vividly described the victimization of women as mothers.[63] Mothers thus could be injured directly or through attacks on their children. Even as the Bryce report chronicled attacks on individual women and girls associated with their role as mothers, its depiction of the overt and multiple violations of women, even "in the market place of the city," suggested the larger, racial and national dimensions of these alleged attacks. Rape as an instrument of war in these accounts became not merely an individual act but a collective and significantly public display of German military strength. Concurrently rape might have been interpreted as also serving to pollute the women of the community. Even if women were left alive after the experience of the "outrage," their experience of procreative sexuality might be forever compromised. One British pamphlet that focused on German atrocities in France rather than Belgium underscored this point by suggesting that what German soldiers had done to French women was "part of a deliberately conceived and organized attempt to Germanize the North and East of France. No class of society has been exempt; wherever the Germans have passed women, young girls, children, even nuns, have been their victims." [64]

From a French or Belgian perspective, women killed after they had been raped could comprise a lost generation of real or potential mothers. Rape in itself could lead to a variety of possible maternal outcomes, all of them directly contradictory to the interests of the nation and, as we have seen in the French debates of 1915, of the nation conceived of as a "race." Thus, the subtext of the reports of the vicious treatment of women and children showed its British audience not only the individual experience of horror but a systematic attack on the present and future of an entire people.

Narrating Atrocities: Wartime Novels and the Politics of Rape and Maternity

Debates about atrocities committed against women not only took shape in philosophical arguments or propaganda. In many senses, their most powerful expositions occurred in the French and British narratives that sought, by fictional example, to inform and persuade readers of the importance of these questions of maternity, gender, and the nation's future. In several popular and well-received novels, the issue of wartime rape was discussed in a manner that linked it even more directly to nationalist and eugenic concerns. [65] Odette Dulac's *La houille rouge* (1916) and Albert Giuliani's *Les berceaux tragiques* (1916) combined stories of rape with the issues of depopulation and maternity. While ultimately on the same side of the debate, Dulac focused on the evils of abortion, and Giuliani focused on the preservation of the life of "children of rape." Lillith Hope's *Behold and See* (1917)—the tragedy of an English nun raped in a Belgian convent—presented a story where abortion was never an option, while Annie Vivanti Chartres's *Vae victis* (1917) considered questions of rape, maternity, and abortion in an even-handed manner: one character has an abortion and the other keeps her child, and neither choice is given a higher moral weight. In all these novels, maternity provided the dramatic proof that rape had occurred even when victims had no memory of the attack, and concern with the fate of the child or potential child overshadowed concern for the woman.

Albert Giuliani, like Odette Dulac, wrote his novel in the midst of French debates about the children of German rape. Giuliani's book was dedicated to his mother, who was "so saintly," and his charting of the story of Marthe Chamblay fully revealed the Catholic moral perspectives on this problem. *Les berceaux tragiques* opens with a first-person narrator, Maître Guirand, receiving an unexpected visit from Marthe Chamblay, the daughter of an old family friend, a beautiful, but deeply troubled young woman married to a reserve lieutenant. She tells him a familiar and harrowing story. After her husband's departure for the battle and the invasion of Lille, she and her young daughter were left behind defenseless. Forced to lodge two German soldiers in her home, Marthe observed their drunken behavior until: "One evening, the terrible thing was done. The beast, more than customarily drunk, had entered and claimed his prey. . . . She had wanted to cry, to struggle, to die. But the child was there, in the next [room], sleeping her innocent sleep. The crime was consummated in the silence of the night, a silence of death, under the drunken hiccups of the triumphant man." [66] Soon after, Marthe was evacuated and learned, after a silence of thirteen months, that her husband, Lucien, was a prisoner of war. However, to her horror, she has also become certain that there is a "new life" within her — "a life which is my death, our death, the death of our love, of our home, of our happiness . . . a life . . . who will kill us" (29). Marthe's despair is further heightened by the fact that Lucien will soon be repatriated.

In describing her plight to Maître Guirand, Marthe remains unable to decide what to do. The different possible outcomes for her situation are debated between men — most notably a priest, Abbé Mauret, and a man of science, Dr. Loriol. The doctor's perspective is clear: the mother should be aided and the "fruit of the violence" gotten rid of (75–77). The author's point of view is made evident by his portrayal of the Catholic perspective. To the abbé, the raped mothers of Belgium and France are saintlike and holy, "martyred like her [Marthe] by the same tormentors and carrying, like her, the cross of a shameful maternity" (81). For Abbé Mauret, there can be no question of accepting the doctor's "sacrificing the product of this conception": "The foetus lives. His right to life is . . . above the right of his parents to happiness. He is above the right of the French family to the integrity of its blood" (84–85). Here the national interests of the French family, the French race, are explicitly subordinated to God's law ordaining the preservation of life. However, the debate extends beyond the question of moral and religious law, to questions of heredity and depopulation, and finally the appeal to God and to the higher, moral law wins out.[67]

Yet the true test of the "French family" awaits the return of Lucien from his imprisonment. Although the abbé, the doctor, and Guirand meet Lucien at the station, they cannot bear to shatter his happiness by telling him the truth about his wife. It is only when he sees her pregnant body that the truth is revealed.[68] Unable to bear the sight of the pregnant Marthe, Lucien descends into a kind of madness. On Christmas eve, the abbé visits the couple and, in a private conversation with Marthe, is told of how Lucien approached her and, thinking she slept, came towards her with a revolver in his hand: "I saw, beyond my lowered eyelashes, the revolver aimed at me, at my chest which Lucien had uncovered. . . . Without moving, I saw the death for which I had called for so long. . . . I saw then the great tears running down his cheeks. . . . He listened, looked at his revolver, looked at me . . . then he returned to his room where all night, I heard him walking" (149–50). Subsequently, rather than actually attacking his wife, Lucien turns his anger towards the church. As Mauret comes to reason with Lucien after Marthe's report, Lucien denounces God: "Here is the benediction of your Blessed Lord to Christian spouses: a son of the Boche in the belly" (156).

In response, the priest uses the overarching justice not only of God but of the Third Republic to convince Lucien to accept what has happened and not to try to get rid of the fetus: "Could you, you a magistrate, condone this crime, this assassination? . . . Could you, you a public prosecutor, condone this insurrection against the law, . . . of which you are the faithful interpreter and indefectible keeper?" (162). Yet Lucien is not immediately persuaded; only subsequently does he become convinced—again by Mauret—that the acceptance of this coming child is also part of the French victory. For victory, he learns, is not only about armies, "it is also [the victory] of right over iniquity, that of civilization over barbarism, that of the Ideal over brute Force" (217).

The priest, delivering his message, conveniently, on Christmas, stresses that this child will not be one of crime "but the child of your mercy, the child of that paternity of the heart that can, so easily, triumph over the other. Oh! What a beautiful, humane, social, French task it will be for you to accomplish" (220). Reconciled to his "paternity," Lucien is able to declare publicly that he is the father of the child, symbolically named Noel (284).

Throughout this novel, Marthe Chamblay—the victim of the atrocity and the mother who has delivered her sainted, French blood to the infant—bows to the will of the men who surround her. Truly a victim, she voices no opinions of her own and tries to placate both her husband and her spiritual father. The heated debates over the product of her attack are waged between men, and the object of their attention is not her plight but increasingly that of her husband. The bravest gesture in the novel comes not from Marthe's quiet acceptance of her fate but from Lucien's response to the question posed by the local bureaucrat for the birth certificate: "Name of the father?" Thus the plot functions as much as a lesson on French paternity—the overarching idea that a child that can be made "French" by a French upbringing and a French mother deserves the recognition of French paternity—as it does as an illustration of German barbarity. The novel presented many of the issues debated in the French press and other nonfictional forums, but, in many ways, any discussion of Germans or the war was subsumed by the question of the permissibility of abortion. By providing a concrete and plausible example of the possible outcome of a "Boche rape," Giuliani suggested the only potentially happy solution, for the French nation and the French family, for this wartime problem: the acceptance of the will of God, however painful it might be.[69] In effect, Giuliani used the stories of the victims of German brutality both to instruct his readers about the higher moral law of Catholic justice and to confront the meaning of paternity.

The theme of Catholic and religious martyrdom ascribed to French atrocity accounts by historian Ruth Harris was not, however, restricted to French examples.[70] Lillith Hope's *Behold and See* was a wartime atrocity novel that also confronted religion and the contest between the law of men and the law of God, but in a British context. Here, German brutality was demonstrated by attacks not just on ordinary civilian women but on nuns. *The Times Literary Supplement* commented in February 1917 that the novel presented "the terrible living fate of an English nun caught by the German invasion in Belgium" and that "it is a moving and poignant narrative, the effects given with restraint and with insight."[71] One might quibble with the characterization of restraint, since the novel begins immediately after the Germans invade Belgium, with the mother superior hearing "[h]orrible tales of blood-lust and rapine," which she initially discounts.[72] Soon, however, the Germans take over the convent, and one soldier, catching sight of Sister Rose, "advanced towards her. A guttural sound escaped him, and his red lips widened in a luscious smile. Like some huge beast of prey he seemed to the young nun" (45). Quickly, the young nuns are hidden in a locked part of the basement, but this proves to be only a temporary protection:

> There was a roar of laughter as the flying steps retraced their way back. The agonized screams of a woman once more split the air. At the sound the terrified nuns sprang to their feet, huddled together like a frightened flock of sheep, and listened with bated breath. . . .
>
> They were coming down the stairs. Thick drunken voices bawled to each other as they descended. . . . The steps were nearing the door. . . . A derisive shout of laughter. . . . A pounding on the door. The bolt held.
>
> Then rifle-butts smashed in the panels of the door (49–51).

Although propaganda typically made clear—by using the terms "outrage" or "violation"—what was happening to women, in this novel, the direct violence, the attacks on the nuns, transpire beyond the reader's sight. Through vividly depicting what is overheard and its aftereffects, Hope implies the criminal bestiality of the German soldiers without ever showing it. In fact, the violation of the nuns is presented to them, by their superior, as a kind of sacrifice: "We, His suffering handmaids, offer our outraged bodies as an expiation for the sins of us all" (56).

To this "martyrdom" is added another: Rose and several of the other nuns find themselves pregnant. In the novel's subsequent section, the first-person narration of Rose temporarily takes over, allowing the reader to witness her agony and growing confusion. At first she describes herself as "an automaton from whom an enemy has despoiled the soul, a puppet with no volition of her own" (83). Like Marthe Chamblay, Rose seems helpless and unable to cope with her fate. Soon, however, her "shame" becomes "her secret joy," and she begins to reconsider obeying the church's orders, which would have her give up her child and retake her vows to resume her former life. Finally at peace with herself, she confesses to her mother superior that though initially "I revolted with the nausea of the evil and shame thrust upon me, . . . God was gracious to me. He awoke in me the divine nature of a mother" (91). Here, unquestionably, the higher calling of motherhood, a divine calling like that of the Virgin Mary herself, is placed before the laws of both church and state.

From this point on, Rose's choice is clear, even though she is warned about the innate evil her child may inherit. Rose leaves the convent, assuming the identity of the wife of a widowed soldier so as to guard her honor and that of her family (101–2). Hope then attempted to portray the birth of the child as a redemptive and inspirational act. Rose finds that "God fashioned me a mother, prepared my body for the holy ordeal. . . . No woman realizes bliss until she feels the soft lips of her own child at her breast" (121–22). Yet, strikingly, these sentiments are contrasted with the revulsion that Rose also feels as she recognizes the features of her attacker in the infant: "I was once again in the vortex of that maelstrom of evil, a hapless victim whirled to destruction. . . . For one sinful moment, I hated the child, the incarnation of a foul crime" (124). Once the child cries, Rose's maternal instinct comes flooding back. The return of pure maternal love does not, however, remove the sense of ambiguity embedded in her motherhood. Systematically, Rose becomes associated more clearly with Mary, as well as with Hagar, both martyred biblical mothers who had been cast out of society.

The second half of the novel traces Rose's attempts, in the secular world of the wartime British countryside, to find a place for herself and her son. Living with her sister-in-law and initially rejected by her devoutly Catholic brother, Rose can never be at ease. Even as her brother warns her that her child — "the child of a German devil" — will always be tainted by his heredity, Rose vehemently claims him as belonging to her alone. At the end of the novel, Rose dies, leaving her child to the keeping of a soldier and his wife — her devoted friends who are featured in a subplot of the novel. Against this backdrop, Lillith Hope firmly stated her concurrence with Rose's claiming the child as hers alone:

> The bacteria of sin which wanders in the blood of one generation to another may have the power to poison the character of that piteous plaything of a cruel fate. Yet even in the immovable law of nature there lies a consolation and a hope.
>
> The child of so gentle and holy a woman as Rose will sense the

influence of those prenatal months of ceaseless prayer and interces-
sion. Heredity will declare itself, the heredity of the mother with all
its ancestral traditions of virtue and honour. (299–300)

Even as the departing soldier goes off "to cleanse the world of German
Kultur and to scourge the Huns into some sense of morality . . . [to]
do my bit to avenge poor Rose upon that scum of the earth," the child
born of rape will be redeemed by maternal virtue (297).

In this atrocity novel written for an audience allegedly far-removed
from the theater of war, Lillith Hope portrayed German brutality in
a most heinous form. Not only did she emphasize Germans attacking
young, innocent women, but by making them nuns, she further called
upon a sense of religious and moral indignation—striving for a story,
as *The Times Literary Supplement* put it, both "moving and poignant." By
having them commit rape in a convent, Hope ensured the Germans
would come across as truly a breed apart, who could profane even this
sanctuary. The question of complicity, of any possible suspicion falling
on her heroines, is answered at the outset. Sister Rose is so virtuous—
is constructed so closely to resemble the ultimate sacrificial and virgin
mother, Mary—that it would have been hard for a wartime reader to
disagree that those who had raped her were indeed immoral "scum of
the earth." Abortion does not even enter in the debates about Rose's
child; the question is never the infant's right to live but Rose's maternal
right to care for it.

While *Les berceaux tragiques* focused on the problem of "tainted
infants" as a question of paternity, *Behold and See* demonstrated the
primary importance of maternity. Motherhood—and in many ways a
motherhood both specifically and ironically English and Catholic—
was celebrated here as the ultimate womanly virtue. Thus, Hope's novel
functioned on several different didactic levels. First, it dramatized the
bestiality of the Germans in Belgium by depicting a lack of morality
so deep that they could violate nuns. Second, it explicitly claimed that
motherhood could determine and shape the future of a child, a family,
and the nation. In contrast to concurrent legal definitions of nationality, in this example, the child, though conceived from a drunken and
brutal act of force, takes after his pure and tragic English mother.
Even though Rose initially feels some revulsion for this child, by the
story's end "Johnnie" has begun to resemble any English lad and will
be raised as an Englishman in total ignorance of his origins. Thus, in
complicated ways, far from supporting the notion of blind heredity or

classic eugenic arguments about the indomitable effects of one's origins, this atrocity tale promoted maternal strength and the capacity of "prenatal . . . prayer" to overcome the most tragic of circumstances. As with the earlier French example, motherhood not only embodied women's patriotism but also produced little patriots, regardless of their paternity.

In some accounts of raped and impregnated women, religious issues were portrayed as being much less important than intensely national questions of the fitness of the population and the need for future citizens. In her novel *La houille rouge,* Odette Dulac blended an antiabortion diatribe with a spy novel, where abortion becomes much more of a crime against the nation than against God.[73] The novel begins with a group of women in the waiting room of a Parisian midwife. They include a married woman whose husband wants no more children, a medical student, and a seduced and abandoned piano teacher; they are all, for different reasons, seeking abortions. The women eventually abort their pregnancies and proceed with their lives, while the midwife, Madame Rhoea (after being arrested and acquitted) is blackmailed into participating in a fanatical spy ring of the Kaiser, which goes by the name of the Houille Rouge (red coal).[74]

The outbreak of war finds the various female characters caught up in the general wave of patriotism and anxiety. As part of her spying activities to infiltrate the heart of French society and prepare the way for the Kaiser's takeover of France, Mme. Rhoea has joined the Red Cross and, at the outbreak of war, is set to journey to the front. As she prepares to depart Paris, Mme. Rhoea encounters two of her former clients, women who were introduced in the novel's opening scene: Madame Breton de l'Écluse and the female medical student, now doctor, Jeanne Deckes. All three women are heading directly into the path of the oncoming German army.

In describing the experiences of these characters once they encounter the invaders, Dulac presents the horrors that befall them as stemming directly from their past abortions. Their sufferings are exacerbated by the shame they feel because of their past misdeeds against the nation. Madame Rhoea ends up near the front and soon in the midst of battle. Here, after witnessing the Germans' total disregard for human life and for the "rules" of war, she is overcome by guilt at her behavior as both an abortionist and a participant in the secret spy organization. She begins to go insane as she listens to a chorus of soldiers' voices calling for "Maman" as they lie dying (126).[75] She even encounters a man at whose birth she assisted, who asks her to help him to kiss the portrait of his mother before he dies, and when she begins to wonder why one would bring children into the world in light of what she sees on the battlefield, she knows the answer: "To save France" (129). Watching the victorious Germans march by, Rhoea begins to comprehend the importance of "numbers," to realize the consequences of *dénatalité* (the decline in the French birthrate), and she finally loses her mind. Screaming out, "It's I who opened the door to this monster. . . . Don't condemn me without listening to me . . . I swear . . . and I repent. . . . [T]oday, they are eating all the infants that I have killed," the midwife-turned-abortionist calls for France to rouse itself (136–37). She wanders, yelling, into the streets, runs into the German troops, and disappears from view.[76]

Meanwhile, Madame Breton de l'Écluse has arrived at her château near Coucy to organize the retreat of her servants and dependents, but she becomes caught up in the calm atmosphere and her work for the Red Cross. Her thoughts, however, keep returning to her son, André, in the army and to speculations about "*the Other*," the one she aborted. The phrase *un de plus* (one more, one besides) keeps going through her head as her conscience is troubled by the idea that the "one" she aborted could have been the soldier who saved her son, the officer in charge of a decisive fight (142). By having given birth instead of having had an abortion, she might thus have provided someone who could potentially save her beloved son, should he be endangered, or even the nation itself.

As in other atrocity novels, the supposed calm is broken by the arrival of German Hussars, who take over the château, including her own room, the symbolic private sanctuary. Even more humiliating is the discovery that their leader, Fritz, was formerly Mme. Breton's clothes fitter at the couture house of Nadoff. Previously, Dulac had attacked the "German" influence on French fashion, implying that couture styles helped to lower the birthrate by distorting the bodies of vain French women. That fashion thus destroyed a woman's natural, maternal shape is one of the themes harped on in the novel, and the character of Fritz embodies the German spy in the house of fashion who has thus done the Kaiser's bidding.[77] As more and more wine is consumed, Fritz, as commandant, orders the others to leave Mme. Breton alone with him. Declaring that he must have vengeance, Fritz informs her that she must be violated, to which she responds "By you? Make me laugh!" Fritz agrees that women do "disgust" him, but he will revenge himself on her nonetheless by ordering his "valet," Hans, to ravish her. Hans obliges, and "what passed, under the eyes of the satiated beast, defies the most impure pen" (153–54).

Three weeks later, both the baroness and one of the servant girls find themselves experiencing strange symptoms of nausea and soon discover that they are both pregnant. As Madame realizes this, she thinks of the child she aborted and wonders how she could have possibly refused a "legitimate maternity" now that she knows that the seed of the enemy is growing inside her (163). Both women conclude that, in the words of the peasant woman who cooks for the household, as "men are equal before death, we [women] are equal before life," and they accept their fates and prepare for their impending motherhood. When her child is born, Madame Breton de l'Écluse demonstrates her full acceptance of her fate by actively embracing the legal fiction that her new son is "a legitimate child," just as if he had been the offspring of her husband.

A similar fate—of rape followed by pregnancy—has befallen Dr. Jeanne Deckes. Having gone to the front to assist the wounded, she finds herself in the midst of a German onslaught and is raped by an enormous and drunken Pomeranian (195–97). Despite her "thirty-nine years[,] . . . during the drama of blood, fire, alcohol and bestiality, the atom of the enemy has taken hold . . ." (200). Believing this fate to be "the worst humiliation," Deckes finds herself in no position to have another abortion. However, when her German captors find out that she is pregnant and possibly by a German, they too find the idea an "abomination. . . . [We] will not let you have this honor" (213). At the idea that the Germans would claim this child, Jeanne Deckes is filled with immense anger and maternal pride, stating defiantly that he "will be French. He is French" (214).[78] After her son's birth she embraces the mysteries and duties of maternal love, giving him the name "Christian" and forgetting all thoughts of his origins.[79]

The novel closes with the doctor's return to Paris, where she gives a lecture in order "to challenge her sisters the women of France" (297) to have children as their patriotic responsibility. Appearing on a public platform at a meeting to which she has invited "all the figures of feminism, the press and the arts," Jeanne Deckes addresses, "above all, intelligent women" (297). Beside her lies Christian, whom she introduces first as one "born of a woman intellectual and a brute drunk on alcohol and crime." After the public reaction of disgust, she states more simply, "It's my son" (299). She then issues a direct challenge to her "intellectual" and "feminist" audience, calling herself and her son symbols and defending her actions as being to the supreme benefit of the race, "since for too long, the 'makers of angels' [abortionists], the love of luxury, the stupidity of fashion and now the cannon have made our Race anemic" (303). Urging her audience to "save France," she calls upon women to "Put life in balance with death. . . . May cradles be the Marseillaise of the hearth: Form the battalions of future epics! . . . Women of France, take for your slogan, these words promising men and victories: Gunpowder and Milk!" (304–6).

In Georges Docquois's account of the debates over the children resulting from German rapes, Odette Dulac claimed that she "had already pleaded the cause of the tragic cradles in her book, *La houille rouge*," but here, too, she reiterated her cry of alarm. Like her character Jeanne Deckes, Dulac appealed to all French women to organize themselves for "life" as men have organized themselves for "death," she outlined a specific plan for the establishment of child care and nursery and primary schools, and she stated directly that "above all, [society must] admit finally that it is as glorious to be a mother as to be a soldier."[80] Attacking those who feared the tainted blood of children produced by the German rape of French women, Dulac declared, "The blood of a Française is pure enough to clean all blemishes, even German ones."

In many ways, Dulac's novel provided an even more compelling presentation of these views, since the travails suffered by her various heroines ultimately demonstrated the necessity, the power, and the glory of French motherhood. The maternal valor of characters such as Jeanne Deckes and Madame Breton de l'Écluse offered an equivalent heroism to that of French soldiers, and the very rejection of maternity was shown to be exactly what the Germans—the emblem of bestiality and violence—had worked for all along.

Such views were met with some skepticism from reviewer Rachilde, who in the *Mercure de France* criticized the novel's representation of the problem of depopulation as stemming from the Kaiser, which she described as "perhaps a pretty patriotism . . . but also much too simple." Despite all the crimes the Kaiser doubtless committed, he did not need to "serve as the emissary" for the sterility of French women. Seizing upon the occasion of reviewing Dulac's text to urge a change in social education as necessary to combat *dénatalité*, Rachilde deemed the end of Dulac's novel, the conference held by Jeanne Deckes, which "offer[ed] the result of enemy violence for the admiration or pity of the public," something "extraordinary." She added that the adoption of "the little boches" should not impede the conservation of "the little French [who were] truly French." [81]

Thus, Dulac rewrote the war—as others also perceived it—as a struggle not solely between soldiers but also between "populations" or even "blood lines." Rather than focusing in any significant manner on the rapes of her mother-heroines, Dulac used the subject of rape-leading-to-maternity as a means of celebrating the supreme importance of motherhood for the survival of the French nation and of maternal blood as insuring the future of a French race. In *La houille rouge,* women's refusal to be mothers proved more personally devastating both to them and to the country than the sexual violence of the German enemy. Even more than *Les berceaux tragiques* or *Behold and See,* this novel promoted motherhood as the most patriotic activity that women could perform, reinscribing this most traditional and seemingly passive of female roles as the most powerful guarantor of nationality and national survival.

While also celebrating motherhood, Annie Vivanti Chartres's *Vae victis*—or, in its American incarnation, *The Outrage*—offered a startling contrast to the fictional accounts previously discussed. Chartres told the story of two raped and impregnated Belgian heroines: one is a married woman who is sympathetically portrayed as choosing to have an abortion, while the other, is a virginal adolescent who succumbs to an overwhelming maternal instinct. This novel, like *Behold and See,* first established a familial idyll in a Belgium untouched by war, but a birthday celebration of the young Chérie is brutally interrupted; Chérie, her sister-in-law, Louise, and her sister-in-law's child, Mireille, are told to flee the invasion.[82] Hesitating too long, the women are at first relieved when their initial glimpse of the Germans is of someone who "did not look like a hellhound. He did not evoke the idea of violence, outrage, and slaughter" (60). But such a depiction only makes ironic the brutality that follows as the German officers requisition the house and terrorize the women. Louise pleads with one of them: "Your children . . . your little girls are in bed and asleep . . . they are safe. . . . As God may guard them for you, oh protect us!" (82). At first moved, despite his intentions, the officer tells them to hide and orders his men to stop tormenting Chérie. However, his fellow officers point out that they have "higher orders." "The German seal must be set upon the enemy's country." And even this potentially sympathetic man decides that "if it isn't I . . . then . . . somebody else. . . . Woe to the vanquished, my poor woman" (85). Thus the systematic attacks on the women are presented as being "ordered" by the high command; individual Germans could show no mercy since they were pledged to obey a brutal regime that legitimized the rapes of women as a way of "setting" the "German seal" upon "the enemy."

At this juncture in the novel, the fate of Louise, Chérie, and Mireille remains a mystery as the scene quickly shifts to Britain, where an English family has taken in three Belgians as refugees, whom the reader soon discovers to be the same three women, now utterly changed by their experience. As a result of the horrors that she has witnessed, Mireille has become deaf and dumb. Equally wretched fates have befallen her mother and young aunt. Only upon hearing news that her husband is safe in Belgium does Louise fully agonize over what has happened to her and the family; she decides that " 'Mireille must be healed. . . . He must never know.' . . . [W]hile the gaze of the child was clear and vacant, the eyes of the mother were wild and wide with some dark horror and despair" (126–27). For Chérie, her memories of what befell her that night are shaded in blackness; in England, she finds herself suffering from a "strange" illness and she is fearful that something has "unhinged" her reason (142). As she confides in a diary, when she thinks back to her birthday, she only encounters "wide blank spaces in my brain" and yet, she senses that "[s]omebody is dead. Somebody has been killed, I know it. I know it. . . . Is it I—is it Chérie who is dead?" (145, 155).[83]

Chérie does not believe she is now pregnant but rather persists in thinking of herself only as someone who has been "murdered," as if the loss of her virginity itself has caused a metaphoric death. Meanwhile, Louise recognizes that "what she had dreaded more than death had come to pass. . . . She knew that the outrage to which she had been subjected would endure; she knew that her shame would live" (165). In despair over what to do, she feels she must die and feels the fetus growing inside to be a monstrous result of "savagery and debauch." She cannot accept that she must bear this pregnancy to term, because "waking and in her dreams she saw it; she saw it crawling like a reptile, she saw it stained in the colour of blood, she saw it . . . frenzied and insane" (167).

It is in this section of the novel, after having presented the horrible consequences of the invasion, that Chartres finally reveals what occurred in August 1914. Louise had awakened at dawn and discovered the family dog with its skull beaten in and the Germans gone. At the foot of the bed Mireille lay "like a little dying bird" and only after rousing her with great difficulty had Louise realized that the eyes of her child were "wild, hallucinated and intent" (169). Mireille had been staring at the red-curtained door of a bedroom; entering the room, Louise had found the unconscious Chérie with her dress "all torn and bloodstained . . . with her two hands stretched upwards and tied to the bedpost above her head. . . . Her face was scratched and bleeding" (170). Safe in Britain, Louise remains haunted by these visions and resolves to terminate her pregnancy.

She goes first to the local clergyman and there confesses her ordeal to him, his wife, and the visiting town doctor. As Chartres described the scene, she offered one example of how presumably ordinary British women and men could respond to Louise's plight: "In that quiet room in the old-fashioned English vicarage the ghastly scenes of butchery and debauch were enacted again; the foul violence of the enemy, the treason, . . . all lived before the horrified listeners, and the martyrdom of the three helpless victims wrung their honest British hearts" (180). At the end of her tale, Louise flings herself at the doctor's feet, begging him "to release and save her." The doctor concludes that Louise is on the verge of insanity and must be helped. The vicar, while offering prayers and material support, tells Louise that, whatever her sufferings, she has "no right . . . to contemplate a crime." Louise herself questions whether "it is a greater crime to drive me to my death" (183). And despite the vicar's insistence that divine laws must be obeyed no matter what, the doctor concludes that such reasoning has no bearing in this case, since "[w]e all know that every law, both human and Divine, has been violated and trampled upon by the foul fiends that this war has let loose" (184).

Here again, as in the debate between the doctor and the priest in *Les berceaux tragiques,* the scientific and religious perspectives on abortion are personified by two men, Dr. Reynolds and Rev. Yule. However, while the clergyman and the doctor mirror the opinions of their French counterparts, in this portrayal, women are also actively present. Louise pleads her own case and, at the very end, when the doctor insists that not only will the child probably be a degenerate but that the birth will kill Louise or drive her mad, the vicar's wife sides with him. As Dr. Reynolds and Rev. Yule face each other in stony silence, Mrs. Yule touches her husband's arm and asks him to "think that she has a husband— whom she loves, who is fighting in the trenches for her and for his home. When he returns, will it not be terrible enough for him that his own daughter has lost her reason? Must she also go to meet him carrying the child of an enemy in her arms?" (186–87). Although her words speak to the plight of Louise's husband and thus to the effect of rape on the man attached to the victim rather than to Louise's condition, it is striking that a *woman*'s voice provides the last, ultimately convincing words promoting Louise's decision to terminate the pregnancy.

Louise herself is overjoyed at the thought of her release, until she realizes that because Chérie is also pregnant, she must now "tell the unwitting Chérie what the future held for her. She must stun her with the revelation of her shame. . . . [For Chérie is s]ullied and yet immaculate, violated and yet undefiled—of her could it indeed be said that she had conceived without sin" (191). Chérie emphasizes this explicit linkage with the Virgin Mary by slowly comprehending her plight and yet refusing to make the same choice as Louise. When Louise informs her that both of them are facing the "shame" and "doom" of this terrible maternity, Chérie revels in the fact that motherhood was the "key to all her own strange and marvelous sensations, to the throb and thrill within her. . . . She heard . . . a child-voice asking from her the gift of life" (205).

Undeterred by the maternal instincts ascribed to Chérie, Louise has her abortion, which is described as a "deed of mercy and of ruthlessness" (206). After recovering from her abortion, Louise becomes persuaded that the family should return to Belgium and tries once again to convince Chérie to end her own pregnancy. But Chérie refuses to consider it because of "the great primeval instinct of maternity," even when Louise harshly urges her to "[t]hink of the brutal hands that bound you, of the infamous enemy that outraged you. Think, think that you, a Belgian, will be the mother of a German child!" (215–16). In the end, Chérie's primitive maternal instinct cannot be silenced and she gives birth on Belgian soil.

Like Rose in *Behold and See,* Chérie is initially the only person to rejoice in her son. Chérie and the child are shunned by Louise; yet the most harrowing encounter Chérie faces comes when, having escaped from the Germans, her fiancé, Florian, flees to the house. Here once again the focus shifts to the impact of the rape on the compatriot soldier, not on the woman he loves. As he realizes what has occurred:

He looked down at her shimmering hair, at the white nape of her neck. . . . The enemy had had her. . . . She whom he had deemed too sacred for his touch. . . . The foul, blood-drunken soldiers had had their will of her—and there she lay sullied, ruined, and defiled. . . . . There she lay, the broken, helpless creature . . . the symbol of his country, his wrecked and ruined country! (269–70)

Unable to bear her cries for death and yet for the child to be safe, he becomes incensed, cursing her child "in the name of Belgium . . . of our outraged women, our perishing children, our murdered men" (273). But when he hears the child wailing, "anger, grief . . . despair, the passion of vengeance and the desire to kill, all dropped out of his soul and left it silent and empty" (275). As he abandons Chérie forever, she realizes that "the comrade and lover of her youth, had vanished—only the soldier stood before her" (275). Here not only did women become transformed into the truest symbol of the vanquished nation, but also men became transformed into true soldiers after witnessing the consequences of rape.

After Florian departs, Chérie concludes that she has nothing left to live for and should kill herself and her child. While she is preparing to depart, young Mireille, who has just returned to the house, creeps downstairs, revisiting the scene of her torment and trying frantically to recover what it is she so fears. The red curtain opens and reveals Chérie and her son, "a Mother and Child" haloed in the light of the moon, and miraculously, Mireille regains her voice and sanity.

As raped and impregnated victims of the German army, Louise and Chérie face the mutual horror of bearing "children of violence." They make diametrically opposed and yet understandable, even sympathetic, choices regarding these pregnancies. Louise is no more criticized within the context of the novel for terminating her pregnancy than Chérie is for carrying her saintlike ordeal to term. *The Times Literary Supplement* concluded its review of the novel by focusing on the more hopeful elements of this "terrible" story:

[T]he case of the child, deaf, dumb, and imbecile through horror, and the cases of the married woman and the girl, each of whom finds herself with child by a German ravisher, are not for the squeamish to contemplate. Whether English surgeons of good repute have run the risk of doing in such cases, what Dr. Reynolds did . . . we do not know; but by means of the one child that reaches birth Mrs. Chartres lifts the darkness and shows the light of hope and love once again dawning.[84]

Without elaborating on the risks that Dr. Reynolds ran, the review did not explicitly condemn his actions; it merely equated the birth of Chérie's child with the possibility of hope and redemption—something the novel itself deliberately evoked. Although, in effect, the review warned readers about the "squeamish" elements of the book, it also proclaimed that "[t]here is truth in this disposition," because it emphasized not the tragedy alone but its aftereffects. As these aftereffects were being played out in Belgium, they were brought directly home to Britain as well. Thus, the power of the novel resided in its ability to communicate the experience of Belgian victims of German attacks to a British audience that needed to be educated and to understand the extent of their sufferings.

It is essential to keep in mind the different national contexts in which these novels appeared. Wartime France itself witnessed an occupation, hence its novels focused on the plight of French women, whereas wartime Britain came closest to witnessing the horrors of atrocities through the tales of those fleeing Belgium for Britain. If government propaganda used atrocities to rally morale or increase recruitment, the novelists considered here—Albert Giuliani, Odette Dulac, Annie Vivanti Chartres, and Lillith Hope—used the rape-resulting-in-maternity plot for other political ends. In France, these novels became part of a wider struggle over the meanings of motherhood and the consequences of *dénatalité*. In Britain, stories of outrage instructed the British about what was (potentially) at stake for British women, implying that knowledge would lead to compassion for Belgian and, perhaps by extension, British, unwed mothers.

All four novels, to differing extents, made use of imagery and language that equated the victims of German rape with the Virgin Mary. Given the strong, overtly Catholic perspectives that these novels contained—the raped women in these novels are largely Catholic—it is important to consider that in both nations Catholicism was only uneasily part of the construction of the nation. For Britain—with the exception of Ireland (and Irishness was often elided in discussions of the war)—Catholics were a distinct minority and anti-Catholicism had a long history in a particular kind of British nationalism, still in evidence during the war. In France, the situation was perhaps even more complex, since Republicans viewed the church as one of its enemies and anticlericalism was long a part of its traditions. Although the *union sacrée* created by the war sought to bring together the entire population of France, incorporating devout Catholics as well as ardent socialists, the explicit support for the religious position in a novel like *Les berceaux tragiques* had overt political implications. Even Dulac's *La houille rouge,* which offered an ostensibly more pro-Republican reason for attacking abortions, also directly linked the children produced by rape to the Christ child. In the British context, *Vae victis* provided its audience with information to understand the "sainted" motherhood of raped Catholic, Belgian women, while *Behold and See* took the atypical character of an English nun to create a victim whose "Englishness" would cause her to be viewed sympathetically. In the midst of a national crisis that required the support of diverse constituencies within the nation, an appeal to all women could be based on their shared victimization and potential or actual motherhood, using the potent imagery of Mary or Mary-like figures to further this end.

If there were similarities in equating their rape-impregnated mothers with Mary, these novels nonetheless contained important differences in the options available to (and chosen by) their heroines. They also provided contrasting ideas about the role of women in making the decisions about maternity. Rose and Chérie not only chose to carry their pregnancies to term but to keep and raise their children as single mothers. Louise herself decided she must terminate her pregnancy, while Marthe Chamblay was persuaded to keep her infant. Both Jeanne Deckes and Madame Breton ultimately saw their children of rape as atoning for their past crimes against the nation, their previous abortions. The range of choices available to all of these female characters suggests a strong association between maternity and women's agency, or perhaps more succinctly, women were granted agency as mothers, an agency they could not exhibit in other realms of life.

It is also extremely suggestive that all the children born to women in these diverse novels are male, raising complicated and related questions about national inheritance and mothers' national function as the producers of future soldiers. The male child also, of course, completes the mother as Mary and child as Christ analogies. However, it is the complicated ideas of paternity and the inheritance of nationality as well as patrimony that the maleness of the children evoke. In order to offer their readers an acceptable model of women giving birth to their enemy's children, both French and British authors presented a vision of motherhood inherently national and immeasurably potent.

Conclusion

Rape served the purpose in all four of these propagandistic texts of proving the distinct barbarism of the German race, but the focus on maternity downplayed much of the wholesale violence against women by paying attention instead to the palpable consequences of sexual assault. The most serious problem for contemporaries came from the impregnation of women through rape, the conquest of the maternal body. As was evident most clearly in French wartime debates over infanticide and abortion, concern about atrocities was linked to anxiety about nationalist eugenics, the birthrate, and the survival of the "race." Given these prevailing interests, attacks on women were more than attacks on unfortunate individuals; they were assaults on the nation's reproductive future.

The widely publicized discussions about rape and atrocities also contributed to the eroding of the line between combatant and noncombatant as well as to creating a sense of "national security" rooted in there being "true" French or British mothers (and thus implicitly future soldiers). The emphasis on *mothers* as the victims of rape and atrocities, seen in French and British propaganda, in French wartime debates on abortion, and in both countries' literature, demonstrated wartime society's overarching concern not with violence done to women but with "racial" mixing and attacks on national honor.

As writers such as Yvonne Pitrois would suggest, the suffering of "martyred" women victims could even be compared to the sufferings of soldiers.[85] And both British and French novels provided a forum for the manipulation of popular sentiment against Germany and to promote sympathy for the alleged and *real* victims of the German invasion.[86] They also offered opportunities to rehearse arguments about the influence of heredity or environment, German ancestry or French soil, upon the population. French proponents of eugenics were particularly concerned with the kind of population that would survive the war: would it be tainted by German seed or rescued by French maternal blood?

Rape as an act of individual violence against a woman remained, of course, a criminal act, and the responses of women to this act, as was evident in both novels and the debates over the products of wartime attacks, were individual as well as national. However, in a world caught up in the "violence" of war and, particularly, a world where the potency of the accusation of rape may have been diminished by its metaphoric and exaggerated uses in propaganda, rape was not treated as sexual violence alone. When commentators looked at the falling birthrate coupled with the rising death tolls, the future of both nations seemed at stake in more than military terms.

Much has been written on the nation as the woman, as in the term "rape of Belgium," but the discourse about atrocities and motherhood demonstrates the significance of women as the nation: suffering, pure, and—because of their capacity for regeneration—greater than the sum of their parts. Thus, in part, the use of rape in wartime propaganda overwhelmingly inscribed women as passive, ultimately sacrificial victims, as the emblems of the traditional home and family that the war was presumably being fought to protect and preserve. The rape of women by the enemy became part of the construction of a set of narratives about atrocities and the war that made the maternal body another site of conflict and the act of motherhood, no matter what the circumstances, the ultimate source of women's patriotism and agency.

Promoting Motherhood and Regulating Women

WOMEN'S LABOR AND THE NATION

The State and Motherhood during Wartime

Through the bodily labor of reproduction, women provided the raw ammunition of war, and, in a variety of public wartime forums, this kind of gender-specific national work was repeatedly underscored. Beyond being urged to provide sons and relinquish them to the war effort, women were also encouraged to exert a related moral influence. In August of 1914, an article rousing support for the war spoke of the patriotic duty of women in the following terms: "To send them cheerfully on their way, and enter fully into their enthusiasms, while minimising their anxieties with regard to those they are leaving behind is a sacred duty which England demands they [women] should perform with the same readiness which she asks of her sons in volunteering for the field."[1] When Britain's "sons" were to go to war, her "daughters," the mothers of these sons, had the "sacred duty" of sending them readily into the fray, as was evident in a range of propaganda posters.

Throughout the war, a variety of social commentators and activists, as well as politicians, reinforced the centrality of motherhood in both Britain and France. Motherhood, in this ubiquitous rhetoric, defined female identity and could provide a means to unify women. As the war's deaths mounted, generalized pronatalist concern with mothers as producers of the national resource of the next generation grew exponentially and erupted in debates about women's moral behavior, especially their alcohol consumption and sexual practices leading to illegitimate births, and, perhaps most significantly, their remunerative war work. Furthermore, the declining birthrate was seen as producing additional casualties of war and, although women continued to make decisions about their pregnancies that contradicted some of their social mandate to reproduce for the sake of their country, they did so in a climate of new urgency for promoting maternity for national, political ends. In many of these arenas, motherhood came to represent for women what soldiering did for men, a gender-specific experience meant to provide social unity and stability during a time of unprecedented upheaval.

Thus during the war, the "maternal body" and its labor became the focus of both family policy and the state regulation of work. This chapter explores several sites in which states' needs to employ women in a variety of new occupations and to preserve the "race" through preserving women's reproductive abilities came into direct conflict. It begins with an analysis of the British policy that paid separation allowances to unwed mothers and the subsequent fears about the war babies that such government largess would produce. It then examines the transnational dilemma of "munitions versus motherhood," a contradiction that the shapers of social policy tried to resolve and social commentators sought to exploit for a variety of political ends.

Given that France had no need to offer support for soldiers' families as an enticement for them to enlist, this chapter begins by focusing on one of the unexpected consequences of British separation allowances. In Britain, allowances paid directly to women whose husbands were serving in the armed forces became a potent means of establishing the principle of state support for families as well as being a useful device for recruiting.[2] As a result of this legislation, debates broke out in Britain over the extent to which the government should therefore regulate women's alcohol consumption or support illegitimate children. These debates cut to the core of how government funds should be properly allocated. The first year of the war brought a heated controversy to Britain over war babies, or the anticipated increase in illegitimate children as a result of the war. As the previous chapter discussed, France had its own version of the debate over illegitimate children and the future of the nation in the crisis of "the children of boche rape." In the context of the paradoxical need to encourage the birthrate and maintain morality, French and British politicians alike initiated discussions about laws re-

"Women of Britain Say—'Go!'" Parliamentary Recruiting Committee poster.
Courtesy of the Imperial War Museum.

garding bastardy and nationality, although legislation would remain largely unchanged.

In addition, state support proposed for mothers ironically served as a pretext for both controlling the behavior and improving the health of women. The British and French governments were concerned with regulating the behavior of the many women that they called into war-related work, especially in factories. However, the focus on women's health and their roles as workers was directly related to the focus on their roles as mothers and, therefore, their place in the nation's over-all health. If women were defined as mothers, even the most radical changes in the workplace could be depicted as temporary deviations from a normative family life. While Chapter 2 explored the maternal body under attack, this chapter will investigate the maternal body's potential to be an instrument of war.

Illegitimacy and the Redemptive Power of Motherhood

As was shown in Chapter 2, the occupation of French territory by German troops raised very specific concerns about the fate of some illegitimate children. Even more serious than the presumed stigma of illegitimacy was the fear of women bearing allegedly "mixed-race, half-Teutonic" children, and this prompted many social commentators to argue for the primacy of maternal blood as making a child French. Legally, however, laws governing legitimacy did not acknowledge this, and, as other French wartime commentators noted in the debates over changing the laws on abortion, German soldiers were not the only producers of illegitimate offspring. Both the British and French governments thus also faced the problem of "homegrown" illegitimacy, although in France, which had a higher illegitimacy rate and a lower birthrate than Britain, children could be made legitimate by the subsequent marriage of their parents.[3] This was not true in all of Britain, particularly not in England, a fact that will become significant in the discussion below. French laws thus seemed more flexible in terms of their treatment of illegitimacy. Yet French politicians concerned with encouraging women to have more children debated further measures to make even more children legitimate. They proposed first that marriage by proxy be permitted and, even, the posthumous legitimating of children if the father was killed fighting for France before he could marry the mother.

In December 1914, the feminist paper *La Française* provided details for its readers about changes enabling a soldier at the front to recognize and confer his name to his out-of-wedlock child. The soldier could do so whether the child was already born or only expected simply by informing the mayor, if one could be found, or an officer already qualified to register deaths who could also register the "recognition" of the child.[4] In March 1915, a law was proposed in the French Senate that would, in the words of its sponsor, Senator Catalogne, be in the "interests of women and children who await a name and a family." For "war had modified the social state; mobilization, in tearing away all valid French citizens from the household and in not giving them the time to take care of their private affairs, had shaken up many things," including postponing marriages, some of which could never take place because of "a glorious death." Catalogne urged that what was no longer possible for the dead should be granted to the living: the right to give their name and to acknowledge their family. This proposal was met with applause and cries of approval. Those in favor of this measure emphasized that such provisions would be solely for the duration of the war, allowing men serving "under the flag" to do the honorable thing toward their offspring.[5] When the proposal was also approved by the Chamber in early April, *La Française,* along with newspapers such as *L'Écho de Paris,* notified the public that soldiers at the front could now be married by "procuration," so long as an engagement, cohabitation, or previous material support of the mother could be demonstrated.[6] French legislators went even further: in mid-1916 they began to debate a law concerning posthumous legitimation of the children of soldiers killed on the field of battle, legislation that was ultimately approved.[7] Again, French concern about illegitimacy in these circumstances, unlike the cases due to German rape, centered on the fact that these were the children of soldiers, not merely native-born men, thus entitled to special treatment under the law.

In British debates on wartime illegitimacy, societal concern did not necessarily result in government intervention, although here, too, the children of soldiers and sailors were viewed as meriting special consideration. These debates were set in motion on 10 August 1914, when Prime Minister Herbert Asquith announced that all wives of servicemen would be eligible for separation allowances.[8] One immediate consequence of the government's maintenance of soldiers' and sailors' wives and dependents was a public debate over whether this then entitled the government to supervise their spending and behavior. Sylvia Pankhurst, suffragette leader and wartime activist among London's poor in the East End, later described "wartime hysterics" giving rise to what she considered unfounded stories of "drunkenness and depravity amongst the women of the masses."[9] Further outcry erupted after a War Office circular of September 1914 established guidelines—repeated in a Home Office circular forwarded to chief constables—that named immoral behavior and child neglect as causes for the denial of the allowances.[10] Writing in December 1914, Rowland Kenney pointed out the main flaw in linking the support of soldiers' dependents to moral concerns: "We must make our soldiers and their dependents moral, if we starve them to death in the process."[11] Such protests did not stop attempts to tie the receipt of separation allowances to women's morality.[12]

The crisis of the war babies that emerged in 1915 revealed British confusion about women's sexuality and their moral contributions to the war. The scandal of this alleged increase in the illegitimate offspring of military men demonstrates just how quickly ideas about reputed "new" female sexual promiscuity that at the time were linked to the other social issue of maternity captured the public imagination in Britain. "War Babies" was the term popularly used to refer to a suspected increase in children born to unmarried women impregnated by men who then joined the military. However, the war baby phenomenon really dealt with two categories of unwed mothers. Some used the term in reference to women who lived in nonmarital but often long-standing partnerships with men who joined the armed forces as a result of the war. Others, more commonly, used the term to refer to young women allegedly impregnated by soldiers and sailors in brief relationships before the men went overseas. Some distinguished between the two circumstances, labeling the former the "problem of the unmarried mother" and the latter the "problem of the war babies," but for most participants in the debates war babies and the women who created them were one problem.[13] Nonetheless, the war baby scandal produced two competing narratives, one concerned primarily with the morality of women, and the other with the morality of a government that legally penalized illegitimacy. The crisis of the war baby powerfully mingled the sexual and the maternal body.

The war baby debate itself originated in the decision to grant separation allowances to some women not legally married to servicemen. The Soldiers' and Sailors' Family Association (SSFA), the voluntary organization created to support soldiers' and sailors' dependents, had aided their illegitimate families during the Boer War if it was clear that the father had made a home for the family.[14] While the SSFA's role was eventually superseded by the government-controlled dispersal of separation allowances, initially during the First World War it became a critical agency in the delivery of relief.[15] Despite the Boer War precedent, a special general meeting of the SSFA was held in London on 28 January 1915 to determine whether support for unmarried mothers should be administered as part of separation allowances under the auspices of the SSFA.

Speakers at this January meeting vigorously debated two opposing propositions. The first was a resolution from Reverend L. Wainwright urging the SSFA to "reaffirm" that aid would only be administered if marriage and birth certificates could be produced. An amendment proposed by Hayes Fisher, a member of Parliament and the vice president of the SSFA's executive committee, instead called for the reaffirmation "that help is given to unmarried mothers and their children where there is a real home, where the children are properly cared for, and where the connection is not merely a casual one, and that this meeting approves the action of the Executive Committee in administering relief on these lines during the present War in collaboration with the Prince of Wales' National Relief Fund." In response, Wainwright urged the members not to allow themselves to be proponents of sin, "keeping a home open for them [unmarried fathers] to come back to, to the evil life in which they have been living." Wainwright further complained about the SSFA's delay in calling the meeting, noting that he had first voiced his objections in September of 1914, and he concluded by threatening to remove his support from the organization if its policy allowed aid for unwed mothers.[16]

Others at the meeting voiced a similar resolve not to promote sin, arguing that unmarried mothers should not be helped by an organization aimed at "families." Mrs. Hicks Beach, identifying herself as the local secretary of an SSFA branch overseeing "rough" areas, recounted her experience during the Boer War: "I do not ever intend to be the Secretary of this Association through another war if we are obliged to help these women who are unmarried. . . . I think it is extremely bad for the *morale* of the population." Miss Connolly, of Wainwright's London parish, asserted that some "respectable wives" of soldiers "thought we were engaged in licensing vice, and . . . asked me very plainly . . . whether we ladies should like it, supposing we were in the position they were in and had to be helped by the Government, if it came before a committee whether we should like to be paid with the mistresses of her husband's friends." Thus, on behalf of respectable women and in order

to uphold the sanctity of marriage, opponents of materially supporting common-law wives from the same funds as "real" wives urged the
SSFA to verify the legitimacy of the women and children who appealed
for aid.[17]

In voicing approval of a more generous approach to unmarried
mothers, Hayes Fisher laid bare not only his version of the moral issues
at stake but also the larger politics underlying the SSFA's claims to
administer relief funds per se. After first expressing his regret at the
meeting's public airing of the SSFA's "domestic differences," Fisher argued that the majority of the population supported efforts to aid all
the families of soldiers and sailors. The ordinary man and woman felt
that unmarried soldiers' dependents for whom these men had provided
a "real home" should be helped, and the SSFA was now acting as an
agent of the National Relief Fund, which strongly endorsed assisting both married and unmarried mothers "where there is a home and
where the children are properly looked after." Given, Fisher added, that
those in charge of the National Relief Fund did "not much like" the
SSFA and would have set up alternatives to it, changing current SSFA
policy would mean the lost opportunity of using its experience to do
good and aid the nation. He further explained, using SSFA statistics
for London, that so far roughly 2 percent of cases (1,350 out of 75,000)
had involved unmarried couples. Extrapolating from these figures, he
implied that one percent of approximately 500,000 cases nationwide,
or 5,000 families—where the father was risking his life—might have
been left to starve if unmarried women were not aided. Furthermore,
because of the SSFA, out of the 1,350 London cases, "no less than 320
have been persuaded to sanctify their lives by the ceremony of religious marriage." This alone, Fisher asserted, was reason enough to
treat established, unmarried couples as if they were married.[18]

The majority of other speakers at the special general meeting supported Fisher and his amendment. Religious leaders voiced their opposition to Wainwright, and women voiced their support of unmarried
mothers.[19] When a final vote was taken, nearly 75 percent of the ballots
agreed that the SSFA should administer separation allowances to unmarried soldiers' dependents.[20] And so the SSFA's War Circular No. 3
set forth in unmistakable terms that "the Committee of the National
Relief Fund have decided that, for the purposes of distributing Relief
out of the Fund, unmarried mothers and their children should be regarded as dependents in cases where the father being a soldier, sailor,

or marine, has actually made a home for them."[21] It also cautioned that in many cases the marital status of the family was not widely known and thus they should be treated with discretion.

The National Relief policy regarding the payment of separation allowances, along with associated efforts to determine how many women and children would qualify for them, accounts for some of the initial public discussion of wartime illegitimacy. Shortly after the SSFA meeting, the *Manchester Guardian* explained the relief work provided by the "War Babies League," a service of last resort for unmarried mothers who had difficulties receiving allowances. Disputing the circulated figures of 39,000 unmarried mothers in London being dependent on soldiers' pay, the secretary of the league declared that since August 1914 the organization had dealt with some 3,500 to 4,000 mothers, of whom about 75 percent were unmarried. Noting that many of these women had formed lasting ties with their children's fathers, the league's secretary claimed that the allowances for wives and children motivated some to enlist and that, where possible, "when the way is made plain the men are pleased enough to marry."[22] Explicit in these early discussions of war-induced births was the assumption that these children were "soldiers'" children, thus able to make unique and potent claims on both charity and the state. War babies, from the start, were deserving because of their paternity.

In a letter to the *Morning Post*, Tory M.P. Ronald McNeill advanced the debate when he proposed the reformation of the bastardy laws, urging that "the mothers of our soldiers' children are to be treated with no scorn or dishonour, and that the infants themselves should receive a loyal and unashamed welcome." He further suggested that these babies "boldly be adopted as the children of the State."[23] Other legislation proposed in the House of Commons by M.P. Dundas White sought to resolve the issue of bastardy by making laws embodying "the principle of the legitimation of children by the subsequent marriage of their parents," which already held in Scotland, consistent throughout the United Kingdom.[24] The subject came up again during question time at the end of April 1915 in the House of Commons, when the government, represented by Reginald McKenna, claimed that the "controversial" nature of the subject prevented it from introducing legislation to reform the laws on illegitimacy. In response, M.P. James Hope asked if it was not "much more important . . . to deal properly with those writers on the subject in newspapers who are suffering from erotic hysteria?"[25]

Whether or not the media, like the public, was suffering from "erotic hysteria," newspaper articles and letters to the editor continued to focus on the wartime plight of soldiers' illegitimate children. In her 1933 autobiography, Vera Brittain wrote with amusement about her response to the war baby controversy, claiming that her thoughts combined "a limited number of independent opinions with inherited remnants of ancestral morality." In April 1915, Brittain described her reaction to the newspaper articles and letters:

> One set of people who write letters are most unmorally moral, want to disgrace the poor girls as much as possible. . . . The other, the hysterical party, absolutely excuses the offence on the score of abnormal conditions . . . hold forth about 'the children of the heroes of Mons and Marne' (which they are not), and even make suggestions of compensation so extremely favourable to the offenders as to encourage others to repeat the sin, and thus undermine our whole social and moral structure.[26]

In Brittain's worldview at this time, "hysterical" support for the mothers of war babies was so extreme as to undermine the very foundation of society. On this issue, the link between sexual morality and social order was obvious, even if one neither approved of attacks on the unfortunate mothers or the loosening of standards for behavior.

Less "hysterical" letters to the editors of papers such as the *Morning Post* and the *Manchester Guardian* offered ideas for ameliorating the condition of unwed mothers. On 14 April 1915, two women involved in aiding such mothers, Lucy Dean Streatfield and Harriet Whitting, wrote to the *Morning Post* in response to McNeill's earlier letter. They portrayed the difficulty facing unmarried mothers who did not wish to give up their infants and solicited support for a "Day-Servant's Hostel," something that would allow unmarried mothers both to work and to keep their children. They even pointed out that "in the turmoil and excitement of the present time, when money is being lavishly subscribed to support schemes for supplying our menfolk (some of whom may be the fathers of these children) with comforts, it is not easy to . . . collect money to keep the girls and their little babies from destitution." If "thousands of pounds" could be "generously given for cigarettes for our men," surely a "few hundred" should be spared for "the lives of these mothers and babies." By associating unwed motherhood with the national cause and by calling the children "war babies" and hinting at a soldier's paternity, organizations and individuals already concerned with alleviating the treatment of illegitimate children and their mothers utilized this connection, whether it was accurate or not.[27]

A letter from Mary Longman, the general secretary of the Women's Labour League, echoed Dundas White's call for changes in the bastardy law. While agreeing that estimates of the number of war babies were probably "very grossly exaggerated," she urged that measures be taken "in whatever way will tend to the best interests of the mothers, the babies and the nation as a whole."[28] Longman linked the need for a plan regarding war babies with the need for a sound policy in support of maternity as a both public health and national issue. Other organizations also took up this cry. Following the official proposals by members of Parliament, suffragette leader Emmeline Pankhurst and the Women's Social and Political Union (WSPU) offered their organization's help to rear some of the unfortunate female war babies under "modern ideas of child culture."[29] Mrs. Pankhurst energetically appealed for aid for this plan: "It is proposed to establish a home in country surroundings and, as a beginning, to assume entire responsibility for the upbringing of fifty of 'the nation's babies.' "[30] However, Sylvia Pankhurst recorded after the war that, despite the WSPU's proposal, they only assisted five infants.[31] While the scant number of war babies aided by the WSPU suggests either the half-heartedness of these efforts or the lack of "real" war babies, the emphasis on female babies is revealing. It underscores that the importance of war babies lay not in the fact that the babies were considered "male" and thus future soldiers, but that they were themselves the offspring of soldiers, regardless of their sex.

Other public commentators, praising McNeill's proposal, took up the reform of Britain's bastardy laws. Writing in May 1915, *The English Review*'s editor Austin Harrison urged that as the nation honored the dead, "surely we should care for the living," for war babies who were "perhaps the only human side of war." Harrison claimed these children resulted from "self or race preservation," and should not be condemned by archaic laws on bastardy to suffer lifelong social ostracism. Instead, they should be thought of as "unborn children . . . left to us in trust by our soldiers." Each one of these children was a potential citizen owed additional honors by virtue of possessing a soldier's paternity. Changes in the laws on bastardy were essential, he continued, because of the growing need for children, and such changes could come by the concerted political pressure of mothers: "There may yet come a time in this country, owing to the war, when motherhood will be a national duty—

in Germany and probably in France it will be a State necessity. The lot of these little ones lies with the legitimate mothers of England. . . . If every man is to be a soldier, let every woman at least think like a mother and have done with this obsolete and cruel legislation."[32]

Before the removal of such "obsolete" legislation, the very facts of the war baby phenomenon were called into question. Although Harrison spoke to the importance of war babies for the nation, and efforts were, theoretically, already in place to care for these illegitimate children, some individuals publicly continued to express doubts about war babies' existence. On April 26, the archbishop of York made reference to the rumors of war babies while addressing the Annual Meeting of the York Rescue and Prevention Association. He declared: "The balance of evidence by those entitled to give it by their expert knowledge was clear in proving that many of the statements made [about war babies] were wildly exaggerated." Fearing that a wave of "sentimentality" would challenge public morals, the archbishop warned that nothing could be worse than allowing the war to encourage tolerance for "moral deterioration" rather than a "moral strengthening."[33]

Some social investigators, such as Dr. Barbara Tchaikovsky, a doctor affiliated with Sylvia Pankhurst's work in East London, set out to determine the veracity of war baby rumors. While Tchaikovsky discovered that accurate estimates were impossible to obtain, she nonetheless offered anecdotal evidence from Glasgow to Plymouth, stating that, given the average rate of illegitimate births, "even if there were not the great increase in illegitimacy which is talked of, a very large proportion of the illegitimate children must be the children of soldiers."[34] Yet her local inquiries suggested that the problem was hardly as great as had been initially feared or reported. Mrs. Arnold Glover, the secretary of the National Union of Girls' Clubs, felt that "the extent of the evil had probably been very much exaggerated," although she did not doubt that "a large proportion of the mothers would be very young girls" and that the phenomenon was not "a purely working-class one," for "the temptation was one to which undoubtedly women of all classes had been subjected."[35] Yet, a few days later, a report in the *Manchester Guardian* declared that in two Manchester parishes, no war babies had been discovered.[36]

Given the contradictory evidence, the archbishop of Canterbury and other prominent individuals established a committee of women to investigate the war baby phenomenon and clarify the extent of the danger.[37] Mrs. Louise Creighton, the head of the National Union of

Women Workers (NUWW), led the committee and used the NUWW to conduct the investigation. The National Vigilance Association (NVA), which campaigned for public morals and social purity, approved this step and described the question of illegitimate children as one of "the many problems forced upon us by the war," an issue that "calls for careful thought and judicious treatment." Asserting the importance of the archbishop's speech and of the need for an inquiry, the NVA denounced:

> the hysterical and sensational statements of irresponsible people who have not given themselves time to think of the serious libel upon the community at large, or of the moral evil engendered amongst the young people of both sexes by making such a serious topic the subject of common everyday conversation.
>
> There will doubtless be an increase in illegitimate births, which is much to be deplored, but to talk of thousands in one town and of hundreds in various small villages is, in our opinion, 'hysterical nonsense.'[38]

The NVA went on to suggest that such stories were being spread by those opposed to "Christian" values, who wanted to speed legislation through Parliament that would overturn laws concerning illegitimate children. Other leaders of the Church of England were thoroughly in accord with these views, as the bishop of Oxford cautioned that "there seems a danger of people going as far as to make a glory out of shame."[39]

However, before the findings of Mrs. Creighton's committee were even known, the linking of attacks on female moral laxity with the production of war babies had elicited a feminist critique of the double standard that blamed women for the creation of war babies. Responding to local charges "that the enemy which we must really fear is the immodest girl," an anonymous Liverpool suffragist offered the counterargument that "no girl can go wrong by herself." She went further, arguing that "men withhold the vote from us on the plea of superiority, yet when it comes to a question of evil influence, then the girl's influence is of unspeakable strength. Is this a proof of superiority?" The solution to this crisis, she asserted, was to train both men and women to be "responsible citizens," which could only be accomplished by making them equal before the law. Only then, the writer observed, would girls cease to suffer "the full price of error, while those who have outraged them walk in our midst as the embodiment of all that is honourable."[40]

In the suffragist's letter a much older interpretation of young women as innocents who are "outraged" by soldiers countered more prevalent images from the war baby debate. This interpretation of wartime illegitimacy made the soldier's paternity the essence of wrongdoing rather than the sole redeeming feature of these unfortunate women and their children. It is especially noticeable that—within a month of the issuance of the Bryce commission's report on Belgian atrocities—British soldiers could even be hinted at "outraging" the young women who bore war babies. The term "outrage" was so prevalent in atrocity propaganda that it became nearly synonymous with the way the treatment of enemy women by the invading German army was referred to. The language of this analysis thus marked it as a clear departure from common wartime assumptions.[41]

Two official reports on the war babies arrived the following month and were publicized at the same time. The first, produced under the leadership of Mrs. Creighton and a Special Committee of Investigation under the auspices of the NUWW, directly investigated the phenomenon. While this special subcommittee was at work, the archbishop of York had convened an even larger committee to consider the findings of the report and make recommendations.[42] Yet even before presenting the findings of the investigative committee that she headed to the archbishop, Mrs. Creighton and the bishop of London spoke at a "largely attended and influentially supported meeting" in London on June 6. Here, Mrs. Creighton censured those who approved of "the excitement and enthusiasm of the French women when our soldiers arrived in their country, [but who] . . . criticised our girls . . . [and] spread reports about hundreds of war babies." Echoing her words, the bishop of London spoke of his "righteous indignation" at the aspersions cast on the men in training, for "the cry raised by the Press about war babies had proved a great delusion. . . . [T]he number instead of thousands, was about twenty." While initially there had been "excited and giddy girls who haunted the camps and caused mischief and scandal," this had not led to immorality on the scale suggested, according to the bishop, and he went on to praise the actions that had been taken by Mrs. Creighton and others.[43] A few days later, the archbishop of Canterbury endorsed the Committee of Investigation's conclusions that reported increases in illegitimacy were based on rumors and not facts.[44] The broader committee therefore concluded that no new laws were needed because no evidence justified assertions that the conditions of war resulted in increased illegitimacy.[45]

The NUWW subcommittee cast a fairly wide net in its inquiry, sending questionnaires to all of its fifty-seven branches—which generated thirty-two full and twenty-three less detailed responses—as well as to fourteen Women's Patrol Committees. It also made use of the separate inquiries of Dr. Barbara Tchaikovsky, the Charity Organisation Society, and the Local Government Board. Contrary to rumors, this committee found that the Local Government Board had not ordered a single new bed for any lying-in hospital and that reports of 500 war baby cases in a single locale yielded only three that could be verified. When individual cases of war babies were discovered, many of the mothers were already thought to have "a bad character . . . having had illegitimate children previously."[46]

Stressing that there were existing organizations aimed at unwed mothers that needed continued support, the committee also stated that there had been "grave cause for anxiety on account of the prevailing low moral standard, as well as on account of intemperance, often the result of thoughtless treating" as well as "much giddiness and foolish excitability among the young girls leading often to most undesirable conduct." It went on to suggest that such developments resulted from "the same spirit of unrest and excitement that makes others ready to believe and repeat the most exaggerated statements without due evidence." The solution lay in finding "wholesome outlet[s]" for girls' "natural excitement and patriotic zeal" and in preventing the spread of false rumors about illegitimacy that were bound to cause harm.[47] Thus, the report also implied that those who acted in an "undesirable" manner were no worse than those who spread tales that portrayed women and soldiers in the worst possible light. If immorality and sexual promiscuity were serious problems for wartime society, so too was the willingness to believe unsubstantiated rumors about them.

Neither the plight of unmarried mothers cohabiting with men now serving the nation nor the ongoing anxiety about the behavior of sexually active girls completely account for the widespread credence given to the idea that Britain would be besieged by illegitimate births.[48] Moreover, the debates were clouded because the same term, "war babies," could be used to refer to the alleged offspring of two different kinds of women. Those involved in stable relationships were construed as both more deserving and more moral than the others, sexually promiscuous young girls. What two such different groups of women shared was their reproducing the children of soldiers.

That such reproduction might result from the inspired sacrifice of conventional morality for the good of the nation became the subject of a play by Marie Stopes. In *The Race: A New Play of Life* (1918), Stopes, better known as the author of *Married Love* (1918), with its pleas for recognizing maternal sexuality, offered her own interpretation of the war baby phenomenon. Stopes's play provided complete justification for war babies by depicting the dilemma faced by her heroine, Rosemary, who is unable to marry her fiancé before he must leave for the battle lines. Instead, she determines that she and her lover must consummate their relationship rather than "murder the child which might be ours."[49]

After seducing her soldier so that he "may live for ever, in thy children's eyes," Rosemary finds herself pregnant with the child of her dead fiancé. While denounced by her parents (representatives of conventional morality), Rosemary defends her actions: "[H]eredity *does* matter. . . . For the sake of our race all fine young men . . . should have children" (61). Furthermore, she directly equates motherhood with patriotism: "[M]y body serves my country. . . . A soldier gives his body to death; a woman gives hers to bring life" (68). Thus, according to this logic, in order for the race to prosper, it must allow the bloodlines of its heroes to be kept alive through their children, legitimate or not. By representing the unwed mother and creator of the war baby as a selfless, patriotic heroine, Stopes made a case for wider "racial" issues transcending traditional morality; illegitimate motherhood could give "healthy children . . . the true riches of the State" to the war-torn nation (95).

In contrast to other writers, Stopes portrayed the decision to have an illegitimate child as supremely rational and even spiritual. Yet one significant feature of the war baby debate was the widespread use of the term "hysteria" or "hysterical" to describe the whole tone of popular discussion. The use of this term suggested that anxiety about these women was somehow both irrational and out of control. As the report of the Special Investigative Subcommittee noted, not only was it uninterested in "illegitimate births" as such, but it also "object[ed] emphatically to the use of the term 'war babies' . . . the supposed increase in the number of such births caused by the present conditions of the country."[50] There was resistance to the use of the term itself because it seemed to make these births somehow acceptable. For while the blame for illegitimacy tended to be placed on women, in the case of war babies, the primary identity of the father as soldier made both these women and these children somehow acceptable, a result that was not to everyones' liking.

Nonetheless, despite campaigns to change attitudes toward illegitimate births as a result of the demographic crisis perceived to be initiated by the war, individual women could not be relied upon to make decisions based on what was presumed to be the national interest. One of the puzzling features of pronatalism and the concern with maternity evident in wartime government social policy was its coexistence with ongoing tolerance for abortion and infanticide, or a reluctance to convict women accused of these crimes.[51] Some wartime legislation, such as the Notification of Births (Extension) Act of 1915, which required the reporting of any stillbirths in Britain, was aimed at increasing awareness of, and thus possibly eliminating, these measures of birth control.[52] And, as discussed in Chapter 2, French debates over infanticide and abortion in relationship to rape provoked a huge outcry, even though the French, too, were more likely to acquit than punish those accused of infanticide and abortion.[53]

The punishment of those accused of infanticide and abortion in Britain continued to be less severe than the anxiety about the future of the "race" and the nation would suggest. These acts persisted, despite the allegedly new national concern over the birthrate and a rhetoric that proclaimed the life-giving mother as the ultimate emblem of female citizenship. That abortion and infanticide were not halted by new material measures designed to aid women and children indicated the extent to which potential mothers continued to make individual, uncontrollable choices.

London wartime court records do not suggest that it was the fear of giving birth out of wedlock alone that prompted abortions and infanticides. These cases contain both familiar and new stories about women's maternal decisions, including evidence that the fear of having an illegitimate child was a common motivation for women's actions. Moreover, the infanticides involved not only some of the traditional defendants in such cases—for instance, the domestic servant separated from her family in a bourgeois home—but also women who had taken on new roles as servants of the state such as munition workers isolated from their families in hostels.[54] If some of the explanations for infanticide and abortion returned to tales of seduction and abandonment, there were also compelling wartime twists to such plots. The court records contain the stories of women impregnated by soldiers, of those who sought to get rid of the product of adultery committed while husbands were serving overseas, and, in one case, of a woman raped and impregnated by a Commonwealth soldier stationed in London.[55]

While some politicians wanted to support all women who bore the children of British servicemen, the government did not change the laws regarding illegitimacy, even as its policies made it more difficult to conceal infanticides. This was in direct contrast to what was happening in France, where politicians made it possible even for dead fathers to make their children legitimate. The reasons for these divergences had a great deal to do with larger debates about both pronatalism and morality. Yet, the war baby controversy revealed the extent to which—despite increased interest in motherhood on the part of the legislators, social welfare workers, and feminists—illegitimate motherhood remained stigmatized. While even French mothers impregnated by Germans could be seen as contributing to the state, not all social commentators thought the every British mother or child, whatever its paternity, was equally deserving.

Pronatalism, Welfare, and Women's War Work

Despite widespread ambivalence about unwed mothers, pronatalists in both France and Britain seized the opportunity that the war provided to launch intensified campaigns about the necessity of women performing the vital service of replenishing—reproducing—the nation as race. As has been well documented, concern about the falling birthrate in both nations had been evident before the war, and France, in particular, was preoccupied by questions of *dénatalité* in relationship to Germany's superior birthrate.[56] As the birthrate dipped during the war and the death toll mounted, the national—not to mention for Britain the more overtly imperial—future seemed increasingly at risk.[57] If pronatalists emphasized that women's fundamental contributions to the war consisted of repopulating the world with a new crop of future soldiers, women themselves used this focus on the position of the mother to argue for increased benefits being paid to women for this work. Wartime contingencies created an atmosphere in which maternal and child welfare received increased attention.[58] Nonetheless, while both British and French commentators lamented the costs of women's wage work to the health of their respective populations, rhetoric was not matched by substantive action.

These concerns produced lively discussion in France about just what women's ideal contribution to the war effort really was. Pronatalism had long influenced debates about women's roles and influence in French society, and the war only intensified these public discussions. A variety of responses to the falling birthrate and increasingly rising death toll were proposed, debated, and enacted. Jules Blouet, addressing the

Jeunesse Catholique de la Manche in 1915, warned that France had two interior enemies, alcoholism and depopulation, and that the remedy for the latter was to honor *familles nombreuses* and insure that those in homes left empty by the war "repeople."[59] There were numerous other warnings of the wartime necessity to repopulate a France devastated by war. In 1916, feminist Marguerite de Witt-Schlumberger argued that "women were privileged to be the creators of life" and had "two principle duties, to raise children without fathers and to give new children to the *patrie*."[60] A year later, expounding on the "particular duty of women," she spoke of women's obligation to provide children for the *patrie;* by so doing, they "represented the power of the future." In spite of the anguish caused by the war, women should be "immensely proud" to have "been able to give to their country [its] many defenders."[61] Other commentators lamented "how many young girls, victims also of the war" would now experience "forced celibacy" and urged measures to support those who could have large families.[62]

In an article appearing in the *Revue Bleue* in January 1917, Raphael-Georges Lévy noted the stirring roles that all French women from "peasants". to "great ladies" were playing in the fields as well as the factories. The French woman fed and armed the nation, and she cared for soldiers, but did "the notion of duty to the *patrie* also modify her views about her proper existence, about maternity, about the family?" In the aftermath of the battles of the Marne, Yser, Verdun, and the Somme the question of infant mortality and maternity was more of a concern than ever. Lévy offered concrete suggestions such as the creation of crèches or "maisons de la Mère Ouvrières,", but, more importantly, he urged women "burning with a desire to make themselves useful and searching for the manner to work for the country" to work with "mothers." There was one type of work above all else that was needed "to remake a France, stronger, more beautiful, more glorious: . . . give her as many children as possible."[63]

Some French commentators went so far as to call for the *mobilisation des berceaux* (the mobilization of cradles), which emphasized the parallels between mothers and soldiers and employed a military metaphor for the home. In *La mobilisation des berceaux* (1917), his book-length study of the dangers of depopulation, F. A. Vuillermet began with a cry to France from the tombs of its fallen soldiers, warning that these deaths would be in vain if France failed to promote large families.[64] Then, reporting the views of living soldiers, Vuillermet quoted one as having learned from fighting that "I was a coward until now. In agreement with my wife, I wanted but one child: it's bad what I did. In the future, I will do my duty, I will have children" (49). Here the responsibility for the national task of insuring population growth is acknowledged as being one both men and women shirked.

Alfred Krug, in a pamphlet titled *Pour la repopulation,* (1918), explained further that the causes of depopulation were not merely physical—alcoholism, tuberculosis, and venereal disease—but primarily "moral." French men and women did not have children, he continued, because "they did not want them," and this attitude had to be corrected at once by teaching the youth of both sexes that their primary duty to the country was to marry and reproduce.[65] Still others, like Marie de Roux attacked everything from voluntary sterility, to the lack of punishment for abortions, to the work of women outside the home as the causes of depopulation, arguing that the wartime crisis might help to change such attitudes and practices.[66]

The dual significance of women's war work as production and re-production can be also found in the wider popular culture, for instance in the images used in official and unofficial posters. A poster from the Cinematographic Section of the French army, for example, depicts "La Femme Française Pendant la Guerre" in the following manner: against the backdrop of an allegorical woman in armor—possibly Victory—there is a woman at industrial work and a rural woman at farm work and, in the center, a breast-feeding mother whose other child holds out a letter, presumably from a soldier. These images suggest an equiva-lence between all these forms of labor but visually make mothering the centerpiece. In several posters for national loans, the female munition worker disappears and the work of women is represented as primarily agricultural and maternal. For instance, a poster for the 1918 Defense Loan depicting idealized women at work in the fields, images remi-niscent of Jean-François Millet's painting *Les glaneuses,* asks for aid in order to maintain "the gentle earth of France." However, the dominant female figure here is also clearly a mother, holding a hoe in one hand while reaching to touch her child with the other.[67]

Concern with mothers and women war workers overlapped in spe-cific discussions of the latter's maternity. A 1915 pamphlet produced by the Association Nationale Française pour la Protection Légale des Travailleurs directly posed the more practical question of what to do about female workers' motherhood. It argued that motherhood's "im-portance grows even more if we envisage the current circumstances, the terrible test imposed at this moment on our country." Comparing

"The French Woman during the War," poster of the cinematographic section of the French army. Reprinted in Hardie and Sabin, eds., War Poster *(1920).*

"To Return to Us Entirely the Gentle Earth of France," poster for the 1918 French National Loan. Courtesy of the Imperial War Museum.

the suffering France experienced due to the war with the fatal blows struck by "the interior enemy"—the "regular and rapid decline of our natality"—this pronatalist document sought to use the intensified decline in the birthrate even before the war's increased death toll to demonstrate a new urgency for the protection of maternity.[68]

Using language designed to suggest the equivalence of mothering and soldiering, the pamphlet referred to a woman recovering from childbirth as *une blessée*—someone "wounded." She was thus in need of "absolute repose" and other kinds of care associated with recuperation, not industrial work.[69] Proponents of these arguments saw the way to guarantee a sufficient birthrate in the creation of laws to promote maternal leave, thereby encouraging breast-feeding and other practices designed to safeguard infant life, particularly among the working class.[70] As Dr. Bonnaire further explicated, in the immediate aftermath of the declaration of war, the Ligue Contre la Mortalité Infantile decided on "its own mobilization" by placing itself under the military government of Paris and guaranteeing that no pregnant woman would lack aid despite the crisis of the war.[71] Once again the concept of "mobilization" signified an association between society's preparing for war and for childbirth. On a more practical level, as historian Mary Lynn Stewart has shown, it was concern about *dénatalité* that led to the French government's interest in the maternal labor of women working in war-time factories and to such innovations as the 1917 law that permitted new mothers to breast-feed their children while at the workplace and, more generally, government encouragement of crèches at work sites.[72] Seen as a matter of life or death for the future of France, the main issue became not the extent to which women should be excluded from or protected within factories but how to reconcile the conflicting needs of women to support themselves and their children by factory work, of the wartime nation to experience no disturbance in work necessary for the liberation of France, and of the country to insure that its future and current mothers were adequately protected.[73] The author of this report, Dr. Jacques-Amédée Doléris, contributed to the larger debates in a 1918 book examining motherhood. Here, he attacked birth control and abortion and appealed to French women: "It can appear strange perhaps that one comes to speak of motherhood in this tragic moment where so many mothers cry. . . . [But if] French mothers . . . can forget the present for an instant in order to think of the future, don't you think that it's precisely because death cuts down the flower of the children of France that the women of this country should not cease to envision the future flowering season?" Doléris thus urged the government to out-law neo-Malthusian measures and abortion and all French women to work to replace the glorious dead and thus regenerate France.[74]

Wielding greater influence, Dr. Adolphe Pinard, a leading pronatal-ist, helped launch more public debates that ultimately produced these changes when he brought to a general audience beyond the Academy of Medicine in early December 1916 his concerns over the "maternal" costs that women paid for war factory work. Provocatively, he proclaimed on page one of a leading Parisian daily, *Le Matin,* that the factory was the "killer of children." Basing his views on statistics about infant mortality and the birthrate in Paris during the first two years of the war, Pinard stated "with an absolute certitude" that factory work was directly to blame for the decline in births. In response to this crisis, he proposed that the government forbid pregnant women, nursing mothers, and those who had given birth within six months from doing factory work. And those concerned about the production of weapons had to recognize that "woman, she, has but one natural aptitude for which she was created: *the production of the child.*"[75] The entire issue was contextualized in terms of widespread concern with repopulation after the war given the loss of men, the declining birthrate, and the rising level of infant mortality.

Looking to the postwar future and the need to rebuild France to insure lasting victory, Pinard had asserted in his initial report to the Academy of Medicine that the children produced by women "were as . . . indispensable for the second victory as munitions were for the first."[76] He maintained that factory work and motherhood were incompatible and that it was shortsighted of the nation to think otherwise. Pinard proposed the exclusion of pregnant and nursing women and mothers who recently delivered from factory work and that, in order to prevent economic hardship, all French women in such conditions receive five francs a day. His most vocal opposition came from Dr. Paul Strauss, a member of the French Senate, who not only argued that there was insufficient evidence that women's factory work caused the decline in the birthrate but also used the studies conducted by Dr. Bonnaire to argue that closing factory doors to pregnant and nursing mothers would produce the antithesis of the desired effect. If having and nursing children became an obstacle to economic survival, potential mothers would instead choose "voluntary sterility, abortion, abandonment."[77] Rather than removing such women from the factories, the state should do whatever it could to protect mothers who had to work in them.

Throughout the winter of 1917, members of the Academy of Medicine debated what specific actions to take regarding motherhood and factory work. Pinard repeated his call for the total exclusion of pregnant and nursing women from factories, while others, like Strauss, insisted that this was not only untenable but also potentially harmful to the war effort. In the end, Pinard's proposals were seen as impossible to enforce and too expensive; members compromised by recommending the following measures: that pregnant women and nursing mothers needed to moderate the type and duration of work and were entirely forbidden to work at night or with toxic substances; they were to be offered medical and hygienic advice from both doctors and newly appointed female superintendents; and, in order to encourage breastfeeding, factories, especially war factories, should create conditions under which women could nurse their children while at work.[78]

Meanwhile, Pinard's article and the debates it inspired also elicited a response in the feminist press. In late December 1916, Mme. Legrelle de Ferrer, on behalf of the Alliance Féministe pour l'Union Sacrée de Mères, insisted that while France was in a state of war even pregnant and nursing women could not stop working. According to her, they did so out of necessity, "because it is the only means aside from stealing or prostituting themselves in the absence of the father to give the necessities to their families." The problem was the insufficiency of state support for children, and Legrelle de Ferrer addressed Pinard, speaking on behalf of "mothers of families, French women and patriots, placed in front of this terrible problem, 'the rapid extinction of the population of France,'" by offering practical remedies. Her specific proposals included increasing financial aid under the Loi Strauss of 17 June 1913, as well as suppressing alcoholism and prostitution; but Legrelle de Ferrer was also adamant that women "did not want to be treated as simple females for reproduction."[79]

Jeanne Bouvier, responding to Pinard in *L'Action Féminine,* blamed not the factory itself for the declining birthrate but the "economic and social anarchy" that caused women to work under such injurious conditions. She expressed her grave concern that closing factory doors to women in need of work would cause far greater social damage. Instead, Bouvier urged the adoption of both changes in factory life specifically aimed at women, like the creation of nursing rooms or crèches, and workplace innovations like eight-hour shifts and the "English week."[80] Feminists in general strongly defended women's right to work, as they had done throughout the war. In the end, the only legislative measure taken in regard to mothers in French factories was to give women time off, with pay, to breast-feed their children, a recognition of the difficulty of not using women in wartime factory work despite the fact that such work curtailed what was regarded as their other national responsibility.[81] This modest compromise measure still represented a wartime step that Britain did not take.

On the other side of the channel, while continuing to speak of motherhood as "woman's first war duty," those concerned with both the British state's and private charities' roles in supporting mothers claimed that "the heaviest burden of the war falls on women. . . . [B]ut as individuals and as a nation we can share the responsibility of raising the children."[82] In the nation's attempt to make it easier to raise not only the children of soldiers but also future soldiers, its self-interest in promoting motherhood was emphasized throughout the war.[83]

Almost as soon as war broke out, leading British feminist organizations such as the National Union of Women's Suffrage Societies (NUWSS) joined forces with the Local Government Board in lending aid to the spread of "maternity centres," originally instituted under the auspices of the Women's Co-operative Guild. Such centers, according to Millicent Garrett Fawcett, were meant to save infant and maternal life by giving material support to pregnant women before and after birth. She stressed that "the work of saving an infant life is surely of immense importance at such a time as this, when there is such a heavy loss of life in war, but it is also . . . a piece of constructive work of national value."[84] However, Britain also called upon even its female subjects to perform other "constructive" work.

Despite exhortations to Britons to "do their bit," wage work relevant to the war was placed in opposition to motherhood as almost a mutually exclusive means of proving national loyalty and providing national service. Concern with the health of working women centered on what kind of production was most important to sustain the war effort. Early in 1915, Austin Harrison proclaimed that "motherhood [was] the first duty of women." Writing of the possible results of continued warfare, Harrison prophetically stated that with even another year of war "we must expect a hecatomb of males, the best, from the standpoint of population, because the youth, of the race. That women will be gravely injured as a result needs no demonstration." Predicting that the war-driven population loss could lead to an end of conflict between the sexes, Harrison further suggested that "[f]or a decade women will react to the calls of motherhood and human sympathy. . . . [T]he first duty of women will be motherhood in the interests of State." He then cited the French example of "Faire des gosses [have children]," claiming it would become a "European watchword" and insisting that "the home [would] become the panacea of Britain." By linking the panacea of the home with women's having children "in the interests of State," Harrison conflated women's domestic, ostensibly private, duty of child-bearing with their public, national responsibility.[85]

Other journalists took such arguments even further, with one stating that "the first business of a good Government . . . is the manufacture of healthy little citizens, and plenty of them. . . . Everything else should be conducive to that."[86] While recognizing that the war had saved "girls from the old conception which regarded them as tame domestic pets," Alex Thompson highlighted the danger of promoting women's new forms of wage work while neglecting "another trade at which they shine unrivaled—and that is the useful trade of motherhood." After detailing Britain's falling birthrate, Thompson told readers that "the overthrow of the British Empire against which our men are so gallantly fighting . . . will be achieved in a few years by the selfishness and cowardice of our women." Thus the article presented the war as the shared struggle of men and women to preserve the empire, in which men excelled in holding up their end of the bargain as fighters, while women "cowardly" refused to do their bit and produce "healthy citizens."[87] He proposed that motherhood be treated as a productive trade and compensated accordingly. According to Thompson, if the government did not encourage "the useful trade of motherhood," it would find itself with "weaklings" and not "heroes." A letter to the editor of *The Times* in September of 1915 also lamented that working married women were raising "the future generation" and urged "the importance of making clear to the mothers that they cannot do a greater service to their country than in raising a healthy race of men and women."[88] Throughout these discussions, the idea of motherhood as a natural, national industry emphasized the preeminent position of women as mothers who produced the state's most valuable commodity and insisted that whatever else women did, motherhood remained their primary way to demonstrate patriotic support of the empire.

Wartime rhetoric insisted that motherhood was a "trade," so Margaret Llewelyn Davies, leader of the Women's Co-operative Guild, which represented largely working-class and lower-middle-class women, helped orchestrate one of the grass-roots efforts to aid mothers in Britain by urging government action to regulate it and by calling for the state allocation of maternity benefits. In 1914, Davies delivered a speech on "Motherhood and the State" to the Metropolitan Branch of the Society of Medical Officers of Health in which she stated: "[I]t is time that married women's lives were so conditioned as to enable them to do *well* their great task for the nation."[89] Explicitly promoting maternity—reproduction—as women's work on behalf of the state, Davies used this argument as the underlying basis of her subsequent demands for the state to replace private and voluntary associations in supporting maternity. In 1915, the Women's Co-operative Guild underscored its demands by publishing *Maternity*, a collection of letters from working-class women that articulated working women's perception of themselves as mothers in need of state support.

Drawing upon correspondence from all over Britain, Davies selected a collection that emphasized the overwork and deprivation experienced by pregnant women and those raising children. All letter writers belonged to the Women's Co-operative Guild, and, in order to stress their financial needs, they included the amount of wages coming into their households and the number of children they had, which followed the text of each letter. Some women made explicit the connections between their own roles as mothers and the future of the nation.

As one put it, "The child is the asset of the nation, and the mother the backbone. Therefore, I think the nation should help to feed and keep that mother, and so help to strengthen the nation by her giving birth to strong boys and girls. . . . I only hope that sick visitors would see that it is the mothers that are getting the benefit of the maternity benefit, and not the husband and often the landlord."[90] Metaphorically, mothers became an ill-treated part of the national body, a "backbone" in need of strengthening; yet the need for mothers' independence was stressed along with their need for support.[91] Others insisted that women should exercise control not only over any financial aid given to them but also over their bodies by making choices as to whether or not to become mothers: "How women, and poor women, can have children year after year, is a marvel to me. . . . [I]t seems terrible, bringing such children into the world, a burden to their parents, to themselves, and to the nation, for they are only wrecks, and fill our hospitals, mental deficiency schools, and prisons."[92] Another woman wrote: "All the beautiful in motherhood is very nice if one has plenty to bring up a family on, but what real mother is going to bring a life into the world to be pushed into the drudgery of the world at the earliest possible moment. . . . There is nothing that is done can ever be too much if we are to have going a race in the future worthy of England, but it will not be until the nation wakes up to the needs of the mothers of that future race."[93] Several different representations of motherhood appeared in these letters. In the opinion of some, the state needed women to reproduce the race. Others felt that, because motherhood was forced upon them, women needed the state to eradicate its burdensome aspects. One salient feature of the letters was the linking of a nationalist eugenics with concern for mothers. In addition, control of fertility by women emerged as a benefit not just for mothers themselves but for mothers as producers, either of children—presumably male and future soldiers—"worthy of England" or of those fit only to fill "hospitals" and "prisons." The choice of what mothers could produce lay not with them, according to this rhetoric, but with the state.

In demanding aid, these mothers argued as a group who contributed to the larger public good, not as individuals demanding rights. The desire for the state to protect its mothers and to recognize the needs of "real" mothers resonated throughout the Guild's campaign for maternal benefits. Furthermore, the book's reception indicated its influence. In a long essay on the state and the mother, in the *Quarterly Review*, *Maternity* was saluted as revealing "the manifold problems of the working-man's home life, the centre and vitals of a nation," showing that "we deserve to have . . . a declining birth-rate," even though the empire needed "a growing and virile population."[94] Advertised as "a book which has caused a Sensation" before going into its second edition, it was promoted by quotations from the *New Statesman* and *The Times* that claimed that "it is scarcely possible to overstate the value of this publication" and that "no man whatsoever ought to animadvert on 'race suicide' until he has read this little volume."[95]

Following this book's account of the shared working-class experience of maternal suffering, the Women's Co-operative Guild issued a "Memorandum on the National Care of Maternity." This document equated the "welfare of the country" with the need for the "enlightened and generous care of Maternity." Addressing those concerned with infant mortality, it stated: "The care of the mother should have equal consideration with that of the infant. Her welfare must be secured so that she may be capable of meeting with intelligence and energy the various responsibilities of motherhood and home life. The claims of mother and child are not antagonistic, but interdependent."[96] Although arguing for "equal consideration," this statement nonetheless collapsed the claims of mother and child into one another. Later in the document, the Guild argued — as did other organizations, including the National Council of Public Morals — that discrimination against unwed mothers must end and that state aid to mothers must transcend misconduct rules. The sharing of the traumatic and bodily experience of motherhood created a bond among women that was meant to supplant traditional notions of respectability and distinctions between married and single mothers and between classes. However, as the debate over war babies made clear, such appeals did not always succeed.

Taking up the effect of war work on mothering, three other women's organizations, the Federation of Women Workers, the Women's Trade Union League, and the Women's Industrial Council, began in 1916 to collect evidence that the new work performed by women would prove injurious "to future motherhood."[97] Once again, the focus on threats to motherhood as threats not to individual women but to the national future identified all women as potential mothers. The medical profession also used its expertise to heighten the sense of danger that women's industrial work posed to the "national" health. Issuing a "warning to women doing men's work," Dr. J. Dulberg cautioned that "in the midst of the patriotic enthusiasm which the women of the country are displaying" the nation should not forget that "after all is said and done, woman's main function in life is to perpetuate the human species." Before undertaking work "which is not quite in keeping with the comparative weakness and peculiarities of her sex," whatever its value and for whatever noble reasons, women had to keep in mind that they ran the risk of rendering themselves "unfit" for their "predestined" role in life.[98]

A long article in *The Quiver* in 1916 posed the question: "Is there a danger that these women workers are jeopardising the wonderful bodies God gave them, and risking the ultimate purpose of those bodies? Are they unfitting themselves for home life . . . for motherhood?"[99] Comparing the privations of soldiers with those of the women in wartime factories, this article suggested that "the point . . . is that the women of this country have actually made far greater sacrifices over the war than any of us realise. . . . [H]ow many women must be denied the babies they wish to bear through the loss of young husbands? Is not this a heavy penalty for the sex to pay for war, and in a country whose birth-rate is one of the lowest in the world?" Insisting on equating women with mothers, the article also associated their specific heroism with that of soldiers: "[T]he war's cost to women will be found to be as great as the price paid by man. . . . [T]he little woman who has put her one wee babe in a municipal crèche and gone a-war working for a dozen hours a day . . . has fought a hard fight, made an heroic sacrifice."[100] The use of military metaphors thus equated the valor and necessity of the factory working mother with that of the fighting man. In another study of war work, aptly entitled *Conflicting Ideals of Women's Work,* Barbara Hutchins noted that debates about women's work were not new, but she also recognized in their modern form that "no one can deny that the service of the childbearing mother is that which is most indispensable to the continued existence of the nation and the state." The problem was that motherhood had "no exchange value whatever," and thus other mechanisms had to be found to support women who had children.[101]

However, one female doctor's response to concern with factory work's impact on potential motherhood reminded readers: "There is a great deal of over-anxiety as to women war workers as future mothers. . . . No one has tried to collect statistics as to how far heavy cleaning, scrubbing, laundry work, and sweeping have harmed women."[102] Nevertheless, as the need for women workers to free men for the fighting line intensified, newspaper articles continued to caution "all those in authority over women workers to guard the future mothers of the race."[103] Solutions to the seemingly incompatible facts that "[w]omen are wanted for munition work . . . [b]abies are wanted for the Empire" included the establishment of factory crèches as a means of insuring the production of both weapons and humans for the imperial arsenal.[104] Such concern led to concrete proposals, as Susan Pedersen has illustrated, for endowments for motherhood espoused by feminists such as Eleanor Rathbone and Maude Royden. In a statement evocative of many discussed earlier, Royden wrote in 1917: "The State wants children, and to give them is a service both dangerous and honourable. Like the soldier, the mother takes a risk and gives a devotion for which no money can pay."[105]

In addition, the National Birth-Rate Commission of the National Council of Public Morals conducted two studies on these questions. The results were published in *The Declining Birth-Rate: Its Causes and Effects* (1916) and *Problems of Population and Parenthood* (1920), which provided ample evidence of a growing sense of urgency regarding the link between the national crisis and fears of a declining population. The first of these two studies was initiated in 1913, which pointed to the prewar concern with these questions, and the members of the Birth-Rate Commission included representatives of numerous religious, medical, philanthropic, and intellectual groups, among them several women.[106] By the time its second investigation had begun, special concern with both the problems of illegitimacy and of wage-earning women as mothers had come to the forefront.

Testifying in October 1918, Miss A. G. Philip, director of the Maternity Subsection of the Ministry of Munitions, explained the problems raised by work rules that sought to dismiss any pregnant woman for her own good. This caused difficulties because pregnant women with other children to support were desperate to keep their jobs. As a result, a woman often tried to conceal her pregnancy, "and in many cases endeavor to get rid of it." In response to fears that women would prevent or abort their pregnancies, factory doctors and supervisors attempted to set up a system for women to keep working until shortly before giving birth by switching them from heavy to medium work at the fourth month of pregnancy, and to light work at the seventh month. Thus women were encouraged to report rather than conceal their pregnancies. In addition, crèches for working women had been established as early as the fall of 1916. In April 1918 treasury funds were actually set aside to accommodate munition workers during prenatal and postnatal periods as well as at birth. Philip insisted, however, that the experience of the Ministry of Munitions suggested that nothing definitive could be done to help working mothers unless conditions within the factory could be affected.[107] The questions following Philip's testimony hinged on whether or not it was a good idea to encourage any married women to continue doing industrial work after the war and what the effect was of treating unmarried and married mothers on the same basis.[108] Philip's responses indicated that, despite the presumed contradiction between factory work and motherhood, allowing pregnant women to remain in jobs where they could support themselves, their families, and their babies could have the desired effect of encouraging women to have more children.

It was not solely government officials who expressed concern about the effect of women's wartime labor on women's productivity as mothers. British manufacturers of baby formula—with obvious commercial motives—paid for the most prominent series of advertisements in the *Woman Worker,* a magazine for women's trade unions and women laborers. Advertisements for Glaxo baby formula explicitly addressed the newly employed female factory worker and insisted on the connection between all women and productive motherhood. The advertisements regarded all women workers as potential mothers and reinforced an imagined contradiction between women's factory work and child rearing. Rather than supporting the economic independence of mothers, these advertisements further attempted to exploit their anxieties and to play upon a presumed universal female desire to put children's needs above all others.

Ad copy such as "deep down in every woman's soul there lies the vision of the dream child which will be a reality one day—when all this war and strife are over and done with" sought to reassure women that the real calling of their "soul"—a baby—would be answered if they produced the tools of war now, which would hasten a British victory.[109] Other advertisements used the wartime context to explain why formula should be substituted for mother's milk: "[I]n these days of strife and worry, Baby's natural food is often not forthcoming."[110] Overall, the entire series of advertisements emphasized that support for mothers aided the war and vice versa. War temporarily displaced women from their "preferred, dream roles" and deprived them of the precious gift of children; however, all mothers, like all children, were necessary to the state.

This attitude came forth most forcefully in the full-page text of another of Glaxo's ads. Under the heading, "Munitions and Motherhood," the advertisers explicitly linked freeing mothers for war work with feeding their children:

> Not even a woman can eat her cake and have it, not even she can make the munitions to save the present and tend the children who are to be the future. But the present day requires that women shall leave their homes, where the future should be made, and should take the place of men in the factories. . . .
>
> Women can take men's places; but men cannot take women's. That is the humiliating truth for the sex-proud men to swallow to-day. . . .
>
> At first we were as blind and reckless of the consequences to the future as we could be. We worked our women seven days a week, . . . and we forgot the children altogether. . . . To-day we are learning some measure of sense; and its substance is this: —
>
> If women in general, who necessarily include mothers, are to make munitions, serve their country . . . in any capacity, high or low, it is necessary for our national future that special steps be taken to guard the children who are the natural, sacred and supreme care of womanhood. Whether it be the child of the munition-worker, or of the most highly-placed woman-worker in the land, the problem is one and the same.[111]

Embedded in this material was the certain fundamental and unchallenged belief that the only role women could *alone* perform, which rendered their services invaluable, was motherhood, the concern of all women.

More than anything else, these advertisements focused on the product of maternity. They expressed general concern with children and with women primarily as conduits to children. "Special steps" needed to be taken "to guard the children," not to guard "womanhood," from being worked seven days a week. The exploitation of women in factories became a problem only because "we forgot the children altogether." All of Glaxo's advertisements helped to deny the importance of women as wageworkers; in fact, they apologized for *not* treating women as mothers. The perceived detriment to children and the interruption of the traditional relationship between mother and child prompted this emotive brow-beating, rather than concern about the plight of mothers. Since these advertisements were prominently and deliberately placed in a periodical aimed at women performing industrial work, the makers of baby formula clearly assumed that women wanted to return to their "traditional" roles, that their primary concern was the well-being of current and future children. Regardless of how women themselves felt about these appeals, defining women as mothers helped to promote the notion that mothers played an equivalent role for states that soldiers did, especially in wartime. In both Britain and France, women's wartime factory work remained something meant to be put up with "for the duration." Their true service lay in other forms of labor.

Conclusion

Given the increased need for women in the wartime factories of Britain and, to a lesser extent, France, the governments of these two nations found themselves attempting a delicate balancing act. On the one hand, they encouraged women's patriotic participation in war work, and on the other, they felt compelled to safeguard motherhood as anxiety about declining birthrates grew as the war's death tolls mounted. When the British government decided to institute separation allowances as a means of encouraging recruitment, they also believed it necessary to insure that such money was being used to support a family. When funds for soldiers' and sailors' families became available to unwed mothers and their children, debates about whether this aid supported the children of heroes or the products of a shameful wartime immorality divided feminists, social workers, and politicians. Finally, when women entered wartime factories, contemporary commentators expressed their concern about the dual obligations being thrust upon women. By viewing women as first and foremost mothers and potential mothers, they were torn between acknowledging wartime female factory workers' vital contributions to the present war effort and agonizing over their essential role in preserving the nation's future population.

It should not be surprising that as the war drew to a close, the safeguarding of motherhood was viewed as crucial by a variety of organizations trying to determine what awaited women in the postwar world. Organizations that had devoted themselves to studying the birthrate warned with renewed vigor of the dangerous gap between births and deaths. The maternal body, discussed in Chapter 2 as a contested space in the armed conflict of the war, became in these debates an instrument of state renewal. While motherhood did not have the same meaning to everyone, "the mother" was viewed by many commentators in both Britain and France as encompassing all women as objects of national concern and state intervention in a manner akin to the way these states viewed all men as potential soldiers.

The state's concern with women, however, was not completely restricted to the married and unmarried women who produced the country's future soldiers. The wartime view of women as instigators of immoral activity caused concern over the threat posed by nonprocreative sexuality and led to government attempts to regulate women, sexuality, and prostitution and to monitor venereal disease. These governments' efforts to promote the war and preserve the domestic order by controlling women's bodies will be taken up in the following chapter.

Women's Wild Oats

SEXUALITY AND THE

SOCIAL ORDER

Gendered Behavior and Social Disorder

In 1919, Catherine Hartley's treatise *Women's Wild Oats* responded to a series of alleged crises about women during the just-completed war that concerned women's moral behavior and the threats contained in and posed by the sexual female body. Starting her book with an account of the celebrations that met the armistice, Hartley commented:

> It was the women that I noticed the most: they were wilder than the men. . . .
>
> The woman without a cigarette was almost the exception. There was no attempt at concealment. But what impressed me was the way of holding and smoking the cigarette that proclaimed the novice. Quite plainly the great majority of these girls were smoking not at all because they desired to smoke, but for a lark. A little thing . . . and yet it is the straw which reveals the direction of the wind.

By tying such a small shift in behavior, the revealing detail of women smoking, to a range of "uncontrollable" activities, Hartley proclaimed "the peril of the future" to be "the problem of unstable woman."[1]

Hartley lamented what prominent journalists, members of the

clergy, politicians, and others had "discovered" during the war: a decline in women's moral behavior and stature. A whole range of behaviors deemed minor vices if performed by men—smoking, drinking, or using foul language or rude gestures—were considered grave problems when women allegedly adopted them in great numbers during the war.[2] By the end of 1917, a defiant article in Britain's *National News* suggested that recent campaigns to encourage women to give up smoking "because there may be a shortage of tobacco for men" were blatantly unfair. Pointing out that women were willing to have smaller bread rations since they ate less, the article argued that "to ask a woman to give up an occasional cigarette that the men who crowd out the tobacco shops shall have all that there is, is yielding up the outward symbol of equality which it took three years of war to win."[3]

Whether or not the adoption of what were seen as men's vices represented women's true move to gender equality, a focus on women's public moral behavior in Britain and France began as soon as war broke out. Criticism of women's smoking, drinking, and public mischief served as precursors to more anxious concern about women's sexuality. As the war progressed, women's sexual behavior, particularly that of so-called amateur girls in addition to prostitutes, came to be seen as threatening to military strength and the fighting man.[4]

The multiple public debates that posed female sexuality as a threat to the fighting man point to the extent to which debates about the female body as the site of temptation and the transmitter of disease became an arena for the expression of anxiety about general social disorder. In contrast to images of French, Belgian, and misplaced British women as victims of male (particularly German) sexual predators, discussed in Chapter 2, women in the so-called home front who instigated sexual misconduct were viewed as internal threats to the nation's welfare. The most stringent response to anxiety over women's sexuality was manifested in the revival of several provisions of the abolished Contagious Diseases Acts (C.D. Acts) in Britain, which stipulated that a woman found to have a venereal disease could be criminally prosecuted for infecting members of the armed forces. This significant British policy shift was at odds with conditions in France. Despite its substantial tradition of regulatory behavior, French concern over prostitution and the spread of venereal disease did not result in increased action by the wartime government directed at women.

In general, despite the wide-ranging opinions expressed about these issues, shifts in notions of moral standards for female sexuality were negligible at best; women continued to be portrayed as either sexual temptresses or innocent victims. Tellingly, although Britain produced more (and more controversial) wartime legislation addressing prostitution, disorder in its capital city, and the spread of venereal disease, France remained the model against which such efforts were measured and attacked. In France, regulated prostitution continued and, for the only time in the twentieth century, according to historian Alain Corbin, the number of *maisons tolerées* (state-regulated brothels) increased.[5] Both nations faced what appeared to be a shared problem: an increase in casual sexual intercourse between girls — *too* well-trained in love of country (and thus of the man in uniform) — and those serving in the military.[6] The British and French governments and many social commentators viewed preserving the strength and fitness of fighting men as their overarching goal. One result of this was a shared and intense focus on women in debates about the perceived decline in moral standards and behavior, and the related increase in prostitution and venereal diseases in France and Britain. This common concern provides yet another powerful example of how interwoven the "separate spheres" of home front and front line were, and the extent to which anxiety about wartime social disorder more generally was played out upon the mores and bodies of women.

"How They Are Working Mischief": Women and Wartime Morality

In both France and Britain, commentators, politicians, and social reformers wanted to channel women's support for the war in ways that preserved the family and the nation. They also seemed aware that such support could be problematic. Changes in women's access to public space and in their behavior once they occupied these spaces were apparent to observers in both countries. In France, popular cultural artifacts like songs, postcards, and works of fiction depicted women as the literal rewards for soldiers' bravery, suggesting a greater acceptance of women's sexual expression there than in Britain.[7] In Britain, terms like "flappers" and "amateur girls" were associated with allegedly new kinds of female sexual activity, even though, as in the war baby scandal discussed in Chapter 3, some people claimed that little had changed with the war. Even in France, however, acceptance, or even tolerance, was not universal, as some contemporaries, especially men, condemned women's allegedly greater sexual freedom during wartime and demonstrated their fears of female sexual betrayal.[8]

Still, it remains difficult to know how contemporaries interpreted such images as "Flirt 1914," which appeared in the magazine *Le Rire* and was then reproduced in a special issue of *Je Sais Tout.* In the drawing, an attractive, young nurse sits at the bedside of an injured soldier; the nurse, we may presume, is French, but the hand she is gently holding belongs to a sleeping colonial African soldier. The title "Flirt" could have been read as ironic; such an image might have been meant to show what had happened to the prewar "flirt." She now embodied the true devotion of the French woman as nurse who cared for all soldiers of France, regardless of status, including race. At the same time, labeling an image depicting a white woman holding the hand of a black man "flirt" suggests some deeper discomfort with the physical closeness now available between men and women, irrespective of class, age, nationality, or race.[9]

A less complex wartime reaction to French women may be found in Paul Géraldy's popular novel *La guerre, madame* (1916), where his hero, a returning soldier, is horrified to discover Parisian widows wearing make-up. He wonders as he passes women on the streets: "Of what are they thinking? Have they husbands and brothers at the front? Are they rushing to some rendez-vous? . . . Have they men who undress them?"[10] Géraldy's soldier finds a world of women who seem to have forgotten the war, a city insensitive to hardship and in love with pleasure, where women seem to exude their (perhaps illicit) sexuality in the streets.

Indeed, the invention of the *marraine de guerre,* whose support of men at the front was discussed in Chapter 1, was filled with sexual promise—potential sexual promiscuity—as well as pure emotional and material aid.[11] In a 1918 history of the *marraine,* Henriette Vismes praised the valuable work they performed but also noted the importance of separating the "true" *marraines* from those who "usurped" their name and acted in a "frivolous" manner.[12] Certainly advertisements placed by men seeking *marraines* that ran in periodicals like *La Vie Parisienne* hardly indicated interest in the role's charitable origins. One *poilu* went so far as to declare: "I have no need for socks, but would be very happy to correspond with a young, pretty, affectionate *marraine.*"[13]

French reformers, including feminists, and politicians also responded directly to the threatening use of alcohol by women, and campaigns against alcohol became a major wartime feminist activity.[14] They were particularly concerned with the dangerous association between alcohol and prostitution, although it was not until October 1917 that laws forbade the presence of prostitutes in all establishments where drinking occurred.[15] Two years earlier, François Dulom had opened his study of prostitution "dans les débits" by quoting the following:

It's in the home of the dealers of liquors and beer
That one can see dancing with the garrison
The famous harlots of ordinary [everyday] life
Who are a terrible poison for our army

The sellers of beer and alcohol in Dulom's attack created an atmosphere that encouraged prostitution and thus "poisoned" France's fighting men. For Dulom, this mix threatened the combined "physical, material and moral health of the society." Most dangerously, establishments selling liquor provided space for the fateful encounters between prostitutes and soldiers, encounters destined to be "even more contrary to military discipline than to the health of the troop of men." Dulom concluded that one of the most efficacious ways to combat this problem was to punish those "who provide asylum to women leading a bad life or reputed to do so," thus implicating the vendors of alcohol in his attack.[16]

If reformers responded quickly to potentially dangerous forms of female sexual expression attributed to alcohol, they also reacted with similar intensity to proposed alternatives to conventional bourgeois sexual morality that attempted to respond to fears about the falling birthrate. Rumors of German proposals in support of bigamy or polygamy in response to the war's death tolls as well as indications that some French people were considering similar ideas provoked a horrified reaction in 1916. Jane Misme, writing in La Française in January, denounced any proposals advocating polygamy as a response to the loss of men. While describing women condemned to celibacy and denied the opportunity to become mothers as no less "victims of the war," Misme denounced accepting polygamy because it would indicate "a singular overthrow of the moral sense." Instead, while admitting that prostitution and adultery already made monogamy "one of the public lies of modern Society," she asserted that the preservation of monogamy remained a worthy feminist goal since any alternative signaled a return to the inequality of "primitive antiquity" and "barbarism."[17]

Other feminist commentators reacted to proposals designed to promote unconventional sexual arrangements such as polygamy by asserting the need for education and for a unified standard of morality for both sexes. In August 1916, Marguerite de Witt-Schlumberger, writing in L'Action Féminine, spoke of the need for a single moral standard as a response to the loosening of morals that always accompanied war. Reacting to "legal bigamy" as one example of relaxed morals, de Witt-Schlumberger denounced the idea as one that, if accepted, "even temporarily," would represent a "retreating of civilisation" and a "degradation of woman." Instead, she advocated that young married women do their "national duty" of having children and that society "accept children that did not have a legal father," without trying to change radically existing social and moral laws.[18]

Later the same year, Jean Pain noted the loud voices celebrating the contributions of women during the war, as if they were afraid to admit to any of women's weaknesses. For Pain observed that war had also contributed to "a relaxing of morals." The danger to morality lay in the fact that women were exposed to a "new existence," which gave some the "taste for prostitution." The solution lay, in part, with a feminism that could instruct women about their corporate, national identity and could thus promote a sense of self-respect strong enough to combat sexual temptation.[19]

Conventional morality was further threatened by other proposed solutions to depopulation, like the encouragement of unwed motherhood. The treatise *Mère sans être épouse,* for instance, suggested that, with the war's losses, the women of France "must sacrifice their prejudices . . . in order to assure the growth of the victorious *Patrie*" by having children out of wedlock. If repopulation was a primary goal for the nation, French women needed to reproduce regardless of their marital prospects and status.[20] The promotion of "free maternity," like proposals for polygamy, was attacked by Jane Misme as "degrading for the woman, humiliating for the man, and noxious for the infant" as well as "dangerous for public order and intimate happiness."[21] Despite fears about depopulation, the greater danger, according to Misme, came from weakening morality. Other feminists concerned about both France's birthrate and threats to morality argued that the time had come to provide moral and sexual education: "[T]omorrow more than yesterday . . . patriotism will not be manifest only on the fields of battle; . . . the dignified preparation of youth to resist temptation . . . will also win the victory."[22]

These "dangerous" ideas and efforts to resist them were not the only attempts to preserve as well as defend the morality of French women on all fronts. In late 1917 the Conseil National des Femmes Françaises's subsection on morality launched an energetic attack on what it deemed an almost "pornographic" document found in the possession of an English soldier. Entitled "Five Minutes Conversation with Young Ladies," the document was described as being one "of the most infamous productions" designed to "facilitate vice by foreign men," notably English-speaking soldiers. It listed a series of phrases, given in both English and French, including such scandalous expressions as "Voulez-vous accepter l'apératif? (Would you accept an aperitif?), Où habitez-vous? (Where do you live?), Notre bonheur sera de courte durée (Our happiness will not last long), Pouvez-vous diner avec moi? (Could you dine with me?), and Permettez moi de vous baiser la main—de vous embrasser (Let me kiss your hand, embrace you)."[23] Feminists attacked the document for the damage it would do to France not only by openly encouraging vice on the part of Allied soldiers but also by provoking the anger of American, Canadian, and British women who lent their men to defend French women and expected them to return "morally and physically pure." Here the affront to women's moral standards put into question some of the previous assumptions about their decline, placing the blame on male behavior.

Further reaction in France to the particular presence of American soldiers and their behavior toward French women can be found in French police reports on the morale of the Parisian population during the war. One of these reports suggested that American men and French women were being equally assertive. Although the following account was written just at the end of the war, it probably reflected immediate wartime attitudes. It claimed that the attitude of American soldiers toward French women was "not at all correct," because "they call upon women quite rudely in the street without being concerned with whom they are addressing." It also noted that "young girls leaving their lessons let themselves be easily approached by American soldiers and engaged in conversation with them under the pretext of being able to speak English." In short, "neither the Americans nor the women . . . have a proper attitude."[24] Like similar reports, this account officially recorded public complaints; some French men and women were upset by the behavior of the Americans. However, crucially, some social commentators believed that it was the "young girls" who, like the soldiers, lacked the "proper attitude" and engaged in conversation, and possibly flirtations. While there were explicit references to the behavior of prostitutes and other moral problems in these reports, as will be discussed further below, these "jeunes filles," like the "amateur girls" of London, were not equated with "real" prostitutes. Nonetheless, women's morality remained a potential source of disorder.

A long study of female sexuality by Dr. Toulouse, published in 1918, took for granted that the war had altered behavior: "[W]ar is inevitably a school of sexual liberty . . . tending to transform morals."[25] War introduced sheltered, middle-class women who volunteered as nurses to "the mystery of the other sex"; it separated men from women while heightening awareness of unforeseen deaths, and, by permitting women to experience "masculine" domains of society, it destroyed the illusion that women needed protection and encouraged the loosening of morals (12, 17). Toulouse, like the feminists discussed above, promoted a single moral standard and proposed this solution: "[I]mpose chastity equally on young people of both sexes" (30, 35). In discussing such dangers as free unions, polygamy, and divorce, Toulouse focused on what would best enable France to achieve a stable population and cope with wartime dislocations, emphasizing that equal expectations of morality from both men and women were the keys to a "true" victory.

Across the channel, public debates about female behavior focused on the effect of mobilization on women left behind as men went off to battle. Women were held accountable for their incomparable moral influence on men, an influence that could be compromised if they drank or acted immodestly in public.[26] Even as women were urged to take on a variety of appropriate feminine, often charitable, activities, London newspapers reported on the possible consequences of "girls in the street" soliciting for charity: "'Who are these girls, young and pretty for the most part, who pester men in busy thoroughfares . . . rattling a collection box for an unknown fund?' was the question asked by the molested public." After investigating the matter, the *Daily Express* reporter concluded that "they were chiefly young women of the superior working class who, though not necessarily of a vicious disposition" were acting far too interested in their customers. Furthermore, after consulting with leading members of the National Union for Women Workers, the London Council for the Promotion of Public Morality, and the National Vigilance Association about the scandalous activities of these women, the paper quoted Arthur Paterson of the Social Welfare Association who warned that girls "are a grave menace to morality . . . all but the most strong-minded of them are in danger of falling victims to vice." Other journalists commented on women's generally pernicious influence on soldiers and noted with approval the inquiry into "the moral aspect of the occupations of certain young women" collecting money in the streets of London. The report denounced their "painted faces" and their "suggestively ogling and hanging on to the arms of khaki-clad soldiers."[27]

In November 1914, an appeal by the wives of the archbishop of Canterbury and the bishops of Rochester and Southwark that appeared in *The Vigilance Record,* the paper of the National Vigilance Association (NVA), noted that the outset of war was a "time of great excitement and anxiety." Encouraging girls to work and pray, the women highlighted the importance of a uniquely female moral influence:

> Many a man has been kept good by thinking of the good straight girl he knows at home who expects him to be good and straight. He is fighting for us women and for our homes. Give him something nice and good and true to think about. Don't let your excitement make you silly and lead you to wander aimlessly about. . . . Be very careful that, so far as you are concerned, no one of them [the men] shall carry away with him as his last remembrance of the women and the girls of England anything but what is pure and gentle and straight and true.[28]

Thus these women defined the motive for going to war as the preservation of women and the home, implying that unless women and girls were "straight" and "pure," soldiers would not only have nothing to fight for but also would themselves go wrong.

The effort to distinguish between prostitutes and women who slept with soldiers out of love or misplaced patriotism was a preoccupation of several reformers. Restrictions on the behavior of young girls initially centered not only on their activities in places such as London but also in the newly established training camps in Britain. Upon the outbreak of war in 1914, the British government instituted a series of measures under the Defence of the Realm Act (DORA) designed to combat internal enemies by eventually allowing for the suspension of many civil liberties.[29] One of its first targets was prostitution. Colonel East, commander of the Severn Defenses, cited DORA when he issued an order in November 1914 to certain women in Cardiff effectively placing them under curfew from 7 P.M. until 8 A.M.[30] The first five women arrested under the order pleaded guilty and were eventually sentenced to detention for sixty-two days; other women arrested for the same offense were sentenced in early December to a total of fifty-six days of hard labor.[31]

These actions prompted a quick public outcry. By late December, newspapers reported that several protesters, including labor leader

George Lansbury, had met with East to protest the military orders. Pointing out that Prime Minister Asquith "had pledged his word that the C.D. Acts should not be introduced," the delegation sought to persuade East to rescind the order. They made the point that such restrictions on behavior, if necessary, should be applied to everyone, not merely women listed by the police. East listened but claimed his interest was in the health of the soldiers and not morals, which led the *Herald* to comment that "his action . . . means that the military authorities only take action to secure the health of the men. The physical and moral degradation of women does not count with them." Urging all who were opposed to East's measures to join in "emphatic protest" against them, the paper indicated that the public, in its view, had no intention of allowing government attempts to regulate prostitution and venereal disease to go unnoticed.[32]

The case of the Cardiff women presented the first use of DORA to regulate the behavior of women suspected of immoral behavior and prostitution. That it was read as a return to the Contagious Diseases Acts was evident in an angry feminist response published in the suffragette periodical *The Vote*. In this article, C. Nina Boyle made use of the popular vocabulary of outrage prevalent in wartime propaganda. She referred to the "Prime Minister and a 'Scrap of Paper' "; that is, she implied that Asquith's refusal to abide by his previous declaration that there would be no return to the C.D. Acts was comparable to Germany's violating the 1839 treaty guaranteeing Belgian neutrality. Worried about the arbitrary nature in which such regulations would be applied, particularly in wartime, and the fact the accused women would be tried in courts-martial, Boyle denounced as "utterly sickening" the way in which women's rights were denied and their good names besmirched. She tellingly observed that prostitution typically went unnoticed, but "[w]hen inconvenient and dangerous—to men, not to girls—there is an immediate resort to persecution of a peculiarly dastardly kind."[33]

In prosecuting the Cardiff women, Colonel East felt that he was acting on behalf of the well-being of soldiers, but others concerned with the behavior of women both around centers of military activity and in major cities and towns believed regulation was no solution to what was fundamentally a moral problem. The National Vigilance Association spoke of the need to appoint "women patrols" to safeguard the behavior of the women and girls around the base in Cardiff.[34] Patrols were also proposed as a solution to "scandalous conduct" in Bristol, where there was "great excitement" among the young women of the city. According to the NVA, "[v]ery young girls, indeed, owing partly no doubt to a kind of silly hero-worship, were trying to flirt, or do something more than flirt, with young soldiers."[35] Thus, innocent excitement about heroes in uniform had the potential to turn dangerous, becoming a kind of morale-gone-too-far. While women were urged to preserve the morale of the fighting forces and the soldier became the epitome of all that was desirable, those concerned with immorality feared that such sentiments could corrupt both young women and men.[36]

This kind of dangerous "hero-worship" persisted after the first wave of enthusiasm. On Monday, 22 November 1915, twenty young women, aged eighteen to twenty-five, were charged at London's Tower Bridge Police Court for "frequenting Waterloo-road for immoral purposes." Not accused of being ordinary prostitutes or prosecuted under DORA, these women were nonetheless charged with "soliciting" and brought before a magistrate, who commented that "for their own safety" the women ought to be sentenced to an indeterminate detention. "It is hopeless and almost worse than useless," he went on, "to treat these cases as if they were *ordinary* misdemeanours. It is not only the girls who require protection against themselves, but the soldiers also call for some protection from persistent solicitation."[37] Other public figures, like Lady Frances Balfour, had in mind less punitive solutions to these "misdemeanors." In an article in a Birmingham paper in March 1915, Lady Balfour offered the following as a "woman's" perspective:

> Tell the worst woman who ever haunted the camps of armies that her conduct helps to make or mar the fighting man, and you will appeal to something that never dies in the heart of womanhood, the instinct to serve, to protect and to strengthen—no branding of pillory, no flogging at the cat tail saved society from the drunken prostitute. No police surveillance, or warning to avoid "women and wine" will serve to strengthen the ideal of comrades in arms against a common foe.[38]

Balfour's solution was to encourage an appeal to innate, patriotic emotions. Perhaps it is due to her stated aim of providing a female voice that she emphasized men's and women's shared antagonism to a "common foe" and called attention to the behavior of men, advocating not that men be warned against "women and wine" but that both sexes be encouraged to treat each other with respect.

During the following year, wartime campaigns to purge London of moral corruption focused on the behavior of women. In September 1916, the Church of England sponsored a "National Mission of Repentance and Hope," which called attention to the plight of wartime London. In a series of addresses, published in a collection entitled *Cleansing London,* Arthur Winnington-Ingram, the bishop of London, elaborated on the city's many problems and what could be done to alleviate them.[39] The image on the frontispiece of the published treatise depicted Christ, standing unmistakably in London, reaching out his arms to an audience that included soldiers, nurses, workers and, at the front, a kneeling mother with a cradled child before her.[40] The bishop opened by proclaiming his glorying in "being a son of Britain to-day" but went on to denounce "the villains more mischievous than German spies, who ought to share their fate, who lie in wait to stain the chivalry of our boys, poison their minds, and undermine their character."[41] Chief among these villains were "the male hawks who walk up and down this very Piccadilly night by night with twenty or thirty helpless and trembling girls under their surveillance, and who take from them the very money the girls earn by their shame" (25). Calling for the raising of the age of consent from sixteen to eighteen, the bishop also urged that laws be enacted that would drive such men from London and, along with them, "the writer of lecherous and slimy productions ranking as stage plays" (25). He attacked the use of other public spaces—specifically theater promenades and parks (in danger, he claimed, of becoming "open-air brothels")—for the purposes of prostitution and the resulting corruption of young men.[42]

The bishop then insisted that noncombatants, both women and middle-aged men should "purge the heart of the Empire before the boys come back" (25). He called for "a change of mind and spirit," for a return to old-fashioned religious morality (28). He challenged the propagation of vice among the young: "Have you asked yourself what God says about fornication—not what your shallow friend says?" And he attacked the restoration of the Contagious Diseases Acts, claiming regulation would only encourage immorality (28–33). He further criticized activities causing the disintegration of home life, particularly infidelity, bad temper, alcohol, and birth control (57). *Cleansing London* became a cry for a purge of offensive behavior not only in the streets but inside homes as well.

Tying all such issues together was the need for religious awakening to counter both public and private "sin." But beyond the religious call was a patriotic one, a linkage between home front and front line as comparable moral as well as physical battlefields. And if it was up to only a certain category of men to "purge the heart of the Empire," it was the task of *all* "the women of London." Calling at one point for a "new Spirit of Fellowship" based on wartime circumstances in which men from all classes "have all fallen side by side," the bishop insisted that such losses would be "a waste of blood and treasure if the old moral dangers of London are left unaltered!" (42). Implicit in the bishop's remarks, as in other commentaries on wartime London, was a sense that women of all classes could (and should) take responsibility for safeguarding against the potential "waste of blood and treasure" by acting as moral guardians. Women were thus both the cause of and the cure for the moral decay plaguing the city and the nation.

The bishop criticized women who did not act to uphold moral standards in his response to a "girl-worker" who objected to his characterization of London and claimed she could walk "unmolested" through the city. Agreeing with her, he added, "[A]ny girl who will mind her own business, and go straight ahead and not loiter about, will be unmolested" (42–43). Thus women were not only responsible for overall moral conditions but were implicitly held accountable for being "molested," as molestation followed from "loitering" or not "going straight ahead." In the final analysis, *Cleansing London* asserted that women had a greater responsibility than men for both their own moral behavior and that of the city—the heart of the empire.

While the Church of England's "National Mission" received a great deal of attention, it was not universally praised. Charlotte Despard, leader of the Women's Freedom League, applauded the idea of a national mission but criticized the bishop's campaign as based wrongly on exclusivity—given that it denied a voice not only to Nonconformists but to all women. According to Despard, the "spiritual, moral, intellectual, economic, [and] political" needs of the nation demanded a mission led "from the hearths and homes of the people," not from bishops' palaces, churches, or cathedrals. Furthermore, Despard asserted that women had a unique role to play in the "new dawn" that awaited England, not because of their innate moral character, but because the woman's movement had been battling for generations "the spirit of domination, through which our beautiful world is being made a charnel-house."[43] Despard kept her focus beyond the streets of London and their moral woes.

The following winter, *The Vote* reported the recurrence of attacks on "the Harpies of London." It complained that a headline protesting

London's "Harpies" had appeared in the *Daily News,* which described London women as being as "voracious as these monstrosities of classic lore." This 1917 discussion of London women was very similar to the intense debate about the Cardiff women in the early months of the war. From a feminist perspective, such attacks were regarded as of a piece, stemming from the old idea that "man's sin is always to be traced to woman's power of temptation." The women maligned as "harpies" were "man-made, for they are the living impersonation of man's vices and woman's compliance."[44] The answer to complaints about female behavior, according to the Women's Freedom League, was a single moral standard for both men and women. By this stage in the war, some writers even suggested the conscription of women, and the "useful" girl was contrasted with the "frivolous" girl, as these two terms came to be identified with patriotic or detrimental behavior.[45] The epitome of the "girl not doing her bit" became personified for some in the flapper, representative of, in one attack, a "very numerous class of women — especially young women, who are absolutely hindering victory through . . . thoughtlessness," for whom "war means nothing but men in uniform with whom they can flirt."[46]

Women's and girl's scandalous public behavior prompted studies that offered solutions to this problem, and several conferences on these questions took place in London during the first half of 1917.[47] The bishop of London presided over one in June, where he again called particular attention to the continued presence of "hundreds of women . . . soliciting for prostitution in the streets," which proved how much was still to be done "to clean up this heart of the Empire." Speakers such as Sir Edward Henry, the chief commissioner of police, addressed specific problems facing London and detailed the misuse of parks as locations where, throughout the night, "couples may be seen behaving in a most scandalous manner." While highlighting his efforts on behalf of soldiers, Henry lamented the lack of alternatives for young girls. Lieutenant-General Sir Francis Lloyd, the officer in charge of London forces, then spoke on behalf of soldiers, urging the audience's tolerance because "it is difficult when you have been working in dirty wet trenches with bullets flying about . . . to come to London with all its pleasures and temptations, and if you are a virile soldier, not to 'have a go' of some sort." Mrs. Louise Creighton, the final speaker, concluded that public action had to support a morally pure London. Not only did Londoners have to fight prostitution, drunkenness, and debauchery, they had to struggle to prevent ordinary boys and girls from becoming practitioners of these vices.[48] The concern here was with the corruption of soldiers and young girls too "weak" to know any better.

Other discussions of "public morality" during the war concentrated on the apparently aggressive behavior of women, laying the blame for immorality squarely on their shoulders. In a study published in the *Nineteenth Century and After*, M. H. Mason offered a range of anecdotal evidence to suggest that soldiers, "far from welcoming the advances of disreputable women and girls, are greatly annoyed by them."[49] What most disturbed them, and Mason, were girls who were sexually aggressive, who kissed convalescent soldiers too helpless or too polite to resist, or who approached men on leave in railway and tram stations (187). Mason even provided one example of "a healthy and innocent boy of seventeen" who, after being accosted by girls, disappeared and ended up "in a Military Hospital, beyond cure and ruined for life" (187). The active agents of vice throughout Mason's discussion were women, and thus Mason's solutions to public morality dealt directly with their potentially dangerous behavior.

However, while denouncing both women and the leniency of current sentencing against prostitutes and other sexually predatory females, Mason also offered excuses for women's behavior. Using rhetoric about prostitutes as fallen women, Mason emphasized that "these unhappy women" had doubtless begun as innocent girls who had become "damaged goods" and would gladly return to respectability, defending flappers as "not vicious, nor intentionally immoral" but overly fond of pleasure, amusement, and "the prestige in each other's eyes of being accompanied by a soldier" (190). The danger of current laxity in laws regarding prostitution, according to Mason, came from the example set by the "hardened" older woman for young and "merely silly" girls. Mason recalled with a kind of horror witnessing a group of girls observe one of these older women kiss a soldier and hearing one proclaim, "Oh! I wish I could get them [the men] to kiss me like that!" (190). Mason attributed their "envy" to the fact that they were too "silly" not to notice the woman was a prostitute and only admired her success in achieving that "fine thing," a soldier's kiss. Given that these "harpies" threatened not only soldiers but impressionable young women, Mason proposed that women who were apprehended soliciting and endangering public morality be not so much punished as truly reformed via "committal to institutions of a really remedial and restorative character" (194). Insisting that innocent women be protected from being summarily arrested, Mason focused on the already "fallen" woman, not the "innocent" flirt kissing soldiers in the street.

Medical professionals also sought to inform their counterparts in other professions of the real dangers caused by wartime transformations in women's behavior. Dr. James Burnet's "Women War-Workers and the Sexual Element" shifted the focus from the girl in the street to the "woman war-worker in male attire" and the "amateur war-nurse, . . . [arguing that] the careful study of these women war-workers will reveal much that the average student of sex problems has scarcely dreamt of." While acknowledging that this criticism did not apply to all women war workers, Burnet insisted that there was obviously a "sexual element" to their work and that, furthermore, "this free intercourse of our sexes has not had altogether a beneficial effect on the morality of the country." Tying together the presence of women in short skirts and women drinking and smoking with lowered moral standards, he lamented that such matters were left to "laymen, . . . clerics and grandmotherly or hysterical women," not in the more capable hands of the medical profession.[50] The response to this article was swift. Novelist May Sinclair wrote that she read the article with "considerable amusement" and took Burnet to task on many points, but particularly pointing out that he had offered no evidence for his conclusions and that in her experience, most women war workers were far too exhausted and well-disciplined to misbehave.[51]

Women workers continued to be scrutinized. However, the behavior of the flirtatious "girl in the street," particularly the streets of London, attracted increased citywide and national interest in 1918 with the arrival of American troops. The *Daily Express* first ran a series of articles in September of 1918 on the scandalous behavior of women in the London streets, urging that the soldiers be saved from the women and the women saved from themselves.[52] The *Express* aimed its call for action at General Sir Nevil Macready, London's new commissioner, urging him to ban "strumpets" from all places of "soldiers' recreation" and instead to send them "to the land, to that good mother earth that is pure and sweet, and there they should be made to save themselves by honest labour."[53] Here again, the distinction between the socially useful "Land Girl" and frivolous "strumpet" illustrated the gap between two kinds of womanhood.

Following this cry to arms, an article by Edward Bok, editor of the American *Ladies' Home Journal,* intensified the debate.[54] In an interview after a two week visit to London, Bok said that nothing "surprised and depressed" him "so much as the apparently uncontrolled solicitation of our boys by women on the London streets." Comparing his time in London with his experience "in a great many large cities," Bok claimed to have never witnessed more "disgraceful" scenes than those he found in London streets, where American "boys [we]re openly solicited, not only by prostitutes, but by scores of amateur girls." All successful efforts to halt the spread of vice and disease in America would be of no use, he lamented, if America's "clean-blooded and strong-limbed" soldiers came "over here only to be poisoned and wrecked in the London streets. We should not be asked to send our boys here to be morally crucified."[55] Bok further commented that while the work of volunteer organizations and women patrols had done some good, the situation was one that called for government responsibility and authoritative action. If an individual soldier, for instance, sought out a brothel, he would be responsible, but "where the temptation is allowed to beset him on every hand in street, hotel and restaurant," then the responsibility was that of the "[g]overnment which allows such a traffic to go on apparently with its sanction." Bok was particularly shocked by the apparent "public acquiescence with this traffic based on the argument that the men who are making the great sacrifice must be permitted certain indulgences while away from home." He found it impossible to believe that moral standards could be so widely divergent between Britain and the United States. Bok, perhaps most threateningly, implied that the failure to eliminate this threat to American soldiers might lead to the withdrawal of U.S. troops for their own safety.

Following a denunciation that so thoroughly questioned the morality of the British, the *Evening News* sought confirmations or rebuttals from various agencies. Perhaps unsurprisingly, some agreed with Bok's remarks and some defended both American soldiers and London: "The official view appears to be that even if solicitation is practised, the solicited need not respond. . . . [T]he temptation of the streets does not come from the woman, as much as it comes from the men." Others clarified the government's legal position that, while prostitution as such was not permitted, a woman could come and go as she pleased in public, provided she was not "disorderly," thus the morality of her behavior would not necessarily lead to her being stopped. Moreover, those defending London noted not only that disease and vice could be found in comparable measures in New York but that "the necessities of war have placed the sexes on a different relationship, and that this freedom which has broken down so much of woman's reserve, appears to . . . be a greater evil than it really is." The problem was thus redefined as one of perception; the behavior of London's women was not immoral. Bok had failed to recognize that the war had created "different" and "freer"—but no less moral—relationships between the sexes.

The *Evening News* appeared to disagree with this line of argument in defense of London's women. Instead, it congratulated itself for having drawn attention two years earlier "to the disgraceful state of London streets, particularly at night, when not only the professional street walkers but a large army of ill-disciplined and shameless young girls lie in wait for the passing soldier." While declaring that there was no need to panic, the *Evening News* urged that action be taken because war required all of the nation's strength and "we should make up our minds not to allow ourselves to become weakened by the idle and the vicious." [56] Once again, morality at home was seen as the key to British victory.

The National Vigilance Association offered its own rebuttal to Bok's comments and to the allegedly deplorable condition of London's streets. It cited with approval the response of Edward Price Bell, the editor of the *Chicago Daily News,* who argued that Bok was wrong in "portraying London and other British cities as *extraordinarily* dangerous to young men in their streets—far more dangerous, in especial, than are the leading cities of the United States." Bell was particularly scornful of the idea that American soldiers were "good enough men to fight the Hun, . . . [but] not good enough men to venture into British streets unescorted." [57] American soldiers themselves echoed such views, and a letter in the *Evening Standard* from an American serving with the Grenadier Guards objected to Bok's portrayal of American soldiers as "Babes in the Wood, with no sense of right or wrong and without will power to overcome various evils." The letter went on to defend London's women as "worth the fight, right or wrong," praising "their cheerfulness, staunchness and self-sacrifice in the hour of need" and protesting that "this rot on London's morals reflects upon their character generally, and we resent it." [58] In addition to defending the honor of London's women against slander, this soldier also asserted men's control over their own morality and their lack of fear of the dangers lurking in London streets. *The Vigilance Record* concurred, lamenting Bok's "wild and unfounded statements." [59] Despite the fact that many British commentators themselves were quite critical of the behavior of women in wartime London, the hyperbolic attack by an American caused an emotive defense.

Certainly, as *The Vigilance Record* and others pointed out, the scandal of London's streets made for "good copy." Scandal indeed sold papers, but the debates about the public behavior of women in the capital were not just about creating news. The reasons for the perceived dangers of London's "amateur girls," particularly for overseas troops, can be explained, in part, by the defensive observation that war had altered the relationship between the sexes and caused freer, and consequently misinterpreted, associations between men and women.[60] These changes in social and public behavior did not go unnoticed, nor as we have seen, unchallenged. Nor was the sexual double standard loosened in these debates; it was, however, shifted. Women were still regarded as the guardians of moral virtue, held to higher standards of behavior, and granted influence over even the most "virile" soldier. If relationships between the sexes had become freer, women, even young girls—and here the language seems particularly significant—could be accused of "molesting," "accosting," and "preying" on soldiers in training or home on leave. Whether such accusations were valid or not, the anxieties disseminated in public about women displayed the extent to which alleged changes in appropriate feminine behavior could send shock waves through the entire society.

It is not possible to evaluate the extent to which the moral standards of women as a whole, particularly the generation that came of age during the war, "declined" or even if their sexual activity increased. The wartime evidence is simultaneously riddled with anxieties, filled with laments, and permeated with defenses and praise. Some wartime commentators celebrated the new comradeship between men and women, while others bemoaned women's lack of morals.[61] Reflecting on such alleged changes in women's behavior caused by the war, Justice Darling of the Old Bailey claimed that "the harm the war had done to the morals of the people . . . was far beyond any material damage that had been done. In nothing had it done more harm than in the relaxation on the part of the women of this country."[62]

Writing in *The Sunday Times,* Lady Burbidge took vehement exception to these statements, although she professed to understand what caused the justice's opinion. Criticizing Darling, Lady Burbidge defended women against "[t]he allegation that the war has brought about a lapse in woman's morals generally," claiming that such laments had been "heard almost from the first day when woman was called upon to play her part in the conflict." She offered her own testimonial to the fact that women were entering new spheres and engaging in new occupations for patriotic purposes, that "girls without any experience of the world were brought into contact with men of all social and moral grades in circumstances strong with emotional appeal," yet they, overwhelmingly, did not yield to temptation. Why then did it appear to some, like Justice Darling, that women's behavior had irrevocably changed? Burbidge claimed that the war "weakened for the time being the barriers restraining criminal activities and immoral tendencies. The less daring of the criminal and immoral types took advantage of this fact," and this encouraged crime and immorality.[63]

She might also have noted that the war intensified the attention paid to a range of social ills and that from the start women were seen as a problem for the state because their support was both necessary and yet never acknowledged as essential in the way that the male labor of soldiering was. That women's morale and morality became such objects of public scrutiny in both France and Britain can, perhaps, be seen as a sign of women's increased importance in this new modern war.

Danger to the Army: Wartime Campaigns against VD

Always implicit and oftentimes explicit in wartime discussions of women's sexual behavior was the fear not only of moral corruption but also of the spread of venereal disease, especially to military men. In Britain, the passage of DORA in 1914 and the public issuance of the report of the Royal Commission on Venereal Diseases in 1916 indicated the government's concern from the outset. In France, the government and members of the public also expressed anxiety about the effects of prostitution and venereal diseases on the strength of the army. In a telling contrast, however, the British government opted to regulate the spread of venereal disease by reintroducing some provisions of the Contagious Diseases Acts in addition to promoting other measures such as the Criminal Law Amendment Bill, while the French government, which already regulated prostitution, did nothing to prosecute ordinary women—presumably lulled into moral lapses by the war— suspected of infecting soldiers.

France already had an established system of *filles soumises* and *insoumises* and responded to the problems of prostitution and venereal diseases and their spread to the army by advocating increased regulation. Historian Alain Corbin argues that it was understandable that the suppression of unregulated prostitution should have increased, particularly because the early years of the war saw a marked "revival of venereal disease." [64] In a contemporary history of Parisian prostitution during the war, Dr. Léon Bizard recorded that while prostitutes initially fled the city, fearing a repeat of the siege of Paris during the Franco-Prussian War of 1870, by mid-Autumn of 1914 they had returned, and Paris regained "if not gaiety, nonetheless movement and life."[65] Although prostitution shifted its geographical location within Paris during the war, the total number of brothels rose after 1916.[66] Bizard himself noted a growth in prostitution and disease during the early years of the war, but conditions deteriorated as the war went on and regulation increased. Offering counter-evidence to those who linked sexual misbehavior to the public spaces that were thought to encourage such immorality, Bizard claimed that the fact that restaurants and cafés closed at nine and that it was forbidden to serve alcohol to those in the military or to women merely encouraged sexual misconduct. Since soldiers and women were barred from public spaces, Bizard claimed that their reasoning was: "What else was there to distract oneself with"—besides sex? Thus, Bizard argued that it was partly due to these regulatory changes that the last two years of the war created conditions that further encouraged "debauchery and prostitution."[67]

The number of houses of prostitution did increase during the war, but the French government made serious efforts to prevent the spread of disease by asking the Academy of Medicine to issue a set of guidelines meant to advise military personnel about what they could do to avoid venereal disease. In a series of discussions in November 1915, members of the Academy fine-tuned the language used in these guidelines, changing, for example, the wording of a sentence promoting sexual continence from "the most sure method" to "evidently the most sure method." While few of the eleven paragraphs provoked more than unanimous assent, the sixth—which advised the use of a "rubber *préservatif*" and described how to wash after sexual intercourse—led to a long debate. There was some disagreement over what to call *préservatifs* and in the end the slang terms "condom" and "capote" were added in parentheses. More significantly, however, a debate over the frankness of the description and the role of the Academy in issuing such orders emerged. One of the more revealing changes between the first and final versions came in an alteration of the opening phrase, which originally stated, "Every time you have sexual intercourse with these women don't neglect to use a rubber *préservatif*." In the final version, it began, "Every time that you have the weakness to be tempted by these women . . ."[68] The shift from the prosaic language of describing the circumstances under which VD was usually contracted to a language of morals—of male "weakness" and women as "temptations"—suggested the extent to which the Academy of Medicine echoed broader concern with moral and social order as much as with the prevention of disease.

Despite these official guidelines for soldiers, individual Parisians expressed their frustration with the public spectacle of encounters between soldiers and prostitutes in written complaints to the Parisian Prefect of Police. In July 1916, a letter from "the wife of a mobilized soldier" complained that the prevalence of prostitutes in the city's streets mocked and insulted "wives and mothers who cried." [69] Comparing the frivolous and debauched prostitutes to virtuous French patriots, another angry letter declared that while national factories lacked workers, official authority had "to be firm and inflexible, because it could not let these new and sad mores be planted." [70] Others suggested in July 1917 that streets like the Rue St. Denis and the Boulevard Sebastopol be purged of "all women who accost men and children and above all our soldiers. It's repugnant!" [71]

Within the Prefecture of Police, reports on the state of the Parisian population collected during the last year of the war also noted the presence of prostitution. Attention was paid to particular districts of the city, where, despite efforts to repress its existence, prostitution flourished along the Grand Boulevards and particularly near the Gare du Nord and Gare de l'Est, where soldiers congregated. [72] In other districts, prostitution was observed to be diminishing. One police report offered the following explanation for this decline: "[I]t's necessary to admit evidently that it's because the men are absent. But it's also quite necessary to admit that prostitution can no longer recruit among women when work, at a high salary, is assured." [73] Yet, rather than addressing such economic motivations for prostitution, the government, throughout the war, continued to support the establishment of *maisons tolerées*.

This regulatory policy was linked to the prevention of disease, something affirmed by physicians and those who instructed soldiers on how to avoid becoming infected through sexual contact. In 1915, Dr. F. Balzer insisted that the surveillance of prostitutes combined with regular medical visits for women in contact with troops was essential to control disease. [74] A 1917 report by Dr. Butte warned of the more pronounced danger of *les insoumises*, whose ranks now included "refugees, married women, [and] female factory workers." [75] Later in the year a review by Dr. Paul Faivre of measures that could prevent venereal diseases also argued for increased surveillance and the maintenance of regulated prostitution. He disagreed with those who protested that regulated prostitution gave men a false sense of security and only encouraged vice.[76] He claimed instead that regulated prostitution protected the population from the more certain danger of the *femme isolée,* or unregulated woman. Faivre believed that although it was difficult to do so, it remained necessary to distinguish between "women who indulged in 'exchanging compliments' in a calm and discreet manner, and those whose attitude constituted a menace to public tranquillity." For example, while female war factory workers were not exactly prostitutes, they nonetheless "gave themselves" to specific men and needed to be watched closely. Faivre's proposed remedy was public education, and he praised the devoted work of M. Pourésy of the Fédération Française des Sociétés Antipornographiques, who preached the purity of morals to soldiers on behalf of the Ministry of War.[77] The influential work of Pourésy, an "ardent apostle of purity of morals," was even reported in the British *Vigilance Record.*[78]

In a study of soldiers' sexual behavior, Louis Fiaux pointed out that the spread of venereal disease due to "moral relaxation, inevitable in time of war" threatened "not only . . . the power of armed combatants but . . . the future of the race." Fiaux criticized *maisons tolerées* for soldiers as promising "uncertain and unreal" benefits and urged the provision of wholesome alternatives and education instead of regulated prostitution.[79] In lectures given to soldiers and later reprinted, Dr. Bizard took the opposite view, placing particular emphasis on the dangers of unregulated women.[80] He warned young soldiers of the "sufferings in a kiss," that disease could result from "a single imprudence, a single minute of forgetfulness" (13). Bizard suggested that one way to prevent such lapses was through maintaining a pious respect for "woman who represents, let us not forget, the . . . interests of the Family and of the *Patrie*" (16). While urging young soldiers to be chaste, Bizard also highlighted the relative dangers of various kinds of prostitutes, noting that the war had caused an increase in women "deprived of direction and good counsel," who turned to prostitution to support themselves (23). It was these unregulated women, he asserted, who often seemed young and healthy, who nonetheless composed the greatest threat to men, thus the safest recourse for those who succumbed to temptation remained the regulated prostitute.

Many feminists objected to regulated prostitution. Although they acknowledged the "great sexual temptations" that beset soldiers, the Conseil National des Femmes Françaises (CNFF) subcommittee concerned with morals complained that houses of prostitution that had tended to "disappear" before the war had returned "with new vigor." They were particularly concerned with the opening of brothels close to the front. Worrying that this would have "disastrous consequences" in terms of the "moral" as well as "physical" well being of soldiers, the CNFF encouraged efforts to teach young conscripts that "chastity was not injurious."[81] The CNFF also denounced the wartime growth in regulated prostitution, while "honest women" and soldiers' wives had great difficulty in trying to visit their spouses. Marguerite de Witt-Schlumberger even attributed the "augmentation in venereal diseases" as well as increased prostitution to the fact that wives could not easily reach their husbands on the war fronts.[82] Such was not the way to promote the war effort or the rise in legitimate births that France needed. And after the French government publicized in a circular of 13 March 1918 its support for creating new authorized brothels, *The Vigilance Record* reported in England that leaders of CNFF and the Union Française pour le Suffrage des Femmes protested strongly to the Minister of the Interior. Writing as "mothers, wives and sisters of soldiers," Julie Siegfried and Marguerite de Witt-Schlumberger denounced the establishment of licensed houses of prostitution as "a gross insult to woman and the family of which she is the guardian. . . . We maintain, with conviction based upon our experience of life, that the regulation of vice will not help to do away with disease."[83]

French *maisons tolerées* received perhaps even more attention across the channel, where the idea that British soldiers serving in France might use these official brothels caused substantial concern. The Association for Moral and Social Hygiene (AMSH) spearheaded the attack after debates took place in Parliament in February of 1918 about whether *maisons tolerées* would be placed off-limits to British troops. In a flyer entitled "The Under-Secretary for War Defends Tolerated Brothels," the organization highlighted quotations from the Parliamentary discussion that suggested that it might not be "such a bad thing to have a certain house where women are registered and kept clean."[84] A conference organized by the AMSH in March 1918 "expressed its shame and indignation at the attitude of the British Military Authorities in permitting tolerated houses for the troops in France." Speakers included Mr. Lees Smith, M.P. from Northampton, who considered the under-secretary's remarks "one of the most revolting pronouncements the House had ever heard." Smith pointed out that the troops were the same men who carried "in [their] soldier's pay book the letter from Lord Kitchener telling them that respect for women is one of the first duties of a soldier."[85]

This response to the mere suggestion that British troops make use of French official brothels indicated the extent to which French and British endeavors to halt the spread of venereal diseases differed. The French retained their prewar system of regulated prostitution, while the British experimented with a number of legal alterations, some of which, like the return of legislation remarkably similar to the Contagious Diseases Acts, ironically went beyond the scope of some of the French measures.

Concern with the spread of venereal disease in Britain before the war had prompted the creation of the Royal Commission on Venereal Diseases (RCVD) in 1913, and war only intensified its importance. The commission, however, concurred with those who opposed anything resembling the Contagious Diseases Acts of 1864; it offered conclusive evidence that the regulatory system imposed by the Acts had no advantage in the fight against these diseases.[86] In its systematic study of venereal disease in Britain, the RCVD estimated that the number of individuals infected with syphilis could not be less than 10 percent of the population in larger cities and that there were perhaps 3 million sufferers in the whole United Kingdom (103). The report also noted the links between the consumption of alcohol, sexual activity, and the spread of disease, commenting that increasing temperance would be an important part of the fight against the disease's spread (26). The report also asserted that as a result of the wartime situation, soldiers and sailors generally received better, earlier treatment than the general population, and it emphasized the need for education (36). Along with education, the suppression of misinformation was deemed essential to the eradication of disease, and Dr. Douglas White, the leading member of the committee, provided a footnote to the reprinted version of the report, pointing out that in May 1917, Parliament outlawed the treatment of venereal disease by anyone except qualified medical personnel. The attack on unauthorized treatment of venereal diseases was itself a result of the war.

Among the RCVD report's contributions to the larger debates about women and their behavior were its conclusions that no practical legislation could prevent the spread of disease among single or sexually promiscuous people (49).[87] Further, it concluded that while these diseases might result from "vicious habits," it was "equally true that large numbers of sufferers are absolutely innocent" (52). By promulgating the information that many victims were not infected through immoral means, the RCVD hoped that sufferers would no longer conceal their illnesses and that they would instead seek proper medical treatment and help to halt the spread of the diseases. Significantly, the RCVD based its call for action on the fact that, along with the "heavy losses of the best manhood of the nation," venereal diseases "must tell heavily on the birth-rate and on the numbers of efficient workers." Efforts to check the spread of VD, therefore, became "of paramount national importance" (58). Thus, the RCVD concluded that the very future of the nation was at issue.

Two organizations took the initiatives called for in the report by producing literature and offering speakers designed to educate the public. The first, the National Council of Public Morals (NCPM), was already in the midst of investigating the declining birthrate, a task it would continue to do throughout the war. The other, the National Council for Combating Venereal Diseases (NCCVD), sprang into action after the outbreak of war in response to "the need to anticipate, and if possible to check that exacerbation of venereal disease which always follows in the wake of a great war."[88] Under the auspices of the NCPM, the president of its Ladies' Council, Dr. Mary Scharlieb, published *The Hidden Scourge,* a work aimed primarily at women to provide them with knowledge about venereal disease.[89] In her opening remarks, Scharlieb explained that she wrote the book because of the national cry to "Save the Babies" in response to the high proportion of infant disability, sickness, and death caused by syphilis. She echoed the RCVD's condemnation of the C.D. Acts, claiming that any such measures had the pernicious effect of "intend[ing] to make wrong-doing safe"—to "enslave" women and to "dupe" men (17–19). For Scharlieb, it was crucial to care for every individual sufferer and not to condemn them for some "mistaken ideas of morality," because the entire community was at risk (35). Along with pleading for better care for victims of the disease, she advocated better education and housing. Most importantly, she emphasized the crucial role of mothers in preparing their children for their great "blessings" and "tasks" of motherhood and fatherhood, especially reminding boys that "any dereliction of duty will bring its own punishment" of physical and moral disaster (53, 80).

Scharlieb made the war's harmful influence on the spread of disease unmistakably clear. She suggested that there was no "doubt that the wave of patriotic feeling and general excitement that passed like a flame over the land during the first months of the war did result in a dangerous heightening of sexual passion" (75).[90] As a result, both men and women "were too often swept off their feet by unrestrained emotion," and, consequently, cases of both venereal disease and infant mortality were on the upswing (75–76). Scharlieb was adamant that the British Empire was at a crisis point, that venereal diseases posed "a national danger as great and more insidious than defeat on sea, on land and in commerce" (78). The first step toward a complete victory was to awaken the nation to this "internal" enemy by providing children with a moral upbringing and fighting against pernicious influences, such as popular fiction (85). With its emphasis on maternal responsibility and education as means of combating the spread of the disease, Scharlieb's text seemed to live up to its aim of addressing women, but Scharlieb did not believe in sheltering them by following rules about what was deemed appropriate for respectable women to know. In her closing arguments, she called for "an honest and a determined effort to know the truth and to bring it home to others" (96). By providing a book meant to be brought "home," replete with detailed information about the causes, spread, and remedies for venereal diseases as well as moral messages, Scharlieb made the topic one of as much domestic as military concern.

Other perspectives, while stressing the need for the "enlightened co-operation of women" in fighting diseases such as syphilis, also emphasized that while human nature could not be changed, it could be regulated. Urging the institution of controlled prostitution, one article declared it was no good to complain about immorality, for "in war there is only one way, and that is State control, to localise the evil, coupled with the immediate clearing-up of all young girls from the streets." It could certainly not be "more moral or dignified to allow 'flappers' to infest the streets and infect the soldiers rather than introduce the system which all Europe knows to be the only preventative measure."[91] Others urged the combination of education and anonymous enlightened treatment. George A. Wade spoke of the vital work that had been done in addressing British and colonial soldiers about venereal disease: "[T]he lectures have been short, terse and practical, and they have been well-received."[92]

After the release of the RCVD's report but before the enactment of legislation in 1917, a group of women launched a letter-writing campaign demanding official notification and compulsory treatment, policies in force for other infectious diseases. Signed by such well-known women as Emmeline Pankhurst, Margaret Macmillan, and Mrs. Lloyd George, the letter spoke on behalf of "soldiers' mothers" who "have given their sons willingly to die for the Empire, but not like this." Urging legislative action on behalf of the "race," the writers invited "the mothers and wives of the Empire to join with us in demanding that these diseases should be treated as other dangerously infectious ones are."[93] In response, Charlotte Despard of the Women's Freedom League and feminists representing the United Suffragists denounced such demands because of the "social ban" attached to sufferers and the fear that notification would cause people to avoid treatment, thus increasing the chance of the diseases' spread.[94] *The Englishwoman* questioned the fundamental mechanism of the proposal in its reporting on the letter "given wide publicity in the press." How, they asked, were the infected persons to be discovered?[95] Advocates of the more lenient guidelines set up by the RCVD continued to stress the importance of education, not notification.

Maude Royden, a leading suffragist, attempted to popularize the newly released information about venereal diseases among civilian audiences under the auspices of the NCCVD. Her *The Duty of Knowledge* (1917) took "social workers," and, by extension, women, as its specific audience. Proclaiming the RCVD report a great step forward, Royden readily endorsed its perspective that those suffering from such diseases be treated rather than punished. Royden, like Scharlieb, emphasized the importance of disseminating information about how many "innocent" victims of venereal infection existed, thus helping to separate efforts to fight disease from moral controversy.[96] Royden, too, denounced any attempts to regulate prostitution as providing men with a false sense of security and punishing women. She reminded her readers that "if men are infected by women, the women themselves must, in the first instance, have been infected by men." She argued that women, particularly because of the wartime crisis, had a role to play in helping the sufferers get aid and should educate themselves about where and how to acquire treatment. In addition to their other wartime roles, Royden also asserted, the volunteer force of women responsible for "rescue, preventative, or reformatory work, in schools for mothers, in crèches, as probation officers" all had a vital role to play in the battle against this indigenous foe.

In its advice to lecturers on its behalf, the NCCVD also emphasized women's special roles and responsibilities in wartime. The organization urged speakers to remind their audiences that "war has intensified existing evils and brought them prominently before us." Not only was "health and efficiency" vital to a community at war, but a "sound race" was needed for postwar rebuilding. Moreover, the NCCVD relied on mobilizing women's moral authority, the idea that "women make fashions and customs" and that women could help "make the country more worthy of sacrifices" by soldiers. The NCCVD also proposed lectures that equated moral conduct with a patriotism demonstrated by doing one's duty to future marriage and children. It offered responses to common questions, carefully separating the morality of behavior from the transfer of disease.[97]

This officially sponsored public dispersal of information was met with comparable discussions in British periodicals and newspapers. Most articles noted the influence of the RCVD's report and of the altered circumstances of the massive mobilization of men and other social upheavals caused by the war. Millicent Garrett Fawcett, leader of the NUWSS, wrote in 1917 that as a result of the war, among other things, "the very feeling of gratitude and admiration for what our soldiers are doing for us has led numbers of inexperienced girls into a frame of mind which makes them think that anything and everything which these men wish for must be given to them." While excusing the girl's behavior as the result of naïveté, Fawcett remarked that the disease could be seen as "one of the penalties which war exacts." Applauding the conclusions of the RCVD report and, in particular, its evidence that the C.D. Acts had not worked and should not be reinstated, Fawcett also raised the issue lurking at the back of many of the debates, that the real enemy to be rooted out was not the disease, but prostitution, and that the core of such a fight was the need for men to exercise self-control and to lead chaste lives.[98] Thus public outcry about venereal diseases and prostitution was turned, not atypically but perhaps with a greater hint of urgency, into a questioning of both men's and women's general, as well as sexual, morality.

After the initial uses of the broader terms of DORA and in the aftermath of the RCVD's report, in 1917 the British government introduced legislation into Parliament to deal with sexual immorality: a new Criminal Law Amendment Bill. A wide range of measures were covered in the bill, including raising the age of consent for women from sixteen to eighteen and introducing penalties of imprisonment with hard labor for knowingly spreading venereal disease.[99] It also criminalized the advertisement of abortifacients and alleged cures for disorders spread by sexual contact. The most controversial aspect of the bill proved to be its provisions, in the infamous Clause 3, that if a girl under eighteen was found guilty of loitering for the purposes of soliciting, of actively soliciting, or of behaving in "a riotous or indecent manner" then "by reason of her mode of life or associations" the court could "in lieu of awarding any punishment, order the girl to be detained until she attains the age of nineteen, or any less period." [100] Clearly this measure responded to the ongoing public outcry over the "scandal of the streets" and the allegedly loosened morals of young girls, and the National Vigilance Association endorsed this idea of reforming rather than merely punishing the girl. [101]

Feminist organizations, on the other hand, quickly denounced the bill as doing more harm than good. They objected to compulsory examinations for venereal disease and pointed out that, despite proponents' claims that both men and women would be subject to the same laws, women were still far more likely to be blamed and punished. Members of the Women's Freedom League insisted that making the transmittal of venereal disease a legal crime as well as a moral one would do nothing for wives infected by their husbands since "very few married women in their present state of economic dependence could afford, for themselves or their family, to dispense with the breadwinner, and many would hesitate to imprison the father of their children." And leaders of the Women's Freedom League, like Charlotte Despard, Florence Underwood, and Elizabeth Knight, attacked this aspect of the bill as being a backhanded way of re-establishing the contagious diseases acts and urged that it be opposed. [102] As a result of this and similar opposition, this provision in the bill was withdrawn. [103]

Although the Criminal Law Amendment Bill was meant to be an indirect means of fighting venereal disease by regulating prostitutes and other suspicious women, it failed to achieve its goals. As an alternative, under DORA, the British government revived certain key provisions of the Contagious Diseases Act of 1864. In the eyes of opponents to the C.D. Acts, the first of these attempts occurred with regulation 35C. This regulation made it possible for the police to "control" or "regulate" the "presence, movement or behavior" of anyone "likely to prejudice the training, discipline administration or the efficiency" of those people engaged in making or "handling munitions of war." Such suspected miscreants could be reported to the police or the military authorities, and anyone who had been "convicted . . . of any offence against public order and decency" could be prevented from residing in the area. [104] Although the wording of the regulation did not refer to either prostitutes or women, those opposed to the C.D. Acts believed not only that the law could easily be turned toward prostitutes but also that it implicitly addressed them.[105] What was at stake in such regulations was *discipline* not disease; indeed, it recast disease as a question of order.

Despite receiving criticism over the ambiguously worded Regulation 35C, in late March of 1918 the government issued a new Defence of the Realm Regulation designed to prevent the spread of disease among the armed forces. Regulation 40D stated that "no woman who is suffering from venereal disease in a communicable form shall have sexual intercourse with any member of His Majesty's forces," nor could she "solicit or invite" such intercourse. Women charged under this regulation could be taken into custody for at least a week and subjected to any medical examination that could ascertain if they were suffering from venereal disease. An accused woman would be "informed of her right to be remanded" and could choose to be examined either by "her own doctor or by the medical officer of the prison."[106] For critics, some of the worst aspects of the Contagious Diseases Act thus returned with 40D, including the fact that women were held accountable for the spread of disease and, even if merely suspected, could be subjected to an intimate medical examination with or without their consent.

Outraged by the sweeping tone of the regulation, organizations such as the AMSH demanded its immediate withdrawal.[107] On 27 June 1918 at a protest meeting in London, representatives from the leading feminist organizations gathered to voice their strenuous objections.[108] Women and "social purity" campaigners did not provide the only voices of protest. An editorial in *The Manchester Guardian* asserted that while the "evil" that was being combated was also "a source of serious military weakness," it did "not follow that the remedy proposed is wise or even tolerable."[109] Like other editorials, the *Guardian* denounced both the inequality of charging women not men, thereby assuming that women were the "solicitors," and the dangerous "French" precedents that were being followed. As an editorial in the *Herald* mused, this was but the slippery slope toward the "logical end" of the "*maison tolerée* with its certified occupants."[110] Although France did not subject any woman suspected of "inviting" soldiers' sexual intercourse to arbitrary arrest and physical examination, its very maintenance of legalized brothels made it the emblem of a system that regulated and thus tolerated the evil of prostitution.

Regulation 40D was not abolished until December of 1918, after the war's end. In the meantime, a number of women were "successfully" prosecuted under its aegis. Cases drew both publicity and public protest, but the Home Office, while responding to criticism, did not alter its policy during the war.[111] Although it has not been widely analyzed, the history of 40D is certainly not a new story, but there are several important things to be learned from its brief life. First, while the British continually compared themselves to the French when constructing policy around venereal disease, eventually the British regulations under DORA were even more widespread in terms of criminalizing nonvenal sex than the French system of regulated prostitution. Within both France and Britain, there were differing strategies, but in Britain a severe split existed between its military and public health directives regarding venereal disease.[112] DORA's regulations 35C and 40D directly contradicted the government's own report from the Royal Commission on Venereal Diseases.

Overall, the range of options regarding venereal disease was similar across Europe, but initially Britain had to establish (or re-establish) elements of a regulatory system that France already possessed. The degree to which laws regulating venereal disease and prostitution were enforced or even enforceable remains open to question. Yet, it is striking that in the debates surrounding the containment of venereal diseases in both Britain and France, the dangers—prostitutes and amateurs—were defined as the same but the techniques used against them varied. British policy, as encapsulated in Regulation 40D, excluded no category of women from potential government scrutiny. France's politicians and social commentators, on the other hand, while acknowledging that all sexually active women might pose a danger to the army, did not alter a policy that saw regulated prostitution as the means to control disease.

One further way to analyze the differing British and French strategies to prevent venereal diseases impeding the army is to look at the larger cultural context in which these actions were interpreted, at the kind of cultural manifestations shaping these debates. Significantly, Eugène Brieux's play *Les Avariés* helped promote public awareness and set the tone—decades apart—in both France and Britain for understanding these diseases. The play first addressed the pernicious effects of venereal disease among the bourgeoisie in France in 1901, and an English translation was published in 1911.[113] However, it was not until 1917 that government censors lifted the ban on *Damaged Goods* (as it was called in English) and that the play was first performed in London. By April of 1917, the play had not only been presented to London audiences but had also been reprinted, according to a notice by Mrs. Bernard Shaw in *The Times Literary Supplement,* because the performance of the play in London had created renewed demand.[114] In a piece entitled "Brieux Triumphant" in the *Review of Reviews,* the London premiere of *Damaged Goods* was lauded as the victorious conclusion of "some of the fiercest battles of the censorship." Responding to the controversy surrounding the play, the critic Norman Croom-Johnson vehemently denied that "its matter is unhealthy or obscene, or in any way unfit for public presentation. . . . M. Brieux's play deals with a terrible subject, the most appalling scourge of civilisation, but it deals with it simply, seriously, and with the most absolute sincerity."[115]

In its London performances, *Damaged Goods* was introduced by a warning. Before any of the play's dramatic action was presented on the London stage, the stage manager read the following statement: "I beg leave to inform you, on behalf of the author and the management, that the object of this play is a study of the disease of syphilis in its bearing on marriage. It contains no scene to provoke scandal or arouse disgust, unless we must believe that folly and ignorance are necessary conditions of female virtue."[116] Having thus warned the audience, the play commenced with a two-character first act in which George Dupont consults an eminent doctor about his physical condition. A casual sexual encounter has given him syphilis, and he is in search of an immediate cure since he is supposed to be married in a month. After being sternly warned by the doctor not to marry until he undertakes a cure of at least three to four years, George exits and reappears in the next act. At the start of Act II, George is married to the innocent Henriette, and they are already the parents of an ailing daughter. The same (unnamed) doctor is called in as a consultant by George's mother and, after diagnosing the little girl with congenital syphilis, forbids the Duponts from using their wet nurse lest she catch the disease from the baby. While George and his mother try to disregard the doctor's orders, the true nature of the baby's illness is discovered by the nurse and eventually by Henriette, who faints as the curtain falls. In the final act, Henriette's father, who goes to the doctor to find evidence against his son-in-law and secure a divorce for his daughter, receives a lengthy lecture on the need for reform of the social system with regard to venereal disease, which is illustrated by a variety of "cases" who are brought on stage to tell their respective stories. The play thus offered both a tragic personal story and scientific and sociological information about the dangers of not only syphilis itself but also the "folly" and "ignorance" demanded by "female virtue."

As the critic for the *Review of Reviews* noted, at the end of the second act "the play, considered merely as a play, may be said to end. We see no more of the guilty husband and of the miserable victims of his miscon-duct. . . . [T]he remainder of the drama is taken up with the application of the moral." [117] And the moral emphasized that the secrecy and shame surrounding such diseases must be ended. At a crucial moment, the doctor, the playwright's spokesman and the play's moral voice, asks the outraged father:

> [H]ow many of these rigid moralists, who are so choked with their middle-class prudery that they dare not mention the name syphilis, or when they bring themselves to speak of it do so with expressions of every sort of disgust, and treat its victims as common criminals, have never run the risk of contracting it themselves? . . . How many do you think there are? Four out of a thousand? . . . [B]etween all the rest and those who catch the disease there is no difference but chance.

Instead of allowing people, the young in particular, to wallow in a complete lack of knowledge about sex, Brieux maintains that "they ought to be made to understand that the future of the race is in their hands." [118] The enemies of a healthy population and a strong state are a too rigid morality and the supreme ailment of ignorance.

Croom-Johnson attested to the riveting effect and "at times extraor-dinary dramatic force" of this message on the wartime London stage, claiming that "*Damaged Goods* is received with a still, tense attention that I have rarely seen in a theatre. Its production in aid of the cam-paign against venereal disease is a most significant event in the history of our stage." [119] An article in *The Vote,* the paper of the Women's Free-dom League, also reported the popularity of *Damaged Goods,* noting, "[P]eople are turned away from every performance . . . [and t]here are usually large numbers of men in khaki in the audience." *The Vote* also urged all "Freedom Leaguers" to see the play and asked whether free tickets could be made available to soldiers or whether the play could be performed free of charge on Sundays for the duration of the war, because its lessons must be learned: "[I]f our race is to continue an Im-perial race, the production of damaged goods must cease." [120]

The impact of Brieux's work also displayed the manner in which attitudes about venereal diseases appeared to be converging in Britain and France, despite the policy differences that remained. The reception of *Damaged Goods* and the fact that it was permitted to be performed for the first time in wartime Britain also attests to the extent to which venereal disease had become an object of not only state but cultural interest as well. Unlike the regulatory apparatus set up under DORA, the focus was not on attacking women willfully infecting men at arms and damaging the war effort but on the publicizing of a decades-old argument against ignorance and the double standard as a threat to racial, national, and pointedly "imperial" health.

Conclusion

Debates about venereal disease reflected concerns with the war's disturbance of the social order in both action and in perceptions of behavior. Female sexual misconduct thus became an issue of discipline and morale, not just of disease, and the response of the British government in its setting up of a regulatory apparatus under DORA suggests that the issue went beyond public health. France continued to provide *maisons tolerées,* but it did not address the issue of diseases spread by women who were not prostitutes. Moreover both policies generated criticism in their respective countries.

During the war, concern with social order and the moral battles that *had* to be won if the war was to be a true victory became intensely caught up with the behavior of women. The appearance of women smoking, drinking, or acting "wilder" than the men, and especially perceived changes in women's sexual expression, suggested to many, throughout the war, that drastic changes in the relationships between men and women were under way. Others insisted instead that the "freer" behavior being discussed reflected a new comradeship between them. However, if the war brought a greater openness in discussions of venereal disease or illegitimacy and in the kinds of public space available to unsupervised women of all classes alone, it also brought a good deal of trepidation and anxiety to those who observed these developments. Both the French and British governments claimed that they needed to control women's sexuality to aid the war effort, even though they had differing strategies and ideas about what this control might entail.

The problems posed by an allegedly rampant female sexuality were threefold. The first concern was that "amateur girls" and increased casual sexual encounters were causing a moral decline in each nations' metropoles and that the countries could be felled by the seeds of moral decay eating away at them from the inside. Second, articles in both the French and British press expressed a shared anxiety about professional female sexuality and particularly with the interactions between prostitutes and soldiers. Their concern was as much with these encounters threatening discipline and order as with their spreading disease, but most at issue was women's, not men's, presumed sexual misbehavior. Finally, however, venereal diseases and their debilitating effect on the fitness of the fighting forces remained old problems, which were met with the traditional, nationally specific responses of regulated prostitution and the eventual return of the forced medical exam of the original Contagious Diseases Acts. While government policy in France and Britain differed, public attitudes in the two countries toward venereal disease and its sufferers may have been converging, as illustrated by the British acceptance—a generation after it was first performed in France—of the French playwright Brieux's *Damaged Goods*.

Throughout this analysis of debates on wartime sexuality, it is evident that what happened behind the front lines was, once again, viewed as integral to the nation's defense. Women's bodies needed to be controlled lest they spread disease or disorder, and transgressions of expected feminine morality challenged states mobilized for total war, indeed, so it seemed to many, challenged the very possibility of victory. Chapters 5 and 6 will explore the challenges provided by women's more overtly political actions, which involved either resisting or insisting upon their further identification with the national cause.

Feminism on Trial

WOMEN'S DISSENT AND
THE POLITICS OF PEACE

Feminism, Pacifism, and Dissent

Both the French and British governments and many women in these nations were deeply concerned with the behavior and moral influence of women, defining them—especially through their motherhood—as central to the war effort. However, throughout the war, a few women used some of the same rhetoric in order to express their opposition to the conflict. These attempts highlighted the variety of women's responses to the war, and they sparked some of these states' most powerful attempts to shape a national identity rooted in feminine patriotism. Feminist pacifism and women's dissent, small in scale though it was, represented an arena where normative ideas about gender—associations of femininity with peacefulness especially rooted in maternity—came into direct conflict with normative ideas about women's wartime status vis à vis the nation.

States increasingly challenged female behavior that linked peacefulness with femininity as the war intensified. By the middle of the war and particularly during 1917, feminist and female opposition to war, especially in France, was rescripted as dissent and even treason. Of course, all resistance to the war, whether by a combatant man or a woman far removed from the trenches, could have been considered treasonous.

However, because of the association between civilians and women, and the importance of civilians to the war effort, women's dissent took on a heightened meaning. In order to interpret this development more fully, after discussing the theoretical antecedents and wartime activities of feminist pacifists in both Britain and France, this chapter will focus on an exemplary case study: the 1917–18 investigation of Hélène Brion, a French socialist, pacifist, and, most importantly, feminist school-teacher, who was tried for treason. Brion's significance lay in the positions that she occupied in wartime France not only as a woman and a teacher but also in the political manifestations of these roles, as a feminist and syndicalist. Brion's trial and the responses to it reveal as much about the expectations of wartime gender arrangements and the state's response to threats to the wartime social and political order as they do about the nature of wartime treason.

Feminist Pacifism in Theory and Practice Prior to 1917

Theoretically, feminist pacifism relied on historical feminist assumptions emphasizing the connection between male or masculine power and the existence of war. Its claims rested on some basic ideas: first, that feminism stood as a "moral force" in contrast to a world ruled by "physical force." It also insisted that women, because of their maternal function, had a unique role in human society and needed to be empowered. Furthermore, it asserted that women, because they existed as a universal subordinate "class," remained outside nationalism and had more in common with each other than with men of their nationality or class.[1] For the most part, this feminist pacifism used "difference-based" arguments whose logic lay in demanding rights for women because of their special, gender-specific characters or social roles.[2] Although rooted in the idea of women's difference, these ideas were not necessarily essentialist. For some, the biological fact that women bore children did not mean that they were naturally pacifists; Hélène Brion, for example, emphasized women-as-mothers' roles as the "first teachers" of language and, by extension, of national identity. The lines between society and biology, which both constructed the "maternal instinct," were thus blurred. Such feminism often sought to emancipate women on account of their maternal qualities in order to effect social and political change.[3]

However, many feminist pacifists called specific attention to women as the mothers of men, dividing the world into those who served the state by fighting and those who served it by producing, in Olive

Schreiner's words, the "primal munition of war."[4] In her influential *Woman and Labour* (1911), Schreiner linked the shared female bodily experience of pain caused by motherhood to the "moral force" of women in opposition to war. She depicted the price in blood and bodies that women pay to produce the lives that men squander on battlefields, using this analogy to fortify her insistence that women must be empowered.[5] According to Schreiner, women's part in war has always been reproduction: "Our relation to war is far more intimate, personal and indissoluble. . . . There is no battlefield on earth . . . which it has not cost the women of the race more in actual bloodshed and anguish to supply, than it has cost the men who lie there. We pay the first cost on all human life."[6] Schreiner linked the possibility of a mother's death during childbirth with the possibility of a soldier's death in battle. Moreover, she equated their production of men with a kind of ownership by women of men's bodies. Maternity allowed women to know the value of life in a way no man could, and this knowledge of the "history of human flesh" was women's alone.[7] Using the emblem of the mourning mother, Schreiner claimed not that women possess an inherent moral superiority but that as mothers, women *know*—through the direct experience of pain—the worth of human life. Such arguments received new force with the outbreak of World War I.

After the outbreak of war, British suffragist Helena Swanwick published a series of pamphlets that took up Schreiner's ideas and presented a feminist perspective on the war.[8] In the first of these, entitled *Women and War*, Swanwick reiterated Schreiner's maternalist pacifist metaphor of women's reproductive labor. In doing so, Swanwick neatly partitioned the world: "[M]en make wars, not women." Women, moreover, suffered disproportionately from war because of their unique relationship to what they produce: "Every man killed or mangled in war has been carried for months in his mother's body and has been tended and nourished for years of his life by women. He is the work of women: they have rights in him and in what he has done with the life they have given and sustained."[9]

In her 1916 treatise *War and Its Effect on Women*, Swanwick concerned herself with another aspect of maternity, arguing that war cost women the right to be mothers. According to Swanwick, war victimized women not only by killing their sons and thus destroying their "very life-blood" but also by destroying their potential offspring, that is, the children who would never be born to a lost generation of fathers.[10] For this reason, Swanwick ran into further essentialist constraints: "If motherhood is woman's supreme function, it is important that it should be denied to as few as possible, and to women should belong its supreme direction. The racial instinct of women is of tremendous importance to the welfare of the race, and it is encouraging to note how scientific knowledge is coming to reinforce much of what is instinctive in the mother" (23). Even as Swanwick acknowledged the "outrage of unwilling motherhood" and the need for modern woman "to be a complete person," she criticized the government for its refusal to legitimate the needs of the mother: "[I]n a State where mothers were rightly honoured, women would have a voice in laws and institutions" (23–26). Motherhood thus remained the source of women's claims to authority in Swanwick's reasoning.

Other explicitly gendered appeals divided the world according to the gender-specific roles of mother and son, granting special weight to the mothering of men. In her 1915 *An Address to the Mothers of Men,* Frances Hallowes put forth one of the most explicit wartime manifestations of this sort of antiwar claim. Hallowes, however, made the implicit gendered separation of mother and child explicit, proclaiming all mothers to be the "mothers of men." In Hallowes's rhetoric, the divisions between men and women were fundamental and extreme: "Men as such seem to have little estimate of the value of human life. Militarism— a masculine invention, holds a man's body as so much hostile stuff to put into use. . . . Women realise deeply the worth and preciousness of life. . . . Thus the full tragedy of war can be only grasped by those who can imagine the silent agony of mothers[,] of the millions of mothers weeping in secret for their sons who were, and are not."[11] Hallowes's antiwar motherhood thus emphasized not women's production but the more passive "agony" imposed on women because of maternity. According to Hallowes, the exclusion of women from politics became the cause of war. On behalf of disempowered mothers, she demanded political rights and redefined patriotism for mothers who were deemed victims of what inevitably resulted when nations and governments excluded the wisdom of mothers. However, she used the biologically determined position of mothers to claim women's superior knowledge and political entitlements.

Other British feminists who opposed the war attempted to unify women's claims through mothers' claims. In 1915, Sylvia Pankhurst responded to the fragmentation in the suffrage movement over the war by addressing her followers and all feminists as mothers:

[T]he Women's Movement is the mother movement, the bringing to the service of the public life of the whole world that which
the best of mothers display towards their own children in wisest and
tenderest moments.

This must surely be the contribution of the Women's Movement
to human progress. . . .

Do not imagine that we can be mother-builders for the children
of the future, if we believe in War and sweating now, or are afraid to
speak against these evils.[12]

Echoing a familiar theme about needing to enfranchise mothers, Pankhurst here both extolled the virtues of mothers and continued to define
mothers as producers whose labor conflicted with war. Moreover, the
intrinsic position of feminists became that of mothers whose place
must be to denounce war and its exploitation of women.

Other writers argued that such gender-based divisions and assumptions contributed to the oppression of women. One tract, *Militarism
versus Feminism,* presented an analysis of militarism's effect on women:
"In every country this dread of being left behind in the ceaseless and
unconsidered production of babies, with its persistent degradation of
so many women to the position of beasts of burden, leads militarist
governments to oppose every effort to reduce the birth-rate. . . . Even
in 20th century Europe this first requirement of woman's freedom, the
claim to be something more than a domestic animal is vigorously denied by every state that is organised for war."[13] Rather than celebrating
motherhood as an ideal or making claims that it induced greater pacifism among women, the authors observed that the imposition of childbearing encroached upon women's rights. Thus, according to this logic,
while some women might oppose war because they were mothers, they
did so not because of war's destruction of their sons, but rather because
of its destructiveness for women. Women should oppose war because
it harmed them directly rather than relationally.[14]

Feminist pacifism was less prevalent among mainstream feminist
organizations in France than in Britain. Instead, it developed more
slowly and was more clearly articulated by women associated with the
far left such as Louise Saumoneau of the Groupe des Femmes Socialistes, which wrote a letter of protest addressed to all women on the
eve of the war urging them to form "a living barrier against murder-
ous and menacing barbarity."[15] Further, some of the few published

examples of French women's opposition to war also made use of maternal imagery. Marcelle Capy's *Une voix de femme dans la mêlée,* with its deliberate play on the title of the best-known French antiwar tract, Romain Rolland's *Au-dessus de la mêlée,* brought a gendered perspective to more general concern about the war.[16] In the second part of her work, entitled "Ceux qui pleurent" ("Those Who Cry"), Capy spoke of the "natural solidarity that unites all women of the earth," that their "hearts are in perpetual revolt against all that destroys their work, all that creates death."[17] Suggesting, like Swanwick, that men are women's creation, Capy emphasized that what united all women was their shared anguish over the fates of their men: "[W]ives, lovers, they [women] have all the souls of mamas."[18] Capy directly addressed the material loss as well as the emotional anguish that war caused mothers, pitying the "poor women from whom the war has taken their husbands and sons, and devoured their last pennies."[19] Finally in her section on proletarian women, Capy demonstrated a congruence between the sorrows experienced by women and their exploitation as workers.

The war also provided important opportunities for the politicization of such beliefs. In 1915, the March gathering of socialist women in Berne and the April International Women's Peace Congress at The Hague laid the foundations for an international movement based on prewar and wartime connections between feminism and antimilitarism. Even before the Berne meeting, a group of socialist feminists, among them Hélène Brion, signed a public declaration, published in *La Française* in February 1915, asserting that to cease to fight now would "betray the cause of right and of justice" while it affirmed the need for women to help disarm Europe.[20] In Britain, the question of whether to support the war or to participate in public antiwar conferences like that at The Hague divided both the militant and nonmilitant women's suffrage movements.[21] Several historians have already discussed British women's participation in the Hague Conference and the organization it inspired, the Women's International League, which became the Women's International League for Peace and Freedom. But more general public reaction to this conference and women's antiwar activities demonstrates that such activities were viewed as threatening not only to the government's operation of the war but to society more generally.[22] Moreover, the idea that women had a particular stake in discussions of peace was not an idea that all women or all feminists found plausible, despite the potent claims made on behalf of women's injuries caused by war.

No French women attended the Hague Conference, and France was the only nation whose feminist movement unilaterally boycotted this event. Feminist leaders like Marguerite de Witt-Schlumberger insisted that this was a simple decision since French soil had been invaded and was still occupied, and the Conseil National des Femmes Françaises (CNFF) in collaboration with the Union Française pour le Suffrage des Femmes (UFSF) published a message to the women of neutral and allied countries insisting that it was not appropriate to talk of peace under the present circumstances.[23] The strong sense of national unity held as, at least initially, the overwhelming majority of French feminists did not challenge the need for unified support for the war. Thus, the link between feminism and resistance to the war evolved more tentatively. While there is little evidence of French women resisting the initial call to patriotism, antiwar responses were carefully monitored and criticized. Following the outbreak of war, some French feminists, such as Jeanne Halbwachs, Gabrielle Duchêne, Marcelle Capy, and, most vividly, Louise Saumoneau — in addition to Brion later on — voiced a pacifism that the vast majority of their compatriots found disloyal and inappropriate.[24] Saumoneau viewed the war as a violation of class solidarity and a betrayal of the internationalist principles of socialism affirmed by the Second International of 1889, and she joined with other socialist women in the March 1915 conference at Berne in calling for peace.[25]

Upon her return from Berne and throughout 1915, Saumoneau spoke of the united efforts of socialist women to say, "[E]nough murder . . . peace." In that way she elaborated the arguments of the conference, that women — who had no political rights, therefore no part in the creation of war — held a unique position from which to demand peace.[26] Other leaflets distributed by Saumoneau on behalf of the Berne International Conference of Socialist Women also addressed "women of the proletariat" by asking them "where are your husbands? where are your sons?" and urging them to fight the war and save their men.[27] Posters, cards, and pamphlets addressed specifically to women appealed to their sensitivity to the suffering caused by the war. Organizations like Le Comité Féminin pour la Paix posted signs asking women if they had had enough of "the horrible carnage," enough "widows and orphans."[28] Throughout 1915, Saumoneau and others continued this appeal in leaflets proclaiming, "Enough dead men, peace" and elaborating this message with a specifically feminist slant: "Women want peace and their rights."[29] By December of that year, the appearance of a short pamphlet entitled "Un Devoir Urgent pour les Femmes" scandalized the socialist party by suggesting that women's "real duty" lay not in their support of the war but in their hastening its end.[30] Such publications and their message that women's duty was to end war, however, voiced the opinions of a small minority, certainly at this stage of the war.

If the threat of feminist antiwar activism remained slim, the French government nonetheless responded forcefully with a lengthy report entitled the "Feminist Campaign in Favor of Peace," issued in October 1915. While acknowledging the limited appeal of the pacifist feminist campaign, the report noted that "its promoters know, in effect, that the influence of woman may be very efficacious, considering that she is called to manifest herself first in the family, then in the feminine element of society where action, less deliberate, is more diffuse, more vehement and more uncompromising than in other settings."[31] The language here demonstrated the government's concern not merely with the few pacifist feminist campaigners but with women more generally. The report then examined three groups of potential activists: middle-class feminists; socialists and socialist women, especially those connected with the Berne conference; and adherents of feminist internationalism. Its conclusions insisted that the roots of pacifism lay in an insidious foreign, notably German, influence and called for vigilance in the face of feminist contributions to a moral decline in the country.[32] The double threat of women organized as feminists, however, remained one of the more striking features of the rhetoric used throughout the document. The text managed to express two prevalent anxieties about women: their alleged "power" within the home and family, and the slipperiness of all that femininity (*l'élément féminin*) represented, since it resisted "deliberate action" and was instead emotional, devouring, uncompromising, and out of control.

The police continued to monitor the activities of antiwar women and women's organizations and to report them to the Sûreté. But they also filed reports on wartime feminist, socialist, and trade union meetings that were not specifically war-related. However, another form of women's potential resistance to war also merits analysis here. If one paramount duty of women remained the bearing and raising of children—particularly of sons as future soldiers—then any attempt to refuse this role, either by eliminating pregnancies or by being a "Malthusian" (a supporter of birth control), could be interpreted in wartime as an act of disloyalty or even subversion. As earlier discussions of the 1915 French debates over changing the law on abortion and the reaction to the infanticide case of Joséphine Barthélemy in Chapter 2 demonstrated, these issues were highly charged even when maternity allegedly occurred as a result of German rape. In such an atmosphere, any suggestions of behavior deviating from "normal femininity" were also read as a threat to the *union sacrée*, the social order.[33]

The Crisis of 1917 and the Case of Hélène Brion

On 18 November 1917, a short article on the front page of the Parisian daily *Le Matin* announced the death of Auguste Rodin and a much larger one announced the arrest of a schoolteacher, Hélène Brion, claiming this dangerous woman had long been guided by the ideas of "Malthusianism, defeatism, antimilitarism, [and] anarchy."[34] While this disparity of attention might have suggested a lack of regard for Rodin, it certainly displayed the extent to which the crime of defeatism and the question of women's moral support for the war had come to preoccupy wartime France.

While supporters rallied to her cause, Brion spent four months in the St. Lazare Prison for women. In March of 1918 she and Gaston Mouflard, a soldier who had been the recipient of Brion's letters and, like her, was active in the syndicalist movement, were charged with publishing and distributing "seditious" propaganda and tried for treason before the First Council of War. After listening to testimony from teachers, socialists, and feminists, the council found them guilty, and while giving Brion a more severe punishment, suspended both sentences.

Although they were on trial for a treasonous violation of the law, their crime was known by a new term, "defeatism."[35] In 1917 France, it had begun to be considered a crime to advocate a negotiated end to the war rather than a fight until victory. Definitions of defeatism encompassed both a willingness to accept peace at any price and any criticism of the conduct of the war. Defeatism also became linked to certain kinds of behavior, expressions, and political associations. In particular, an undated pamphlet—presumably from late 1917—made explicit the connection between defeatism and feminism. Émile Janvion's *Le féminisme défaitiste* specifically referred to the *paciboche* and *défaitiste* leaders of feminism, such as Brion, Séverine, Marguerite Durand, Hubertine Auclert, and Nelly Roussel, and stated that "the history of defeatism, when it is known, will demonstrate superabundantly that feminism will there merit, I dare say, the place of honor."[36]

Of course, the state's concern with controlling its citizens and their opinions during wartime was not unique to the Great War. However,

World War I accelerated this process and intensified the repression of civil liberties.[37] In his study of French society during the war, Jean-Jacques Becker persuasively showed that consensus in favor of the war had to be both manufactured at the onset and sustained through the duration.[38] Given the agenda of both the socialist and feminist movements prior to the outbreak of the war, one might expect some continuation of their internationalist pacifist stance. However, the initial reaction to war, even among socialists, reflected almost total commitment to the war effort. Only slowly were voices of opposition raised. Moreover, the extent to which these cries in the wilderness influenced the general public hardly seemed significant. Censorship made the spread of these ideas difficult, and, at least initially, "anything but unqualified support for the war was exceptional."[39]

However, 1917 represented a new crisis point for the French war effort; it was a year of strikes, which included women munition workers, mutinies, and the gradual emergence of political and social antagonism to continuing the war.[40] Although neither the mutinies nor the weariness of workers proved disastrous, they suggested that French morale could be assailed. In response to these threats, civil and military authorities paid even closer attention to public opinion.[41] Under the combined influence of the Russian Revolution, Russia's potential and then actual leaving the alliance, and an indigenous crisis of morale, both the possibility of open opposition to the war and the growing support by socialists and radicals for an immediate, negotiated peace seemed to present a real threat to *union sacrée*.[42]

The 1917 and 1918 treason trials thus reflected a larger, perceived moral as well as political crisis, and Brion's case formed a crucial part of this crisis because her trial called to the forefront the particular role of women.[43] The trials occupied a center space in Parisian newspapers as news of arrests, speculations of guilt, and excerpts from the trials appeared on an almost daily basis through the fall of 1917 and the spring of 1918. Yet details of the elements contributing to the intensity of the government's crackdown, for example full accounts of how widespread strikes and mutinies were, failed to reach the public. Moreover, the "Affaire Bolo," "Affaire Malvy," "Affaire du Bonnet Rouge," and "Affaire Caillaux" probably aroused interest as much for the stature of the participants as for the issues at stake. Among the accused was Joseph Caillaux, a former prime minister and the leader of the Radicals, and Louis Malvy, minister of the interior.[44] Essentially, anyone found to be publicly in favor of a compromise peace rather than a total military victory and caught espousing these ideas was subject to charges of defeatism and treason.[45] To oppose war was thus to bring into question one's loyalty, one's identity as a citizen of France. Only by fighting could one's love of country be *unconditionally* validated, even if one desired an immediate peace.[46] For women against the war, the situation was even more complex. Because they could not fight, they had no way to prove their patriotism, except as providers of moral support.

However, much more was at issue in the trial of Hélène Brion than the question of support for the war. The importance of Hélène Brion's case comes from the precise nature of her status as a feminist activist and of the place of women in supporting or resisting the war effort. At its core, her trial concerned itself with debates about political rights in wartime, with the responsibility of women to stand between society and children in order to both inculcate and embody virtue, and, fundamentally, with whether it was possible to be "feminine," "feminist," and "French."

With the war's evolving emphasis on civilian morale came attempts to redefine the identity of women and their proper role during the war. Women remained, despite the presence of male noncombatants, the quintessential civilians, and civilians remained necessary to a successful outcome of the war. Thus Brion was perceived as especially dangerous because as a feminist and a woman who dissented she overtly challenged certain norms, most significantly those concerning civil rights and national identity. In essence, Hélène Brion transformed her trial into an arena in which to debate feminism, the rights of women, and the notion that a world of enfranchised women would be a world without war. Her trial therefore provides a means of exploring how for women "war crystallizes contradictions between ideology and actual experience," particularly as far as national loyalty was concerned.[47] It is both exceptional, because few people were actually tried for treason, and representative, because the issues Brion's case raised for women were far from unique.

Why did Hélène Brion become the focus of such a prominent, national trial? A partial explanation can be found in both who she was and what she represented. Fundamentally, Brion was on trial as a "woman," not just as a "citizen," because she represented the potential dangers posed by women to an ungendered patriotism. Both her sex and her profession made her an obvious target of government interest. However, her unrepentant feminism and socialist trade union loyalty caused her to be perceived as a leader, someone who could influence women, the working-class, and teachers. Her personal history also came into play. Born in 1882, she was orphaned at an early age and reared by her grandmother in the Ardennes. For a woman of her generation, she received a high level of education, attending the École Primaire Supérièure Sophie Germain in Paris. After her graduation, she took a teaching position in 1904 and became involved in both socialist and feminist politics.[48] Brion led a busy life in Pantin, a Parisian suburb, supporting herself as a teacher and devoting herself to numerous organizations. She held administrative positions in the Federation of Trade Union Teachers, the Worker's Orphanage Society, the General Committee of the Confédération Générale du Travail, and the local socialist party, and she actively participated in the feminist organizations of the day, including working on the electoral campaigns of feminists Hubertine Auclert and Madeleine Pelletier.[49] Brion thus possessed impeccable feminist and syndicalist credentials.

Despite her activism in her union and in the socialist movement, she identified herself as a feminist first and foremost. In 1913, in the pages of a socialist-feminist journal, a heated debate developed between Brion and Louise Saumoneau, in which Saumoneau attacked Brion for siding with "bourgeois" feminists over workers.[50] Brion felt that female solidarity transcended class solidarity, a position she again articulated in her 1917 *La voie féministe,* which criticized the inability of the socialist party or the Confédération Générale du Travail to incorporate the struggle for the rights of women into their agendas.[51] As one of her personal endeavors, she compiled a feminist encyclopedia, wherein in protest against "patriarchal" structures she arranged its subjects by first rather than last name, and, in 1919, she founded a weekly paper, *La Lutte Féministe.*[52] Her primary political identification lay with feminism, but her feminism led her to socialism and, eventually, to antimilitarism.[53] As was true of many socialists, her initial stand was to support the *union sacrée.* However, she increasingly became disillusioned, and ultimately, as secretary of the militant national teachers' union, she came into conflict with the war effort.[54]

Teachers had played an important role in the formation of the Third Republic. As schooling became compulsory, secular, and free in the early 1880s, it formed an essential component of Republican policy.[55] Moreover, it offered one of the few professions for women, although women were restricted primarily to teaching girls.[56] The state thus expected teachers to be not only exemplary models of Republican virtues but also conveyors of a nationalist sense of identity. Furthermore, as lay educators, public school teachers were perceived as being servants of the Republic, politically aligned with the Left as opposed to the more Catholic-identified Right. Few, however, were active socialists or militants.

For militant teachers, the Federation of Trade Union Teachers proved a stronghold. Their union created what historian Thierry Flammant has described as a progressive counterculture.[57] Through their journal, *L'École Emancipée,* the National Federation expressed internationalist, feminist, and even pacifist opinions up until the eve of the war. With the outbreak of war, however, the government expected teachers to help maintain morale.[58] From the onset of the conflict, the government ordered teachers to inculcate French values and a belief in the certainty of French victory. In a circular of September 1915, the Ministry of Public Instruction stressed that instructors "already know how important public education is in the struggle of our armies." The directive encouraged teachers to incorporate the war in all educational activities, including daily readings of "judiciously selected extracts from the correspondence with soldiers" in order to "fix the spirits of students on the daily phases of the war and to elevate their sentiments as to the heights of heroism deployed by our soldiers."[59] The explicit connection between militarism and a primarily right-wing nationalism and educators having a professional duty to "preach" this doctrine contributed to the problems of antiwar teachers. It may help to explain why Brion herself originally joined with the great majority of teachers—and feminists—in supporting the war effort.[60]

Despite their official mission, antiwar activist teachers such as Marie and François Mayoux from Dignac became increasingly vocal. Their 1917 pamphlet, *Les instituteurs syndicalistes et la guerre,* spoke for pacifist teachers who questioned the schoolroom propaganda attacking Germany and glorifying war. Assailing dishonesty in education, they challenged the very foundations of French wartime rationale. They recommended that children be taught instead that "[w]ar is immoral, inhumane, ruinous."[61] Praising the efforts of the federation—and mentioning Brion by name—they called for teachers to criticize war openly. The reaction to this document came swiftly. The Mayoux were arrested in July 1917 and tried for an infraction of the law of 5 August 1914—a violation of wartime censorship.[62] In October, the Mayoux each received a sentence of a fine of Fr 100 and six months in prison.[63] And they were not the only teachers to face charges under this law.[64]

As head of her union, Brion had her own role to play in these antiwar endeavors. In her capacity as secretary of the teacher's union, Brion revived union activities in January 1915. By June of that year, some teachers began to organize opposition to the war. Led by Marie Mayoux, these "revolutionary" teachers came to the federation's congress in August to urge full union support of antiwar agitation. Following long debates at the August congress, the federation and Brion adopted the more radical pacifist stance, joining the socialist minority, where most French antimilitarism had its roots.[65] From this point on, militant teachers and their union, led by Brion, worked on behalf of a negotiated peace settlement, even when threatened with revocation of their credentials to teach.

As soon as Brion's support of the socialist minority's opposition to the war became evident, the government began a surveillance of her correspondence and kept track of meetings that she attended. Even as she began her antiwar work, Brion recognized that within the pacifist movement women's voices were in danger of being marginalized and suppressed. In December 1915, she co-authored a letter to protest the suppression of a feminist antiwar publication, noting that "this is once again the case where the propaganda of women is prevented when that of men on the same subject is let alone."[66] She became convinced that opposition to the war was necessary as a socialist and as a union leader, but even more decisively as a feminist.

By the end of 1916, Brion's increasing activism on these three fronts led to her name being listed among those "notorious individuals known for their pacifist propaganda."[67] Throughout 1916 and 1917, the Prefecture of Police accumulated lengthy documentation about her work and letters to Brion were copied and carefully recorded.[68] Brion not only had a major role within the teachers' union, but her aid and influence were also solicited in the spring of 1917 in support of striking women workers in the Seine.[69] As noted by Dubesset, Thébaud, and Vincent in their study of the "munitionettes" of the Seine, the actions of women workers in stopping the production of arms also implicitly threatened the war effort as a whole.[70] Jean-Jacques Becker has argued, in contrast, that the strikes of 1917 reflected general fatigue and concern with economic privation, not necessarily antiwar sentiment per se. Yet, as Laura Downs has more recently argued, the women's strikes of May–June 1917 were as much politically as economically motivated, and were read nervously by authorities as signs of defeatism.[71] And as other letters to Brion and comments recorded in her police file reveal, Brion was involved in "destabilizing" campaigns, and not only on behalf of women in the trade union movement. By July 1917, when the government mounted its "preliminary" investigation against Brion, she had already been characterized as a "woman of slovenly behavior, hysterical in word and pen, who stimulates the ardor of her syndicalist comrades throughout the territory."[72] This description both belittled her and pointed to her potential danger as a "hysterical," immoral, and persuasive woman.

Already committed to the militant minority's antagonism to the war — and, if not publicly, at least in the eyes of the police, notorious for it — Brion continued to distribute pamphlets, most notably that by the Mayoux. No doubt her being mentioned by name in the Mayoux's pamphlet contributed to the authorities' interest in prosecuting her, although her own activities and words in and of themselves probably called enough attention to her. She had attended the Zimmerwald Conference of Socialists, which became associated with socialist "pacifism." Furthermore, her 1917 treatise *La voie féministe* expressed the potentially threatening idea that women shared a desire to end the war, although they were unable to act on this desire because they were deprived of civil and political rights.[73] As the official investigation against her intensified after July, her school in Pantin — where she had worked since 1911 — became concerned and suspended her in October 1917.

The prosecution built its case against Brion between July and November, and Brion was called to court on November 17. Authorities arrested her when she refused to answer questions without the presence of her lawyer and charged her, along with fellow teacher Suzanne Dufour and Gaston Mouflard, of the crime of spreading "defeatist" propaganda. Imprisoned in Saint Lazare, Brion was subjected to a psychiatric exam, to which she protested, and she remained there until March 1918, when she and Mouflard were tried together before the First Council of War. Charges against Suzanne Dufour, a teacher in Joigny, were dropped after doctors testified to her precarious state of health. Meanwhile, Brion's lawyer, the well-known attorney Oscar Bloch, argued that she should be tried in a civil court, but his motion was denied.

This bare outline of the facts cannot illuminate the tremendous impact of her arrest. Parisian daily newspapers, ranging from the radical, right-wing *L'Action Française* to the socialist *L'Humanité,* instantly reported the arrest of this seemingly obscure teacher. "Defeatist Propaganda: Two Teachers and One *Mobilisé* Are to Be Prosecuted," read the headline of a small article in the *Petit Parisien* on 18 November 1917. It reported that Mlle. Hélène Brion "sent to the front and to factories, tracts, brochures, leaflets, all printed in Lausanne or Geneva, with the object of [spreading] the most active defeatist and even revolutionary propaganda."[74] Other Parisian papers denounced her as a follower of "Malthusianism, defeatism, antimilitarism, and anarchy . . . a member of revolutionary groups." The front page of *Le Matin* attacked her under the heading "Suffragette!"[75] *Le Figaro*'s column entitled "Crimes against National Defense" discussed the defeatist teachers, and Clemenceau's paper, which had just changed its name from *L'Homme Enchaîné* to *L'Homme Libre,* under the heading "Treason," spoke of the "arrest of a teacher" for "antimilitarist, defeatist, bochophile and Malthusian" propaganda.[76] Beneath the headline "Defeatist Propaganda," *L'Action Française* angrily demanded to know how such unpatriotic tracts could reach France and expressed surprise that Brion had not been previously arrested. *Le Petit Journal* contained a small article entitled "Prosecutions against Defeatism," and *L'Écho de Paris* reported that a propagandist of defeatism had been arrested.[77] Before the trial, it seemed as if the press had already convicted the defendant of the crime of defeatism.

By the following day, Brion's case occupied the front pages of *Le Matin, Le Petit Journal,* and *Le Petit Parisien,* and they, along with other newspapers, regularly featured details of the progress of her "affair" for the next week. These front page articles—including one complete with a photo of "Hélène Brion in Masculine Costume"—presented Brion as an agitator who was the focal point of an organization "constituted for propagandizing defeatist ideas in France."[78] Clemenceau's *L'Homme Libre* carried this idea further by repeatedly—and mistakenly—suggesting that twenty accomplices would soon be implicated in the Brion affair.[79]

A more balanced view of the case appeared in *Le Petit Journal,* which mounted its own inquiry and presented "both" sides in two columns: "what her accusers say" and "what her friends say." Its account began with a fellow teacher who attacked Brion for receiving in her room "all sorts" of people, for traveling to Paris to distribute her tracts at revolutionary meetings, and for participating in anarchist and feminist groups. The anonymous teacher characterized Brion as "doubly dangerous" because she managed to befriend and convert other teachers to her ideas. An unnamed friend of Brion, a co-worker at the soup kitchen, offered a counterdescription of Brion as a helpful woman who aided feminist teachers and bicycled; this last statement could and would be used to explain away her appearance in unconventional, masculine garb such as a bicycling outfit. Furthermore, the friend recalled

"Hélène Brion in masculine costume," photo that appeared on the front page of Le Matin, *19 November 1917. Courtesy of Association pour la Conservation et la Reproduction Photographique de la Presse, Paris.*

that Brion had told an English suffragette, a Miss Fell, that she would not go to the international feminist peace congress at The Hague because "the time was not yet right." The paper added, "One must believe that Mlle. Brion has since changed her views."[80]

The language and images used in the various accounts of Brion's arrest suggest the importance of gender in her case. Other than the persistence of the accusation of "Malthusianism" and her having some neo-Malthusian pamphlets, little evidence suggests that Brion was primarily involved with the birth-control movement. "Defeatism," "anarchy," "antimilitarism"—these terms merely proclaimed left-wing activity, but "Malthusianism" took on a peculiarly gendered tone, a code word in pronatalist and particularly wartime France for the worst fears about feminism. By associating feminism with Malthusianism, the feminist could thus be attacked as refusing the most central and natural patriotic role for any woman: maternity. With the initial news of her arrest, Brion as a woman and as a feminist was on trial. The reproduction of her portrait labeled "in masculine costume" further illustrated the extent to which her "femininity" as much as her "Frenchness" was being called into question.[81]

While angrily condemning Brion's harmful, unpatriotic actions and attacking her "femininity," the daily papers also emphasized her profession and attempted to separate Brion from other teachers. On 20 November *Le Petit Journal* ran an interview with a Mme. M., secretary to the director of schools in Paris, who described Brion as a "temptress" trying to enlist the aid of co-workers in her odious work. Although M. acknowledged Brion's considerable intelligence and service, that she "loves the children," she stressed nonetheless that Brion was "very proud" and "very dangerous."[82]

By the time Brion's home had been searched and more damaging evidence uncovered—in the form of pictures of Lenin and Trotsky and copies of "defeatist" literature and correspondence—the attention paid to her in the daily press had dwindled. Yet the cumulative portrait that emerged from this barrage of negative press was filled with contradictions. Brion was described as both hysterical and masculine, irresponsible and dangerous, tempting and hard, in other words, qualities loaded with both masculine and feminine connotations. Brion thus was blamed for both being "naturally" female—a hysterical, irresponsible temptress—and "unnaturally" male—masculine, dangerous, unflinching.

These attacks, especially what was implied by the photograph of her in "masculine costume," quickly evoked a response from her supporters.[83] In an article in *L'Humanité* on 20 November 1917, friends of Brion sought to correct misinformation printed in at least five Parisian newspapers.[84] They charged that those interested in prosecuting Brion were permitted "to create in the public [mind] false sentiments and to establish a presumption of guilt. These proceedings are infinitely regrettable, above all because the facts thus insisted upon by journalists have not been verified."[85] Brion was the secretary of Pantin's Workers' Orphanage Society, and a petition was circulated by the society protesting both her arrest and the attacks made on her in the press. It called upon "we who love her, we who have for her a high and deep esteem, a profound admiration, [to] not let her be unjustly beaten"; they stated her case as one of "right, liberty and democracy" and collected signatures on her behalf.[86] Brion herself wrote a letter to the editor of *Le Matin* in early December refuting the accusations made against her.[87]

Two weeks after Brion's arrest, Madeleine Vernet, Brion's friend and the founder of the worker's orphanage in Pantin, produced a pamphlet in which she presented Brion's case, among other things, as a new Dreyfus affair.[88] In thirty pages, Vernet sought to present the "facts" concerning Brion's persecution and to counteract the negative publicity: "From this tissue of infamies," she wrote, "it came out that Hélène Brion was a dangerous and suspicious character — Anarchist, revolutionary, Malthusian, anti-militarist, defeatist. . . . The word spy, which was not directly pronounced, was visible between the lines."[89] In face of such calumny, Vernet presented a counterportrait of a dedicated, generous, beautiful soul — who also happened to be devoted to aiding children, workers, and women. She quoted Brion's teachers and colleagues attesting to her intelligence and moral character. Always, though, she emphasized Brion's "feminine" nature. Responding to the photo of "Hélène Brion in masculine costume," Vernet asserted that Brion was merely wearing a cycling costume, which she did when "she had a large task to accomplish," such as working at the soup kitchen.[90] Since most women did not cycle, the fact that Brion wore a cycling costume and thus admitted that she cycled may have implicated her in potentially nonfeminine behavior, but Vernet diffused this by suggesting Brion wore it to do such feminine work as feed the poor. Despite the insinuations made against Brion because of this outfit, Vernet insisted to "messieurs les journalistes" that Hélène Brion "is a woman, essentially a woman. Her qualities are all feminine qualities. . . . [She has] the heart of a woman, — of a strong and noble woman."[91] Vernet addressed the crux of the issue: Brion's virtuous womanhood. This need to prove Brion's femininity signifies just how much her gender was associated with the notion of the depth of her crime.

Vernet's defense occurred during a severe crackdown on resistance to the war, when tolerance for criticism, indeed for all oppositional voices, had been curtailed. Thus, Vernet wished to show Brion as not only true to herself but equally true to an acceptable feminine ideal. By questioning why Brion had been singled out, Vernet not only attempted to illuminate the difference between Brion's pacifism and true defeatism but also to portray Brion as a martyr to a cause larger than herself. Brion represented a pacifist idea—which was not, Vernet underscored, defeatist but instead based on love of country and of humanity (24). Vernet alluded to Brion's adherence to a feminist belief that asked, "Should not, in the natural order of things, woman be the irreducible enemy of war? Woman, creator of life, eternal source of the race, beacon of the future?" (4). Yet, in her final comparison of Brion with Dreyfus, she made no mention of feminism. Instead, she emphasized that the attack on Brion, the lies published about her ideas and about her private life, as much as the arrest itself, appeared to be part of a vicious campaign against all militant activists, against any voices opposing the government and speaking for justice and peace (30–33). As Vernet correctly observed, Brion was not the only militant prosecuted for articulating and publicizing subversive ideas. Further, Vernet suggested that the emphasis on "scandals" and "trials for treason" simply and deliberately drew attention away from questioning the war itself (31).[92]

Brion on Trial

After a build-up in the popular and political press, the trial of Brion began in the spring of 1918; she and Mouflard were tried together in proceedings that lasted for five days in late March 1918. Given the ongoing German offensive, Brion's trial took place during an even more tense period for the French war effort than at the time of her arrest. This may account for the fact that while daily résumés of witnesses and testimony appeared in the press for each day of her trial, they were not the leading news items and, just as suddenly as word of her trial appeared, the scandal apparently faded away. Yet Brion's trial received enough attention to warrant a special edition of the journal *Revue des Causes Célèbres: Les Procès de Trahison,* created solely to provide full accounts of the treason trials. An entire issue was devoted to "Pacifism and Defeatism: The Hélène Brion Affair."[93] While the *Revue* also reprinted in multiple volumes the "Affair of the *Bonnet Rouge*" and the "Affair Malvy," Brion was the sole feminist, indeed the sole woman to be so honored.

The *Revue* first described Brion as looking like a schoolteacher in neat and very simple attire (131). The popular press also paid close attention to her physical demeanor, and each paper voiced its own opinion about Brion's personality and her conduct in court. On the whole, they portrayed Brion more sympathetically during her trial than during her arrest and at the initial news of her crime. That Brion's "was a nervous and quasi-indignant voice that answered before the First Council of

War" was how one newspaper described her on her first day in court.[94] Yet even *L'Action Française* depicted her with a kind of grudging respect: "To all this [courtroom activity] Hélène Brion seems to attach little importance, of intelligent mien, expressing her thoughts with assurance and facility, a lively eye, a rapid reply, she contented herself, for an instant almost turning her back to the Council, with casting a seemingly detached glance into the room . . . searching there for faces sympathetic to her cause." More surprisingly for a paper of the nationalist right, *L'Action Française* noted her seeming "good morality" and "strong intelligence."[95]

In one of the few photographs of her during her trial, appearing in *Le Petit Parisien,* Brion sits in the dock, looking tired and leaning on one arm. The text beneath read: "Alone, Mlle. Brion sat on the bench. She had come there with a bare head, typical of her class, clothed in gray . . . a cravat of deep blue. . . . The face is at one moment smiling, and the next contracted to the point of severity." The papers and the *Revue* never pictured Brion with a hat on, although *Le Petit Journal* provided details of her costume on a daily basis and described her on the second day as wearing a brown outfit, complete with a small round hat. Presumably the image of a hatless Brion was significant, emphasizing her class, as *Le Petit Parisien* suggested, and perhaps also her nonconformity, or her alleged masculinity, her status as a "radical" and a "feminist."[96] As to her character, *Le Figaro* noted later in the week:

> However much she protests at each instant against the prosecution of which she is the object, Hélène Brion is consciously or unconsciously happy to appear before the Council of War, in front of the judges and the public, where she expresses herself freely and where her love of discussion can be given free reign. She argues about everything for the pleasure of arguing. One senses that she is satisfied with herself, satisfaction that manifests itself with a little smile . . . after each one of her discussions.[97]

And however much the papers denounced her crime and remained convinced of her guilt, they emphasized Brion's energy—whether nervous or not—and her intelligence. Even the *Revue* allowed Brion moments of humanity, of tears, agitation, and emotion.

The trial opened with an interrogation of Brion. After clarifying the law used against her—Articles 1 and 2 of the law of 5 August 1914— the prosecution asked detailed questions about the contents of and methods she used to distribute the "defeatist" propaganda in question.

Immediately, Brion demanded to know why she and not the author of the brochure in question was being tried. And in response to suggestions that she was on trial for deliberately initiating a campaign against morale, she defended herself by claiming that she wrote and sent tracts to persons she assumed to be as reasonable as she (132).

In a statement quoted in several newspapers, Brion affirmed her right to free speech: "I have the right to think and the duty to think clearly."[98] Two papers also mentioned an interchange that the *Revue* left out: one recorded Brion as saying she was being attacked because she was a woman, and the other stated that "the accused seems to pose herself as a victim of the adversaries of feminist ideas."[99] At this first interrogation and throughout the trial, Brion insisted on her feminism and her intelligence as an educated woman, playing upon the discrepancy between her nonexistent rights and the influence she was thought to wield. She herself pushed the subtext about gender to center stage.

Immediately following the brief testimony of Gaston Mouflard, Brion called approximately sixty witnesses who, as the *Revue* explained in the typical pattern of treason trials, would testify as to her character and to the validity of her ideas. Some of the most provocative discussions during the trial occurred during the interplay of Brion and the witnesses, including the following exchange with Mme. Daridan, another schoolteacher in Pantin. In response to the question, "Did she [Brion] say 'civil war will save us from a foreign war?,'" Daridan replied, "Yes, I remember that. . . . She told me that it would be necessary to have a revolt of women in order to bring about peace. Then, I responded: 'But there would be revolution,' and she added that that would not matter, provided that one would have peace.'" Brion interrupted, "But blood in the streets, Madame Daridan?" Asked to clarify her question, Brion continued, "I would like to ask Mme. Daridan what she understands when she proclaims to have heard me say[,] that I would like a revolution?" Daridan replied that she understood that Brion "wished the revolt of women." Brion protested again, asking if Mme. Daridan really felt her capable of "using violent means and of saying to people 'Kill in order to make peace?'" Here the commissioner intervened in order to establish that Brion's ideas, being anarchist, were in favor of civil war, but Brion asserted her right to defend her ideas: "It is obvious that I am against the spilling of blood between people. . . . I am against civil war, because all of my propaganda for twenty years is a revolt against violence, a call to reason and to justice" (143). Brion then characterized her position as an advocate of a peaceful revolution of women, that they revolt through words. Brion expressed her faith in the reason of "empowered" women, and her feminism remained unmodified: after the feminist revolution, there would be peace.

In order to suggest that her *révolte des femmes* meant "civil war" and violence in the streets, Daridan and the council had to deliberately misinterpret Brion's intentions and statements. Indeed, basing her entire defense on her twenty years of nonviolent agitation, Brion stressed that the essence of her feminism was based on appeals to reason and justice. Hence, her indignation—"not blood in the streets?"—and her insistence on a broader definition of "revolution," thus setting the terms of the debate on the nature of feminist politics. It was not without irony that Brion was accused of both promoting pacifism and advocating violence.

Conveying the perception of a "feminist revolution" was thus more important than uncovering what kind of social change Brion supported. Other testimony, like that of Mlle. Daridan (presumably Mme. Daridan's daughter), undercut prior statements implicating Brion in "revolutionary" activities. When asked about her knowledge of Brion's "revolutionary ideas," Mlle. Daridan replied: "She told me one day that if all women revolted, the war would end all at once and I could get married" (144). Such evidence clearly undermined what Brion's prosecutors believed to be a link between women's liberation and their potential power to end war. Moreover, Mlle. Daridan's reply and the laughter it invoked in the audience found its way into the daily papers. *Le Petit Parisien,* for example, quoted it with relish.

At the start of the trial's third session, a more radical exposition of Brion's ideas occurred. Another colleague of Brion, the widow Mme. Ruehl, described Brion's reaction to mobilization:

> She told me: "It's finished. If women had shown themselves more active in the last few years, when we signed petitions in favor of a lasting peace, maybe we would have been able to 'pacify' the conflict. Now, we have to resign ourselves. Have courage." These are the words of Hélène Brion on that day. She was magnificent. Jeanne Séguin [another teacher] went to the piano and played the Marseillaise. That is how she discouraged us that day (144).

Yet again, this testimony emphasized Brion's faith in enfranchised women's capacity to forge lasting peace, a goal rather different from sabotaging the war effort. Along with Ruehl, more than thirty friends and colleagues came to Paris to attest to Brion's good name. *Le Matin* described how witnesses "enumerated the qualities of the heart and spirit of their comrade: frankness, concern, goodness, gentleness, intelligence and courage."[100] The newspaper's account of this testimony, including that of Mme. Ruehl, who described Brion surrounded by her students as "a mother hen in the midst of her little ones" (144), thus allowed a more sympathetic and, more importantly, "feminine" portrait of Brion to emerge.

Other fellow teachers concurred that Brion would never advocate defeatism. Witnesses among the socialists of Pantin spoke of her idealism. Mme. Girondon, concierge of the school, stated that Brion "never propagandized" (147). And furthermore, according to Mme. Desour, a charwoman, "To women who waited in line for coal, she preached patience and not revolution" (147).

The press paid more attention to the presence of famous witnesses, notably M. Dalbiez, Deputy of Pyrénées-Orientales. In particular, *L'Humanité* praised Dalbiez for "excellently defining what should be the rights of citizens, even in time of war."[101] Dalbiez's testimony raised several crucial points, including his thesis that "citizens should be able to speak and agitate during war" (145). This held especially true, he asserted, since the war had lasted so long: "[W]e know that errors have been committed, thus the public opinion of militants like Hélène Brion and others perceives that the government has not taken all the action it could or should take" (145).

One contributing factor to the public interest in Brion's trial may also have been the notoriety of feminist witnesses called in Brion's favor. Those who testified, Séverine, Nelly Roussel, and Marguerite Durand, were among the most well-known leaders of the bourgeois women's movement.[102] Séverine had already published articles supporting Brion and in her statements to the court made a dramatic linkage between Brion and famous communard Louise Michel, noting their mutual courage and persecution.[103] Yet, the *Revue* provided little of Séverine's detailed testimony, focusing on such humorous elements as her protest against the court's use of letters received by Brion: "If one had judged me by the letters I've received, a long time ago I would have been guillotined" (149). A fuller presentation appeared in *L'Humanité,* which described Séverine's "ardent, passionate" defense and especially that she quoted a passage on the liberty of opinion and the dangers of military justice, written by none other than Clemenceau.[104]

Marguerite Durand, editor of the feminist newspaper *La Fronde,* called attention to Brion's sitting in the dock for believing in a pacifism that she had come to understand when it was considered a virtue (152). Like Séverine, Durand did not make Brion a special case solely because she was a feminist. Although, according to *L'Action Française,* Durand gave a "vibrant, academic profession of feminist faith" when she mentioned Brion's bravery in fighting for the liberty of women workers against the tyranny of masculine syndicalists.[105] Durand attested to Brion's determination and idealism and drew a parallel between her courage in combating "male" tyranny and the tyranny of war.

Nelly Roussel, who at this point was still vice president of the Union Fraternelle des Femmes, and an outspoken advocate of birth control and maternity rights, spoke of how Brion "inspired me at once. . . . I know that she is the author of a great number of clear, clean, spiritual, generous writings, in a word *bien français*" (148). After explaining the difference between military and civil heroism, Roussel extolled the virtues of Brion as representative of the latter category: "I am proud as a woman and as a feminist and I am proud—I insist strongly on this point—I am proud of her as a French woman, because the glory of a people is made not only by the warlike valor of soldiers but . . . also by the greatness of soul and generosity of heart. . . . Hélène Brion brings honor to France; she is a pure and true *Française*" (148–49). Throughout her testimony, Roussel insisted upon Brion's status as a true countrywoman, a faithful daughter of France, thus someone who was incapable of treason. Roussel concluded her arguments by pleading that the court remember France's sacred role in the defense of liberty, emphasizing the underlying issue of civil rights at the trial, and asking that the court consider Brion simply "as a woman faithful to her ideal, who dared to say that she hated war and desired peace" (149). This idealization of Brion represented as well an idealization of, rather than a challenge to, the specifically female task of instructing others in virtuous behavior. Also implicit in this testimony was an adherence to prewar links between feminism and opposition to war. Roussel thus suggested that the ideals to which Brion had remained faithful could be seen as "feminine," "feminist," and "French." They were "feminine" in their desire for peace, "feminist" in their belief that women needed to act in the public, political arena for such a goal, and "French" in their advocacy of liberty and civil rights for all.

At the next and final session of the trial, Brion delivered a statement in her own defense that rendered explicit the connections between her feminism and her opposition to war and the question of women's rights and citizens' rights in time of war. Throughout her trial, Brion had been shifting the focus of the case away from the question of whether or not she distributed pacifist literature—and what it said—toward a passionate plea for the empowerment of women. In her declaration, Brion developed several key arguments.[106] First, she pointed out that as a woman she had no legal status. She claimed to possess none of the rights of citizens nor a say in what laws were created, hence the legal system was glaringly inconsistent in punishing her for a political crime when she had no political rights. As the law had ignored her political rights, it should have ignored her "political" crimes: "Because I am a woman, I am classed . . . by the laws of my country as inferior to all the men of France and of the colonies. In spite of my intelligence . . . in front of the law, I am not equal to an illiterate negro of Guadeloupe or the Ivory Coast. He can participate, by means of the postal vote, in directing the affairs of our common country, and me, I cannot do this. I am outside the law" (5). Challenging the very nature of how citizenship was defined, Brion played upon certain French assumptions about race and imperialism in order to illustrate just how "dangerous" the denial of women's rights was for the nation. Not only had men created a world run for and by them to the detriment of everyone, but they had even denied the most fundamental truths of what constituted citizenship: "If the peoples, conquered and dispersed by force, . . . have maintained their particular soul, is it not above all else thanks to the energy of women, of mothers, the first and most powerful of teachers, determined to defend the hearth and inculcating, from the cradle, in the child, love of a language, of a country, of a race?" (15). Given this all-important task, she continued, how could a world, in which those who perform this service were rendered powerless, hope to have anything other than war? Brion thus linked the denial of women's rights to the "frightening" power that even men of the colonies *allegedly* had over French women, to the persistence of war and the inability to recover from its costs, and, ultimately, to the denigration of motherhood and especially the mothers of France, the women who perform this all-important symbolic and literal task.

Thus, for Brion, pacifism resulted directly from a particular brand of feminism: "I am above all and before all else a feminist, . . . and it's because of feminism that I am the enemy of war" (6). Her pacifism, she maintained, dated from 1914, while feminism had been her raison d'être for twenty years (8). She opposed the war primarily because as a feminist she knew that "war is the triumph of brute force; the feminist can not triumph except by moral force and intellectual valor. There is absolute opposition between the two" (8). And the consequences of war, which, according to Brion, arose from masculine domination, included immorality, prostitution, and the mistreatment of all women in invaded territories.[107] "Peace," she insisted, "does not dishonor us! But what does dishonor us, what is a disgrace without name for all of masculine humanity is the godless continuation of this massacre, without one word of reason dared to be heard" (12). Reversing the commonly expressed association of women with irrationality, Brion asserted that war was the consequence of immoral, irrational thought and her work, her feminism, was "above all an appeal to reason, never to violence" (18).

After her long speech, the trial concluded anticlimactically. The prosecution, in its summation, reminded the court not to judge the person of Hélène Brion and her moral character but her actions. The prosecutor noted that "it pleases me to state that Hélène Brion has a generous heart, no one disputes that. . . . [T]he moral portrait of Hélène Brion as a young Louise Michel, as a witness testified, is exactly the impression I have" (154). However, he insisted, blind pacifism is defeatism, and he quoted long passages from *Les instituteurs syndicalistes et la guerre* to demonstrate its defeatist message. Further, in an interesting inversion of gendered ideas of legal culpability, he characterized Brion's strengths as being a terrible danger in that she influenced Mouflard, which thus, in part, excused him. Finally, Brion's lawyer, Oscar Bloch, made a passionate plea that if Brion had to be found guilty, the court should be lenient. After all, "if she made a mistake, she did it without personal interest, she was mistaken out of goodness, the nobility of her soul" (167). Moreover, she had "endured four months of harsh imprisonment in St. Lazare, prison of thieves and prostitutes. . . . [S]he has weathered them courageously, gently. She has now largely expiated the little of wrong that you reproach her with" (167). The court must have been partially persuaded; Hélène Brion was sentenced to three years imprisonment, Gaston Mouflard was sentenced to six months, and both sentences were suspended.

Even the press, whose characterization of the final audience varied a bit from paper to paper, did not express surprise at the verdict, although it downplayed the fact of suspension. On the Right, *L'Action Française* noted that Brion became "aggressive, even violent at times" when reading her defense and that "she made the trial about actual society which is the work of man, created by man, for the profit of man." The newspaper also reported the presiding court official's response: "[Y]ou have above all defended feminism, but in order for your ideas to triumph, our soldiers must be victorious."[108] In an account equally hostile to Brion's final words, *Le Figaro* mocked Brion's "good feminine sense" and the idea that "according to her, war is the result of masculinism. She traces the program of feminism and devotes herself, of course, to violent attacks against men."[109] Thus Brion's feminist arguments were ridiculed as "violent" and irrational attacks on men, implying once again how important ideas about gender were in this case. Whether ignoring or criticizing her comments, no paper seemed to have taken them at all seriously. Even the feminist *La Française* spoke of the justice of the decision, not the content of Brion's defense.[110] With the news of her verdict, the case of Hélène Brion vanished from the mainstream press, except for a small article in *Le Petit Parisien* of March 31, which reported that Brion's certificate to teach had been revoked.[111] It would not be reinstated until 1925.

Brion's trial wove together many of the problems with civilian morale that the government had sought to remedy by publicly purging the nation of its internal enemies. If, as we have already seen, the 1917 upsurge in strike activity, expressions of popular discontent, and mutinies provided one context for these trials, then the continued and even increased actions of feminists might also provide a particular grounding for Brion's case. Some of this other feminist activity also came to the attention of the police and, subsequently, the Sûreté. For example, wartime police files contained propaganda from *Le Bataille Syndicaliste,* which, in an effort to link an explicit appeal to women in their "natural" role as mothers with one to class solidarity, and perhaps an implicit reference to the mutinies, put the following question to mothers: "An officer knocks your son, he's acquitted, your son strikes an officer, he's shot. EQUALITY???"[112] This antimilitarist propaganda must also be considered in the context of anonymous letters sent to "Femmes Françaises" that specifically called upon women to put an end to war.

Some examples of these appeals to all women, and to working-class women in particular, during this time period were confiscated and sent to the central government, contributing to a fear of women sowing the seeds of dissension. Some of these texts went beyond connecting women with motherhood to directly addressing them as workers: "Women of France!!! You are the strength and the will!!! of the nation!!! . . . Refuse to work at munitions!!! Each time that you receive your pay!!! You receive the price in blood of those whom you love."[113] The file on such evidence at the National Archives contains several examples, including a "letter" directed to women that emphasized their roles in the family, not the public workplace: "Enough blood! Not a family in France is without a sadness or a mourning. Our fathers, our brothers, our husbands, all our children are sent to [their] death[s] and this butchery has already lasted three years!"[114]

Police did not restrict their surveillance of women to those actively engaged in pacifist or socialist agitation. Morale—more broadly interpreted as the sustaining of the war effort—was also thought to be affected by the behavior of civilians (women) and by their ordinary actions. Thus reports on "antiwar" activities throughout the nation took careful note of what one might construe as mere gossip. Nonetheless, the reports themselves provided evidence of how quickly and unofficially information was transferred among women, perhaps signaling why such minor infractions were thought worthy of investigation. Thus reports to the Special Commissioner in Dieppe noted "alarmist noises in Eu," which included such seemingly minor infractions as Mme. Lalleve telling Mme. Dellys, the baker, that she was stocking up on provisions because a (female) neighbor had told her the Germans were about to strike Yser and would be in Eu in three months.[115] If spreading pessimistic "news" about the war situation merited surveillance, so too did criticism of the government from more patriotic quarters—religious Catholic women critical of state provisions for the orphans of the war.[116] Reports on the "Esprit of the Parisian population" for the last years of the war recorded how women were responding not only to fears about German success but to the cost of living and the availability of housing and work.[117] Thus, Brion's actions and those of other self-identified feminist pacifists were considered part of a continuum that led from complaining to committing treason.

In the radical socialist women's journal *La Femme Socialiste,* Louise Saumoneau, in her capacity as editor, though occasionally censored, continued to issue appeals for the end of war. In 1917 through 1918, she also commented on the persecution of "pacifists" such as the teachers Mayoux and Brion. One satirical piece that appeared in May 1918 under the heading "Chronique Médicale" discussed the occurrence of a new disease called "Clemenceauphobie." Among other symptoms of the disease were the "continual vision of a terrified animal," a lack of revolutionary spirit, and irrational fear; the disease was linked to the trials of the Mayoux and Brion.[118]

In light of other socialist-feminist statements made against the war, what seems striking about Brion's final statement in her trial was not how she articulated two distinct strands of feminism—of women being deprived of rights, hence standing outside both the law and politics or war, and of women's moral force as naturally pacifist—but the way in which she linked these arguments. In other words, feminist pacifism during the war often drew on a difference-based feminism. Brion used equal rights–based arguments and yet also employed a rhetoric that still insisted on certain gender distinctions between men and women. Unlike other feminist appeals against war that were addressed to mourning mothers and used, or perhaps even subverted, a rhetoric similar to the propaganda about women and their wartime duties, Brion insisted on her intelligence, her rationality, her rights, and her "reasonable," feminist hostility to the irrational, male violence of war.

A British Feminist on Trial

The plight of Annie Pimlott, a socialist feminist, offers an additional example of feminist opposition to war, a British counterpart to Brion's affair, and the shared danger of women's dissent.[119] Pimlott's treasonous offense can be traced to the complex use of atrocities in wartime propaganda: she stated at an Independent Labour Party (I.L.P.) meeting that British soldiers also committed rape, like their German counterparts, only that this information was suppressed by the British press.

As the organizing secretary of the Independent Labour Party in Yorkshire, Annie E. Pimlott became the object of official inquiries after she gave a speech in Dewsbury on 10 December 1918.[120] An article in the *Batley Reporter* recorded the details of these "very important criminal proceedings," which stemmed from a violation of the Defence of the Realm Act: "spreading by word of mouth at Dewsbury a certain false report in relation to the conduct of the British Army."[121] The offense, the prosecution noted, was "about as grave a breach of the Defence of the Realm Regulation, No. 27, as one could well imagine."[122] During the general election, Pimlott addressed a meeting at St. James Mission Room, Vulcan Road, Dewsbury, and in the course of speaking, stated:

> You have read of the awful slaughter and atrocities, and everything else. If you could go to Germany, you would find the same thing about England. It is all the outcome of the war. A discharged soldier said: "You have read a lot about German atrocities. I'll tell you something they dare not put in our papers. It is quite a common thing if the soldiers met a woman they simply outraged her, and after they had done that to her, rather than she should go forward and tell the tale that it was an Englishman they have taken a bayonet

and pierced her through the heart. You might wonder why they did not shoot her, but if a British Tommy shot a Belgian or German or French woman they would have found the British bullet."

After this speech was reported, some of the highest military and civil authorities decided that "it would be wrong to the common soldiers of this country to allow the statement to go unpunished and unrebuked."[123]

At Pimlott's trial in Dewsbury Police Court, authorities such as Major General B. E. W. Childs, C.M.G., director of Personnel Services at the War Office and former assistant adjutant general at General Headquarters in France from August 1914 to February 1916, testified that no cases of rape and murder, nor even of rape alone, occurred during his tenure in France. Brigadier General K. Wroughton, the assistant adjutant general, traveled from France "specially for this prosecution" and testified that "until the present day there was only one case of a British soldier in France or Belgium being charged with rape."[124] Under cross-examination, Pimlott defended her actions. She asserted that she only reported what she had been told and, after a long pause, said she could not name her source of information and that she herself did not believe the account. Nonetheless, after a short deliberation, Annie Pimlott was found guilty, sentenced to three months in prison, fined £50, and ordered to pay an additional £25 in expenses.

Most remarkable about the prosecution of Annie Pimlott is that, at great effort and expense, the army and government felt obliged to use such forceful means to prosecute a woman who, it appears, was not very powerful or influential. A trial at a police court hardly seems to have merited the presence of one brigadier general and one major general as witnesses for the prosecution, particularly since the trial took place after the successful conclusion of the war. Pimlott's crime can hardly have threatened military or civilian morale, since her speech occurred a month after the armistice. One way to make sense of this prosecution would be to contextualize it in terms of both national and gender politics. If British soldiers could also commit "outrage" and "murder," then the power of rape as a particular national weapon of war would diminish, and the particular "racial" construction of the German enemy would fall apart. Moreover, the battle lines would shift from those of the nation or race to those of gender. Pimlott's speech, arrest, prosecution, and conviction demonstrate how women's challenging the state-sanctioned "truth" about war remained a threat.

Conclusion

In 1918, the French government tried Hélène Brion as a defeatist and a militant pacifist who used feminism to conceal her obviously treasonous acts of distributing pacifist propaganda to soldiers. As far as popular reaction and the popular press were concerned, Brion's gender and consequently her feminism were also significant points of contention. Thus, the popular press explicitly and the government implicitly also placed her gender on trial. Brion herself transformed her trial into an arena to debate women's political rights. Supporters may have rallied to Brion's cause as socialists, pacifists, trade unionists, or feminists, but she herself saw feminism as the most important cause, and evidence from the trial suggests that she convinced others of this as well.

Brion also clearly presented a more direct challenge to the state, one based on gender. Given the notion of citizenship that based itself on rights and provided the cornerstone for nationalism, could a woman — who claimed to have no "rights" — ever be "patriotic?" By placing herself "outside the law," Brion also placed herself outside the nation. In doing so, at a time when, more than ever, women were necessary for French survival, she called into question the potential loyalty of all women. All of Brion's arguments provide another possible explanation for the hostility that met her arrest and for the desire to "defeminize" her.

It can be argued that Brion's trial was about how feminism could be seen as inseparable from the treason of "defeatism," and, more generally, how women's dissent from gender norms and feminism itself during the war could be seen as potential threats to the social order. Questions about feminist and female loyalty also reverberated in debates about the proper role of women in maintaining morale. This is evident in the reaction of the British and French mainstream feminist movements and presses to the Hague Conference of 1915, as well as to the case of Hélène Brion and to other French and British feminist pacifists and their activities. Continued anxiety about the stability of the moral order can also be found in discussions about education — in schools and the home — and the family. Brion's trial brought into focus several of these related concerns at once, since she occupied a dual position as a woman and a teacher and, in the politicized equivalents of these roles, as "feminist," "socialist," and "union leader." The case of Hélène Brion serves as one potent example of the impact of the war on the relationship between women and their national identities.

Additionally, in debates over women's suffrage before the war, women's inability to provide military service had been used as an argument to deny them the vote, even though Britain did not have a tradition that every male would be a citizen soldier, as did nations like France. Turning the antisuffrage premise around, some feminists argued that one of the virtues of giving women the vote would be their standing for a "moral force," in contrast to the "physical force" of men. Women's lack of participation in the military was thus made a virtue.[125] Before and during the war, antisuffragists also argued that women's so-called natural exclusion from the military permitted their exclusion from the national political sphere.[126] This would further complicate efforts to define women's roles in their wartime nations, as will be seen in the following chapter, which explores struggles over the emblems, privileges, and rights of citizenship during the war.

National Service
and National Sacrifice

CIVIC PARTICIPATION,

GENDER, AND NATIONAL

IDENTITY

Wartime Women and the Question of Political Rights

The First World War provided British and French women with new forums in which to protest their exclusion from national political life and to assert an often transnational feminist pacifism. At the same time, it presented them with opportunities to identify themselves more fully with their nation, which in turn gave women a new basis for claiming citizenship. When historians have considered women's citizenship claims during the war, they typically have focused on debates over women's suffrage.[1] This focus has created an obvious contrast between the experiences of women in these two nations because some British women gained the right to vote in 1918, while French women were to wait until 1944. Although the outcome of women's suffrage in the two nations varied substantially, women's wartime services and sacrifices were widely acknowledged as a potential basis for political rights in both France and Britain.

In 1914, the political rights and military obligations of British and French male citizens differed significantly, and this helps explain how a parallel rhetoric about women and the war might yield such different outcomes. At this time, France had universal manhood suffrage and used military conscription as the basis for its armed forces. This helped make military service an obligation of enfranchised male citizens. In contrast, Britain, alone among the major combatant nations, possessed a volunteer army at the war's outset. Further, since Britain grounded the franchise in property qualifications as well as age, significant groups of men did not possess electoral rights at the beginning of the war. As a result, British debates about what constituted citizenship and what qualities and/or actions then entitled citizens—including women—to vote became increasingly caught up with how military service and patriotic action were to be recognized, especially after the introduction of conscription in 1916.[2] When the British government altered the franchise in 1918, the significance of patriotic service was illuminated by the disenfranchisement of conscientious objectors and, for some observers, by the enfranchisement of certain categories of women.

Against this backdrop, this chapter analyzes debates over women's suffrage that emerged as a result of such wartime innovations, but it locates them as part of a wider discourse about women's national service and patriotism.[3] In Britain, the question of electoral reform resurfaced when it became apparent that not all soldiers could participate electorally.[4] In France, the war's huge death tolls led to calls for a "suffrage for the dead," which would guarantee that families of dead soldiers would still be represented, as well as to suggestions that the voting age be lowered from twenty-one to twenty to guarantee that all soldiers could vote.[5] All of these debates were inseparable from discussions about citizens' and women's proper contributions to the wartime nation.

Starting with an investigation of controversies surrounding some aspects of women's national service in Britain and France, this chapter will demonstrate that wartime debates over suffrage drew upon a preexisting rhetoric of women "serving" the state either by direct action or by "sacrificing" the men they loved. While stressing the importance of women identifying completely with their national cause, many contemporaries in both nations also sought to limit the claims for equal citizenship that could be made by and for women. And although contemporaries in Britain and France made strikingly parallel arguments about women's suffrage—about the equivalency of military and maternal service for instance—these generated divergent political and social outcomes.

British Women and the Emblems of Citizens

The First World War provoked a reworking of the claims made by patriots and citizens in Britain. At the war's outset, Britain alone among major participant nations had needed to raise its army through recruiting. When war was declared in 1914, some British women began responding to patriotic appeals by participating in formal and informal military recruitment.[6] To send men to war became, as the *Evening Standard* put it, "the patriotic duty of the women of England." And it quoted women declaring: "Single young men . . . should be made to feel that Khaki is the only fashionable colour . . . [for it is] the royal robe of heroes."[7] Immediately, wearing khaki was linked to heroism, patriotism, and the military, which embodied male national service.

As part of their recruiting efforts, some women insisted that if men would not enlist, they would do so in their place. As a letter to the *Evening Standard* commented: "Many women are already good shots, and, though they may not have the strength and physique of the men, they would at least have the pluck and patriotism, which seem almost extinct in Young England now."[8] The *Daily Graphic* reported that "there is a widespread feeling of discontent among women" who felt that "the disabilities of their sex" were all that kept them from "finding their way to the firing line."[9] Such expressions of patriotism were in keeping with other recruiting efforts, such as the white feather campaign, which sought to shame men into action.[10]

Reports of such female enthusiasm soon gave way to those of women forming overseas battalions. In February 1915, under the heading "Le loyalisme des suffragettes," France's *Le Figaro* described the creation of two "regiments" of British suffragettes calling it a gesture "made to touch our hearts." It also noted their "ambition to be treated as citizens" and equated their costume with the kilt of Highlanders.[11] Drawing upon this account and other reports in the French press, several British papers began to embellish the story, with claims that a battalion of "Amazon" suffragettes had landed in France ready to help the Allied cause. The *Daily Express* claimed to have consulted several suffrage organizations on the matter, only to have received the response: "We know nothing of them; we should like to, it is so very interesting."[12] Even at this early stage in the war, these activities were linked — by the use of the term "suffragette" — to women's struggles for political rights. These groups of women volunteers, however, insisted on a patriotism not linked to political rewards since they argued for their very right to exist.

The alleged direct presence of thousands of militarily attired women serving overseas attracted attention in the press, but the locus of female military activities remained Britain itself. Soon after the war's outbreak, women began organizing themselves into voluntary forces designed to help protect the United Kingdom against invasion or otherwise serve the nation. One of these groups, the Women's Emergency Corps (WEC), quickly produced a more popular offshoot: the Women's Volunteer Reserve (WVR). As scholar Jenny Gould has noted, the military-style activities of these groups sparked a hostile reaction.[13] By early spring of 1915, images of women drilling on village commons prompted accusations that they were wasting effort and time; as one letter to the *Newcastle Chronicle* put it, "These 'Lady Kitcheners'" were "playing at soldiers."[14] Opponents of women's military activity criticized them for not taking up nursing, an occupation for which they had a "natural qualification." Unlike other necessary women's work, they asserted "playing at soldiers was a far more congenial occupation. . . . Rifle shooting afforded good sport and opportunity for elegant postures. . . . [T]he one all-important fact . . . [was] that they were worse than useless."[15] A longer article in an August 1915 *Ladies' Pictorial* was more explicit about the significance of the women's voluntary groups' use of khaki uniforms: "Never, surely, was there a time when we had greater reason or need to display respect to the trappings which mark men as the servants of their country, the soldiers of their King. Yet at this time when women are urging men to don this uniform, when they are rightly vaunting the glory and honour and distinction of wearing it, they themselves in many instances are rendering it ridiculous by adopting it for themselves and playing at soldiers."[16] This comment thus defined what the "King's uniform" represented: it literally "mark[ed] men as the servants of their country." Women in uniform were not just useless or simply aping men, but, more insidiously, they were appropriating the garb of the King's soldier, the nation's servant. Women's wearing of uniforms thus demonstrated their inability to understand the duties of true—that is male—citizens at war.

Those critical of women in khaki regarded the fabric itself as only suitable for those who could have it stained in blood. For women to appropriate it was therefore an insult to the "real" work of war done by soldiers overseas. As one 1915 commentator stated: "We stupid males will continue to think that the wearing of khaki had better be left to persons who may be called into the fighting-line."[17] In wartime Britain, putting on the khaki of the King's uniform represented patriotic service: "Khaki is sacred to those for whom it forms a shroud; . . . it is the garb of the fighting man who goes out to war risking life and limb for England, home and his women-kind; and it should not be lightly donned."[18] Such language presumed that women could never be asked to make the ultimate sacrifice of laying down their lives for the country. While this presumption ignores the presence of women under fire both in England and overseas and those who died while serving the nation as war workers, the implication is clear: women did not deserve to wear khaki since it would never form "their shroud," and they were thus not full participants in the war, not full citizens. It is worth noting here too that the criticism that women would "lightly" don this color suggested a gendered frivolity to women's wearing of khaki, a "posturing" that male wearers would not possess. Furthermore, "women-kind" and "home" were explicitly portrayed as what men in khaki were "risking" themselves for; as the objects that inspire military action, women by definition could not participate in such action themselves.

Women who joined military-style organizations and wore khaki uniforms reacted vigorously to these complaints. In its recruiting literature, the WVR asserted that the organization "crystallizes into outward form the patriotism of women, and gives them a distinct place in the service of the state. . . . The attainment of physical fitness becomes a patriotic duty . . . made possible by the provision of drills in military uniform."[19] The WVR also issued regulations informing recruits that wearing jewelry or low-necked blouses with their uniforms exhibited a "lack of good taste," and explained that the uniform was "not merely a form of dress . . . [but] something to be respected."[20] An article in the *Brixton Free Press* provided a more mundane and common justification for the WVR costume itself: while "[t]he uniform of the corps has called forth considerable discussion, . . . it is a serviceable dress and its colour does not show dirt."[21]

A more profound defense of women in uniforms appeared in a December 1916 edition of *The Gentlewoman* in a poem by an anonymous member of the London Battalion of the Women's Volunteer Reserve:

> When we are gone
> You will remember then
> We wore the Sacred Khaki soberly
> As did the men.
>
> Quite well we know
> All that its colour shows—

Dust of the earth, to dust we all return
As also those

Who died; and so
To Mother Earth returned,
Gathered all tenderly unto her breast,
Their rest well earn'd.

We only work—
Yet if the work will stand,
Part have we too in this great Sacrament
Hand strength'ning hand.

For outward Sign
The colour shall suffice
The inward spirit of the Sacrament,
A Sacrifice.

The poem modestly claimed that women "only work"—and while it did not suggest a true parallel to a soldier's wearing of khaki—women's work nonetheless could be seen as being part of the national sacrifice.[22] The writer insisted that women wore the "sacred khaki soberly"—as men did—that it was not lightly donned. As an "outward Sign" the khaki color became an emblem of women's "inward spirit" of "Sacrifice." Nevertheless, the ultimate actor, the one who made the ultimate sacrifice, remained the fighting man, and the sexual division of patriotic labor remained unchanged. Beneath these verses, *The Gentlewoman* commented that this "should silence once and for all any adverse criticism on the Corps or its uniform."[23]

While claiming their right to wear uniforms as emblems of their service and sacrifice, women of the WVR had to defend themselves against charges that their actions were politically motivated. A February 1915 article in *Ladies' Pictorial* asserted that the WVR promoted "the ideal of comradeship among women regardless of social position," and photographs appearing in *The Bystander* the same month contrasted two types of "militant" behavior: that of prewar militant, out of control suffragettes and orderly of ranks of women in uniform, "militant servants" of king and country in 1915.[24] An April 1915 letter to the editor of the *Bournemouth Echo* argued further that women's uniforms could erase class differences: "In the Reserve we have no politics whatever, and no class distinctions, and every girl is welcomed who is able to pass the medical exam."[25] The denial of political motives for women's patriotic

The Bystander, February 17, 1915

Tempora Mutantur!

WOMEN BEFORE THE KING'S PALACE THEN AND NOW!

MILITANCY AS IT EXPRESSED ITSELF AT BUCKINGHAM PALACE LAST SUMMER

Two different versions of "militancy" that appeared in The Bystander, *17 February 1915. Courtesy of the Imperial War Museum.*

service was made even more explicit in a recruiting speech given in York by Mrs. Charlesworth, the head of the London branch of the Reserve. Charlesworth responded to objections about the Reserve's "military" activities, uniforms, and alleged "suffragette" links: "Some one would probably say: 'I know why you are doing this; I know what you are: You are a suffragette organiser.' As a matter of fact they were nothing of the kind. They were absolutely non-sectarian and non-political, and after the war was over they were not going to knock anybody down. (Laughter)."[26] Differentiating the WVR from the militant suffragettes who "knocked" people down and from associations with the women's suffrage campaign, the leadership of the Reserve aligned the WVR with a different kind of politics, one based on military service. They denied that women in uniform posed a political, that is, feminist, threat, even while some public commentators began to assert that women's military service could form the basis for claims to citizenship on par with men.[27]

Over the next year and a half of the war, the terms of the debate over women and military service began to shift. First came the failure of voluntary military recruitment, which was preceded by the creation of the National Register in 1915—established through a Parliamentary bill

MILITANCY AS IT EXPRESSED ITSELF AT THE SAME PALACE LAST WEEK
When the Women's Volunteer Reserve marched past the scene of former violence as militant servants of

that required householders to report the occupations and particulars of both men and women between sixteen and sixty-five. Since the war's outset, some women had argued for their right to serve the nation, and their arguments saw some success with their inclusion in the National Register.[28] That women were being counted in the register, however, did not meet with universal approval, and critics believed that women had other, more important national responsibilities, like caring for children. It might also be argued that the inclusion of women in the National Register made it seem less like a direct link to the Military Service Act of January 1916 and the eventual conscription of first unmarried and then married men made possible by this and subsequent legislation.[29] Some accepted the idea of compulsory service for women as a further means of freeing men for the fighting line around the same time that male conscription was enacted. In March 1916 in the *Pall Mall Gazette*, May Bateman proposed such compulsory service as a way for women to assume a "legitimate share of the common burden." A series of letters to the *Gazette* in response mainly supported the use of the register to achieve this end, although some objected that there were "limits to woman's effort which no amount of patriotic zeal will remove without serious results ensuing" and, in particular, that a woman's physical work should not come "at the expense of her children."[30]

Despite the exclusion of women from compulsory service, their contributions to the war effort received an important symbolic, national recognition in 1916 when they were allowed to receive military medals. As noted in the *Pall Mall Gazette,* this development recognized that women "should not be overlooked in an age when their tests and trials are almost of the same order of those of the men in the trenches." This decision, it continued, was not meant to spur the creation of "a race of Amazons springing from the barely cold ashes of Victorianism" but to reward "the ready enthusiasm, the calm heroism and devotion for which no medal is too great as a national recognition."[31] Service, a selfless dedication to the nation, had thus become something expected not only of men but also of women, and something that could be acknowledged in an equivalent manner.

Women in military uniforms also became more acceptable when, in the aftermath of instituting conscription, the government created the Women's Army Auxiliary Corps (WAAC)—which became the Queen Mary's Army Auxiliary Corps (QMAAC)—to free men for the fighting line.[32] Thus, only after men were subject to military conscription did the government endorse women's military service. The creation of the WAAC in 1917 made women in military uniform an increasingly familiar and, to an extent, an officially sanctioned, sight. Nonetheless, controversy continued over the appearance and behavior of women in uniform.

WAACs' wearing of khaki, interestingly enough, passed without comment when the organization's original leaders, Helen Gwynne Vaughan and Mona Chalmers Watson, proposed that the corps wear a "coat and skirt of Officer's khaki."[33] However, the suggestion that WAACs display insignia representing military rank provoked debate because wearers of "recognised military badges of rank" had to be saluted.[34] As the uniform's finishing touches were determined in late April 1917, the War Office insisted that "so long as it is clear that *military uniform is not to be adopted,*" it did not really matter what distinguishing badges were used.[35] Ultimately, WAAC officers of different grades wore a distinct number of embroidered emblems featuring a rose and/or fleur-de-lis. Although WAACs were technically serving the military, they were not in "military uniform" and could not be saluted, thus demonstrating that they were far removed from men in uniform.

Despite attaining the privilege of wearing khaki, WAACs continued to come under intense public scrutiny. The viability of the organization was called into question by a series of rumors of rampant sexual immorality, including reports of WAAC pregnancies and of WAACs serving as prostitutes.[36] As part of her analysis of the hostility "toward militarism in women," Jenny Gould has argued that "[d]uring the First World War people drew links, either consciously or unconsciously, between displays of militarism and masculine women, feminism, and lesbianism."[37] This was also the case with WVR members, who felt they had to defend their image as contributors to the national good by combating accusations that they were militant, mannish suffragettes in disguise.[38] Perhaps, then, the scandals about the WAAC, especially the heterosexual behavior of its rank and file overseas, were in some way a means of combating possible suggestions of lesbianism or "mannishness" in the women's army.[39]

However, the very suggestion of any sort of impropriety was viewed as causing a drop in recruitment and led the minister of labour, G. H. Roberts, to appoint a commission of inquiry. The WAACs were defended not just by government leaders like Roberts, but by important public figures like the archbishop of Canterbury. In January of 1918, the *Daily Sketch* asserted that the rumors about immoral relations between WAACs and those in the regular army were "so mischievous, that they are surely of pro-German or pacifist origin."[40] When the commission appointed to investigate the WAAC issued its report on 20 March 1918, it gave the corps a clean bill of health.[41]

Quite apart from the alleged scandals about the WAAC, the WAACs and the QMAACs—and their uniforms—elicited interest from the popular media. Writing for the *Ladies' Pictorial,* Ella Hepworth Dixon insisted that "[t]here is no coquetry about their working kit, but it is seemly and sensible."[42] Female reporters also visited WAACs in France and sought to reassure the fears of a potentially pessimistic audience, which worried that "when the girls come home [from France] . . . the country will be overrun by cigarette-crazed, mannish, self-opinionated creatures with short hair . . . and a distaste for domestic life." But, one reporter suggested, the "discipline of Army life . . . cannot smother the woman's heart beneath the khaki overcoat, cannot eradicate that homing instinct that is her birthright."[43] Even critics who commented that the khaki uniform gave women a snobbishly (and falsely) superior sense of themselves also suggested that "in nine cases out of ten, a tender heart beats beneath those manly trappings."[44]

As women in military-style uniforms became more acceptable, in part because they were constructed as quintessentially feminine, the woman out of uniform became suspect. By the last half of the war, the patriotism of the women in uniform was even more insistently contrasted with the lack of that of the shameful "slacker in petticoats."[45] In 1916, a correspondent for Britain's *Daily Mail* suggested that a popular recruiting poster be revised to picture a girl with her mother rather than her father so that "no idle girl . . . would be able to pass without twinges of conscience the picture of a grey-haired woman confronted by a pertinacious daughter demanding of her, 'Mother what did you do in the great war?' "[46] In October of 1917, following a speech by Sir Auckland Geddes on the need for recruits to the WAAC, several articles in the popular media began to critique "Women Slackers." In these pieces, the more traditionally dressed woman, the woman out of uniform, was now criticized for her lack of morality and patriotism.[47] In addition, proposals began to appear anew in the press in late 1917 arguing for the conscription of single and idle women, one suggesting that if conscription seemed harsh, then "National Service for Women" should be required.[48] By the spring of 1918, suggestions about conscripting women again appeared in the national and regional press. Proponents such as Lady Askwith argued that women would welcome conscription, "rejoicing that she is deemed worthy to serve in whatever capacity is deemed necessary."[49] Others, while denouncing the continued presence of women leading a "butterfly life" in England, argued that "there is no need for compulsory service on the lines suggested by certain well-meaning feminists, but there is a strong moral obligation on the part of women" to be willing to serve.[50]

While "slacking" had been a term that previously described men who refused the call to arms, its transposition to women helped establish national service as the norm for them as well. More importantly, it defined women's service as not a voluntary charity (a luxury) but the fulfillment of an obligation to the country. An image that appeared in the *Bystander* in February of 1918 under the heading of "The New Gallant" underscored this point. It approvingly noted the role reversals conjured by women in uniform by portraying one such woman giving her seat up to a well-dressed, overtly feminine "madam." The masculinity of the "new gallant" was evident not so much in the uniform—especially since she still wore a skirt—but in the masculine role she had taken on. There also seems to be an implicit criticism of the "madam" in the smirks of the crowd of men and women in the omnibus in response to the uniformed woman's gesture. Showing such images as the woman in uniform as a source of nonthreatening behavior helped to promote the permissibility of such wartime innovations in gendered behavior.[51]

The New Gallant

"TAKE MY SEAT, MADAM"

An image that appeared in the 6 February 1918 edition of The Bystander *depicting a woman in uniform giving up her seat on a bus. Courtesy of the Imperial War Museum.*

An insistence on the fundamental and unchangeable femininity of these women, despite their "mannish" costume also helped validate this altered behavior. In a 1917 article entitled "'WAACS' and Weddings," Hilda Love argued that even if women were dressed in "overalls, breeches, [or] uniforms," with their hair hidden away or cut, in whatever role they played as "national workers," nothing could hide their "bright faces and shining eyes." She also claimed that "of all the romantic unions of the war, surely none pleases the eye and the heart of the onlooker more than the wedding of a khaki man and a khaki-clad girl."[52]

At the outset of the war, women in militarized or masculinized uniforms were criticized as being somehow not normal and were even linked to questionable sexuality or morality, although some of these attitudes would change once male conscription was adopted. This resulted in a great deal of effort to demonstrate that women in uniforms, participating in work of fundamental national importance, were still quintessentially feminine. Uniformed women's efforts to assert that they were directly participating in the war were constantly undermined by a rhetoric that claimed that women's, even military women's, main contribution was to serve the men serving the nation.[53]

The Civic Virtues of Les Françaises

Although French women did not form voluntary battalions or join the military as British women did, they were called upon to participate actively in supporting the *union sacrée*. In creating charitable organizations and performing a myriad of tasks, they demonstrated their service to the nation. Earlier chapters in this book have analyzed fictional representations of women's service and debates about female factory workers, and research by historians such as Laura Lee Downs, Françoise Thébaud, and Margaret Darrow have examined women's patriotism as expressed through such activities as war work and nursing.[54] More generally, a range of contemporaneous public commentary from across the political spectrum attempted to address the women of France and to document their contributions to the nation, highlighting both their "services" and their "sacrifices." Although French women's war service was largely less controversial than British women's military service, French women nonetheless found themselves figuring out how to express their own versions of patriotism in an acceptable manner.

While French women did not don military uniforms, French feminists reacted positively to the idea of British women's military service as early as 1915. In a front-page article in *La Française*, editor Jane

Misme noted that the warm welcome shown to members of British women's volunteer associations like the WVR by French public opinion was "miraculous" given the hostility with which the idea had been initially received. She also criticized earlier reports that insisted that these women were "suffragettes," implying that only women courageous enough to "break windows" in pursuit of their rights were capable of serving in uniform. She rejected the idea that militant feminism was behind the feminist triumph of having women serve in the army, which allowed women to choose their path to national service. Instead, she asserted that, given the upheavals of war, the WVR represented "the first *révanche* of feminine nature." To those who said such actions would never be seen in France, Misme responded that this resulted simply from the difference between living in a country with conscription and one without. It was not because "feminine aptitudes were different in France," argued Misme, citing requests from women in the Puy-de-Dôme and elsewhere who were willing to perform any type of service that "would prove that they were as courageous and disciplined as soldiers." Misme concluded by insisting that "[i]n France also, if one wanted, one could have feminine regiments of practical service for the army."[55] Another commentator, after retelling the story of brave Parisian Denise Cartier, a fifteen year old injured in an air raid, noted that here was proof that "if the women of France, as in England, could be formed into regiments for active service in the army . . . no doubt that Paris would furnish a fine regiment."[56]

Such assertions aside, French women only slowly found ways to serve the military directly. In early 1916, feminist groups were singled out for their patriotic work, for doing everything from sewing for soldiers, to sustaining "morale" throughout Paris (by providing alternatives to more decadent and costly amusements), to creating the "Corps Volontaire de Défense Nationale des Femmes Françaises et Belges" in order to train women to serve as military auxiliaries.[57] A year after Misme's discussion of the WVR, Thérèse Casevitz-Rouff, writing in the same journal, spoke of how proposals that women do auxiliary military work had gone from being controversial to becoming a "poignant reality." Women had begun to help cook and do other work in military hospital units, without agitating; they "silently" performed these tasks "with all their force, all their intelligence and all their devotion."[58] Headlines in *Le Petit Journal* in November of that year would praise such women serving the army for "doing the housekeeping of France."[59] By the end of 1916, leaders of the Conseil National des Femmes Françaises (CNFF) had begun to promote and publicize the notion of a civil mobilization of women, asking them "to consecrate themselves to the national defense" by creating an "army of women" ready to serve France.[60] Others predicted that French women would be as capable as British women of forming "regiments" of "active service" in the army.[61]

At a meeting of the group Action des Femmes in 1916, some feminists sought to promote the additional idea that the war had both led to a "more tight collaboration between man and woman" and further allowed women to prove their physical strength, that they were not "feeble being[s]." Speakers also criticized men for insisting that women remain delicate and praised British women for their physical development. However, this comment prompted a man in attendance to cry out: "[T]he English woman is not agreeable to a man, she more resembles a male than a female." The meeting was then so disrupted by conversation that it came to an abrupt end, suggesting that the model provided by "amazonish" and patriotic British women did not meet with complete approval.[62]

Many writers focused on two central themes regarding the war and the women of France. They praised the *mater dolorosa,* and the brave sacrifices made by sisters, wives, and, of course, mothers. Often at the same time, though, writers self-consciously called attention to the fact that something "new" was happening to women, something unexpected. Loyalty to the French nation not only transcended political, religious, and class differences but also, as these works tenuously expressed, sex differences. An article by Émile Bergerat proclaimed: "[T]he woman of 1915 will have liberated the fair sex and, this time . . . by the sole exercise of her proper virtues, by being [a] woman." In contrast to the feminist agitation experienced at the end of the turn of the twentieth century, "honor" had returned to French women. They had "stoically" replaced the warriors that the *patrie* had taken from them and had preserved "our laws, our mores, our vital institutions . . . even our soil." Bergerat singled out for praise the woman who carried her "little ones on her back" while making the factories hum.[63] Later in the war, the kinds of "new" behavior that women exhibited were recorded in articles that compared women who simply maintained family businesses to "new amazons."[64]

Laudatory evocations of the sacrifices made by the women, particularly the mothers, of France appeared in a number of book-length texts. Yvonne Pitrois's *Femmes de 1914–1915* detailed women's patriotic volunteer work but also paid close attention to the mother, who was "giving more than her life" by giving her son to the nation. Pitrois illustrated this point by recounting an anecdote of a group of police officers coming across a sobbing old woman near Verdun kneeling beside a newly made grave. When questioned, the woman explained that all six of her sons had been killed in the war and she had come to cry over the grave of her sixth and youngest. "Profoundly moved, not knowing what to say in the face of such distress," the men presented arms to the woman, who cried out through her sobs, "Vive la France, quand même!" Pitrois believed that the overwhelming majority of French women had shown themselves ready for "all sacrifices," even though she acknowledged the "astonishing" existence of women who were still "vain" and "frivolous," an indication that not all slackers in petticoats were British. However, such "sacrilege" in no way diminished the significant contributions of mothers, who were "the first victims of this atrocious war." Maternal suffering meant that "[r]ich or poor, great ladies or women of the people found each other in their identical abnegation."[65]

Women's femininity and even their frivolity found some defenders. A front-page article in May 1917 in *Le Figaro* exonerated women who acted like women, by buying new dresses for instance. In general, writers who extolled the virtuous solidarity of women across class lines noted their shared sacrifices.[66] As Jacques Flach of the Collège de France put it in his introduction to the 1916 *Les jeunes filles françaises et la guerre:* "From women of fashion to women of the people, from religious to lay works, everywhere there is the same enthusiasm, the same patriotic fervor, the same spirit of absolute sacrifice, simple and delicate, gracious and serious. The young girl will devote herself until death with the same natural ease and charm that she showed in times of peace in the most simple activities of life." This emphasis on women's capacity for self-sacrifice reified traditional notions of their "feminine" qualities. The wonder of these young girls for Flach was that they had "a largeness of soul equal to the exploits of our soldiers."[67] Woman's sacrifice for family had been deliberately shifted to sacrifice for the nation, a notion consistent with a prewar republican ideology that had become even more important during the war. The young women of France were also praised for their capacity to act with the "same" ease and charm, as if war had affected nothing. Thus, the role of women was not only to be capable of new sacrifices unto death, done with grace and delicacy, but to maintain the necessary illusion that war had "altered nothing," that the "home" was preserved and that they, despite their "new" activities, remained unchanged. Indeed, Jules Combarieu stressed that women demonstrated their capacity for great courage that arose from a "collective mentality where the passionate desire to be useful was not the sum but the product of individual desires, multiplied one by another."[68]

In his *La maison anxieuse* (1916), Lucien Descaves also noted that the war "has provoked among women an admirable movement of solidarity" all dedicated to serving France and, as significantly, to holding on (*tenir*), which he defined as equaling two things: "believing" and "being quiet." Descaves described the many tasks performed by women but suggested that the *patrie* "had no rival more redoubtable than the mother. She had the last word. She gave her son; she takes him back when he is no longer good for anything—only for a mother." Yet her heroism was such that it demanded neither admiration nor condolences.[69]

Through their focus on women's—primarily mothers'—sacrifices of their menfolk, many of these works even echoed feminist pacifist appeals by locating women in relation to men and to suffering, a suffering that now ennobled and even empowered them. Wartime calls for their assistance laid claim to *all* women, regardless of class, age, region, or political affiliation, often by focusing on their familial responsibilities. National unity meant that the *patriote* superseded all other categories, a notion that was confirmed by nonfictional accounts of French women and the Great War that exhibited a striking singularity of purpose across political lines. All of these texts aimed to persuade women that through their substitute work, their sacrifices, their ability to "hold on," they vitally demonstrated their "feminine" services to men and the nation. The politicization of these ideas in more explicit debates about women's suffrage would become a common and shared theme in both France and Britain.

British Women's Suffrage and the War

While scholars no longer agree that British women's support for the First World War gained them the vote, the limited enfranchisement of British women in 1918 continues to be associated with changes in both women's wartime roles and the general perception of these contributions. Historians such as Ellen DuBois and Susan Kent have emphasized that women's asking for the vote was a radical demand. However, the wartime rhetoric attached to women's public activism as well as to the struggles for women's enfranchisement demonstrates that even radical demands could be recast by wartime gender ideology.[70] Moreover, British feminists in all the major suffrage organizations were divided over whether or not to support the war at its outset, and especially over whether or not to utilize the link between motherhood and women's peacefulness that was already part of the prewar feminist movement.[71] Paradoxically, one route to patriotic political action came from the prewar link between motherhood and militarism, specifically as the engine of imperialism.[72] And both of these aspects of women's relationship to politics as mothers were evident in wartime debates about British women's services and sacrifices and their political rights.

From the war's outset, feminists began to appeal for an officially sanctioned form of political participation for women. On 8 August 1914, Sylvia Pankhurst wrote an editorial for the newspaper of the East London Federation of Suffragettes that denounced Europe's decline into "barbarism." Pankhurst insisted that women "will bear the harder part of the suffering. . . . All the women of the world need votes. They need a powerful voice in moulding the policy of nations. To-day all the women's organisations of the World call for peace, but the men-made Government's [*sic*] of Europe rush heedless on to war."[73] Despite this claim, there was little unanimity and no overwhelming, one-sided stand for "peace" taken by the "women's organisations of the World."

As discussed earlier, many women and many feminists rushed eagerly to demonstrate their capacity to serve the nation and argued for the right to do so in national uniforms and as officially sanctioned members of the armed forces. Suffrage militancy was suspended, and suffragists and suffragettes found themselves being praised in daily newspapers as "Voteless Patriots" doing "Great Work in National Relief."[74] As early as November 1914 journalist Ella Hepworth Dixon found it remarkable that suffragists had thrown their organization and resources into the national cause: "In so acting, as political bodies, they have shown . . . themselves more patriotic and public-spirited than the men who refuse them the vote. . . . This war has proved once and for all that the women are as useful to the State as the men." Dixon emphasized what would become a fairly common wartime refrain: by demonstrating their "usefulness" to the state, women deserved to receive full political rights.[75]

Given the nature of women's contributions to war, a variety of public figures used the war as an occasion to change—at least publicly—their opinions about suffrage for women.[76] Newspapers and periodicals not only reported the "extraordinary" contributions of women, they also noted the conversion experiences of those who had previously opposed women's suffrage. As a February 1915 article in the *Nation* observed: "Wars . . . are not supported merely by soldiers; behind them stand a great body of non-combatants. . . . Women have their full share. . . . The exclusion of women from political life is, therefore, not a smaller, but a greater injustice in times of war and of great political disturbance than in a period of peace."[77] Writing in response to this article, Holford Knight offered his perspective: "In my view, this horrible war destroys the grounds on which Liberals have resisted the inclusion of women in the electorate. At the close of the war there is bound to be a shifting of electoral issues to . . . domestic questions in which women will be not only directly interested but actively participant in their settlement."[78] And in June of 1915, the *Sheffield Daily Telegraph* reported a statement from an unnamed general: "I was clean against the franchise for women before the war, but if a woman was to ask me now to support that movement I should not be able to find it in my conscience to refuse. Women's work out here has been magnificent."[79]

Given prewar controversy over the women's vote and these newly expressed sentiments, once the issue of electoral reform emerged during the war, proponents of women's suffrage argued that their demands had to be considered. When rumors began to circulate in early 1916 that legislation was being considered to allow all men serving overseas to vote, the largest women's suffrage organization, the NUWSS, decided to take action.[80] With the Executive Committee's help, Millicent Garrett Fawcett, the NUWSS leader, drafted a letter to Prime Minister Asquith drawing attention to suffragists' efforts to "alleviate distress arising out of the war" and to their "active, self-sacrificing and efficient national service."[81] In reply, Asquith denied that such legislative changes to the franchise were contemplated but recognized that any such alterations would have to take into account "the magnificent contribution which the women of the United Kingdom have made to the maintenance of our country's cause."[82] The NUWSS nonetheless mobilized suffragists by creating an umbrella organization of women's suffrage groups that would be ready to respond quickly to franchise reform in the spring of 1916. A memorandum from this Consultative Committee of Women's Suffrage Societies in August 1916 urged Asquith that if new qualifications for voting were "to be established based on services in the war then the claim of women to share in such a qualification cannot be ignored." Significantly, however, the memorandum not only noted the contributions of women war workers but also added that "there is another body of women who deserve, we think, even better of the country . . . and they are the women who have given their husbands and sons ungrudgingly."[83]

By the summer of 1916, the issue of franchise reform, which included women, was on the table. Accounts of prominent converts, like Asquith, to women's suffrage appeared in publications like the *Observer* and the *Weekly Dispatch*.[84] Commenting on Asquith's change of heart, the feminist writer Cicely Hamilton offered this perspective on what the possible granting of the vote would mean to women:

> [W]hat would once have been a triumph will now be merely an event. . . . I seem to remember from pre-war days many fervid and doubtless honest speeches which more than hinted that the parliamentary vote in the hands of woman would be a key to a new resplendent heaven and most amiable earth. . . . [T]his generation has . . . learned by fiery and bitter experience the actual small value of its vote. . . . [W]e shall take it . . . not as a talisman, but soberly and without illusion.[85]

Two years into the war, some feminists had already lost confidence in women's influence as voters. However, this did not prevent others from using older, prewar arguments or pressing women's right to the franchise, even in the midst of war. The lead article in *The Englishwoman* in November of 1916 outlined one crucial means by which women could argue for the vote, particularly during wartime. It discussed the newly popularized idea that "National Service" should form the basis for the franchise and, thus, women could not be excluded from any potential changes therein.[86]

The ways in which the terms of debate were set by members of Parliament echoed wider discussions about how women's services made them the equals of the men in the armed forces, men who were universally seen as having earned the franchise. The first wartime discussions of electoral reform in the House of Commons made evident how the idea of women's service could be explicitly connected to their receiving the vote. As, by now the former prime minister, Asquith put it in March of 1917: "Short of actually bearing arms in the field, there is hardly a service which has contributed, or is contributing, to the maintenance of our cause in which women have not been at least as active and as efficient as men, and wherever we turn we see them doing, with zeal and success, and without any detriment to the prerogatives of their sex, work which three years ago would have been regarded as falling exclusively within the province of men."[87] Here, as in other aspects of the debate, Asquith made the notion of "active" and "efficient" service, short of bearing arms itself, the cornerstone for women's participation in politics. However, this service alone did not suffice, because he also called attention to the fact that women had not acted with "any detriment to the prerogatives of their sex," which seemed clearly to be familial, if not overtly maternal, responsibilities. Other converts such as Walter Long referred to women's serving the men serving the nation, "women who have meant so much to our soldiers in the trenches, and who have suffered so much with our soldiers, . . . women who have not only suffered and died for their country in many of the fields of war, but, let there be no mistake, without whose heroism, self-denial, skill and physical strength and endurance, this country would never have successfully faced the crisis."[88] Despite some continued opposition, the majority of M.P.s adopted the principles of electoral reform, and voted later in 1917 to approve the Representation of the People Bill, giving the vote to women over the age of thirty who had certain property qualifications.[89]

Commentators reacted swiftly to the passage of franchise reform in the House of Commons on 19 June 1917. Margaret Heitland was quick to point out the effect of the war on this victory. She argued that the war had revealed "that every man and every woman, too, must join the forces directly or indirectly. . . . All the vapid talk about 'women's place being in the home' . . . revealed itself as mere emptiness." For, as Heitland further explained, war had not so much altered the significance of women's contributions as shown "the need which arises for making the most of all effective citizens by a state or nation whenever that state particularly needs support."[90] Nonetheless there was continued public objection to the granting of the vote to women, particularly without the say of those serving overseas.[91]

Still, a volume of important essays published in 1917 acknowledged that the granting of the vote to women seemed imminent. This collection included essays on the consequences of the war for women's voting and other issues. Collectively titled *The Making of Women,* it included essays by Maude Royden, who discussed both "modern love" and "the future of the woman's movement," and by Eleanor Rathbone, who wrote on "the remuneration of women's services" and outlined the plan for endowment of motherhood, a topic examined briefly in Chapter 3. What is significant about this taking stock of feminism as women's suffrage was being debated is how closely women's services were tied to motherhood. Rathbone wrote that the two most important bodies of women to be considered after the war were "the industrial workers and the working-class mothers."[92] And when Royden was considering the future of the women's movement, she pointed out that while war was the enemy of feminism and women, the nation had now discovered that "war itself can no longer, under modern conditions, be carried on successfully without their help." Royden was confident as well that since the state needed children, it would encourage motherhood, and, furthermore, as women entered political life they might strengthen it by bringing "their peculiar quality and experience for the enrichment of the State."[93] In an essay directly concerned with women's suffrage, Ralph Rooper cautioned against expecting too much of the women's vote, although it would represent a step towards greater justice. Rooper accepted that many people had been won to the cause "by the sight of uniformed women carrying on the nation's business" when they had not been persuaded by peacetime arguments. He did offer the hope that since "war on a modern scale has gone far to upset any differentiation between the sexes" in terms of their necessity to the state in securing victory, "the political recognition of women cannot but help to acclimatize the idea that force is not the only and final arbiter of human relationships."[94] Not all would agree with his assessment, however.

Opponents of women's suffrage pointed out in January 1918 that women's responsibility to the nation during the war was not a factor in the bill that Parliament had been debating. Rather, they argued, "this large majority of women workers under thirty years of age are not to be enfranchised. . . . [A]lthough the nation has made its chief call upon them, and although they have responded so fully, they are yet not regarded as qualified to vote. . . . [I]nstead of giving votes to these younger women, we enfranchise their mothers, and aunts, and grandmothers. The position is as illogical as can be imagined."[95] While one could attack this limited enfranchisement as "illogical," feminist leaders such as Millicent Fawcett capitalized on these ideas, suggesting the important "domestic" expertise that women would bring to the polity.[96]

When the Representation of the People Bill reached the House of Lords, which had long been the center of opposition to women's suffrage, proponents there again made the association between women's service and enfranchisement. This idea was then rebuffed by Viscount Bryce: "Was it for the sake of it [the vote] that they [women] gave us their services so freely in such a noble and unselfish spirit? . . . To think this would be to disparage their sense of duty and their sense of patriotism."[97] In other words, only unselfish and uncalculated actions counted as true service. These words echo those of WVR members, who insisted that their service was apolitical and not done for "suffragette" reasons. Lord Sydenham similarly declared that women did not have the franchise in mind when they aided the country in its hour of need. He also implied that these actions did not entitle women to vote, as he compared British women with "the women of France [who] have shown just the same shining patriotism, and . . . [whose] burden of additional work . . . cannot be less than that which our own women are now so bravely bearing."[98]

Challenging this line of argument in general and the claims of Bryce in particular, other members of the Lords insisted that while women doubtless gave their all with no expectation of reward, they still deserved the vote. They merited it for demonstrating "as high a conception of the duties of citizenship as the men, and [for] hav[ing] been as willing as the men, to the extent of their power, to face its perils and bear its burdens."[99] In later debates, those opposed to women's suffrage suggested that men "had an indescribably greater share in the sufferings of war" and thus changes in the suffrage law should be restricted to enfranchising fighting men. To this Lord Buckmaster responded: "[I]f women have not been called upon to lay down their lives for the sake of their country, they have been called upon to bear the loss of lives far dearer than their own." Buckmaster also referred to the women of Belgium, who endured "their persons violated . . . their houses ruined, their children slain before their eyes. . . . I do not for a moment accept the principle that the vote can be determined by attempting to weigh and to measure the different degree of suffering which men and women have to bear in the appalling tragedy and calamity of war."[100] The Lords, too, approved the final passage of the Representation of the People Bill. In 1918, British women over thirty, who themselves qualified as local electors or were married to those who did, finally gained the parliamentary franchise as a right of citizenship.[101]

R. M. Wilson answered critics of the passage of women's suffrage with images not only of the work that women contributed to the war effort but also of the sacrifices that they had suffered as mothers. Wilson's 1918 study *Wife: Mother: Voter* begins by recounting the battle of Ypres. What did this battle have in common with women's suffrage? The answer was dramatically provided:

Upon the plains of Ypres and of all France our dead are sleeping, the sons of the mothers of England who bore them and suffered for them through all the hard days of child hood. . . .

Not men alone are sleeping there on the fields of France. Women, too, mothers . . . have mingled blood with the fallen on the stricken fields.

"You cannot conduct an A1 Empire with a C3 population." But, thanks to the Mothers of England, the numbers of C3 men were smaller by far.[102]

It was because of this that all must understand how "well" it was "that the wives and mothers of England shall wield the Balance of Power" in the postwar era.[103]

Attributing the success and bravery of British men to the mothers who "bred" them, Wilson argued for a secure maternity that women's votes would bring about. Proclaiming motherhood as women's "greatest glory," Wilson nonetheless suggested that its sacrifices might be too high and that one of the urgent tasks of new women voters would be to secure state support for motherhood. Wilson was confident that the "women of Britain" would even defend the unmarried mother. In viewing women voters as insuring reforms for women and children, Wilson insisted on the equivalency of the activities of mothering and soldiering, and on children as national assets: "If shells and guns are to be obtained only by paying wages, is it an unreasonable proposition that the men behind the guns, the women behind the shells, should likewise be obtained by paying wages. The producer of a man is at least as worthy of remuneration as the producer of a shell or a gun."[104] Thus, the idea that women's suffrage would create radical social change was muted by insisting on women's primacy as mothers.

Wilson's efforts to make sense of women's enfranchisement in this way also resonated among feminist leaders. Millicent Garrett Fawcett suggested in a speech in 1918 that the newly enfranchised women over thirty could represent a specific group of women: "No one is likely to forget that a very large proportion, fully five-sixths, of the new women voters are wives and mothers. . . . From some points of view it may almost be regarded as a motherhood franchise."[105] And she was not the last to point out this connection. Nearly a year later, *The Labour Woman,* reporting on efforts to fully enfranchise women, quoted this statement: "There is no greater, grander word in the English language than that of 'mother.' We have conceded the vote to the older mothers and let us now concede it to the younger and the potential mothers."[106]

Thus the manner in which women gained this part of the full rights of citizens continued to be interpreted in terms that highlighted the femininity of new women voters, their fundamental difference from male voters. Despite controversy surrounding conscripting women and thereby treating their contributions to the nation as being as necessary as men's, women's services—either voluntary or remunerative—remained largely separate from those of men. Ultimately, it was their relationship to men and to the state as mothers that remained the core of their claims to national identity.

The Politics of French Women's Sacrifices

The idea that women deserved political recognition because of their wartime services or sacrifices was not restricted to Britain. In France, as in Britain, from the initial days of the war, women were called upon to serve the nation. As early as 25 August 1914, the two leaders of the influential Conseil National des Femmes Françaises wrote to their members to implore them to do "their duty and more than their duty" in the midst of the nation's trauma. "We will go to work like our soldiers to the fire, without reproach and without fear," they continued, "we will be proud to be women of our time, those who have finally become the true companions of man."[107] Promoting feminist support of the national cause did not necessarily suggest women were men's equals; rather, at least initially, being men's "true companions" was deemed sufficient.

Yet as the war progressed, discussions of women's contributions became linked to suggestions that their services might lead to political rights. For example, one writer reflecting on what the war had done for women emphasized the war's transformative effect on women and linked this with the concept of citizenship: "[T]he energy of women has become a magnificent reality. . . . Rich or poor, ignorant or learned, those who still have youth and those who can no longer remember it, all, [are] inflamed and ennobled by the revelation of their new roles, . . . finally female citizens, and not only wives, mothers, sisters or daughters of citizens."[108] In one phrase a decisive leap occurs between women being attached to male *citoyens* to being *citoyennes* in their own right. Women who were more overtly feminist also spoke of women gaining the right to be *citoyennes*. A large meeting organized by the Ligue des Droits de L'Homme in April 1916 focused on "showing" the role played by women during the war and "indicating what rights should result."

At this meeting, speakers noted that women "had shown . . . that they were capable of achieving in the best manner the title of *citoyenne*."[109]

As the war continued, feminists themselves used their work and their loyalty as evidence that they deserved political rights. In April 1916, Marguerite de Witt-Schlumberger, speaking at the annual congress of the Union Française pour le Suffrage des Femmes, put forth the idea of a narrow correlation "between the war and the rights reclaimed by feminists." Since suffrage for women was based on "justice," its "triumph" was "intimately linked" to the war, to "our work and our efforts for the country and her defenders." Moreover, as others at the meeting noted, only when women had the right to vote could they ameliorate certain conditions that the war had exacerbated. While not wishing to disturb the nation during its struggle to win the war, feminists urged women not to forget the need to create a strong feminist movement, particularly in the provinces.[110]

Further, the complicated links between maternity and women's worth predominated in how sacrifices were tied to political expression. These ideas appeared in a range of writings on women, whether written from the perspective of a noted right-wing member of the French Academy, such as Maurice Barrès, or from that of Léon Abensour, Clemenceau's secretary and historian of feminism. In many of these wartime views, the language and content were remarkably similar.

However, few commentators were as extreme in their opinions as Barrès. In one of the frequent articles he wrote for his column, "Chronique de la grande guerre," appearing in *L'Écho de Paris* in February 1916, Barrès popularized the idea of directly associating women's political rights with their bodily sacrifices for the nation. He proposed that "the widows of soldiers who have died for the *patrie* receive the ballot paper of him who is no longer able to protect the interests of his small family."[111] Wives and, in the cases of unmarried men and the absence of another male head of household, mothers would inherit the rights of their "gloriously fallen" husbands and sons in recognition of their sacrifice for the nation. A woman who had lost a close male relative would thus receive a kind of "suffrage for the dead." For, as Barrès elaborated several months later, "by what more noble door would [the women of France] wish to enter public life? . . . The mother receiving the powers of her son, the wife of her husband, the daughter of her father, what grandeur! *Les voilà citoyennes* [There they are citizens]."[112] Although other writers had suggested that women might earn full political rights by *service* to the nation, few of them had equated this acquisition with the loss of one's husband, son, or father.[113] Thus what could be seen as the ordinary virtuous behavior of women became politicized, resulting from either a reconception of women's public role or an extreme glorification of the sorrowing mother.

In either case, a number of feminists rejected these arguments. Responding almost immediately to Barrès's proposal, Jane Misme editorialized in *La Française* that while he "judged that mothers and widows of the war could vote so that the will of the dead could be heard . . . all women like all men should vote in order that the will of the living be heard, so that no interest could be neglected."[114] A letter responding to Misme, in contrast, said that "glorifying the dead by according the right to vote to mothers and widows was good, [yet] it was necessary to replace those who had disappeared. Why not compensate mothers of more than four children by also conferring on them the right to vote?"[115] Thus would women who served the nation by providing as well as sacrificing children be honored. Some feminists sided with Misme and were appalled by the idea of gaining political rights through death. Nelly Roussel responded: "No, M. Barrès, we women of conscience do not want your injurious generosity. We do not want to think for another, to speak for another."[116]

Other feminists agreed with Barrès. At a 1916 meeting of the Union Française pour le Suffrage des Femmes, Marguerite de Witt-Schlumberger "expressed the opinion that the widows and mothers of soldiers fallen in the field of honor should have the right to vote in the place of their husbands and sons."[117] The issue continued to be discussed by feminists into 1917. At a meeting of the group Action des Femmes, Anne Léal displayed her displeasure with any and all such "half-measures" when women had "in a certain measure contributed to the defense of the country."[118] Despite disagreement on this particular point, the vast majority of feminists felt that they were aiding the cause of women by their cooperation in the war effort, whether or not they expected their services or sacrifices to be noticed and rewarded.[119]

Léon Abensour's *Les vaillantes* presented a view of the wartime transformation of women's worth that was more sympathetic to feminist aims. After citing the tasks in all aspects of life that women had performed so well, Abensour wondered if the future would bring "complete equality"—suggesting a possible rewarding of women's new roles by the granting of political rights. Concluding that this remained unknowable, he nevertheless suggested that women be given a municipal vote: "One has seen women discussing in an assembly, directing a village, administrating a city, safeguarding immense interests in perilous times. Proof has been shown that with their different qualities, . . . they are as able as men to govern the city. . . . France, victorious but exhausted, should, for its large effort of renewal, requisition all its strength, all its intelligence." He came close to proposing new rights for women based on their wartime contributions and potential to provide future aid to the nation. However, Abensour also ridiculed the writers and publicists who "have shown us woman totally transformed by the magnificent virtue of the war." He observed that, before the war, most women were already "mothers of families, conscious of their duties," and they deserved praise for their "maternal" qualities, for raising the soldiers of France. By early 1917, one concrete and important recognition of women's receiving some new rights along these lines can be seen in the "loi Violette," which for the first time authorized women to be guardians of their children.[120]

The idea of giving women a municipal vote also divided feminists. At a meeting of Action des Femmes in July 1917, Irma Perrot complained about various plans to give women partial votes. She then attacked the organization Suffrage des Femmes for being satisfied with women receiving a municipal vote; Action des Femmes called for an "integral vote" or nothing.[121] In 1917, a new organization, Comité d'Action Suffragiste, led by Jeanne Mélin, began to agitate for suffrage for women on the same terms as men. At their meetings throughout the winter of 1918, speakers such as Mélin urged renewed agitation for women's suffrage. Even if a municipal vote might have been acceptable prior to the war, she argued, women now needed full political rights and, in order to achieve them, they had to act. Mélin, comparing France to other countries, declared: "French women, who had perhaps suffered most, had neither the rights of election nor the eligibility!" In a "civilized" nation, added another speaker, this should be a source of "shame."[122]

More public debates concerning women's suffrage continued to offer the alternative of giving women a vote *debout les morts* or a vote *familial*. The question of women's suffrage had been reopened in France—as in Britain—in 1917 with these proposals and alternative ones suggesting that women receive the vote at the later age of twenty-five, not twenty-one, and that they be barred from electing senators. At the 1917 annual congress of the Union Française pour le Suffrage des Femmes, Pauline Rebour reported on the ideas of *suffrage des morts* and *suffrage familial*, as well as alternatives proposed by the Chamber of Deputies'

Commission du Suffrage Universel. Rebour then urged that women be granted the right to vote in the next municipal elections. Deputy Louis Marin also spoke of the proposed measures regarding women's suffrage, protesting against placing more age restrictions on women than on men.[123] In December 1917, at a meeting of the Comité d'Action Suffragiste, Alice La Marzière declared that, given the important roles women had undertaken during the war, they should receive the right to vote, placing them on an equal footing with men.[124]

Developments across the channel also inspired French feminists. Writing in April 1917, Marie Grimmer noted that in Britain the valuable work being performed by women had been recognized by Parliament and that in France there had been similarly "a sensible augmentation of the partisans of Suffrage in the Chamber and the Senate." A woman, continued Grimmer, would not be content only to be admired. "[S]he must profit by this admiration in order to obtain the right to preserve in the future the race to which, adding this ancient duty to her new task, she continues to give birth." [125] As the war approached its end in the autumn of 1918, other French feminists turned to the example provided by Britain in granting women's suffrage and to the reasons why a comparable measure in France was so urgently needed. In an article in *La Voix des Femmes,* Monette Thomas concurred with Grimmer: women needed to "protect life" and to "save humanity" once they had political rights. The "current goal of 'suffragism' was to soon admit women to civic equality with men . . . to aid them . . . in establishing peace." With both sexes voting, they could "collaborate" on helping France rebuild, repopulate, and "stop the carnage and prepare peace." [126]

Political figures like Joseph Barthélemy, both a professor of constitutional law and a deputy in the Chamber, also began to consider the question of women's voting in light of the war. In a series of lectures given in late 1917 through 1918 and published as *Le vote des femmes* (1920), Barthélemy put forth detailed arguments in favor of women's suffrage. After noting in his preface that the "cataclysm" of war could have underlined the inequalities between the sexes but had instead enlarged "the horizon of women," he went on to offer a "scientific" study of the woman's vote and its possible consequences.[127] Barthélemy carefully considered various special cases in which the interests of women might require political representation; he surveyed issues ranging from girls' education, to the rights of single women, to the question of married women's nationality, to the problems faced by mothers and, in view of the war's costs, widows. He noted that the "global war" had caused women to be "uprooted from the hearth" and that many, regrettably or not, would not resume their places there. Thus the female worker needed the vote to defend her livelihood and her rights.[128] Once he had detailed the reasons that women should possess the right to vote, Barthélemy took on objections to this line of reasoning, including the argument that women's failure to provide military service disqualified them from voting. After weighing various aspects of this issue, he concluded that nature "has imposed on women a social service more important, as painful and as dangerous as military service: that's maternity service."[129] The final chapter of *Le vote des femmes* emphasized that no compelling argument existed to deny men and women equal suffrage.

Legislative proposals, however, despite the renewed efforts of French feminists, lagged behind their British counterparts. There have been several significant historical interpretations of the debates over women's suffrage in the French legislature between 1919 and 1922. Steven Hause has emphasized the lack of a grassroots, provincial, and thus truly national French women's suffrage movement. A more recent interpretation by Paul Smith has returned to older arguments about republican anticlericalism and fears that, because of their greater Catholic religiosity, enfranchised women would vote according to their priests' dictates. However, Smith has also stressed that women's suffrage was simply unacceptable to key political figures, especially among Radicals, and that Radical opposition meant that the "republican consensus" was at stake in these discussions. The potentially disunifying cost of women's suffrage on any scale was seen as too high.[130]

However "inevitable" the failure of women's suffrage in France may thus have looked, it is worth examining how, after the war's end in May 1919, key political opinions had shifted so that women's suffrage as well as women's ability to stand in municipal elections came up for a vote in the Chamber of Deputies. In the course of these debates, the familial vote, as an alternative to "integral" suffrage, almost passed. As discussed earlier in this chapter, the familial vote was based on the idea that the head of the family had a vote in order to represent that family and thus widowed mothers might require the vote since they served as replacements for the absent male head of the family.[131] Yet as these discussions continued, the Chamber eventually adopted a bill that called for the vote for women on the same terms as men.[132]

The French Senate, like the British House of Lords, had long been a serious obstacle preventing women's suffrage. Yet, unlike its British counterpart, the Senate proved resistant to new efforts to enfranchise women in the context of the war. However, in response to proposals in the Chamber of Deputies, the Senate did discuss the different terms upon which women might receive the vote in the immediate aftermath of the war. In a delaying tactic, the bill passed by the Chamber in May 1919 was put to a special Senate subcommittee, where it languished. Yet that same month, right-wing senator Dominique Delahaye expressed dismay over the lack of action on his proposal *debout les morts,* which would give "the vote to the replacements of those who had died in the war." After citing the tolls of two million men dead or missing from the war, Delahaye passionately argued that "these widows deprived of their husbands, these mothers deprived of their children, these daughters deprived of their fathers, these sisters deprived of their brothers had no one to offer them a hand." He further suggested that with the Chamber's proposition of a "generalized" vote for women, his measure "would be the sole line of retrenchment." [133] A discussion of the vote *familial* later in 1919 met with no more success than did Delahaye's proposal. [134]

With great reluctance, as historians have documented, in early October 1919, the Senate's commission that had been considering the Chamber's proposal on women's suffrage and eligibility, under the leadership of Alexandre Bérard, brought forward its report. In what became known in the feminist press as Bérard's "fourteen points," he detailed the reasons that women's suffrage and eligibility for elected office should be denied by the Senate. These points included the idea — akin to Viscount Bryce's argument in the British House of Lords — that women's service during the war had sprung from national devotion and that women thus would be "insulted" with a vote designed to reward them for their wartime actions. However, Bérard's points also mentioned the dangers posed by women's greater sentimentality, Catholic faith, and responsibility to the family. [135]

Other proposals that sought to recognize women's wartime contributions in an official manner demonstrated the extent to which women's sacrifice of "husbands, sons, fathers and brothers" had become politicized. While such "sacrifices" were not ultimately guarantees that political rights would follow, in October of 1919 the French Senate passed a resolution attesting to the heroism of women that acknowledged that "French women and young girls had justified the confidence of the country." In proposing this measure, Senator Magny, noting that "we have all seen the *oeuvre* of French women and girls during the war . . .

substituting for combatants, gone to the front," asked the government "not to forget the services rendered by the women and girls of France." Speaking in support of this measure, Senator Louis Martin urged a recognition of "the unforgettable services of the heroes of the front with those of the heroes of the *arrière* [home front]." While lauding French women through the ages, Martin was interrupted by Senator Henry Chéron, who cried with disbelief, "And one does not want to let them vote!" and by Senator Flaissières, who asserted, "One will let them." Concluding his remarks, Martin stated that the question of women voting would soon be examined, "because it will be extremely necessary that the French woman also vote. In any case, if we are divided over the question of votes for women, this is a point on which we are unanimous . . . that's to give homage to the great qualities of heart, intelligence and devotion of the French woman. She has incarnated the *patrie* in the most difficult circumstances. In the name of the *patrie,* we salute her respectfully. (Well done and loud applause)."[136] With the adoption of this resolution, women received an official acknowledgment of their contributions, which some senators clearly believed should be tied to future debates over the issue of granting them full political participation.

Opponents of women's suffrage in the Senate managed to avoid discussing the Bérard report or indeed any arguments for women's suffrage for another three years. At that point, it had the models of women's suffrage as introduced in Britain and much of the rest of Europe and the United States and its results to consider as well. Such issues among others would emerge when the Senate finally debated the entire question of women's voting rights in November 1922. On November 7 the discussion began with Louis Martin, who cited various famous commentators on women's citizenship going back to Condorcet, then asked his fellow senators to consider the role of women during the war, those who when the workshop was deserted went to the workshop, and who worked the earth when it, too, was abandoned.[137] Yet, he continued, "one wronged woman when one considered her role from 1914 to 1918 as exceptional," implying that her wartime service was in keeping with her previous contributions to the nation. Martin used the example of women's wartime services as part of his counterarguments to the attack on women's civic capacities and rights contained in Bérard's report. In particular, Martin responded to fears about the abandonment of motherhood by women bent on public, political participation by insisting that women would continue to be guided by their "maternal instinct." Furthermore, he added, in countries where women did vote (including England) there was no crisis of natality; indeed, infant mortality in England was on the decline. Martin concluded his appeal by urging the Senate to return France to its rightful place as the "head" of nations by granting women liberty and justice.[138] Martin's successor in the debates, Senator Antonin Gourju, noted that in 1921, 138 million women had political rights and that he was "ashamed to say that not one was French!" He also took advantage of the English example of Nancy Astor, the first female member of Parliament and "the mother of five children," proving that "political life did not impede women from having children." Gourju continued to praise the work of distinguished French women (including Marcelle Tinayre, Lucie Delarue-Mardrus, Séverine, and Nelly Roussel) and to reiterate the argument equating women's maternal service with men's military service to the state.[139]

On 14 November, as the debate continued into the next session, Gourju was joined by Senator François Saint-Maur and others who supported some measure of women's suffrage. However, this session also provided François Labrousse with a forum to aggressively denounce women's suffrage. Labrousse asserted that women did not want the vote, and here he echoed Gustave Rivet's response to Louis Martin's suffragist petition of 5,000 signatures: "5,000 women out of 11 million."[140] Attacking women's character, Labrousse argued that the consequences of granting them the vote would be seriously damaging for the nation's moral as well as political life. He concluded by declaring — to loud and prolonged applause — that he wished neither to play with "the race" nor "the family" nor "the Republic" by agreeing to so "imprudent" a measure as women's suffrage.[141]

Two subsequent days of debate on 16 and 21 November did little ultimately to advance the cause of the women's vote. When Alexandre Bérard spoke to defend his report, he rejected the model provided by England because, he claimed, many British people now "regretted" granting women's suffrage since "women had completely overturned the ranks of political parties."[142] Other senators, such as Fernand Merlin, intervened with praise of both women's wartime service and their role as mothers. And some senators tried to resurrect the familial vote. However, fears raised about the future of the republic due to the decline of the population from the war, the falling birthrate, and, more significantly, the alleged influence of the church over women would all combine to end the debate on 21 November (although the final vote to abandon the bill had a majority of only 22).[143] Women's suffrage on any terms was thus finally dismissed at the end of these sessions and would not become a serious possibility for the rest of the interwar era.[144]

That some French senators recognized women's services and their sacrifices is evident in a variety of ways: in their support for the idea of granting women a familial vote or suffrage for the dead; in the 1919 proposal that paid homage to the French woman; and in the rhetoric of the November 1922 debates. Yet, praise for women's service—even when it was equated with men's military service—did not imply that women were necessarily deserving of the vote. Indeed, for the majority of the senators, neither women's services nor their sacrifices were themselves enough evidence that women had "earned" the franchise. This may suggest how problematic these activities were as a basis for political rights.

Conclusion: The Meanings of Citizenship

Sacrifice and service formed the core of many arguments for women's political rights during and after the war in both Britain and France. Emotive appeals based on ideas of women's suffering or service—that women had worked for the common good, risked their lives for its sake, or suffered grievous loss—came into play as members of both houses of Parliament debated enfranchising most British women over thirty. Some French politicians expressed similar attitudes. That legislation giving women a national vote won approval in Britain but not in France should not suggest as wide a gap between the two countries in the understanding or status of women's political rights as might be read from merely thinking in terms of a British feminist victory and a French feminist defeat. In both legislative and wider cultural debates, certain qualities exhibited by women during wartime were seen as central to their claims for patriotism and, potentially, for citizenship usefulness and the vote. These focused on women's contributions, their duties and responsibilities—to differing extents in Britain and in France—as workers for the national good, as sufferers from the tragic costs of war, and as mothers of the nation's sons.

Given the ostensibly new roles assumed by women during the war, changing notions of women's wartime civic behavior in Britain and France prompted new debates over the relationship between service and citizenship. In Britain, a nation without universal manhood suffrage at the war's outset, these debates became increasingly caught up with how military service and patriotic action were to be recognized, especially after conscription was introduced in 1916. However, some French politicians also realized that age qualifications meant, by the war's end, that a few men who actually fought in the war also did not have full political rights. Politicians on both sides of the channel voiced their rising concern that no fighting man should be deprived of the franchise, a concern that would become the impetus for possible electoral reform in the United Kingdom and France, including proposals to lower the voting age for those serving in the military. But this transnational concern with connecting service to the state with full citizenship rights had different meanings because of specific national politics. It is not as if crucial players among the British Liberals or French Radicals debating the enfranchisement of women had been selected for office because of their views on women's suffrage. However, once the idea of changing the basis of the franchise was raised, women's right to possess this key trapping of citizenship emerged as a privilege that might be granted or denied based on conceptions of what women had done during the war and on abstract, perhaps specifically national, notions of civic rights and responsibilities.

Debates about women in uniforms, their military service, their contributions to the polity, and their civic responsibilities reveal essential assumptions about notions of patriotism and claims of rights for women during the war. They point to the fact that citizens were defined not just by their possession or lack of political rights but also by the cultural and social understandings of their contributions to the "public" and "national" good. If citizenship can be determined by a set of social obligations, then the debates concerning the "emblems" of citizenship gain in significance, because they suggest how much more is at stake. The fact that British women met considerable resistance to their wearing of khaki reaffirmed the continuing link between military service, maleness, patriotism, and, by extension, citizenship.

The end of the war was thus a crucial moment: new forms of female patriotism seemed to open the possibility for gender as well as class equality in terms of political rights. Yet women in uniform, and especially in khaki, further embodied the fear that the gulf between the sexes — and specifically between combatants and noncombatants — was in danger of eroding, if not disappearing. British women's wearing khaki uniforms thus provoked discussion about the potential for *all* women to be represented in, as well as to represent, the nation.

Ultimately, both French and British women were seen as being able to claim a positive patriotic role, but this did not manifest itself directly in terms of a new understanding of their citizenship. Further, if female patriotic service could support normative ideas about femininity, would it then serve as the basis for ideas linking all public service to wider claims for citizenship? This chapter has uncovered evidence in a number of public debates—about women as military workers, civic participants, and voters—that suggests the ambiguous legacy of the war for French and British women. The differing outcomes of attempts at franchise reform in France and the United Kingdom by the early 1920s suggest that wartime efforts to view women as citizens focused on differentiating women's contributions to the war effort from those of men. Both French and British feminists during the war believed that popular sentiment had been won over to their side, whether by virtue of women's services or their sacrifices, and they further felt that this would yield concrete results. Yet comparable national recognition of their contributions was not forthcoming. The restrictions placed on their full political rights in the one case and the absence of such rights in the other suggest that women's identifying themselves fully with the national cause did not make them, in the eyes of their governments, the political equals of male citizens.

Public Spaces
and Private Grief

ASSESSING THE LEGACY

OF WAR

Mothers, Mourning, and Memory

At the end of the First World War, women across Europe engaged in acts of recovery, restoration, and remembrance. Given the extent of the war's losses, mourning and the marking of grief became public expressions as much as private ones. In discussions about the ways to distinguish the bereaved, presumably female, survivors of military men and in postwar attempts to recover their bodies, create rituals, and provide monuments to commemorate the fallen dead, women's mourning came to have a deeply political overtone. Not only did wartime and postwar efforts to provide spaces in which to mourn the dead highlight, in many cases, the particular loss experienced by women and mothers, but the monuments and rituals themselves also made the mourning mother a bearer of memory for the nation of her fallen son. Comparing the ways in which French and British women actively came to terms with the war's human losses provides an opportunity for examining one of the war's most significant legacies for women.

As Jay Winter's recent study of mourning and memory during and after the war stresses, "The history of bereavement was universal history during and immediately after the Great War in France, Britain, and Germany." [1] This history expressed itself in numerous cultural forms:

personal letters, mementos and memoirs, more public "texts," and rituals of belief and mourning. Given that both Britain and France forbade the exhumation of military corpses during the war and that Britain continued to ban their repatriation after the war, new cultural forms attempting to preserve the memory of the lives behind these absent bodies arose.[2] Perhaps most overtly and enduringly these took the form of war memorials themselves. The construction of these monuments, as Daniel Sherman and Catherine Moriarty have shown, was a communal activity, often circumscribed by finances but nonetheless an expression of public mourning and memory.[3] Postwar pilgrimages to such shrines as well as to war graves and battlefields also meant, according to David Lloyd, that mass death served to unite men and women.[4]

This chapter analyzes the wartime and, more significantly, postwar responses to the war's death tolls that particularly involved mourning women. How mothers, both of soldiers and of soldiers' children, were used to commemorate the war's losses in national and local ceremonies illustrates how society used women to express collective grief.[5] The representation of women on monuments themselves provides other examples of how mothering could be equated with soldiering as a form of service to the state. There was little inherently natural about these mourning processes or images, and, in fact, women's responses to or recognition of the war's plentiful losses required direct interventions so that they could be channeled in appropriate ways.

"The Mothers of Dead Heroes": Memorials and Mourning in Britain

On 10 June 1915, according to London's *Morning Post,* the bishop of St. Asaph spoke to members of the Mother's Union, paying "manly tribute to a silent nobility which the country is perhaps rather prone to take for granted." "The courage of mothers who send their sons to the war," he said, "is no matter for loud acclaim or conventional adulation; yet it were a shame if it were by men forgotten in this hour. Amid the stress and tumult and the shouting of war there is something which has been from the beginning and is now the inspiration of heroism, and it is the courage of the women." He emphatically affirmed, "It is better to be the mother of a dead hero than of a living coward." As we have seen, the bishop was certainly not alone in extolling the special role of women as mothers in inspiring action or being themselves worthy of praise as heroic. In this instance, he specifically recognized the contribution of the mother, who saw "neither sense nor reason in the slaying or maiming of those whom she has brought into the world" but who gave her sons "without a word," with "no reproach," and with "noble endurance."[6]

How was women's "noble endurance" to be recognized? Almost as soon as the war began, an article in *The Times* raised the issue of how to provide a "distinctive form of mourning" for "the relatives of soldiers and sailors killed in the war."[7] On September 4th, *The Times* printed a letter from a Red Cross worker containing "perhaps the most interesting and comprehensive suggestion," the wearing of "a black band bearing a miniature Union Jack. The women might be induced to let their menfolk and children wear this, if they themselves had 'proper mourning.'"[8] Elevating the status of the implicit maternal mourner and making all women synonymous with mothers, the use of women in rites of mourning and ceremonies of commemoration demonstrated the cultural power of women as mothers, not as "citizens," in their relationship to the costs and experiences of the war.

A letter to the editor of *The Times* in July of 1915 even proposed that women be rewarded for their reproductive labor. Referring to those who have "died gloriously or fallen mortally wounded," the author asked if "his mother might not be permitted to wear (as a brooch or otherwise) the decoration or medal thus posthumously awarded to the gallant son she had given to her country. It is not suggested that any other relative except the hero's mother (without whom he could not have been borne) should be entitled to this unique privilege."[9] As in much of this kind of rhetoric, the role of fathers was notably absent, and only "the hero's mother" in place of the absent hero was deemed worthy of wearing a "medal" to document her sacrifice. Mourning mothers, by thus publicly representing the experience of bereavement due to war, were meant to be *visibly* giving notice of their patriotism. While mourning dress had always served a semiotic purpose, as the 1914 discussion in *The Times* highlighted, what was at issue here was distinguishing between combatant and noncombatant death. That mothers' experience of grief was acknowledged in proposals to grant them the medals of their fallen sons or to provide them with distinctive forms of mourning made explicit their gendered significance as some of the most important vessels of memory for the war.

Mothers could also serve as forces of social unity in ceremonies of commemoration. As the functional equivalent of the soldier—as the producer of Britain's dead heroes—the mother became not only the wartime ideal for all women but also the embodiment of the civilian experience of war. Mothers represented a solidarity of British woman-hood meant to transcend differences of class, religion, and region in the face of modern, total war. And nowhere is this more evident than in the ways in which motherhood and mothers were used to commemo-rate the nation's fallen sons.

Thus in ceremonies of remembrance and on monuments to the war dead, motherhood could occupy a central place. For it was women as mothers—or as wives with their motherhood left implicit—who, as the living embodiment of the antithesis of war, were depicted on war memorials and who participated in national and local ceremonies. Yet the images of motherhood could be used in many ways. These ranged from the association of mothering with peace to the hope that memorials could instruct future generations, linking maternity and civic virtue.

One of the innovations of this war's attempt to deal with its dead took the form of the tomb of the unknown combatant, where the body of a certified "unknown warrior" could stand in for the "everyman" and "everyson" killed in battle.[10] In Britain, debates about who would be al-lowed to attend the dramatic ceremony of interment of this anonymous soldier in the symbolically powerful grave began almost as soon as the project itself was announced. The prominence of the ceremony, held on Armistice Day for obvious symbolic reasons, raised the question of who had the right to witness the stirring spectacle.[11] A Cabinet Memo-rial Services Committee meeting on 19 October 1920 established that any seats for the interment of the unknown warrior, aside from those reserved for members of the official procession, would be allotted "not to Society ladies or the wives of dignitaries, but to the selected widows and mothers of those who had fallen, especially in the humbler ranks." A proposal for a ballot to choose these seats noted three categories meeting the Cabinet Committee's approval: "(a) Women who have lost husbands and sons or only son (b) Mothers who have lost all sons or only sons (c) Widows."[12]

A letter of 28 October 1920 from the secretary of this committee requested Prime Minister Lloyd George's approval for its plan. Given that no fewer than 36,000 officers and well over 600,000 of the rank and file fell in France alone, the secretary explained, "there will easily be be-tween 2,000,000 and 3,000,000 relatives of the fallen to be considered when we allot the miserably scanty accommodation that is available in the Abbey [Westminster] and near the Cenotaph." The letter also noted that a criterion had to be set for selecting seating, and it presented the decision of the committee to accommodate only bereaved mothers and widows as follows: "First Category: Women who have lost all their sons and their husband. Second: Women who have lost all their sons[.] Third: Widows who have lost their only son." The letter added that, according to War Office estimates, at least 3,000 people would fit under these three categories. It suggested that thus "first consideration would be given to those who were entitled to it: it would be a bold and dramatic stroke, because you might find the Duchess next the charwoman; and it might even have its effect, however small and imperceptible, upon the industrial situation."[13]

This was assuredly a bold stroke, one emphasizing how much the government sought to maintain the national unity and the erasure of class differences allegedly provided by the war. Such arguments also showed how gender politics played into the overall politics of mourning and ceremony, suggesting that society potentially could be held together by the gender-specific, primarily maternal experience of mourning. The three categories established by the committee made women synonymous with mothers and used the common loss of sons as a means of transcending social differences.

The Cabinet Memorial Services Committee considered allowing men to attend, but only as adjuncts to the grieving mothers. It reconsidered limiting seating for women once "it was pointed out that, in view of the great emotional strain under which the relatives would be suffering, prior to and during the two Services, it was desirable . . . [that] a certain number of bereaved fathers and male relatives should also be admitted to the Abbey."[14] Yet, in the end, the government decided to exclude men and the original categories were used to determine seating in early November. The number of applications for tickets "exceeded 15,000," including 99 from "women who [have] lost husband and one or more sons," and 7,506 from "mothers who had lost only sons or all sons."[15] Thus for this most important national ceremony, motherhood and mourning coalesced into a powerful emblem of collective grief.[16]

The Tomb of the Unknown Warrior provided the scene of national mourning, but nearly every town, village, and church produced local sites and ceremonies for communal mourning. And as they did in the ceremony interring the unknown warrior, citizens in each locality participated in the unveiling ceremonies of local memorials. And these regional and civic ceremonies did not neglect to emphasize the special role of women and of mothers in commemorating the war dead. In general, military men and local civic and religious leaders unveiled memorials, but women who had no other significance than having sacrificed their sons or provided the service of their sons were also selected for the honor of unveiling these emblems. For instance, at the 29 April 1923 unveiling of a memorial in Crompton, "Mrs. Hopley (Mother who had eight sons serving in the war)" placed the second of five wreaths.

In other instances, solely grieving mothers unveiled the memorials. The program for the unveiling of the Lytham War Memorial on 14 January 1922 noted that "Mrs H Wakefield . . . through losing three sons in the War, had the honour of unveiling the Memorial."[17] The memorial committee for Leicester's Arch of Remembrance felt "the whole sacrifice of the War should be recorded. The maimed, the halt and the blind, men and women, indeed 'all who served and strove and those who patiently endured.'" At the unveiling ceremony on 4 July 1925, the program stated that "the memorial be unveiled in the name of all those who have lost their dear ones, by A Bereaved Mother." The typeface for these last three words was several times larger than the rest of the text.[18] Programs for other unveiling ceremonies also indicated that a woman unveiled the monument where the unmistakable names of male relations were recorded on the roll of honor.[19] Some of these monuments were thus unveiled by less anonymous, although no less symbolic, "bereaved mothers." The mourning mother could even take her place beside the nobility, as in Manchester, where, on 12 July 1924, "[t]he Earl of Derby [was] assisted in the ceremony of unveiling the Memorial by Mrs. Bingle of Ardwick, Manchester. Mrs. Bingle's three sons were killed in action in France."[20]

Representations of women also occasionally and significantly appeared on the memorials themselves. Their appearance remained atypical, however, for a simple cross and a roll of honor usually marked the community's already obvious losses. According to Catherine Moriarty, few monuments were more elaborate than this. Sculptures were atypical, often following the patterns of prewar funerary images, and if not, were far more likely to depict a soldier than any other figure.[21]

Yet even the emblematic fighting man could highlight the maternal mourner. The description of the Manchester memorial indicates that "the figure of a fighting man with equipment at his side and feet and a greatcoat thrown over the whole convey[s] to those who stand below no individual identity and so in truth 'every mother's son.'"[22] The link between anonymity and the "everyson" quality of the fallen soldier also appeared in the description of Rochdale's War Memorial, which was described as a cenotaph with "a Sarcophagus upon which is laid to rest

Two views of Port Sunlight War Memorial, Liverpool. Courtesy of the National Inventory of War Memorials, Imperial War Museum.

the figure of a Fighting Man, possessing to those who stand below, no individual identity, and so, in truth, the son of every mother who is bereaved."[23]

When a few memorials sought to represent the experience of women or used contemporary images of women, they either presented contemporaneous variations of *mater dolorosa* or used women and children to show whom the war was fought to protect and preserve. In some of these rare cases, memorials visually as much as verbally suggested women's suffering in and through war. The monument at Croyden not only showed a mother cradling her child but also explicitly acknowledged "the men and women who died and suffered."[24] Again, the programs that described unveiling ceremonies self-consciously proclaimed their allegiance to these "models." The program for the Renfrew War Memorial, which was unveiled in August 1922, explained that "Duty and Defence" are denoted "by the figure of a soldier in the attitude of doing duty in defending the weak against Might represented by women and children in the rear appealing for his protection from the enemy."[25] Later the same year, a description of the St. Saviour, Southwark War Memorial elaborated upon the monument's significance: "At the North end, the mourning figure of a woman plays homage to the fallen, and is symbolic of the grief of the present generation, whilst a babe reaching to a dove, suggests the hope of peace to future genera-

tions."[26] Other monuments, such as the sculpture at Eccleston Park, Liverpool, showed both a man in khaki and a woman in mourning and elaborated the role of each in the words carved in stone: "The Laurels Of The Sons Are Watered From The Hearts Of The Mothers."[27]

Two other British memorials reinforced the quintessentially gendered ways in which men and women presumably experienced the war. At Port Sunlight in Liverpool, the figures of women, children, and armed men surrounds the base of a tall pillar. The soldiers' bayonets are extended and at the ready, the seated mother clutches a baby in her arms, while two small children cling to her skirts. Beside the woman, a small girl and her smaller brother lean against the pillar fearfully. The entire scenario seems lifted not from victorious Britain but vanquished Belgium, suggestively turning the "home" front into a potential war front.

Another memorial, at St. Annes-on-the-Sea in Lancashire, unveiled in 1924, also incorporated both the fighting man and the mother. Its description in the unveiling ceremony's program left little to the imagination:

> [The soldier expresses] the constant nervous strain of continuous trench warfare. . . .
>
> The Mother and Child are intended to show the agony of mind caused to Womanhood by the tragedies of the War. The mother sits in anguish and sorrowful reverie, quite unconscious that her babe

Memorial at St. Annes-on-the-Sea. Courtesy of the National Inventory of War Memorials, Imperial War Museum.

V.sual division of men +women

Mother and child on the memorial at St. Annes-on-the-Sea. Courtesy of the National Inventory of War Memorials, Imperial War Museum.

is looking to her for a mother's love. She looks, as it were, into the unknown future, realizing what her sacrifice means, and wondering why.[28]

Even without the program's decoding of the sculpture, the mother's indifference to the child—her arm lies outstretched and empty on her lap not cradling the child which clings to her—is obvious. Her completely inexpressive, almost unnatural face suggests a grief too profound for words. That the sculpture was placed on the monument at the base of the pillar opposite the soldier and underneath a woman with outstretched arms—"the crowning figure [who] typifies the birth of a new life evolved from hard and fierce struggles"—also suggests the separation of this maternal grief from either the fighting man or the newly, optimistically "evolving" life. Taken as a whole, with its images of male heroism and female sacrifice, the postures showing male action and female passivity, the monument delivered some clear messages. The mother can not even actively care for her child, thus a purposeful silencing of the mother also, ironically, occurred.

Throughout Britain, scattered memorials helped to reinforce the significant role women played as grieving mothers. In these instances the "unknowable" sufferings of fallen soldiers were depicted as only to be experienced through the intense grief of their mothers and the mothers of their children, who could be seen to understand both the bodily pain of sacrifice, because of their own experience of the pain of childbirth, and the promise of renewal, which procreation also symbolized. They "alone" could represent a postwar world renewing—remaking—itself, an act analogous to childbearing. Beyond this, the soldier/mother dyad served as a familiar, potent way to inscribe gender roles after enormous upheaval. For many women who viewed these monuments and participated in the commemorative process, these public spaces must have provided not just acknowledgments of their political or symbolic importance but also places where they could grieve for Britain's fallen sons.

Representation and Recovery in Postwar France

Significantly, in France, as in Britain, grieving remained a crucial element of the tasks assigned to wartime and postwar women. A 1916 book addressed to "war widows," already in its fourth printing, urged such women to overcome their grief by "raising your children. It's the sacred task to which you will entirely devout yourself." In so doing, women could let their offspring know their father and "how he lived, how and why he died."[29] Such "maternal duty" was to be women's first consolation, and part of their job included staying faithful and keeping the lost soldiers' memories alive. The act of more "public" commemoration as well as the representations of what was being commemorated, as Daniel Sherman has pointed out, also reveal the crucial role of gender in how the war's losses were to be understood and experienced.[30] Although some British monuments used women allegorically to stand in for peace, victory, justice, or even Britannia, this practice had perhaps an even stronger tradition in France.[31] As the work of Maurice Agulhon has shown, the utilization of Marianne as the feminine emblem of the French Republic was both tremendously popular and multivalent, including the idea of "Marianne-mère"—Marianne as mother of the nation.[32] As a result of the war, however, in part because of the rapprochement that then occurred between Catholics and Republicans, both Marianne and Jeanne d'Arc appeared in monuments to commemorate the war.[33] Still, as in Britain, the majority of memorials to the dead did not contain figurative sculptures. Rather, they usually consisted of the simple stele and were more likely to depict the *poilu* (soldier). However, memorials commemorating the Great War in France also represented women as mothers. This symbolism could be read as having a republican connotation, since Marianne could also be seen in a maternal context, but it also could be associated with traditional images of the Madonna and Christ child, which would be perhaps less surprising in an overwhelmingly Catholic nation.[34]

Given the geographical placement of French women both behind as well as beyond the front line, monuments in the occupied zones of the north and east of the nation offered rolls of honor that recorded the names of the civilian war dead, including women.[35] Yet monuments in these areas also used powerful images of grieving mothers. At Péronne, a sculpture by Paul Auban shows a woman in the garb of a countrywoman leaning over a fallen *poilu,* her arm out-stretched and her hand clenched in a fist. While this mother is clearly patriotic, she is not sobbing with grief or love of France but is vividly demonstrating her animosity to those who have killed her son.[36] Nonetheless, as noted in the collection *Monuments de Mémoire,* such a figure was "atypical."[37]

Perhaps more typically, mothers appeared with small children, not with dead soldiers but with soldiers' living legacy. In such renderings, mothers appeared to instruct the children—as the nation's future—to remember those who died for the country. In Hangest-en-Santerre in the department of the Somme, a sculpture features a woman with her arm around her small son; she holds the helmet of a soldier, and he what could be laurels or an olive branch. The mother and son are both mourning and remembering the man symbolized by the "empty" helmet. A mother and son giving homage to the dead can also be found in the war memorial at Ardentes in the department of the Indre and at Compiègne in Oise. The monument at Bully in Pas-de-Calais presents

"To Our Dead," Péronne War Memorial. Photo by Graham Farthing, courtesy of the National Inventory of War Memorials, Imperial War Museum.

a variation of this theme, portraying a standing woman, while a man with his arms around a child points out the names of the dead inscribed on the roll of honor; here the family unit mourns its losses.[38]

In Equeurdreville, a monument sculpted by Emilie Rodez represented another family. This one was fatherless; the woman clutches a baby, which clings to her, with one arm, while she shields a young boy beside her with the other. Carved beneath this image are the words "Que Maudite Soit La Guerre [The Bitterest Curses Make War]." Not only was this monument a tribute to the children of Equeurdreville fallen for the nation, it also delivered a didactic message for the surviving children.[39] As Annette Becker observes, Rodez was one of the few women to sculpt a memorial to the dead, and she implies that Rodez's message was one of "militant" pacifism.[40] Although Becker does not explicitly suggest this, perhaps Rodez's was a pacifism, like the maternal and "teacherly" sort discussed in Chapter 5, that professed a distinctly gendered perspective.

Indeed, the most explicitly gendered act could be mourning itself. While images of the mother predominated in the few British monuments depicting mourners, from the evidence available in two substantial French collections documenting First World War memorials, the mourning woman—portrayed either allegorically or more realistically—stood on her own, holding a wreath and forever crying for the dead.

In Saint-Florent-le-Vieil (Maine-et-Loire) she is seated at the base of the monument itself with her head bowed and her hands folded across her lap. In Ascain (Pyrénées-Atlantiques) she is a peasant woman, stoically standing, looking at the ground, and in the department of Indre, at Buzançais, she leans, seemingly crying into her arms, against the monument itself. In similarly hooded poses, her form occupied the summit of the monuments of Compan in the Hautes-Pyrénées and of Fotenay-sous-Bois in the Val-de-Marne.[41]

The politics of motherhood resonated in explicit and implicit ways in the uses to which images of women were put in commemorating the dead and the war. Given the losses suffered by France during the war, it seemed appropriate to provide a public recognition of the sorrow that women experienced. As a police report on the *esprit* of Paris on Armistice Day recorded, "Some women, in remembering their deceased of the war, have had crises of tears and nerves on the public way."[42] Both symbolically and literally, depictions of grieving women, particularly as mothers of soldiers and of soldiers' children, highlighted their importance for the nation, and their role as the equivalent—not equal— of the soldier.

There was one area, however, where women's actions regarding the deaths of their men, particularly sons, came into specific conflict with the laws of the French state. British corpses were not and could not be independently repatriated, and, during the war, French corpses could not be exhumed from the zone of the armies.[43] This did not prevent French families from asking if exceptions could made. Moreover, when such prohibitions were extended in February 1919 for a period of three years, some families took matters into their own hands.[44] A practice of "clandestine exhumations" began, which were documented by local prefects who sought the guidance of the minister of the interior about how to respond to such cases.

After the declaration of February 1919, a letter from "a group of mothers and widows" asked the minister of the interior to give them the corpses of their sons and spouses with the briefest possible delay. Claiming to understand the difficulty of retrieving those fallen in the lines, the women demanded the bodies of their "dear disappeared" who had died in ambulances or behind the lines.[45] Some women were not content to wait for permission, and the police commissioner of Montmorency (Seine et Oise) also requested that the minister of the interior modify the February 1919 prohibition. Because the "cult of the dead is so deep-rooted in France," he asserted, no financial sacrifice or danger could stop families, who knew the location of the tomb of their loved ones, from exhuming them and carrying them off. The commissioner cited as an example a mother who went in search of her son, exhumed his corpse herself during the night, carried it home by train, registered as "baggage," and then reinterred her son's remains in the communal cemetery. Clearly, a prohibition "violated with such frequency and such energy was no longer a prohibition." The commissioner therefore sought permission to allow such exhumations so that authorities could supervise the proper identification of corpses.[46]

Other departmental prefects forwarded reports of clandestine exhumations to the minister of the interior later in 1919, and, in several of these cases, widowed mothers were responsible for violating the law and bringing "home" their sons. In July 1919, the mayor of Courpalay reported to the prefect of Seine-et-Marne that the widow Terrouet had arrived with the corpse of her soldier son, Raymond, intending to bury him in the local cemetery. The mayor did not blame the local authorities who permitted this but sought to find and punish the person who had assisted her in digging up and transporting the corpse of her son. Mme. Terrouet claimed to be ignorant of the name of the person whom she hired to assist her, and since the "operation took place at night in a deserted place it did not arouse attention." Nonetheless, the authorities were determined to find a M. Tanguy, whose name was "on all lips" and who "had already rendered services of the same genre to other families in the region."[47]

These mothers, unlike those depicted in stone carvings, actively mourned and demonstrated a willingness to defy the law and disrupt the containment of their grief. Despite the interrogations recorded by the police, there was a tacit understanding of their actions, even a kind of permission. By not overtly punishing these women and by questioning the prohibition on exhumations, even those required to uphold the law implied that the rule had to be altered in such a way that it could be enforced in the face of such determination. Given their geographic proximity to their war dead, some French mothers, unlike their British counterparts, were able to reclaim their dead sons' corpses, actions that challenged the state's authority and the more passive depiction of their grief on the war's memorials.

Conclusion

War memorials in Britain and France similarly sought to preserve the memory of those who died for their national cause. Given this goal, both nations' monuments not only tended to exclude all women but also largely ignored their contributions as nurses and war workers. There were few representations of women wearing uniforms or doing war work of any variety on war memorials.[48] The establishment of numerous local monuments, however, revealed the public nature and importance of mourning. Therefore, the depiction of women as emblems of grief and as mourners on these structures provides some evidence of the continued ambiguity of popular attitudes toward women and the war. On the one hand, women could represent the potent forces of peace, victory, and the nation itself. On the other hand, the images of grieving women left a powerful symbol of a feminized loss and the devastating costs of war in the postwar world.

Postwar acts of commemoration turned battlefields, memorials, and monuments, places meant to allow communities on both the local and the national level to join together in their collective grief, into sites of pilgrimage. Official guides to the war zone appearing in 1920 described the strip of land stretching "like a Sacred Way whose milestones are martyred towns and villages, . . . saturated with the blood of heroes, these broken and distorted masses of stone." Such landscapes were meant to evoke "a voice of supreme Pity and supreme Hope," to call upon the living to "*never forget!*"[49] Although the number of pilgrims along such paths would ebb and flow throughout the interwar era, as David Lloyd has shown, bereaved relatives—especially women—and veterans had particularly privileged roles in such pilgrimages.[50] These two groups were brought together by shared losses that transcended the alleged insurmountable divide between the "fronts" in which they had, for the most part, respectively experienced the war.

With the construction of monuments to the dead throughout Britain and France, the fronts were bridged and the war came home in one final way. While the bodies of British soldiers were left close to where they had fallen, those of some French soldiers were eventually allowed to return to their families. Despite this difference, in local communities across these two nations, men and women shared in the process of creating spaces for public mourning and commemoration. It is not surprising, given the centrality of motherhood to women's wartime roles as well as the emphasis in both countries on repopulation as the key to postwar recovery, that sorrowing mothers occupied so prominent a position in these rituals and places. They were the ones whose attendance at the national unveiling ceremony of the Tomb of the Unknown Warrior in Westminster Abbey in Britain was meant to be prominent and who were excused for exhuming and reburying their dead in France. Thus, women, especially mothers, were singled out to express collective grief in some of its most overt forms.

Commemoration that makes us forget about women

CONCLUSION

During the First World War, the women of the two main European Allies confronted total warfare on an unprecedented scale. Yet despite these changes, the end of the war found that their societies' expectations of and for them had changed remarkably little. While this study has acknowledged important differences between the women of France and of Britain as they faced this war based on differing traditions and policies within these two nations, some wartime experiences did transcend national borders. Although France's conscript military and Britain's voluntary one at the war's outset influenced divergent expressions of civilian patriotism, and the responses of the French and British feminist movement to the war varied, I have suggested that we not read too much into the partial success of women's suffrage in Britain and its failure in France. Certainly, this study has shown how specific national circumstances, such as the invasion and occupation of France and the creation of the Defence of the Realm Regulations, with their reimposition of aspects of the Contagious Diseases Acts, in Britain, directly affected the women of each nation in separate ways. However, despite these obvious and significant national differences, debates about women in both countries consistently demonstrated striking parallels in their assumptions about women's gender identity.

While both governments drew upon traditional notions of gender to exclude women from combat, they were willing to shift other assumptions about gender in order to enlist women's support for specific aspects of the war effort. By the war's end, some women wore khaki uniforms, and unmarried men and women of all classes—all meant to be engaged in national work—had greater unsupervised contact. At the same time, enormous casualties further swelled anxieties about national and imperial futures. Because women were held directly accountable for the falling birthrate in both France and Britain, and because all facets of life on the so-called home front became directly tied to the successful outcome of the war, ideas about how women should best respond to the national crisis came into conflict with one another. For instance, both of these states instituted new measures to support or even empower mothers and children, but these in turn led some to fear that such policies encouraged unwed motherhood, immorality, and thus social decay. Others decried that women could not simultaneously manufacture weapons and care for their children. Similarly, peacefulness and femininity had long prewar associations, yet now women, such as Hélène Brion, who dissented from the patriotic norm were seen as threats to both national and gender orders. In other words, states as well as individual women tried to maintain an uneasy balance between preserving the home life, which the war was allegedly being fought to defend, and fostering changes in behavior so that women could temporarily join men in sustaining their nations at war.

By highlighting the complexity of debates on women's roles during the First World War in these two nations, this book has revealed some changes to prewar discussions about gender and women, but mostly it has discovered continuities. In contrast, the recent historiography on women in postwar Britain and France by Mary Louise Roberts and Susan Kent has emphasized the "reconstruction" of gender in the interwar period.[1] By looking at the gender system from the war's outset, this study has argued instead that the war did not shatter gender relations and identities in such ways that they then needed to be reconstructed in the postwar period. Rather, such "reconstruction" was a constant and ongoing process from the first day of the war.

World War I was, in many ways, a new war. It was the first war that allowed governments to take advantage of the mass media and mass culture of the early twentieth century to reach increasingly literate men and women in the farthest corners of Britain and France. It was the first European war shown in cinemas and presented to this more literate public through a vast array of newspapers, journals, and popular literature. Through these cultural means, women received constant messages about how they should answer their nations' calls to arms and sustain their countries through the long years of war. As we have also seen, individual women, be they feminists Jeanne Mélin and Millicent Fawcett or novelists Berta Ruck and Odette Dulac, responded to such appeals in diverse and complex ways.

Despite the multiple, often contradictory messages about gender contained in such media, motherhood consistently became a major rhetorical tool with which debates about women and the war were conducted in both nations. Although motherhood was a central theme of relatively conservative wartime gender politics, women's own articulations of motherhood sometimes managed to escape these agendas. They did so when maternal imagery was used by feminist pacifists or when mothers violated the law by carrying home the corpses of their sons. While several historians have previously traced the establishment of state policy on motherhood to this war, this book has sought to demonstrate the enormous variety of both political and cultural uses to which motherhood was put.[2] Since the possibilities of motherhood were so widespread and divergent, they need to be analyzed and historicized in their specific manifestations.

Here I want to point out that this study has assiduously avoided the term "maternalism." Given the extensive range of uses to which maternity was (and is) put, I have found the term, with its suggestion of some sort of cohesive ideology or practices, more confusing than useful. Despite scholarly efforts to refine the meaning of this term, they seem to oversimplify a far more complex political and cultural terrain.[3] It is not just that the specific mothering of sons formed the basis for women's diametrically opposed political claims of patriotic militarism and defiant pacifism during the First World War, or that concern with mothers cut across so many lines as to make defining what "maternalism" meant in this context a problematic task. Rather, as this study has shown, motherhood—as an essential component of gendered and national identity—was figured and reconfigured during the war to speak to every aspect of women's lives by an enormous range of voices.

This book has also demonstrated that the allegedly separate and inviolate spaces of home front and war front, where, respectively, women and men were meant to experience the war, were inherently unstable. This war came directly home to the victims of rape in occupied France, to those who came into contact with the injured or read their letters, to those who mourned their absent men, and, particularly, to those subject to that new instrument of war: the air raid. The ability of civilians to hold out, keep up morale, supply the basic necessities of war to those on the firing line, and sustain the war effort proved essential to the war's outcome. This is not to suggest that all experiences of the war were the same or that some were not easier or more terrible than others. However, this book does argue that historians must view the experience of war along a continuum, rather than divide it into the categories of "front line" and "home front," as if one type of war experience was somehow more authentic than another.

In the end, it would be misleading to say that nothing changed for women; they did achieve some significant political and cultural gains. However, the war's lasting influence on gender was more conservative than innovative. For many women, changes in fashion, or some new occupational opportunities, or even the possibility of voting paled in importance when contrasted with the common experiences of surviving, laboring, and mourning, activities that prevailed across the borders between men's and women's experiences of war. The cues that women received—and that some women themselves actively propagated—encouraged them to continue to see their roles as mothers, particularly as producers of future soldiers, as central to their identities. That this held true in both Britain and France despite their differences reveals that the gender system was not a casualty of the war.

NOTES

ABBREVIATIONS

AIR 1	Royal Air Force Records, Public Record Office
AMSH	Association for Moral and Social Hygiene Collection, Fawcett Library, London Guildhall University
AN	Archives National, Paris
APP	Archives de la Préfecture de Police, Paris
BDIC	Bibliothèque de Documentation Internationale Contemporaine, Paris
BHVP	Bibliothèque Historique de la Ville de Paris
BMD	Bibliothèque Marguerite Durand, Paris
CCWSSC	Consultative Committee of Women's Suffrage Societies Collection, Fawcett Library, London Guildhall University
CRIM 1	London Central Criminal Court, Public Record Office
DPP	Director of Public Prosecution, Public Record Office
HLRO	House of Lords Record Office, London
HO	Home Office Records, Public Record Office
IFHS	Institut Français d'Histoire Sociale, Paris
IWM	Imperial War Museum, London
NUWSSC	National Union of Women's Suffrage Societies Collection, Fawcett Library, London Guildhall University
PRC	Parliamentary Recruiting Committee
WO	War Office Records, Public Record Office
WVR	Women's Volunteer Reserve
WWC	Women's Work Collection, Imperial War Museum, London
WORK	Public Works Records, Public Record Office

INTRODUCTION

1. There is an ever-growing literature on the meanings of gender, feminism, identity, experience, and agency for historians, and I could not possibly deal adequately with all of it and its debts to both feminist and poststructuralist theory here. For works problematizing the category of "women," see Alcoff, "Cultural Feminism versus Post-Structuralism"; Canning, "Feminist History"; Liu, "Teach-

ing the Differences"; and, most especially, Butler, *Gender Trouble;* Riley, *"Am I That Name?";* and Scott, *Gender and the Politics of History;* and the responses to some of these in Valverde, "Poststructuralist Gender Historians," and Auslander, "Feminist Theory and Social History." See also the summation of some of this historiography in Coffin, *Politics of Women's Work,* 9–13.

2. Berta Ruck, "The Shirker," in Ruck, *Khaki and Kisses,* 200, 208–9.

3. Other historians have also charted the significance of motherhood for securing normative gender identity in states at crucial political and cultural moments. For studies of this in twentieth-century Europe that I have found particularly useful, see De Grazia, *How Fascism Ruled Women;* Koonz, *Mothers in the Fatherland;* Moeller, *Protecting Motherhood;* and essays in the comparative volumes Bock and Thane, *Maternity and Gender Policies,* and Koven and Michel, *Mothers of a New World.*

4. For before and after the war, see the collections of the Fawcett Library and, for during the war, the Imperial War Museum. For the creation of the most wide-ranging collection on women assembled during the First World War, see Wilkinson, "Patriotism and Duty." The collections in the Bibliothèque Marguerite Durand and the Fonds Marie-Louise Bouglé at the BHVP are also crucial but less comprehensive than their British counterparts.

5. See Bock and Thane, *Maternity and Gender Policies;* for prewar French anxieties see Cole, " 'There Are Only Good Mothers' "; for an important analysis of the significance of British anxiety about population in a prewar and imperial context, see Davin, "Imperialism and Motherhood."

6. Fussell, *Great War and Modern Memory;* Eksteins, *Rites of Spring;* Winter, *Great War and the British People;* Jean-Jacques Becker, *Great War and the French People;* Hynes, *War Imagined.*

7. See Kent, *Making Peace,* and Mary Louise Roberts, *Civilization without Sexes.*

8. Pedersen, *Family, Dependence;* Downs, *Manufacturing Inequality.* For a comparative study of the French and British labor movements during the First World War, see Horne, *Labour at War.*

9. Gender, of course, refers equally to "masculinity" and the "male" body. A good deal of attention has already been focused on men's identities and behavior during the war in Fussell, *Great War and Modern Memory;* Leeds, *No Man's Land;* Audoin-Rouzeau, *14–18, les combattants des tranchées;* Bourke, *Dismembering the Male;* and Leonard V. Smith, *Between Mutiny and Obedience.* For discussions I have drawn upon to problematize "women" and define gender, see especially Butler, *Gender Trouble;* Laqueur, *Making Sex;* Riley, *"Am I that Name?";* Joan Scott, "Gender: A Useful Category of Historical Analysis," in Scott, *Gender and the Politics of History;* and Nicholson, "Interpreting Gender."

10. An overview of some debates about women and the First World War in Britain can be found in Woollacott, *On Her Their Lives Depend,* 14–15. See also Robert, "Women and Work"; Thom, "Women and Work in Wartime Britain" and "Tommy's Sister"; Higonnet et al., *Behind the Lines;* Braybon, *Women Workers in the First World War;* Bonneau, "Les ouvrières et l'industrie de guerre"; Darrow, "French Volunteer Nursing"; and Dubesset, Thébaud, and Vincent, "Les muni-

tionettes de la Seine." For work on the representation of women in First World War propaganda, see Gullace, "Women and the Ideology of War."

11. For uses of these terms that I have drawn upon, see the following: for "ideological work of gender," Poovey, *Uneven Developments;* for "cultural work," Mary Louise Roberts, *Civilization without Sexes;* and for "emotional work," Chapter 1, below.

12. For studies of wartime cultural media, see Huss, "Pronatalism"; Silver, *Esprit de Corps;* Eksteins, *Rites of Spring;* Sweeney, "Harmony and Disharmony"; Fussell, *Great War and Modern Memory;* Mosse, *Fallen Soldiers;* Hynes, *War Imagined;* and Field, *British and French Writers.* In addition to these, analyses focusing on women, culture, and the First World War include several essays in Cooke and Woollacott, *Gendering War Talk;* Cooper et al., *Arms and the Woman;* Higonnet et al., *Behind the Lines;* Melman, *Borderlines;* Gilbert, "Soldier's Heart"; Marcus, "Asylums of Antaeus" and Corpus/Corps/Corpse," afterword to *Not So Quiet;* Margaret Higonnet, "Cassandra's Question" and "Not So Quiet in No-Woman's Land"; Goldman, *Women and World War I;* Ouditt, *Fighting Forces;* Raitt and Tate, *Women's Fiction and the Great War;* and Tylee, *Great War and Women's Consciousness.* Starting points for the more general theoretical literature on gender/women and war include Elshtain, *Women and War;* Elshtain and Tobias, *Women, Militarism, and War;* and Enloe, *Does Khaki Become You?* and "Feminists Thinking about War."

13. See Fussell, *Great War and Modern Memory.*

14. For more on the meanings of feminism and the feminist movement in the early twentieth century, see Nancy F. Cott's introduction to her *Grounding of Modern Feminism.* See also Hause, *Women's Suffrage;* Paul Smith, *Feminism and the Third Republic;* Bard, *Les filles de Marianne;* Holton, *Feminism and Democracy;* Pugh, *Women and the Women's Movement;* and Kent, *Making Peace,* ch. 4. For some of the most significant feminist perspectives on motherhood, see the essays in Trebilcot, *Mothering,* Glenn et al., *Mothering;* Badinter, *Mother Love;* Rich, *Of Woman Born;* and Ruddick, *Maternal Thinking.* Of particular relevance here for the discussion of mothers and soldiers and of the pain-ridden body, see Scarry, *Body in Pain;* Huston and Kinser, *À l'amour comme à la guerre;* and one of the essays translated from this book, Huston, "Matrix of War."

CHAPTER ONE

1. The second edition of the *Oxford English Dictionary* describes "home" or "domestic" as adjectives first used to modify the military term "front" or "organized sectors of activity" during the Great War, citing *Punch*'s 1919 *History of the Great War. Oxford English Dictionary,* 2d ed., s.v. "front." See also ibid., s.v. "home-fire."

2. Allen, *In the Public Eye,* 8–9, 60–67. See also Table A.7.

3. McAleer, *Popular Reading and Publishing,* 7–9, 41, 53, 93, 244, 249–54.

4. For a discussion of French wartime literature—particularly male-authored texts—that argues for the separation of home front and war front, see Mary Louise Roberts, *Civilization without Sexes,* 21–32. For accounts based on British literature that also emphasize the different and conflictual experiences of the war for

men and women, see, most notably, Gilbert, "Soldier's Heart," and Longenbach, "Women and Men of 1914."

5. I am adapting the term "emotional work" from contemporary sociology; for a definition, see Hochschild, *Managed Heart,* 7.

6. See Fussell, *Great War and Modern Memory.* For such postwar texts see Wilfred Owen, Richard Aldington, Robert Graves, and Céline; Remarque, *All Quiet on the Western Front;* Brittain, *Testament of Youth;* Helen Zenna Smith, *Not So Quiet;* and Rathbone, *We That Were Young.* For offerings produced for and by soldiers in trench newspapers, see Audoin-Rouzeau, *14–18, les combattants des tranchées,* and Fuller, *Troop Morale and Popular Culture.*

7. Barbusse, *Under Fire.* Further references to this book are made parenthetically in the text itself. I am using the standard English translation but have checked all references with the French original; see Barbusse, *Le feu.* The Prix Goncourt was one of France's most prestigious literary prizes.

8. See Field, *Three French Writers,* 37. See also Hynes, *War Imagined,* which claims that *Under Fire* "was the first novel to reach the English public with an unameliorated rendering of the horrors of the war" (203–5).

9. Reviews of *Under Fire* in *The English Review* (Sept. 1917) and *The Times Literary Supplement,* 19 July 1917. See also the review praising it as a book "which must contribute towards making war impossible" in *The Englishwoman,* no. 99 (Mar. 1917).

10. For more on Barbusse as bearing witness, see Relinger, "Feu d'Henri Barbusse," 53–65. For more on the legacy of Barbusse, see Leonard V. Smith, "Masculinity, Memory."

11. A footnote by the translator explains the reference for the quote. See also Jean-Jacques Becker, *Great War and the French People,* and Mary Louise Roberts, *Civilization without Sexes,* 233 n. 39, where she links the phrase directly to its origins in a well-known cartoon by Forain entitled "Inquietude" published in *Le Figaro,* 1 Sept. 1915.

12. The episodes in *Le feu* involving the portrayal of the spectral refugee Eudoxie also demonstrate the presence of women in and around the battlefield — at her death, she is found literally mixed with the mud and guts of an abandoned trench — and the impact of women on fighting men. See Barbusse, *Under Fire,* 56–58, 77–80, 196–98; Grayzel, "Writers of La Grande Guerre," 181–89; and, most recently, Tate, *Modernism, History,* 85–87.

13. Barbusse, *Le feu,* used as title page epigraph to Sassoon, *Counter-Attack and Other Poems.*

14. "Mr. Sassoon's Poems," *The Times Literary Supplement,* 31 May 1917. See also Sassoon, "The Hero," in *Old Huntsman and Other Poems,* 48.

15. Sassoon, "A Working Party," in *Old Huntsman and Other Poems,* 27.

16. Sassoon, "Dreamers," in *Counter-Attack and Other Poems,* 19.

17. Sassoon, "The Glory of Women," in *Counter-Attack and Other Poems,* 32. The poem is also discussed in Kent, *Making Peace,* 45.

18. Sassoon, "Remorse," in *Counter-Attack and Other Poems,* 57.

19. The last stanza of the poem concludes: "grant your soldier this: / That in good fury he may feel / The body where he sets his heel / Quail from your downward darting kiss" (from Sassoon, "The Kiss," in *Old Huntsman and Other Poems,* 21).

For French representations of sexualized weapons, see Sweeney, "Harmony and Disharmony," ch. 3; see also the images in Huss, "Pronatalism."

20. As indicated earlier, this chapter cannot do justice to the full range of fiction written by men and women during the war. For some other wartime novels by women set in Britain and not discussed here, see Delafield, *War Workers;* Mary Agnes Hamilton, *Dead Yesterday;* and Kaye-Smith, *Little England.*

21. Sinclair, *Tree of Heaven,* 300–301. Further references to this work are made parenthetically in the text. That Sinclair's novel, published in London in 1917, was reprinted in America suggests the trans-Atlantic appeal of her work. For other discussions of Sinclair's novel, see Ouditt, *Fighting Forces,* 103–8; Tylee, *Great War and Women's Consciousness,* 131–33; Kent, *Making Peace,* 63, 72; Beauman, "'It Is Not the Place of Women,'" 146; and Laura Stempel Mumford, "May Sinclair's *The Tree of Heaven:* The Vortex of Feminism, the Community of War," in Cooper et al., *Arms and the Woman.*

22. Some authors criticized this insistence; see, for example, the disastrous war marriage that forms the basis of Syrett, *Wife of a Hero.* The couple's lack of communication is signified when he refuses to let her do "unfeminine" war work.

23. Macaulay, *Non-Combatants and Others.* Further references are made parenthetically in the text. For other discussions of this novel, see Kent, *Making Peace,* 15, 19–20; Tylee, *Great War and Women's Consciousness,* ch. 4; Ouditt, *Fighting Forces,* 161–67; and Beauman, "'It Is Not the Place of Women,'" 145–46.

24. West, *Return of the Soldier.* For a nonfictional account of shell shock published in Britain during the war, see Smith and Pear, *Shell Shock and Its Lessons.* For an influential analysis of shell shock as "male hysteria," see Showalter, *Female Malady,* ch. 7. For an analysis stressing that "war neurosis" crossed the lines between home and war fronts, see Tate, *Modernism, History,* ch. 1.

25. Sassoon, "Suicide in the Trenches," in *Counter-Attack and Other Poems,* 31.

26. *The Times Literary Supplement,* 21 Sept. 1916.

27. Wells, *Mr. Britling Sees It Through,* 335, 356–57.

28. Ibid., 411, 430.

29. Gaston Rageot, "L'Ame Anglaise par un Anglais," *Revue Hebdomadaire,* Sept. 1918.

30. Swan, *Woman's Part,* 277. Swan had previously published a collection of supposedly nonfictional letters to a woman whose marriage to a soldier would make "his arm . . . all the braver and more powerful" (see *Letters to a War Bride,* 12).

31. *The Times Literary Supplement,* 31 Aug. 1916.

32. For another interpretation of British women's romance novels that deals with Ruby Ayres and Berta Ruck as well, see Potter, "'A Great Purifier.'" Potter also provides the illustrated covers for Ayres, *Richard Chatterton, V.C.,* and Ruck, *Khaki and Kisses.*

33. Ayres, *Richard Chatterton, V.C.,* 264–68. Further references are made parenthetically in the text.

34. *The Times Literary Supplement,* 1 July 1915.

35. See Swan, *Woman's Part;* Ayres, *Richard Chatterton, V.C.;* and Ruck, *Khaki and Kisses.*

36. Ayres, *Long Lane to Happiness,* 272–73.

37. Ruck, *Courtship of Rosamond Fayre,* 281. Further references are made parenthetically in the text.

38. Cross, *Evelyn Hastings,* 58, 103–5, 108–13, 156–57.

39. André Beaunier, "Le roman et la guerre," *Revue des Deux Mondes,* 1 Apr. 1916; Alice Berthet, "Les livres," *La Française,* 26 June 1915.

40. For a survey of women's writing before the war, including several of the novelists mentioned here, see Waelti-Walters, *Feminist Novelists.* In the process of completing this manuscript, I was alerted to two recent articles dealing with French women's war writing: Cardinal, "Women and the Language of War," and O'Brien, "Beyond the Can[n]on." From the footnotes in Cardinal's article, I learned that Tinayre, *Les veillée des armes,* and some other significant novels by women not discussed here, such as Marbo, *Le survivant,* and Yver, *Mirabelle de Pampelune,* and stories by Delarue-Mardrus, were translated into English during the war.

41. Tinayre, *Les veillée des armes,* 274. Further references are made parenthetically in the text.

42. Delarue-Mardrus, *Un roman civil.* Further references are made parenthetically in the text. For more on Delarue-Mardrus's war experiences, including family losses and nursing experience, see Plat, *Lucie Delarue-Mardrus,* ch. 7. For another novel with a nurse as heroine, see Duhamelet, *Ces dames de l'hôpital 336.*

43. "Revue de la quinzaine," *Mercure de France* 118 (Dec. 1916).

44. O'Brien, "Beyond the Can[n]on," also discusses this passage as delivering a message of "female subservience" (207).

45. See the appeal of "sister Mary of the Angels" to Jean in Delarue-Mardrus, *Un roman civil,* 133.

46. For more on the *marraine,* see Chapter 4, below. See also the chapter devoted to *les marraines* in Perreux, *La vie quotidienne des civils,* and Vismes, *L'histoire authentique et touchante des marraines.* See also "L'arrière qui fascine" in Audoin-Rouzeau, *14–18, les combattants des tranchées;* Thébaud, *La femme au temps,* 141–47; and Grayzel, "Mothers, Marraines, and Prostitutes."

47. Rachilde had previously praised Landre as possessing an imagination "not only of a woman, but of a *lettrée* (lettered person) when reviewing Landre's earlier war novel, . . . *Puis il mourut.* See Rachilde, "Revue de la quinzaine," *Mercure de France* 115 (June 1916).

48. Rachilde, "Revue de la quinzaine," *Mercure de France* 122 (July 1917).

49. Landre, *L'école des marraines.* Further references are made parenthetically in the text. See also advertisement for *L'école des marraines* in *Le Figaro,* 2 June 1917. Other cautionary tales about *marraines de guerre* appeared in newspapers; see Pierre Valdagne, "La marraine," *Le Journal,* 18 Feb. 1915, and Louis Marsolleau, "Marrainissime," *Le Figaro,* 6 Sept. 1917. See also the comic and popular play, Hennequin et al., *Madame et son filleul,* and the discussion in Grayzel, "Mothers, Marraines, and Prostitutes," and in Chapter 4, below.

50. This rebuke can be found in a number of male-authored texts, but perhaps the most widely read account would be Barbusse. See the previous discussion in this chapter and in *Under Fire,* 152–59.

51. This female-authored novel thus also acknowledges the presence of neur-

asthenia or shell shock, a parallel to its appearance in works by British women like Rebecca West and Rose Macaulay.

52. Stern, *Le baptême du courage*. Further references are made parenthetically in the text.

53. For Hynes's discussion of the DORA case against Allatini and C. W. Daniels, the publisher, see Hynes, *War Imagined*, 232–34. Tylee discusses it in *Great War and Women's Consciousness*, 121–27, focusing on the antecedents for its portrayals of homosexuality and pacifism. She also makes a greater claim for the efficiency with which the British authorities destroyed the original edition of the novel by wrongfully stating that no copy can be found in the British Library (121). In fact, the novel can be found in the British Library under the pseudonym A. T. Fitzroy, which Allatini used in 1918 to publish the book.

54. Hynes, *War Imagined*, notes that Allatini had "previously published one book" under her own name (232), and Tylee, *Great War and Women's Consciousness*, states that Allatini had written several books previously, but only "conventional love stories" (122). Both assertions are misleading; Allatini had published *Payment* in 1915, a novel that would hardly qualify as a "conventional love story," and she wrote another elegiac account of a young man lost to war in *Requiem* in 1919.

55. Allatini, *Despised and Rejected*, 190–96, 301. All further references are made parenthetically in the text. Note, too, how the depiction of the treatment of conscientious objectors resembles that of prewar suffragettes imprisoned for civil disobedience. See the discussion of this in Mayhall, "Creating the 'Suffragette Spirit,' " and in autobiographies such as Lytton, *Prisons and Prisoners*. Feminists were quite active in supporting conscientious objectors; see Kennedy, *Hound of Conscience*.

56. For one of many examples of this role as documented in wartime propaganda, see Paget, *Woman's Part*, 4–5: "It is perhaps at this moment that we realize fully all that is meant by the 'pain & peril of childbirth.' . . . We do not give ourselves but those who are far more precious than ourselves. . . . [But] we give not in resignation but faith."

57. Mrs. Humphry Ward, preface to Yerta, *Six Women and the Invasion*, v. The French edition, *Les six femmes et l'invasion*, lists only one author, Marguerite Yerta. Throughout this discussion I will alternate between the English version, and English title, and the French original, using the French title.

58. "Under the Heel," *The Times Literary Supplement*, 29 Nov. 1917.

59. See "Bibliographie," *Revue Hebdomadaire* (May 1918).

60. "Under the Heel"; *Athenaeum*, no. 4625 (January 1918).

61. Quoted in an advertisement in *The Times Literary Supplement*, 29 Nov. 1917.

62. Yerta, *Six Women*, 27.

63. Yerta, *Les six femmes*, 19.

64. Yerta, *Six Women*, 28.

65. Yerta, *Les six femmes*, 30.

66. Yerta, *Six Women*, 105–6. Yerta also described one other encounter in which she and one of her sisters-in-law are almost caught by a German, who was able to force his way into the house (see Yerta, *Les six femmes*, 259–61).

67. Yerta, *Six Women*, 202–3.

68. Ibid., 206–12.

69. Ibid., 327. (Yerta, *Les six femmes*, 245, refers more overtly to the Laonnois suffering a "minimum of horrors.") Yerta's account of rapes in the region focused on attacks on older women (328–29), stressing that they fell victim because they were less able to run away and because the Germans had no respect for the aged.

70. Yerta, *Six Women*, 329.

71. Yerta, *Les six femmes*, 247.

72. Yerta, *Six Women*, 330.

73. Gromaire, *L'occupation allemande en France*, 274, 277. Gromaire states that over 20,000 people were deported under this "horrible tyranny" (277). See also the discussion in Annette Becker, *Oubliés de la Grande Guerre*, 68–77.

74. "Les femmes françaises aux femmes de tous les pays," Dec. 1916, in documents on the "Deportations des femmes en Avril 1916," assembled by the Union Française pour le Suffrage des Femmes, 15 Apr. 1919, in DOS 940.3 GUE, BMD. See the note explaining that this appeal was read by Mme. Brunschvicg of the UFSF at a demonstration organized by the Ligue des Droits de l'Homme.

75. [Ministère des Affaires Étrangères], *Deportation of Women and Girls*, 5. Further references are made parenthetically in the text.

76. "Bibliographie," *Revue Hebdomadaire* (Aug. 1918).

77. Celarié, *En esclavage*, 104–6.

78. Ibid., 36.

79. Ibid., 33–34, 71, 77, 120, 136–37. This point was also underscored in testimony collected after the war; see documents on the "Deportations des Femmes en Avril 1916," assembled by the Union Française pour le Suffrage des Femmes, 15 Apr. 1919, in DOS 940.3 GUE, BMD.

80. Celarié, *En esclavage*, 130–31, 51, 129.

81. Ibid., 123, 56–58, 59 (emphasis in the original).

82. Celarié, *Slaves of the Huns*, 2. The words "within seven hours of London" appear above the title on the cover. For a full discussion of W. S. Stead's "The Maiden Tribute," see Walkowitz, *City of Dreadful Delight*, chs. 3 and 4.

83. Celarié, *Slaves of the Huns*, 32 and 51. Other italicized passages include "ten soldiers to carry off one child" and "I am suffering all this pain and fatigue for the Germans, to feed them and enable them" (110 and 150).

84. Celarié, *Slaves of the Huns*, 195; also *En esclavage*, 182.

85. "Come Where You Will," Dec. 1914, in *Mr. Punch's History of the Great War*, 15.

86. Marion Ryan, "The Women's Splendid Courage in the Raided Areas. How They Met Frightfulness from the Sky Alone and Unprotected," *Weekly Dispatch*, 1 Oct. 1916. See also "Women Raid Helpers," *Leeds Mercury*, 15 Dec. 1917, on proposals to train women to look after women and children taking refuge during air raids, and articles in the *South London Press*, 21 Dec. 1917, which include accounts of women's bravery as well as of women and children killed or injured because of the bombing.

87. Lady Frances Balfour, "The Women Are Ready—A Plea for Opportunities of Service," *Birmingham Gazette & Express*, 20 Mar. 1915.

88. PRC 29, IWM: POS 5089. Another poster depicting a zeppelin flying over

Big Ben stated plainly: "It is far better to face the bullets than to be killed at home by a bomb" (IWM: POS 3283).

89. IWM: POS 5119.

90. Coroner's Depositions, Testimony of Margaret Wells, 26 Dec. 1917, in CRIM 1 171/1, 7. The medical officer at Holloway prison also commented on the effect of air warfare on Violet Cambridge, another woman charged with infanticide in June 1916. As he noted, "[S]he appeared to have been terrified at the thought of Zeppelins. . . . [W]hen the subject inadvertently arose, she exhibited extreme signs of apprehension and terror and burst into tears." See "Report of Francis Edward Forward, Medical Officer," 23 June 1916, CRIM 1 161/4.

91. Coroner's Depositions, Testimony of Mary Freeman, 26 Dec. 1917, in CRIM 1 171/1, 2. A recent interpretation of the production of "war neuroses" in civilians in relationship to new forms of warfare and particularly as represented in HD's writing can be found in Tate, "HD's War Neurotics," 241–44, 256, and *Modernism, History,* ch. 1.

92. Coroner's Depositions, Testimony of Edmund Burke Holland, registered Medical Practitioner, 26 Dec. 1917, in CRIM 1 171/1, 10.

93. Medical Officer's Report, 5 Jan. 1918, in CRIM 1 171/1.

94. See the account of Parisian women responding to air raids in Alice Berthet, "La réponse des parisiennes au raid des Gothas sur Paris," *La Française,* 9 Feb. 1918.

CHAPTER TWO

1. For an analytical overview, see Porter, "Rape—Does It Have a Historical Meaning?" An important if problematic treatment of rape in war remains Brownmiller, *Against Our Will.* For useful discussions of rape in the context of World War II, see Tröger, "Between Rape and Prostitution"; Naimark, *Russians in Germany,* ch. 2; and Grossmann, "Question of Silence." For more recent wars, see Ruth Seifert, "War and Rape: A Preliminary Analysis," and Cynthia Enloe's afterword, both in Stiglmayer, *Mass Rape.*

2. This has been analyzed in Kent, *Making Peace,* chs. 1–2, and Gullace, "Sexual Violence and Family Honor," and for the uses of atrocity accounts on film, see Morey, "Sexuality, Maternity, and Femininity." On posters, see Curtis, "Posters As Visual Propaganda," and Dutton, "Moving Images?"; and on propaganda in general in Britain, see Haste, *Keep the Home Fires Burning;* Sanders and Taylor, *British Propaganda;* and Messinger, *British Propaganda and the State.* For a recent reassessment of the validity of atrocity accounts, see Horne and Kramer, "German 'Atrocities.'" For immediate postwar reaction, see Posonby, *Falsehood in War-Time.* Like Posonby, writers of postwar histories of wartime sexuality viewed wartime hysteria as the cause for invented or imagined stories of rape. See Hirschfeld, *Sexual History of the World War,* 321–26, and Fisher and Dubois, *Sexual Life during the World War,* 461–67.

3. Harris, " 'Child of the Barbarian,' " 170. This was also true for France during the Franco-Prussian War; see Reshef, *Guerre, mythes et caricature.* The "rape of Belgium" was used to refer to the violation of this neutral nation's frontiers; France was symbolized as a victimized women but not referred to as a "raped" nation.

4. See, for Britain, Committee on Alleged German Outrages, *Report of the Committee,* and for France, *Documents relatifs à la guerre.*

5. For a recent elaboration of this point, see Gullace, "Sexual Violence and Family Honor."

6. As Brubaker has demonstrated, French laws about nationality hinged on the notion of jus soli, that is, it was enough to have been born in France to become a French citizen; by the end of the eighteenth century one had to prove either a French birthplace or a French father, and as ideas about citizenship developed in the nineteenth century, they had a strongly assimilationist component. However, the blood of the father or French paternity itself could also transmit nationality. See Brubaker, *Citizenship and Nationhood,* ch. 5, esp. 85–93.

7. Thébaud, *La femme au temps,* 58. It is a topic not mentioned in her comparative essay, "La Grande Guerre." Scholars, such as Wishnia, in "Natalisme et nationalisme"; Harris, in " 'Child of the Barbarian' "; and, most importantly, Audoin-Rouzeau, in *L'enfant de l'ennemi,* have begun to reexamine this issue more fully.

8. Docquois begins his book with the following song lyrics: "Let's make love, let's make war / These two metiers are full of attractions / War, to the world, is a little expensive / Love reimburses all its costs / May the enemy, may the shepherdess / Be, each in turn, pressed hard / Oh my friends, can one do better / When one has depopulated the earth / Than to repopulate it after? / Behold the ravishers" (Docquois, *La chair innocente,* iv–v; quotation is on vi).

9. Quoted in Docquois, *La chair innocente,* 3. Harris also begins her discussion of this debate with this article, noting that *Le Matin* was a widely read daily, but she does not discuss the appearance of the official government report of atrocities in the press. See Harris, " 'Child of the Barbarian,' " 191.

10. "Les crimes de l'armée allemande," *Le Figaro,* 8 Jan. 1915; see also "Les atrocités allemandes," *L'Éclair,* 8 Jan. 1915, and "Atrocités allemandes: Un document officiel," *L'Écho de Paris,* 8 Jan. 1915. See also the response in "Femmes outragées," *La Française,* 16 Jan. 1915.

11. "À la nation," *Le Matin,* 8 Jan. 1915.

12. *Documents relatifs à la guerre 1914–1915, Rapport I,* 12, 16–18, 36, 43. See also the influential pamphlet by Bédier, titled *Les crimes allemands,* for accounts of rape and murder allegedly based on German evidence. For more on this pamphlet's dissemination and influence, see Hanna, *Mobilization of Intellect,* 75, 86, 260 n. 108, and Horne and Kramer, "German 'Atrocities.' "

13. Quoted in Docquois, *La chair innocente,* 7–8. See also the material from *La Bataille Syndicaliste* in Fonds Arria Ly, Box 7, Fonds Bouglé, BHVP.

14. Georges Montorgueil, "Les mères outragées," *L'Éclair,* 11 Feb. 1915.

15. See the discussion of these measures in Berger and Allard, *Les secrets de la censure,* 11.

16. Léon Frapie, "Les réprouvés," *La Guerre Sociale,* 10 Feb. 1915.

17. See Camille Mauclair, "La menteuse," *Le Journal,* 28 Feb. 1915, and Michel Provins, "L'horrible secret," *Le Journal,* 14 Feb. 1915.

18. "Communication du dépot de propositions de loi," *Journal Officiel: Sénat, Débats Parlementaires,* 18 Feb. 1915, 37. This change would have affected paragraphs 1, 2, and 3 of article 317 of the penal code. This is also discussed in Thébaud, *La femme*

au temps, 58, and Harris, " 'Child of the Barbarian,' " 191. Martin also proposed the reintroduction of *tours*—rotating devices that allowed women to abandon their babies anonymously.

19. Docquois, *La chair innocente,* 61, 73.

20. "Femmes victimes des violence allemandes," Confidential Circular, 14 June 1915, Ministry of the Interior, AN F23 3.

21. "Rapport . . . du Préfet de la Seine sur la situation générale du département au 24 Août 1915," AN F7 13354. This report covers the months February to August 1915. The Department of the Seine included Paris, on which this report focuses. The 24 March 1915 Circular of the Ministry of the Interior was reprinted in "Textes et documents officiels relatifs à l'hygiène publique parus pendant la première année de la guerre," *Revue Pratique d'Hygiène Municipale Urbaine et Rurale,* no. 8 (August 1914–15). See also Harris, " 'Child of the Barbarian,' " 192.

22. "Rapport . . . du Préfet de la Seine . . . 24 Août 1915," AN F7 13354, 554–59.

23. Misme is cited in Thébaud, *La femme au temps,* 58–59, and the latter quote is from Jane Misme, "La leçon du crime," *La Française,* 13 Mar. 1915.

24. "Que fera-t-on des petits indésirés? Divers réponses," *La Française,* 20 Feb. 1915.

25. Jane Misme, "La défense de petits indésirées," *La Française,* 27 Feb. 1915.

26. Jane Misme, quoted in Docquois, *La chair innocente,* 44.

27. Jeanne Schmahl, quoted in Docquois, *La chair innocente,* 42.

28. Both Karen Offen and Ruth Harris have emphasized the strong streak of maternalism in French feminist politics. Harris links maternalism to Catholic moral arguments in this specific case. See Offen, "Depopulation, Nationalism and Feminism," and Harris, " 'Child of the Barbarian,' " 194–95. For a critique of maternalism, see my concluding chapter, below.

29. Quoted in Docquois, *La chair innocente,* 71–72. See also Colette, "L'enfant de l'ennemi," in *Les heures longues* (1917), cited in Cardinal, "Women and the Language of War," 161.

30. Both Delarue-Mardrus and Yver are quoted in Rabier, *La loi du mâle,* 29–30, 34.

31. Quoted in Rabier, *La loi du mâle,* 36–37, 44.

32. Dr. Filliette, *Caducée,* 15 Mar. 1915, quoted in Docquois, *La chair innocente,* 68. Such debates also relied on a set of suppositions about what kind of children would result from conceptions due to rape.

33. Jean Finot, letter, quoted in Docquois, *La chair innocente,* 89–92. The author of the original story was Jehan Rictus.

34. Annabelle Melzer's recent work would seem to suggest, however, that when it came to representing sexual relations between French colonial troops and French women, women were portrayed not as victims but as willing participants. See Melzer, "Spectacles and Sexualities."

35. Rabier, *La loi du mâle.* For a discussion of Rabier's treatise, emphasizing its views on these children as emblems of defeat and on male behavior, see Harris, " 'Child of the Barbarian,' " 199–200.

36. Rabier, *La loi du mâle,* 14–24.

37. Ibid., 62–64.

38. "La maternité consécutive aux viols allemands," *Journal du Droit International* 43 (Sept–Dec. 1916), 898–99. This article cites *Le Matin*, 24 Apr. 1915, as the source of the information about the league's resolution; but see also the account of this meeting in the "Rapport sur la réunion de la Ligue Nationale des Femmes Françaises," 23 Apr. 1915, AN F7 13266.

39. "L'opinion," *Le Figaro*, 6 Feb. 1916, is also cited in *Journal du Droit International*, 898. The article in *La Depêche*, 10 Feb. 1916, can be found in the Fonds Arria Ly, Box 7, Fonds Bouglé, BHVP. I have been unable to ascertain the validity of the alleged German offer. However, its appearance in a major French newspaper as well as its repetition suggests French willingness to spread information that such an offer was possible. See the related discussion on *La houille rouge*, below, and of women under occupation in Chapter 1, above.

40. A previous infanticide case at the Cour d'Assises de l'Aveyron was discussed in "La maternité consécutive aux viols allemands," 898, which cited a case of a young woman of the region around Péronne who was violated by a German soldier and who strangled the infant that resulted from this attack. She received a two-year, suspended prison sentence. The case is cited as being reported in *Les Débats*, 28 Mar. 1916. See also the articles about this case from *Le Midi Socialiste*, 29 Mar. 1916, and *La Croix de l'Aveyron*, 26 Mar. 1916, in Fonds Arria Ly, Box 7, Fonds Bouglé, BHVP. However, no mention was made of this precedent in the publicity surrounding the more notorious case of Joséphine Barthélemy.

41. Barthélemy's case is discussed in some detail in Audoin-Rouzeau, *L'enfant de l'ennemi*. For contemporaneous accounts, see Docquois, *La chair innocente*, 153–76, and Dr. Gustave Drouineau, "À propos d'un infanticide," *Revue Philanthropique* (Feb. 1917); for newspaper coverage of Barthélemy's 1917 trial, see, for example, "Gazette des tribunaux," *Le Figaro*, 24 Jan. 1917, and "L'enfant du barbare," *Le Journal*, 25 Jan. 1917. With regard to pregnancies resulting from German rape, Drouineau had previously written about the dangers of abortion in "Les femmes victimes des allemands," *Revue Philanthropique* (Apr. 1915).

42. See Docquois, *La chair innocente*, 173–75; Drouineau, "À Propos d'un infanticide," 49; Barthélemy's own evidence quoted in *Le Figaro*, 24 Jan. 1917; and the events as summarized by Barthélemy's lawyer. The fact that she alleged the child never cried is significant, since the lack of a cry could suggest a stillbirth.

43. Quoted in *Excelsior* and cited in Docquois, *La chair innocente*, 155.

44. Loewel, "Plaidoire, Cour d'Assises de la Seine," 190, 187–89. My thanks to Stéphane Audoin-Rouzeau for this reference.

45. Docquois, *La chair innocente*, 173–75, cites the original interrogation by police.

46. "Devant le jury l'enfant du boche," *Le Matin*, 24 Jan. 1917. See also *Le Figaro*, 24 Jan. 1917, and *Le Journal*, 25 Jan. 1917.

47. *Le Figaro*, 24 Jan. 1917; *Le Matin*, 24 Jan. 1917.

48. *Le Journal*, 25 Jan. 1917; Docquois, *La chair innocente*, 156–57.

49. De Witt-Schlumberger and Pinard quoted in *Le Journal*, 25 Jan. 1917, and Docquois, *La chair innocente*, 162–63.

50. Drouineau, "À propos d'un infanticide," 50–54.

51. Drouineau comments on her lack of intelligence (ibid., 49, 51), as do several commentators cited in Docquois, *La chair innocente,* 156.

52. Docquois, *La chair innocente,* 159, 161.

53. These debates would not end with the war. For an immediate postwar discussion of "the bastards of the war," see J. Laumonier, "Les batârds de la guerre dans la population française," *Gazette des Hôpitaux,* 20 Feb. 1919.

54. Curtis, "Posters," 50. See also Dutton, "Moving Images?"

55. See Gullace, "Women and the Ideology of War"; Haste, *Keep the Home Fires Burning;* Kent, *Making Peace.*

56. PRC 69, IWM: POS 247, in Catalog of PRC Posters. These were reprinted in "Four Questions to Women," PRC Leaflet no. 31, and expanded upon in "Women and the War," PRC Leaflet no. 23, IWM: K 33304, Misc. Recruiting.

57. IWM: PST/0071, Non-Parliamentary Recruiting Committee Misc. Catalog.

58. All references here to IWM: PST 6066.

59. The association between male sexuality and men as "beasts" also has a more complicated history as illustrated by the fin-de-siècle feminist campaigns about sexual morality; see Bland, *Banishing the Beast.* For an example of French propaganda using such motifs, see the drawing *Nouvelle Consigne* by A. Willette appearing in *Le Rire* and reproduced in *Je Sais Tout,* 15 Mar. 1915.

60. Bryce's integrity and the creation of the Committee on Alleged German Outrages are discussed in Trevor Wilson, *Myriad Faces of War,* 183–84.

61. Committee on Alleged German Outrages, *Report of the Committee,* 29, 16, 22. For another account of these types of atrocities, see Le Queux, *German Atrocities,* 5, 14.

62. Committee on Alleged German Outrages, *Appendix to the Report of the Committee;* see a21 for the rape of a nine-month pregnant woman, 7; a33 for the rape of a woman after her child had been decapitated in front of her, 12; and c39 for the rape of a woman in front of her child, which results in pregnancy, 43.

63. Gullace, "Women and the Ideology of War," notes that Germans were thought to attack "motherhood in the ritual mutilation of women's breasts" (80, n. 42).

64. Weston, *Germany's Crime,* 20.

65. Albert Giuliani's novel *Les berceaux tragiques,* for instance, had gone into sixteen printings by 1923. Works by Annie Vivanti Chartres and Lillith Hope received favorable reviews in the influential *The Times Literary Supplement,* as will be discussed below.

66. Giuliani, *Les berceaux tragiques,* 27–28. Further references are made parenthetically in the text.

67. It is worth observing that the pro-abortion position taken by Dr. Loriol is further presented as immoral, because immediately following this heated exchange, he goes off to see his mistress—whom we later discover to be a German spy—while the priest returns to church in order to pray.

68. This scene suggests the importance of pregnancy as providing "visual" proof of the rape.

69. That such a religious claim could exert a universal influence is itself part of

the wartime *union sacrée,* which urged a reconciliation between radicals and socialists (who were notoriously anticlerical) and true believers.

70. Harris, " 'Child of the Barbarian'," 175–76.

71. *The Times Literary Supplement,* 22 Feb. 1917, 95.

72. Hope, *Behold and See,* 39. Further references are made parenthetically in the text.

73. Dulac, who was in her fifties during the war, was a singer before becoming a writer "dedicated to defending the feminine sex." See Temeron, "Dulac."

74. On the title page, the expression "Les enfants de la violence" (the children of violence) is placed above the actual title. "Houille Rouge" is the name of the secret German spy society that occupies a significant part of the novel. However, the expression "red coal" is given many different meanings in the course of the novel. It is stated, for instance, that "blood is the red coal of civilisation" (73); red coal is also used as the spark that will start the fire that will destroy all of France and as a metaphor for abortion—Mme. Rhoea claims that as an abortionist, "J'ai brûlé de la houille rouge" (137). I will be discussing only a few of the many complicated strands of this plot. References to *La houille rouge* are made parenthetically in the text.

75. Dulac's vivid portrayal of dying soldiers calling upon their mothers is echoed in the more "realistic" source of trench newspapers. See the excerpt from *L'Écho du Boqueteau,* 12 Mar. 1917, quoted in Audoin-Rouzeau, *14–18, les combattants aux tranchées,* 87–88.

76. She is later encountered by Jeanne Deckes, utterly mad, describing herself as one "who eats children," and is eventually shot and killed; see Dulac, *La houille rouge,* 204–8.

77. See Dulac, *La houille rouge,* 84–86 and 149–52.

78. Like the alleged German general's offer reported in *Le Figaro,* the Germans even offer to pay a price for the child, since they suspect he was, in their words, "the fruit . . . of a German favor"; see note 39, above. Deckes insists that he is "French, since I am French" (285).

79. The naming of this child "Christian" is parallel to the naming of the child "Noel" in *Les berceaux tragiques;* the names associate these infants with the Christ child.

80. Quoted in Docquois, *La chair innocente,* 164–65. Once again, such reasoning made motherhood and soldiering equivalent, gender-specific roles during wartime.

81. Rachilde, "Revue de la quinzaine," *Mercure de France* 117 (Sept. 1916).

82. Chartres, *Vae victis,* 45–47. Further references are made parenthetically in the text. The full text of the British edition of *Vae victis* was reprinted by Knopf in New York in 1918, under the title *The Outrage.* This trans-Atlantic publication also suggests the importance of the novel since it could reach and persuade Americans as well.

83. The diary excerpts that constitute chapters 11 and 12 are written in a breathless, chaotic style that mirrors the horrors Chérie tries to remember (158).

84. *The Times Literary Supplement,* 1 Nov. 1917.

85. Pitrois, *Femmes de 1914–1915,* 133, 140.

86. Anger against Germany was also stirred up by narratives portraying rape victims who died as a result of German attacks; see Floran, *L'ennemi,* and Cicely Hamilton, *William.*

CHAPTER THREE

1. "The Call to Arms," *Evening Standard,* 26 Aug. 1914. This message can also be found in recruiting posters; see the maternal images in "Go! It's Your Duty Lad," IWM: POS 5162, and "Women of Britain Say Go!," IWM: POS 0313.

2. The usefulness of allowances for recruiting is illustrated by the posters and leaflets created for this purpose, promising aid to the wives and children of married soldiers and dependents—including children—regardless of the legal relationships of unmarried soldiers. See IWM: K 33304, Misc. Recruiting, and "Soldiers' Separation Allowances," IWM: POS.

3. For information about comparative birthrates, see Figure 7.1 in Offen, "Body Politics," 139. This chart reveals a precipitous drop in the birthrate during the war years in Britain, France, and Germany, followed by a postwar rise. For statistics on French wartime illegitimacy in the nonoccupied territories of France that indicate that this number decreased from the prewar period and rose during the war from 8.4 percent in 1913–14, to 11.2 percent in 1915, to 14.2 percent in 1917, see Thébaud, *La femme,* 196. See note 48, below, for British illegitimacy rates.

4. "Un soldat sur le front peut reconnaître un enfant," *La Française,* 12 Dec. 1914.

5. See "Discussion d'un projet de loi relatif au mariage par procuration," *Journal Officiel: Sénat, Débats Parlementaires,* 18 Mar. 1915, 104–7. The Senate adopted the law and the Chamber would follow. Quote above is from 105.

6. "Les soldats sur le front pourront se marier par procuration," *La Française,* 10 Apr. 1915, and "Le mariage par procuration," *L'Écho de Paris,* 10 Apr. 1915. The Chamber voted on this legislation on 1 April 1915.

7. This was first announced in "La légitimation posthume des orphelins votée au Sénat," *La Française,* 1 July 1916, and modifications in the law were reported in "Légitimation posthume des orphelins de la guerre," *La Française,* 2 Dec. 1916, and "Au Parlement," *La Française,* 10 Mar. 1917. See also the discussion of "la légitimation des enfants dont les pères sont décédés aux armées" in De la Hire, *La femme française,* 207–8. Soldiers at the front also rejected children attributed to them; see "Gazette des tribunaux," *Le Figaro,* 11 Mar. 1917, where a soldier was reported to deny being the father of a child born to his wife because of the "physical impossibility" of his having cohabited with her since he was at the front.

8. Pedersen, "Gender, Welfare and Citizenship," 989. See also her *Family, Dependence.* Details of measures taken to create the National Relief Fund can be found in *Memorandum on the Steps Taken for the Prevention and Relief of Distress Due to the War.*

9. Pankhurst, *Home Front,* 98. Pankhurst claimed to have found instead an increase in sobriety in all classes, "accelerated by the shortening of public house hours, the reduction in the strength of beer, and other factors."

10. Pedersen, "Gender, Welfare and Citizenship," 996–97 n. 47. See also "Soldiers' Wives," *Leicester Mail,* 14 Dec. 1914.

11. Rowland Kenney, "Soldier's Dependents," *The English Review* (Dec. 1914), 117.

12. Pedersen, "Gender, Welfare and Citizenship," 997–99; "Police Advice to Soldiers' Wives," *The Vigilance Record* (Dec. 1914). For a wartime critique of these measures, see H. Wilson Harris, "The Soldier's Wife: A Liberal View," *The Englishwoman*, no. 74 (Feb. 1915).

13. See the use of this distinction in Soldiers' and Sailors' Families Association, *Thirtieth Annual Report*, 13–21.

14. For details, see ibid. The support of unmarried mothers was publicized in "Separation Allowances for the Unmarried," *The Vigilance Record* (Dec. 1914). See also Pankhurst, *Home Front*, 175.

15. For a full account of the administering of separation allowances, see Pedersen, *Family, Dependence*, 112–13.

16. Report of Soldiers' and Sailors' Families Association Special General Meeting, 28 January 1915, in The Soldiers' and Sailors' Families Association, *Thirtieth Annual Report*, 1874–78.

17. See comments of both women in ibid., 1894–95.

18. Speech of Mr. Hayes Fisher in ibid., 1880–85.

19. See Rev. Thomas Elliott quoted in ibid., 1893, and Miss Wiseman quoted in ibid., 1888.

20. Ibid., 1897. The actual numbers were 329 out of 449.

21. SSFA, War Circular No. 3, reprinted in ibid., 1917.

22. "The Unmarried Mother," *Manchester Guardian*, 23 Feb. 1915.

23. Ronald McNeill, letter to the editor, *Morning Post*, [1915], quoted in Pankhurst, *Home Front*, 175. E. Sylvia Pankhurst, in her history of the war years, claimed that McNeill initiated the controversy surrounding war babies eight months after Britain's entry into the war.

24. White's resolution was quoted in "Care of War Babies," *Daily Chronicle*, 23 Apr. 1915. See also *Parliamentary Debates*, Commons, 5th ser., vol. 71 (1915), cols. 963–64.

25. *Parliamentary Debates*, Commons, 5th ser., vol. 71 (1915), col. 833–34.

26. Brittain, *Testament of Youth*, 141. She is presumably quoting from her diary.

27. Lucy Deane Streatfeild and Harriet Whitting, letter to the editor, *Morning Post*, 15 Apr. 1915. For another plea for the support of unwed mothers and their infants under the rubric of appealing for war babies, see Mary Drew, letter to the editor, *Manchester Guardian*, 26 Apr. 1915.

28. Mary Longman, letter to the editor, *Manchester Guardian*, 26 Apr. 1915.

29. "The Suffragettes and the War Babies," *Herts Advertiser*, 15 May 1915. The article further noted that "the women Suffragists are certainly showing their fitness for the franchise by their quiet helpfulness in this time of danger and need." The article neither explained nor questioned why Mrs. Pankhurst wanted to help only female infants.

30. "Women and War Service," *Daily Telegraph*, 2 June 1915.

31. Pankhurst, *Home Front*, 175.

32. Austin Harrison, "For the Unborn," *The English Review* (May 1915), 231–36.

33. The archbishop quoted in the *Daily Express* and subsequently in "The Problem of the Unmarried Mother," *The Vigilance Record* (May 1915).

34. "The War Babies: No Definite Information Obtainable," *Manchester Guardian*, 27 Apr. 1915.

35. Mrs. Arnold Glover quoted in ibid. She further asserted that "it was, generally speaking, the unattached girl with few interests in her life who succumbed to temptation."

36. "The War Babies," *Manchester Guardian*, 29 Apr. 1915.

37. A copy of a statement to this effect issued from Lambeth Palace on 26 April is quoted in "Problem of the Unmarried Mother."

38. Ibid.

39. Quoted in "Primate's Speech," *Manchester Daily Dispatch*, 28 Apr. 1915.

40. "United Suffragist," letter to the editor, *Liverpool Courier*, 3 May 1915. All quotations in this paragraph are from this letter.

41. For uses of such rhetoric in the prewar suffrage campaign, see Kent, *Sex and Suffrage*, and for more general use, see Bland, *Banishing the Beast*.

42. "Archbishop of York's Report," *Standard*, 18 June 1915.

43. Louise Creighton and the bishop of London quoted in "Bishop and the War Baby Delusion," *Morning Advertiser*, 7 June 1915, a report of a meeting held at Mansion House the previous day. The bishop and Mrs. Creighton were followed by Sir Edward Henry, the metropolitan police commissioner who signaled out the women patrols for especial praise for their help in "suppressing unseemly conduct." See Levine, " 'Walking the Streets,' " for more on the women patrols.

44. "Archbishop of York's Report."

45. Ibid.

46. This statement and the above information comes from "Report of the Sub-Committee," quoted in ibid.

47. Ibid.

48. Kent, in *Making Peace*, 28 and 30, quotes both historians and contemporaries in regard to these fears, as well as articles on war babies in the *The Common Cause*. They are also mentioned briefly in Woollacott, *On Her Their Lives Depend*, 147–48. Despite the anxiety, the overall increase in wartime illegitimate births was quite small. A chart reproduced in Pankhurst, *Home Front*, 176, shows that in England and Wales from 1911 to 1914 illegitimate births went from 43 per 1,000 of all births to 52 per 1,000 total births from 1915 to 1918, while in Scotland the rate stayed at 73 per 1,000 births from 1911 to 1922.

49. Stopes, *Race*, 48. Further references to this work are made parenthetically in the text. Another, more pessimistic imaginative attempt to deal with the different issues raised by the war baby question can be found in D. O. G. Peto, "The Return," *The Englishwoman*, no. 83 (Nov. 1915). In Peto's "sketch," set in a 1917 postwar world, the future happiness of a surviving soldier and his sweetheart is shattered by the knowledge that he had an affair with another woman while he was undergoing his training. For a fuller discussion of these texts, see Grayzel, " 'The Mothers of Our Soldiers' Children.' "

50. "Report of the Sub-Committee," quoted in *Standard*, 18 June 1915.

51. For a discussion of this phenomenon, see Lionel Rose, *Massacre of the Innocents.*

52. This act was also recommended by the Royal Commission on Venereal Diseases as a way of obtaining better information about venereal disease rates and their impact on the next generation. See Douglas White, "Synopsis," *Report of the Royal Commission on Venereal Diseases,* 18.

53. See the discussion in Audoin-Rouzeau, *L'enfant de l'ennemi,* and in Chapter 2.

54. See CRIM 1 168/1. See also Woollacott, *On Her Their Lives Depend,* 150–51.

55. See CRIM 1 168/2, 168/3, 167/6. I do not have a large enough sample to determine how common each of these explanations was and how representative. However, I am suggesting that for every infanticide or abortion that was "discovered," and particularly in the case of abortions, similar cases probably existed. I am using these records not to determine how many women sought to terminate their pregnancies or their maternal responsibilities but to probe women's decisions regarding motherhood.

56. See chart on "Births per thousand population in seven European Countries, 1880–1950," in Bock and Thane, *Maternity and Gender Policies,* 17, for evidence of comparative birthrates. See also Cole, "'There Are Only Good Mothers'"; Cova, "French Feminism and Maternity" and "Les droits des femmes"; Offen, "Body Politics" and "Depopulation, Nationalism and Feminism"; Soloway, *Birth Control and the Population Question* and "Eugenics and Pronatalism in Wartime Britain"; McLaren, *Sexuality and Social Order;* Ronsin, *La grève des ventres;* Mary Louise Roberts, *Civilization without Sexes;* and Dyer, *Population and Society.*

57. For the wartime birthrate in the U.K., see charts in National Council of Public Morals, *Problems of Population.* For contemporaneous concern about Britain's imperial future, see Marchant, *Birth-Rate and Empire.*

58. See Pedersen, *Family, Dependence;* Koven and Michel, *Mothers of a New World;* Bock and Thane, *Maternity and Gender Policies;* Dwork, *War Is Good for Babies;* and Ross, *Love and Toil.*

59. Blouet, *Deux ennemis de l'intérieur,* 13, 15.

60. Marguerite de Witt-Schlumberger quoted in "L'action sociale et morale en faveur de la maternité," *La Française,* 25 Mar. 1916. Recognition of the importance of motherhood was also highlighted in S. Carr, "En l'honneur des mères," *La Française,* 6 May 1916, which spoke of mothers immense suffering in war as entitling them to special "Journée de la Mère," an honor that would be realized after the war.

61. [Marguerite] de Witt-Schlumberger, "Le devoir particulier des femmes," *La Française,* 12 May 1917.

62. Verdier, *Le problème de la natalité,* 6.

63. Raphael-Georges Lévy, "L'enfant de la guerre," *Revue Bleue* 55, no. 2 (Jan. 1917).

64. Vuillermet, *La mobilisation des berceaux,* ch. 1. Further references to this work are made parenthetically in the text.

65. Krug, *Pour la repopulation,* 3–4, 6.

66. De Roux, *L'état et la natalité.*

67. The use of Millet's image in World War One propaganda such as this poster is mentioned in Vardi, "Construing the Harvest," 1424. See other posters from

1917 and 1918 in the collection of the IWM. In posters for postwar "peace loans" of 1920, rural women were again featured, but here they were shown breast-feeding their children, not performing other kinds of work; see Paillard, *Affiches 14–18*, 275.

68. Association Nationale Française . . . , *La maternité ouvrière*, 9. See also the concern expressed by Gaston Rageot, in a section entitled "La mère ouvrière" in *La Française dans la guerre*, 26–30.

69. Ibid., 11.

70. Ibid., 15–17.

71. Dr. Bonnaire, address to Association Nationale Française . . . , *La maternité ouvrière*, 5. Bonnaire was chief obstetrician at the Maternité de Paris; see Downs, *Manufacturing Inequality*, 168.

72. Stewart, *Women, Work, and the French State*, 193–94. See also Downs, *Manufacturing Inequality*, 168–72, and Cova, "Les droits des femmes," ch. 6. The "Loi concernant l'allaitement maternal dans les établissements industriels et commerciaux," 5 Aug. 1917, was also reprinted in *Revue d'Hygiène et de Police Sanitaire* (July–Aug. 1917), 522.

73. Jacques-Amédée Doléris, "Sur la proposition de voeux relatifs à la protection maternelle et infantile dans les usines de guerre," *Bulletin de l'Academie de Médecine*, 30 Jan. 1917, 116–19.

74. Doléris, *Néo-Malthusianisme, maternité*, 16–18, 73–74, quote from 73.

75. A. Pinard, "L'usine tueuse d'enfants," *Le Matin*, 6 Dec. 1916. Italics in the original.

76. A. Pinard, "De la protection de l'enfance pendant la deuxième année de guerre . . . ," *Revue d'Hygiène et de Police Sanitaire* (Jan. 1917), 36. This report was delivered to the Academy of Medicine and also printed in the *Bulletin de l'Academie de Médecine*.

77. Paul Strauss quoted in *Bulletin de l'Academie de Médecine*, 2 Jan. 1917, 30–31.

78. "Sur la proposition de voeux relatifs à la protection maternelle et infantile dans les usines de guerre," *Bulletin de l'Academie de Médecine*, 13 Mar. 1917, 367–68. A copy of the final report by Dr. Jacques-Amédée Doléris was reprinted in *Revue d'Hygiène et de Police Sanitaire* (Apr.–May 1917), 277–83, and was also issued separately under the title "La protection des femmes et des enfants dans les usines" (Paris: Acad. de Médecine, 1917). A copy of the latter can be found in AN F22 444.

79. See the response from Mme. Legrelle de Ferrer in "Bulletin des sociétés féministes," *La Française*, 23 Dec. 1916.

80. Jeanne Bouvier, "L'usine de guerre, tueuse d'enfants," *L'Action Féminine*, no. 47 (Mar. 1917). For more on Bouvier's wartime activities on behalf of women wageworkers, see Coffin, *Politics of Women's Work*, ch. 8.

81. See "Loi concernant l'allaitement maternal," 522.

82. "Woman's First War Duty," *World's Work* (June 1918).

83. An important analysis of state interest in mothers and soldiers and the development of the welfare state can be found in Skocpol, *Protecting Mothers and Soldiers*.

84. Mrs. Henry Fawcett, "Mobilizing Women," *Church Family Newspaper*, 25 Nov. 1914.

85. All material in this paragraph is from Austin Harrison, "Motherhood the First Duty of Women: Biological Crisis of the Next Decade," *Sunday Pictorial,* 21 Mar. 1915.

86. Alex M. Thompson, "Fresh Calling for Girls: The Useful Trade of Motherhood Better Than Acting As Taxi-Drivers," *Sunday Herald,* 18 Apr. 1915.

87. The use of the word "citizen" in this article is suggestive of its associations, particularly during the war, with military service. For a fuller discussion of this issue, see Chapter 6, below.

88. Ronald Carter, letter to the editor, *The Times,* 21 Sept. 1915. He concluded his letter by stating that the "work" of motherhood "is of even greater importance than the manufacture of shells."

89. Davies, "Motherhood and the State," 1.

90. Davies, *Maternity,* 154.

91. To some extent, this resembles the metaphoric use of the maternal body in propaganda—the threat to the motherland represented as a threat to the maternal body.

92. Davies, *Maternity,* 131.

93. Ibid., 89–90.

94. "The State and the Mother," *Quarterly Review* (Oct. 1917), 465–68. See also the review in *The Englishwoman,* no. 83 (Nov. 1915).

95. Advertisement for Davies's *Maternity, Women's Industrial News* 20, no. 72 (Jan. 1916), 4.

96. Women's Co-operative Guild, "Memorandum on the National Care of Maternity," 1.

97. "Will War Work Harm Motherhood?" *Weekly Dispatch,* 17 Sept. 1916.

98. Dr. J. Dulberg, "Warning to Women Doing Men's Work: Plain Speaking Necessary to Check a Menace," *Umpire,* 5 Dec. 1915.

99. A. C. Marshall, "The Woman Who Pays: A Thoughtful Study in National Sacrifice, and the Ultimate Penalty to Be Paid for Women's War Work," *The Quiver* (Apr. 1916), 539.

100. Ibid., 544–45.

101. Hutchins, *Conflicting Ideals,* 11.

102. "[O]ne of the best known women doctors" quoted in "Will War Work Harm Motherhood?"

103. "Overworked Women," *Gentlewoman,* 29 Sept. 1917.

104. "Come out of the Home!" *Evening Standard,* 25 Jan. 1917. Support for these crèches can be found in longer essays such as Arthur James, "Saving the Nation's Life-Blood," *World's Work* (June 1918). For more on the link between concern with mothers and concern with the empire, see Davin, "Imperialism and Motherhood."

105. A. Maude Royden, "Mothers' Pensions," *The Common Cause,* 29 June 1917. Royden went on to say that even if the mother could not be compensated for her risk, she should not as a result be "dependent." Also quoted in Pedersen, *Family, Dependence,* 146. Royden would also testify in front of the National Birth-Rate Commission on these matters. For their discussions of the endowments for motherhood in prewar and wartime Britain, see Dyhouse, *Feminism and the Family,* 98–99, and Pedersen, *Family, Dependence,* 140–52.

106. For a list of the members, see the preface to the National Council of Public Morals, *Declining Birth-Rate.*

107. "Statement of Miss A. G. Philip, Director of the Maternity Subsection, Ministry of Munitions," Monday, 28 Oct. 1918, in the National Council of Public Morals, *Problems of Population,* 134–35. Philip noted that the danger of women trying to have abortions—to avoid being dismissed because they were pregnant—had already been recognized in France, where, in January 1917, "the French Minister of Munitions issued a circular to the heads of all munition factories pointing out this very danger in great detail, and explaining what the munition employer must do to avoid it." See also the French evidence discussed above.

108. Ibid., 136–41.

109. Advertisement for Glaxo appearing in *The Woman Worker* (Aug. 1917).

110. Advertisement for Glaxo appearing in *The Woman Worker* (Apr. 1918).

111. Advertisement for Glaxo appearing in *The Woman Worker* (June 1918).

CHAPTER FOUR

1. Hartley, *Women's Wild Oats,* 9–10, 19.

2. For articles discussing changes in women's manners, see the following examples: Jean Pain, "La guerre et les moeurs," *La Française,* 14 Oct. 1916; Jane Ramsay-Kerr, "Strong Language by Women," *Daily Express,* 5 Dec. 1916; Max Pemberton, "Are Women Losing Men's Respect?" *Pearson's Weekly,* 29 Sept. 1917; and "Foul-mouthed Bellona" and the responses to this article in *The Bulletin,* 3 and 7 Sept. 1917.

3. M. O. Kennedy, "Women's War Sacrifices: Will They Give Up Smoking?" *National News,* 2 Dec. 1917.

4. Angela Woollacott discusses British anxiety about sexually promiscuous young girls under the rubric of "khaki fever," in Woollacott, " 'Khaki Fever.' "

5. Corbin, *Women for Hire,* 335.

6. For more on this, see Woollacott, " 'Khaki Fever.' " For more on the use of patriotic sexuality, see the imagery surrounding the *marraine de guerre* discussed in Sweeney, "Harmony and Disharmony," ch. 3. For an interesting discussion of these issues in Second World War Britain, see Sonya Rose, "Sex, Citizenship, and the Nation."

7. See the many examples of sexual postcards cited in Huss, "Pronatalism," and the images and song lyrics cited in Sweeney, "Harmony and Disharmony," ch. 3. See also the images of "L'offensive en chambre" and "L'artillerie de l'amour" in Gervereau and Prochasson, *Images de 1917,* 131, and others on 130 and 159.

8. See Mary Louise Roberts, *Civilization without Sexes,* 32–39.

9. Fabiano, "Flirt 1914," *Le Rire,* reprinted in *Je Sais Tout,* 15 Mar. 1915, 50. For a brief overview of efforts to restrict contact between French women factory workers and colonial labor, see Downs, *Manufacturing Inequality,* 60; and for concern about French women mixing with colonial troops and of much more salacious images of their interactions, see Melzer, "Spectacles and Sexualities."

10. Géraldy, *La guerre, madame,* 34–37 and 29–33. See also Mary Louise Roberts, *Civilization without Sexes,* 28, 34, 239 n. 89.

11. See, for instance, Landre, *L'école des marraines,* and the discussion of the *marraine de guerre* in Grayzel, "Mothers, Marraines, and Prostitutes."

12. Vismes, *L'histoire authentique et touchante.*

13. Advertisement in *La Vie Parisienne,* 21 Apr. 1917.

14. The feminist anti-alcohol campaign was regularly reported in *La Française* throughout the war; see, for example, articles published on 15 May 1915, 6 and 16 Jan., 12 Feb., 1 Apr., 18 May 1916, and 28 Jan. 1917.

15. The law of 1 Oct. 1917 is described in Corbin, *Women for Hire,* 335. Local decrees already restricted this in specific areas of France.

16. The original French is: "Chez les débitants de liqueurs at de bière / Que l'on peut voir danser avec la garnison /Ces fameuses catins à la vie ordinaire / Qui sont de notre armée un terrible poison." Dulom, "La prostitution dans les débits," 2, 6, 10.

17. Jane Misme, "Les Français seront-ils polygames?" *La Française,* 23 Jan. 1916.

18. Mme. de Witt-Schlumberger, "Unité de la morale et repression de la traite des blanches," *L'Action Féminine,* no. 45 (Aug. 1916).

19. Pain, "La guerre et les moeurs."

20. De Torina, *Mère sans être épouse,* 23.

21. Jane Misme, "Mères libres," *La Française,* 27 Oct. 1917.

22. Avril de Sainte-Croix, *L'éducation sexuelle,* 40.

23. Quoted in "Un étrange manuel de conversation," *L'Action Féminine,* no. 51 (Dec. 1917).

24. "Rapport sur l'état d'esprit de la population parisienne: 5ème District," 25 Nov. 1918, APP Ba 1614.

25. Toulouse, *La question sexuelle et la femme,* 15. Further references are made parenthetically in the text.

26. See "Women and the War: How They Are Working Mischief," *Daily Call,* 19 Nov. 1914. The argument that follows differs from that of Susan Kent, who claims that only the first phase of war witnessed scandals along the lines of "khaki fever" and widespread representation of sexuality (see Kent, *Making Peace,* 28–30), and of Angela Woollacott, " 'Khaki Fever,' " in that it uncovers discussions about the public moral behavior of women that lasted throughout the war, with important consequences.

27. See "The Girl in the Street," *Daily Express,* 3 Nov. 1914, and "Women and the War," *Daily Call,* 19 Nov. 1914. Woollacott, " 'Khaki Fever,' " and Levine, " 'Walking the Streets,' " develop the points raised in the *Daily Call* article.

28. Edith M. Davidson, M. Dorothy Harmer, and Evelyn Burge, "A Nation's Appeal to Our Girls," *The Vigilance Record* (Nov. 1914). See Levine, " 'Walking the Streets,' " for more on the workings of the NVA.

29. The DORA was originally enacted in 1914 "for securing the public safety and the defence of the realm." Regulation 13, one of the original provisions, allowed for the arrest without warrant of anyone suspected of acting or having acted contrary to "public safety" or possessing any suspicious article, book, or document. Regulation 21 forbade promulgating by speech or writing "reports likely to cause disaffection or alarm." These regulations were updated throughout the war, and the latest regulations were then published monthly in *Defence of the Realm Regu-*

lations: Acts and Regulations and consolidated in *Defence of the Realm Manuals,* issued between July 1915 and Sept. 1919. The entire run of regulations and manuals can be found in the IWM.

30. The order was issued in November 1914, and the first women arrested were brought before a court-martial on 28 Nov. 1914. This information was reported in "Undesirable Women and the Army," *The Vigilance Record* (Dec. 1914).

31. That the women pleaded guilty was recorded in "Undesirable Women and the Army." Information about sentencing can be found in WO 32 5526/040564.

32. "The Cardiff Outrage," *Herald,* 19 Dec. 1914. The *Herald* was Lansbury's paper.

33. C. Nina Boyle, "The Prime Minister and a 'Scrap of Paper': C.D. Acts Reestablished in a New Form," *The Vote* (Dec. 1914). Indignation over the German chancellor's tearing up the treaty as if it were only "a scrap of paper" fueled prowar sentiment and became a pivotal part of British propaganda; posters reprinting the treaty's signatures and labeled "The Scrap of Paper" were circulated in Britain. For a reproduction of the poster, see Rawls, *Wake Up, America!,* 44; for a reproduction of the poster and a discussion of the "scrap of paper," see Gullace, "Sexual Violence and Family Honor."

34. "Cardiff and Women Patrols," *The Vigilance Record* (Dec. 1914). See Levine, "'Walking the Streets,'" on the formation of the women police out of a number of such patrols.

35. "Bristol Vigilance Association," *The Vigilance Record* (Mar. 1915). The article attributed a change in this kind of behavior to the early closing of pubs and the creation of woman patrols. The following month the *The Vigilance Record* approvingly cited the warning of a judge from the Gainsborough County Court to young girls who should be kept indoors at night for their own good.

36. See Woollacott's analysis of this phenomenon in "'Khaki Fever.'"

37. "Soldiers and Young Women," *The Vigilance Record* (Dec. 1915). Emphasis added.

38. Lady Frances Balfour, "The Women Are Ready—A Plea for Opportunities of Service," *Birmingham Gazette & Express,* 20 Mar. 1915. Balfour is referring to warning against "women and wine" issued by Lord Kitchener. Note how much the "instincts" to which Balfour refers resemble maternal instincts, or those mothers are meant to possess.

39. Winnington-Ingram, *Cleansing London.*

40. The image, designed by Eric H. Kennington, a well-known war artist, can be found in ibid.

41. Ibid., 24–25. Further references to this work are made parenthetically in the text.

42. For an interesting historical overview that includes references to complaints about sexual misbehavior in London parks during the war, see Dreher, "'Courting Couples' or Courting Disaster?"

43. C[harlotte] Despard, "A Real National Mission," *The Vote,* 1 Sept. 1916.

44. "Adam and the Apple Again: She Gave Me of the Fruit," *The Vote,* 16 Feb. 1917.

45. There are numerous articles on this subject, such as these examples from

1918: Lady Askwith, "Should Women be Conscripted?" *Answers,* 23 Mar. 1918, and "Conscription for Women," *Evening Gazette,* 8 May 1918. See the further discussion in Chapter 6, below.

46. Mrs. Flora Annie Steel, "Women Who Are Hindering Instead of Helping," *Sunday Herald,* 10 May 1918.

47. One conference was sponsored by London Borough authorities on 2 March, and another, "The Moral Condition of the Streets of London," which took place on 27 June, was sponsored by the National Vigilance Association. See "Conference on the 'Moral Conditions of the Streets of London.'" The conference was adjourned and continued on 30 July, as reported in *The Vigilance Record* (Aug. 1917).

48. Bishop of London Arthur F. Winnington-Ingram, Sir Edward Henry, Lieutenant-General Sir Francis Lloyd, and Louise Creighton (leader of the National Union of Women Workers) all quoted in "Conference on the 'Moral Conditions of the Streets of London.'"

49. M. H. Mason, "Public Morality: Some Constructive Suggestions," *Nineteenth Century and After* 32, no. 485 (July 1917), 187. Further references are made parenthetically in the text.

50. All material in this paragraph is from Dr. James Burnet, "Women War-Workers and the Sexual Element," *Medical Press and Circular,* 22 Aug. 1917.

51. May Sinclair, letter to the editor, *Medical Press and Circular,* 5 Sept. 1917.

52. "Scandal of the Streets," *Daily Express,* 20 Sept. 1918.

53. "The Land Cure," *Daily Express,* 20 Sept. 1918.

54. "London Street Women—An American Editor's Endictment," *Evening News,* 24 Sept. 1918. The interview was originally published in the *The Times,* which this article acknowledged, and reprinted elsewhere. Further references in the following two paragraphs are to this article.

55. Bok added that it was unfair not only to the soldiers but to "the American mother" and that an outcry against the war could result too if news of the condition of London reached "the American woman."

56. "The State of Our Streets—A Warning from America," *Evening News,* 24 Sept. 1918.

57. Edward Price Bell quoted in "The Moral Condition of the London Streets," *The Vigilance Record* (Oct. 1918). Emphasis in the original.

58. G. S. Graves, letter to the editor, *Evening Standard,* reprinted in *The Vigilance Record* (Oct. 1918).

59. "Moral Condition of the London Streets."

60. "London Street Women."

61. For those predicting a new, closer relationship between men and women, see Arnold Bennett, "The Sexes after the War," *Sunday Pictorial,* 14 Mar. 1915, and Marie Corelli, "The New Comradeship," *Daily Graphic,* 23 June 1915. For more critical voices, see note 2, above.

62. Quoted in Lady Burbidge, "Woman And The War—Has She Degenerated?" *The Sunday Times,* 1 June 1919.

63. Ibid.

64. Corbin, *Women for Hire,* 335.

65. Bizard, *Les maisons de prostitution,* 2.

66. Corbin, *Women for Hire,* 335.

67. Bizard, *Les maisons de prostitution,* 5.

68. "Rapport sur la distribution dans l'armée de notices relatives à la prophylaxie des maladies évitables," *Bulletin de l'Académie de Médecine* 16 and 30 Nov. 1915.

69. "Une femme de mobilisé," letter, 4 July 1916, to the Prefect of Police in APP Ba 1689.

70. "Un de vos bons amis," letter, 9 Sept. 1916, to the Prefect of Police in APP Ba 1689.

71. Letter, 12 July 1917, to the Prefect of Police in APP Ba 1689.

72. "Rapport sur l'état d'esprit de la population parisienne: 7ème District," 12 Aug. 1918, and "Rapport sur l'état d'esprit de la population parisienne: 8ème District," 5 and 26 Aug. 1918 and 9, 13, and 23 Sept. 1918, APP Ba 1614.

73. "Rapport sur l'état d'esprit de la population parisienne: 6ème District," 9 Sept. 1918, APP Ba 1614.

74. Dr. F. Balzer, "Prophylaxie et traitement des maladies vénériennes en temps de guerre," *Revue d'Hygiène et de Police Sanitaire* (Nov. 1915), 1060–61.

75. Dr. L. Butte, "La surveillance médicale de la prostitution à Paris pendant la guerre," *Bulletin de l'Académie de Médecine,* 13 Feb. 1917.

76. For a feminist argument along this line, citing the work of the Ligue Française pour le Relèvement de la Moralité Publique, see de Witt-Schlumberger, "Unité de la morale."

77. Dr. Paul Faivre, "Prophylaxie des maladies vénériennes," *Revue d'Hygiène et de Police Sanitaire* 39 (Sept.–Nov. 1917), 657–704.

78. "M. Pourésy's Work in France," *The Vigilance Record* (Mar. 1918).

79. Fiaux, *L'armée et la police des moeurs,* vii, 16–17, 23, 194, 207.

80. Bizard, *Les maladies vénériennes.* Further references are made parenthetically.

81. De Witt-Schlumberger, "Unité de la morale," 93–94.

82. "Rapport de l'Assemblée Générale du Conseil National des Femmes Françaises: Unité de la morale," *L'Action Féminine,* no. 50 (Sept. 1917), 204. The danger of sexual vice leading inevitably to venereal disease as a threat to population growth is detailed in C. Colson, "Tâche de demain· La population," *Revue des Deux Mondes* (Apr. 1915), 870–75.

83. This letter was used to gather international support and thus translated and reprinted as part of "The Women of France and Morality," *The Vigilance Record* (Sept. 1918), the version that I rely on here.

84. Association for Moral and Social Hygiene, "The Under-Secretary for War Defends Tolerated Brothels!" [Feb. 1918], Box 313, AMSH.

85. "Moral and Social Hygiene: Protest against Double Standard," *The Vote,* 8 Mar. 1918. Among the supporters of the opposition to official brothels were: Bernard Shaw, Charlotte Despard, eleven bishops, the chief rabbi, General Smith Dorien, and several women doctors, including Lady Elizabeth Barrett. Speakers at the meeting included Maude Royden. For a more widely publicized scandal concerning the opening of a brothel specifically for British soldiers, see Edith Picton-Turberville, "The Cayeux Scandal," *Daily News,* 14 Mar. 1918.

86. The Acts were suspended in 1883 and completely repealed for Britain in 1886. Douglas White, "Synopsis" of the Royal Commission on Venereal Diseases,

Report of the Royal Commission on Venereal Diseases, 5–6. Further references are made parenthetically in the text. For more on the original C.D. Acts, see Walkowitz, *Prostitution and Victorian Society.* The reintroduction of the equivalent of the C.D. Acts can be directly attributed to pressure from Dominion military leaders; see Buckley, "Failure to Resolve"; HO 45, 10802/307990 and 10894/359931; and the discussion below.

87. It suggested that venereal disease was grounds for annulling a marriage, and if the annulment resulted in the children becoming illegitimate, then the state should insure "that disabilities of illegitimacy should not follow" (47).

88. Douglas White, H[elen] Wilson, et al., Draft of Letter on "the Inaugural Meeting of the National Council for Combating Venereal Diseases," 21 Oct. 1914, Box 311/1, AMSH. The first meeting, according to this letter, was scheduled for 11 November 1914 at the Royal College of Medicine. The NCCVD thus began distributing leaflets in advance of the publication of the RCVD's report.

89. Scharlieb, *Hidden Scourge.* Further references are made parenthetically in the text. The book's foreword was by the bishop of London. Scharlieb also publicized these ideas in two articles: "New Remedies for Old Diseases," *The Englishwoman,* no. 88 (Apr. 1916), and "Royal Commission on Venereal Diseases: Education," *The Englishwoman,* no. 89 (May 1916).

90. Scharlieb brings this up in reference to war babies, a subject that is examined in Chapter 3, above.

91. Civis, "A Word about Venereal Disease," *The English Review* (Dec. 1916).

92. George A. Wade, "The National Campaign against Venereal Diseases," *World's Work* (Feb. 1917).

93. Letter to the editor, *Manchester Guardian,* 25 Oct. 1916. The letter originally appeared in *The Times,* 23 Oct. 1916. A press cutting of the *Manchester Guardian* copy can be found in Folder 15, HO 45, 10802/307990.

94. See letters to the editor, *Manchester Guardian,* 25 Oct. 1916. Also in Folder 15, HO 45, 10802/307990.

95. "Echoes," *The Englishwoman,* no. 95 (Nov. 1916).

96. Royden, *Duty of Knowledge,* 4.

97. Ibid., 9–20, 22. For example, to the question of whether promiscuous sexual intercourse caused venereal disease, the RCVD instructed the lecturer to answer: "Not in itself; one party must already be infected in order to transmit the disease" (32).

98. Mrs. Henry [Millicent Garrett] Fawcett, "The Problem of Venereal Diseases," *Review of Reviews* 55, no. 326 (1917), 155, 158.

99. The bill received a good deal of attention from various "moral" organizations, and its various clauses were reprinted and discussed in *The Vigilance Record* (Mar. and Apr. 1917). See also HO 45, 10711/244320, for a discussion of attempts to promote comparable legislation in the spring of 1914 and of the dangers of doing so during the war.

100. Clause 3, Criminal Law Amendment Bill, reprinted in *The Vigilance Record* (Apr. 1917).

101. "Opposition to Clause 3," *The Vigilance Record* (Apr. 1917).

102. The copy of a letter sent to the prime minister, the home secretary and members of Parliament, and the press from Despard, Underwood, and Knight was reprinted in *The Vote,* 2 Mar. 1917. *The Vote* also recorded that the NUWSS, the Free Church League for Women's Suffrage, and "many prominent individual women" also opposed the measure.

103. An overview of debates surrounding the Criminal Law Amendment Bill can be found in E. M. Goodman, "The Criminal Law Amendment Bill," *Review of Reviews* (Apr. 1917); see also Dr. Jane Walker, "Recent Proposal on the Moral Question," *The Englishwoman,* no. 100 (Apr. 1917), and "Beware of Constructive Legislation," *The Englishwoman,* no. 115 (July 1918).

104. Reg. 35C, Defence of the Realm Act, 14 Apr. 1917. See H. M. Government, *Defence of the Realm Regulations* (1917).

105. It could also be used against aliens, an issue that was brought up in a statement from the National Council for Civil Liberties sent to the Association of Moral and Social Hygiene. See Box 311/1, AMSH.

106. Reg. 40D, Defence of the Realm Act, 22 Mar. 1918. See H. M. Government, *Defence of the Realm Regulations* (1918). This regulation was further publicized in *The Times,* 27 Mar. 1918, and reprinted in *The Vigilance Record* (Apr. 1918).

107. Alison Neilans, secretary, letter, 28 Mar. 1918, Box 311/2, AMSH.

108. These included Helena Swanwick (representing the Women's International League), Florence Underwood (Women's Freedom League), Mrs. Broadley Reid (Women's Liberal Federation), and others from the Catholic Women's Suffrage Society, Friends Social Purity League, and National Union of Trained Nurses. See the account of the meeting dated 27 June 1918 in Box 311/2, AMSH. Other letters in the AMSH collection demonstrate opposition from the National Union of Women Workers. The AMSH both amassed press cuttings concerning 40D and actively sought out information as to the impact of 40D on local communities.

109. *Manchester Guardian,* 27 Mar. 1918. Reprinted in "Extracts from Editorial Notes," Box 311/2, AMSH.

110. *Herald,* 6 Apr. 1918. Reprinted in "Extracts from Editorial Notes," Box 311/2, AMSH.

111. For more on 40D, see HO 45, 10894/359931. Reg. 40D was amended on 19 July 1918 to include not only members of "His Majesty's Forces" but also those "of any of His Majesty's Allies" and was revoked on 25 Nov. 1918. See Reg. 40D in *Defence of the Realm Regulations Consolidated* (1920), 151.

112. Buckley, "Failure to Resolve," 81, notes that this split accounted for some of the inefficiency with which venereal disease was fought.

113. Mary Louise Roberts notes that Brieux's play was linked to antivenereal societies' campaigns to provide sexual education aimed at young men and boys; see Roberts, *Civilization without Sexes,* 320 n. 75. For more information about Brieux in France, see Rf. 53, Fonds Rondel, Bibliothèque de l'Arsenal, Paris.

114. *The Times Literary Supplement,* 19 Apr. 1917. This second edition used the same translation by John Pollock and preface by George Bernard Shaw as the previous edition of 1911.

115. Norman Croom-Johnson, "Brieux Triumphant," *Review of Reviews* 55, no. 328

(Apr. 1917). These censorship battles had revolved around all of Brieux's plays. The lifting of the ban on *Damaged Goods* was hailed as part of a liberalizing trend by W. L. George in *Royal Magazine* (May 1918).

116. Quoted in Croom-Johnson, "Brieux Triumphant, and in Brieux, *Damaged Goods,* 186. The version cited in the *Review of Reviews* as being presented in London was slightly abbreviated from the published form.

117. Croom-Johnson, "Brieux Triumphant."

118. Brieux, *Damaged Goods,* 241, 249.

119. Croom-Johnson, "Brieux Triumphant." The popularity of the play on the West End may account for its being turned into a British silent film in 1919; an American film version was made in 1915 (see Kuhn, *Cinema, Censorship and Sexuality,* 55–63).

120. C. S. Bremmer, "Damaged Goods," *The Vote,* 11 May 1917.

CHAPTER FIVE

1. For one of the most influential evocations of feminist pacifism, see the best-selling novel of 1889, Suttner, *Lay Down Your Arms,* whose English translation was still in print in 1914. For prewar examples of the moral force argument, see Swanwick, *Future of the Women's Movement,* and Despard, *Woman in the New Era.* Contemporaneous discussions of internationalist feminism can also be found in *Jus Suffragi,* the organ of the International Women's Suffrage Alliance.

2. For an important theoretical perspective on "equality" versus "difference" within feminism, see Scott, *Gender and the Politics of History,* ch. 8, and the discussion of needing to go beyond the paradox of equality and difference in Scott, *Only Paradoxes to Offer,* ch. 1.

3. For a comparative discussion of this as "maternalism," see Koven and Michel, "Womanly Duties." For an overview of British women writing as maternal pacifists, see Ouditt, *Fighting Forces,* 139–68.

4. Schreiner, *Women and Labour,* 169.

5. Schreiner also wrote directly in response to her experience of the Boer War. See the introduction to her *Women and Labour* and First and Scott, *Olive Schreiner.*

6. Schreiner, *Women and Labour,* 169.

7. Ibid., 173.

8. Helena Swanwick had been editor of the *The Common Cause,* the journal of the National Union of Women's Suffrage Societies, and had resigned over the issue of whether or not to support the war.

9. Swanwick, *Women and War,* 2. Further references are made parenthetically in the text.

10. Swanwick, *War in Its Effect upon Women,* 20–21. Further references are made parenthetically in the text.

11. Hallowes, *Address to the Mothers of Men,* 47. Frances Hallowes's contributions to feminist antimilitarism are also discussed in Liddington, *Long Road to Greenham.*

12. E. Sylvia Pankhurst, "The Peril of Prejudice," *The Woman's Dreadnought,* 30 Oct. 1915.

13. [C. K. Ogden with Mary Sargent Forence], *Militarism versus Feminism*, 56. C. K. Ogden was the signatory to a shorter version, "Militarism and Feminism," published in *The Common Cause*, 26 Feb. 1915. The authors' attributions are explained in the preface to the reprinted edition; see Margaret Kamester and Jo Vellacott, introduction to *Militarism versus Feminism*, 21–34.

14. This perspective, a relatively uncommon one in feminist texts of the First World War, is expounded upon by Virginia Woolf in her antimilitarist *Three Guineas*.

15. See the "Letter of Protest" signed by the Groupe des Femmes Socialistes in *L'Humanité*, 31 July 1914. *L'Humanité* also reported in December 1914 that the letter from Clara Zetkin addressed to Socialist women everywhere was censored. See *L'Humanité*, 14 Dec. 1914. For an overview of French feminist opposition to the war, see Charles Sowerwine, *Sisters or Citizens?*; Bard, *Les filles de Marianne*, 89–108; and the documents in Sowerwine and Sowerwine, *Le mouvement ouvrier*.

16. Romain Rolland wrote the preface to her work; see Capy, *Une voix de femme*. See also Rolland, *Au-dessus de la mêlée*.

17. Capy, "Ceux qui pleurent," in *Une voix de femme*, 24. This text was censored in numerous places throughout.

18. Ibid., 25.

19. Ibid., 43. The rest of the page and quote were censored.

20. "Une déclaration des femmes socialistes françaises," *La Française*, 27 Feb. 1915.

21. Liddington, "Woman's Peace Crusade"; Oldfield, *Spinsters of This Parish*, ch. 9; Wiltsher, *Most Dangerous Women*, ch. 4; Liddington, *Long Road to Greenham*, ch. 5.

22. See the following newspaper and journal articles: Rene H. Feibelman, "Peacettes and Profits," *Daily Express*, 3 May 1915; "The Congress of Women at The Hague," *Yorkshire Observer*, 27 Apr. 1915; "War Speeches at Women's Congress," *Daily Mail*, 1 May 1915; "Women and the Hague Conference. Mrs. Henry Fawcett's Comments," *Yorkshire Post*, 30 Apr. 1915; "Mrs. Pankhurst's Ideas on the Peace Conference," *Herts Advertiser*, 15 May 1915; Margaret Ashton, Margaret G. Bondfield, Margaret Llewelyn Davies, Susan Lawrence, Gertrude Russell, H. M. Swanwick et al., letter to the editor, *Daily Chronicle*, 30 Apr. 1915; "Women's Congress at The Hague," *Herald*, 15 May 1915; Lady Margaret Sackville, "Comments on the International Women's Congress," *Everyman*, 6 Aug. 1915; and "The International Congress," *Preston Chronicle*, 2 June 1915.

23. See letter from Marguerite de Witt-Schlumberger to Jeanne Mélin, 17 Mar. 1915, in Fonds Mélin, Box 39, Fonds Bouglé, BHVP, and the statement of the CNFF and UFSF, "Aux femmes des pays neutres et des pays alliés," Apr. 1915, reprinted in several newspapers and also found in DOS 396 CON, BMD. For more on the CNFF and feminist reaction, see "Le Congrès pacifiste de la Haye," *L'Action Féminine*, no. 38 (May 1915), and "À propos du Congrès de la Haye," *La Française*, 24 Apr. 1915. For discussions of French feminist reaction to the Hague Conference, see Hause, *Women's Suffrage*, 195–97, and Bard, *Les filles de Marianne*, 94–99. Some French women who did not attend were not unsympathetic to its aims; see the 1915 correspondence of Jeanne Mélin in Fonds Mélin, Box 39, Fonds Bou-

glé, BHVP. See also the mixed responses to French feminists' refusal to attend the Hague Conference in the nonfeminist press, ranging from "Le Congrès International des Femmes," *La Bataille Syndicaliste,* 9 May 1915, to "Le refus des femmes françaises," *L'Écho de Paris,* 24 Apr. 1915, to "Il est trop tôt pour parler de paix," *Le Petit Parisien,* 15 June 1915.

24. Hause, *Women's Suffrage,* 192–93. Thébaud, *La femme au temps,* 247–51, discusses their actions and briefly touches on the theoretical motivations of several individual women. For more official government concern, see the "Rapport au sujet du 'Congrès International des Femmes' à la Haye," 27 Apr. 1915, in APP Ba 1651. This document includes the appeal from the CNFF and UFSF noted above.

25. Charles Sowerwine, *Sisters or Citizens?,* 144–48.

26. "Femmes du prolétariat," speech delivered at La Conférence Internationale des Femmes Socialistes (Berne: March 1915). Other appeals to women have such titles as "Le monde crache du sang." See Sowerwine and Sowerwine, *Le mouvement ouvrier,* for copies of these documents. Saumoneau was drawing upon the arguments of German socialist-feminist Clara Zetkin.

27. "Où sont vos maris? Où sont vos fils?" La Conférence Internationale des Femmes Socialistes (Berne: March 1915), in Sowerwine and Sowerwine, *Le mouvement ouvrier.*

28. Le Comité Féminin pour la Paix, "À bas la guerre femmes," in Sowerwine and Sowerwine, *Le mouvement ouvrier.*

29. Noted in Albert, *Le procès Malvy,* 67–69.

30. Section Française du Comité International des Femmes pour la Paix Permanente, "Un devoir urgent pour les femmes," 8, in Sowerwine and Sowerwine, *Le mouvement ouvrier;* see Charles Sowerwine, *Sisters or Citizens?,* for the socialist reaction.

31. "Rapport sur la campagne féministe en faveur de la paix considérations générales," Oct. 1915, AN F7 13266, 1. A copy can also be found in the Police Archives; see APP Ba 1651.

32. Ibid., 58.

33. The government was concerned about threats to the *union sacrée* coming from women on the Right as well as the Left. See the reports to the Prefect of Police concerning activities of the Ligue Patriotique des Françaises in AN F7 13216.

34. *Le Matin,* 18 Nov. 1917.

35. A history of the term "defeatist" and its uses in the popular media during the war can be found in Slater, *Defeatists and Their Enemies,* 42–113. Slater dates the widespread emergence of *défaitiste* to June/July of 1917. Slater's study, however, makes no reference to gender, to any women accused of "defeatism," or to those who linked feminism and defeatism.

36. Janvion, *Le féminisme défaitiste,* pamphlet found at F Rés. 319/2, BDIC. Anxiety in feminist circles about associations between feminism and attacks on the war had already prompted lengthy discussions in 1917 in *La Française;* see "Faut-il parler de la paix?" and "Opinions des Françaises sur la paix" in *La Française,* 28 July 1917.

37. Paxton, *Europe in the Twentieth Century,* 120–22.

38. Jean-Jacques Becker, *Great War and the French People,* 3–4. For an exploration

of French prewar anxieties about antimilitarism, see Jean-Jacques Becker, *Le carnet B.*

39. Jean-Jacques Becker, *Great War and the French People*, 82–83. For a discussion of the flexible practice of censorship as applied to cultural media such as songs, see Sweeney, "Harmony and Disharmony."

40. Jean-Jacques Becker, *Great War and the French People*, 204. For the classic study of mutinies in the French army during 1917, see Pedroncini, *Les mutineries de 1917*, and for a more recent analysis, see Leonard V. Smith, *Between Mutiny and Obedience*. For strikes, particularly by women, see Downs, "Women's Strikes."

41. Jean-Jacques Becker, *Great War and the French People*, 236.

42. Ibid., 248, discusses the development of a "patriotic gloom," where no one wanted the war to continue but thought a premature peace would be far worse. While Becker does not discuss the political shifts in power, Wright, *France in Modern Times*, 321, points out that by returning Georges Clemenceau to power on 16 November 1917 not only a "civilian dictatorship" but also an all out attack on those in favor of a quick peace was established. See Paxton, *Europe in the Twentieth Century*, 121, for a brief synopsis of how this led to the treason trials of the minister of the interior, Louis Malvy, and former prime minister Joseph Caillaux.

43. Extensive coverage of the trials in daily papers reflected either public interest or government efforts to interest the public in them. In any case, whether manufactured or genuine, public demand resulted in a special series of the *Revue des Cause Célèbres* on the *Procès de Trahison*. Advertised in *L'Action Française* for a price of Fr 1.25, "The Treason Trials" claimed to serve the audience who wanted the full details of every trial "that will purge our country of its internal enemies." See *L'Action Française*, 24 March 1918; and *Revue des Causes Célèbres Politiques et Criminelles*, no. 1 (1918), 2. For a historical perspective, see Jean-Jacques Becker, *Great War and the French People*, 308–10, and Paxton, *Europe in the Twentieth Century*, 120–21. I have found no statistics on the number of people accused of "defeatism." For some contemporary accounts of the treason trials, see Adam, *Treason and Tragedy;* Dejean, *[Les Complices];* and Albert, *Le procès Malvy.*

44. Moreover, Caillaux's wife, Mme. Henriette Caillaux, had herself been the subject of a sensational trial immediately before the war. See Berenson, *Trial of Madame Caillaux.*

45. For more on the meaning of treason and the trials, see Slater, *Defeatists and Their Enemies;* Albert, *Le procès Malvy;* and the *Revue des Causes Célèbres.*

46. Rolland, *Au-dessus de la mêlée*, provided the most noteworthy example of early antiwar writing by men. The teachers' union, of which Brion was in charge, enthusiastically endorsed and circulated his ideas. For a discussion of Rolland as a "defeatist," see Debran, *Monsieur Romain Rolland.*

47. Higonnet and Higonnet, "Double Helix," 41.

48. Biographical information concerning Brion comes from Huguette Bouchardeau's preface to the reprint of Brion, *La voie féministe*, and Dubief, "Brion, Hélène, Rose, Louise," 295–96. See also Wishnia, "Feminism and Pacifism," 103–4; Flammant, *L'école emancipée*, 384; and Bard, *Les filles de Marianne*. Brion's roles within various feminist and socialist organizations were further extolled in Vernet, *Hélène Brion.*

49. Her emergence in socialist-feminist circles and within the militant teacher's union receives some attention in the histories of these movements. For her feminist activities, see Hause, *Women's Suffrage;* for her work as a syndicalist teacher, see Ferré, *Histoire du mouvement,* and Flammant, *L'école emancipée;* and for her contributions as a feminist teacher and pacifist, see Wishnia, "Feminism and Pacifism."

50. Sowerwine, *Sisters or Citizens?,* 132–35. See also *La Femme Socialiste,* no. 12 (Oct. 1913).

51. Brion was on the central committee of the Confédération Générale du Travail, hence her focus on its actions. For more on her feminist activities, see Hause, *Women's Suffrage,* and Bard, *Les filles de Marianne.*

52. Brion also wrote feminist travel guides and collected a newspaper archive of information about women and feminism that is now housed in the Fonds Brion, IFHS, and BMD, which also houses her encyclopedia.

53. For more on Brion's later feminist-pacifist activities see Thibault, *Non à la guerre disent elles,* 142.

54. See Flammant, *L'école emancipée,* 240–41, and Brion, *La voie féministe,* 33–35. Brion was not the only feminist teacher to get into trouble for antiwar activities. For a fuller discussion of teachers, see Wishnia, "Feminism and Pacifism," and for list of feminist-pacifist activities collateral to Brion's, see Armogathe, "Historique," 47.

55. Magraw, *France, 1815–1914,* 216. Schoolteachers also became secularized, and to an extent schools were seen as places to inculcate patriotism and unity. A particularly important set of changes occurred when secondary education was established for girls; see Margadant, *Madame le professeur.* See also Weber, *Peasants into Frenchmen,* for the nationalizing role of education in the Third Republic.

56. Wishnia, "Feminism and Pacifism," 104–6. For background on women as primary teachers in the nineteenth century, see Margadant, *Madame le professeur,* 18–20.

57. See Flammant, *L'école emancipée.*

58. These expectations did not stem directly from the war and can be seen in prewar debates about what was to be taught. See Ozouf and Ozouf, "Le thème du patriotisme."

59. Ministère de l'Instruction Publique et des Beaux Arts, "Circulaire du 10 Septembre 1915," 17. See also Audoin-Rouzeau, *La guerre des enfants,* for more on wartime propaganda directed at children.

60. Ferré, *Histoire du mouvement,* 176. Brion initially advocated continuing the war until there was an Allied victory.

61. Mayoux and Mayoux, *Les instituteurs syndicalistes et la guerre,* 10. A copy of the pamphlet can also be found in Sowerwine and Sowerwine, *Le mouvement ouvrier.*

62. This law concerned the censorship of the press and made it an offense to publish "alarmist" propaganda. For more on this legislation, see Berger and Allard, *Les secrets de la censure,* 79.

63. On appeal, their sentences were prolonged and then dismissed. See Ferré, *Histoire du mouvement,* 180–81.

64. Aside from Brion herself, in March of 1918, at the Council of War in Grenoble, Louise Colliard, a fellow syndicalist schoolteacher and an internationalist,

came to trial under virtually the same charges and received a sentence of two years imprisonment.

65. Marie Mayoux again presented the pacifist case in "Manifesto of Unionized Teachers," an unpublished document that demanded an immediate peace. For details, see Jean-Jacques Becker, *Great War and the French People*, 151–53, and Ferré, *Histoire du mouvement*, 174–80.

66. Letter from Hélène Brion to Madame Haumenier, 4 Dec. 1915, 091 BRI, BMD.

67. "Individus Notoirement Connus pour Leur Propagande Pacifiste," 24 Oct. 1916. She also received mention in "Les Instituteurs Pacifistes," 18 Dec. 1917. Both in AN F7 13575.

68. The police also collected evidence of a campaign for peace directed specifically at women. See AN F7 13575 and APP Ba 1639; for many letters to and from Brion, see APP Ba 1561–62.

69. Dubesset, Thébaud, and Vincent, "Les munitionettes de la Seine," 216, esp. n. 108. See also Downs, "Women's Strikes."

70. Dubesset, Thébaud, and Vincent, "Les munitionettes de la Seine," 216–17.

71. Jean-Jacques Becker, *Great War and the French People*, 211–12. Downs, *Manufacturing Inequality*, ch. 4, and "Women's Strikes." See also Jean Rabaut, who discusses the strikes in the context of "resuscitated antimilitarism" (*L'anti-militarisme en France*, 109–12).

72. "Les instituteurs syndiques et la guerre," AN F7 13575.

73. Brion, *La voie féministe*, 93. For her perspective on internationalism, see 94–102. In many ways this document foreshadows her defense at her trial; see especially page 103.

74. *Le Petit Parisien*, 18 Nov. 1917. This information was false; however, the linkage between defeatism and revolution intensified in response to the situation in Russia.

75. *Le Matin*, 18 Nov. 1917.

76. *Le Figaro*, 18 Nov. 1917. *L'Homme Libre*, 19 Nov. 1917. For information about *L'Homme Libre*, see Slater, *Defeatists and Their Enemies*, 188.

77. *L'Action Française*, 18 Nov. 1917; *Le Petit Journal*, 18 Nov. 1917; *L'Écho de Paris*, 18 Nov. 1917. Most accounts seem to rely on information from *Le Matin*.

78. *Le Matin*, 19 Nov. 1917.

79. *L'Homme Libre*, 18 and 19 Nov. 1917.

80. *Le Petit Journal*, 19 Nov. 1917. Brion's friend was undoubtedly referring to the visit of Eleanor Fell to France in April 1915 to try to rally French feminist support for the Women's Peace Conference at The Hague. See the "Rapport au sujet du 'Congrès International des Femmes' à la Haye," 27 Apr. 1915, in APP Ba 1651, which mentions both Fell's visit and Brion's attendance at this meeting. The main wartime feminist newspaper, *La Française*, would wait until early December before commenting on Brion's arrest. An article by Jane Misme tried to separate Brion's actions from those of other feminists, expressing hope that "Brion and her partners would be . . . guilty only of error" but condemning their actions just the same. See Jane Misme, "Hélène Brion et la propagande défaitiste," *La Française*, 8 Dec. 1917.

81. For an overview of ideas about French femininity circa World War I, see Berenson, *Trial of Madame Caillaux;* Martin-Fugier, *La Bourgeoise;* and McMillan, *Housewife or Harlot.* For ideas about masculinity, see Maugue, *L'identité masculine.*

82. *Le Petit Journal,* 20 Nov. 1917.

83. Masculine clothing, although in Brion's case a cycling suit, was linked with nonfeminine behavior, i.e., lesbian, antimale, subversive activities. Madeleine Pelletier, a leading feminist and a friend of Brion's, wore short-cropped hair and masculine attire and felt that her appearance caused more trouble during the war than at any other time. For details about Pelletier, her "costume," and her friendship with Brion, see her war diary cited in Boxer, "Socialism Faces Feminism," 260–61, 276, 288, and Gordon, *Integral Feminist,* 132–52. For more on Pelletier's feminism, see Bard, *Les filles de Marianne* and *Madeleine Pelletier,* and Scott, *Only Paradoxes to Offer,* ch. 5. For a discussion of changes in feminine appearance as a result of the war, see Mary Louise Roberts, "Samson and Delilah Revisited" and *Civilization without Sexes.*

84. *L'Humanité,* 20 Nov. 1917.

85. Ibid. This article quoted comments made about Brion that specifically refuted that she had anything to do with anarchy or Malthusianism. More importantly, the story stressed that Brion had nothing to do with the other treason trials, as several papers tried to insinuate by seeking to link her with other well-known alleged traitors such as Bolo or Almereyda.

86. "Lettre Ouverte aux Societaires de l'Orphelinat Ouvrier" (Paris, 1917), AN F7 13376. The police also noted the agitation of syndicalist, socialist, pacifist, and feminist groups on her behalf. See APP Ba 1639 and Ba 1562 and AN F7 13575.

87. *Le Matin,* 5 Dec. 1917.

88. Vernet, *Hélène Brion.* The Dreyfus affair, stemming from accusations of treason against Jewish army captain Alfred Dreyfus, polarized France at the end of the nineteenth century, and Dreyfus's eventual vindication was seen as a triumph for the Third Republic and for such principles as the defense of individual rights against even military authority.

89. Ibid., 8. By using the word "espionne" (female spy), Vernet may have been evoking the most well-known such figure in France, Mata Hari, who was executed in October 1917. To date I have found no evidence linking the cases, but the audience for Brion's trial was doubtless aware that being a woman was no guarantee that one could escape the ultimate punishment for treason. For more on Mata Hari, see Wheelwright, *Fatal Lover.*

90. Vernet, *Hélène Brion,* 18. She maintains that the "infamous" photo was taken at the local soup kitchen.

91. Ibid., 18–19. Further references are made parenthetically in the text.

92. Presumably, Vernet deliberately chose not to emphasize Brion's feminism but to portray her as an "activist" for peace so as to appeal to a larger audience. However, her final arguments appear to have feminism as a subtext; "militant" seems to refer to feminist in particular. Even if Vernet did not make the feminist-pacifist connection explicit, Brion did in the context of her trial.

93. I am relying on the "transcript" of the trial as reported in the *Revue des Causes Célèbres,* no. 5 (May 1918) (hereafter referred to as the *Revue* and cited paren-

thetically in the text). Published in Paris in 1918, the journal lists no editors and no bylines, thus my use of this document is not unproblematic; however, I have checked the *Revue*'s account against those of many newspapers in order to provide fuller citations when there are discrepancies.

94. *Le Figaro,* 26 Mar. 1918. *Le Petit Journal,* 26 Mar. 1918, also characterized her as "a small, nervous woman."

95. *L'Action Française,* 26 Mar. 1918.

96. *Le Petit Parisien,* 26 Mar. 1918; *Le Petit Journal,* 27 Mar. 1918.

97. *Le Figaro,* 27 Mar. 1918.

98. *Le Matin, Le Figaro,* and *Le Petit Journal,* 26 Mar.1918.

99. See *Le Petit Journal* and *L'Action Française,* 26 Mar. 1918, where Brion was quoted as emphasizing that the charge of antimilitarism masked the fact that her trial was about militant feminism.

100. *Le Matin,* 28 Mar. 1918.

101. *L'Humanité,* 28 Mar. 1918.

102. For further biographical information on these women, see Hause, *Women's Suffrage,* and Bard, *Les filles de Marianne.*

103. Séverine would also make these points in the pages of *Verité.* She wrote a column discussing them in February of 1918, which appears among Brion's own press clippings about her trial. See *Verité,* 13 Feb. 1918, Fonds Brion, IFHS. Séverine also spoke against Brion's arrest at a meeting on 7 Jan. 1918 and against the war at a meeting organized by Madeleine Vernet for the Orphelinat Ouvrier on 4 Mar. 1918. For details of these meetings and more on Séverine, see her dossier, APP Ba 1660.

104. *L'Humanité,* 28 Mar. 1918. It is probably not surprising that a socialist paper such as *L'Humanité* would find this testimony so compelling and worthy of full coverage.

105. *L'Action Française,* 29 Mar. 1918; *Revue,* 152.

106. In discussing Brion's defense, I will use the pamphlet form of her speech printed after her trial, which is more complete than the version that appeared in the *Revue des Cause Célèbres.* All references are made parenthetically in the text. Brion, "Déclaration lue au premier conseil de guerre." These arguments are also foreshadowed in a letter to Jeanne Mélin; see letter from Hélène Brion to Jeanne Mélin, 6 Mar. 1918, in Fonds Mélin, Box 39, Fonds Bouglé, BHVP.

107. Brion noted and attacked the loosening of morality and increase in prostitution caused by war and stated that "our savage allies" would treat the women of invaded countries "exactly" as German soldiers had done in this war (see Brion, *Declaration lue au premier conseil de guerre,* 16–17).

108. *L'Action Française,* 30 Mar. 1918.

109. *Le Figaro,* 30 Mar. 1918.

110. *La Française,* 13 Apr. 1918.

111. *Le Petit Parisien,* 31 Mar. 1918. Brion protested this revocation in a letter to the minister of public instruction, which was also reprinted in *L'Humanité,* 18 May 1918. In May of 1920, a meeting of a group of feminists in Pantin, attended by about 500 people, protested the revocation of Marthe Bigot's teaching certificate as well of that of Brion. See "Meeting de Protestation Contre la Révocation de Marthe Bigot et d'Hélène Brion," 16 June 1921, APP Ba 1651.

112. "Mère, un officier frappe ton fils . . . ," included in the Report of the Prefect of the Department of Isère, 16 June 1917, AN F7 13376.

113. A copy of this letter, dated 19 Sept. 1917, sent to the wives of soldiers in Angers was forwarded indignantly to the police. See "Copie d'une lettre communiquée à la 4è brigade de police mobile, le 19 Sept. 1917" enclosed in the report dated 16 Oct. 1917 sent on to the Sûreté, AN F7 13375. An identical letter was sent to a Mme. Perochaud in Nantes and forwarded to Paris (see ibid.).

114. "Assez de sang!" [11 Jan. 1918?], AN F7 13375.

115. Inspector Parmentier to the Special Commissioner, Head of the Service for Dieppe, [Report] investigation, 7 Jan. 1918, AN F7 13373. The report notes that Mme. Tournois, epicière, also heard Mme. Lalleve repeat similar statements and records its interrogation of Mme. Lalleve and her two "informants," including sixteen-year-old Elise Langlois.

116. The same folder in the archives containing the information discussed above also contains records of the distribution to "Widows of the War" of a pamphlet denouncing the state's appointment of "Conseiller de tutelle" to help those widowed by the war to raise their children. This document claimed that this not only insulted the mothers of France but was a dangerous—antireligious—precedent. See letter from the Prefect of Cantal to the minister of the interior, 15 Apr. 1918, AN F7 13373.

117. See scattered references throughout APP Ba 1614 and Ba 1639.

118. "Chronique médicale contre la Clemenceauphobie," *Femme Socialiste*, May 1918, [3–4]. Saumoneau herself was also arrested for her antiwar activities. For more on this, see Sowerwine, *Sisters or Citizens?*, and Bard, *Les filles de Marianne*.

119. There really was no exact British counterpart to Brion and her cause célèbre, although there were certainly British women accused of treason during the war. The most notorious case may well be that of Alice Wheeldon, who, along with her daughters and son-in-law, was tried for plotting to assassinate Prime Minister Lloyd George in 1917. That case did not directly address gender. See Sheila Rowbotham's interesting account of the case in *Friends of Alice Wheeldon*. For the government records on the case, see CRIM 1 166. I am using the more obscure case of Pimlott because of the issues that it raises.

120. Annie E. Pimlott's name appears in the "Weekly Intelligence Summary of the Northern Command" on 22 Jan. 1919, where her position and address are recorded, as is the note that the "Attorney General has decided to prosecute her" (AIR 1 557/16/15/53). For this citation and for information about Pimlott's case—and particularly for bringing it to my attention—my thanks to Julian Putkowski.

121. "Sensational Charges against Soldiers." Note the parallels between this and some of the arguments made about soldiers by Brion; see Brion *Declaration lue au premier conseil de guerre*, 16–17, and the discussion in note 107, above.

122. "Sensational Charges against Soldiers."

123. Ibid.

124. Ibid.

125. See, for example, the discussion of moral force versus physical force in the writings of the influential American activist Addams in *Newer Ideals of Peace*, 208, as well as those of British feminists Despard in *Women in the New Era*, 49–50, and Swanwick, in *Future of the Women's Movement*. For one British and one French

example of this argument, a not atypical one during the war, see also Gollancz, *Making of Women,* 15–17, and Maurice de Walette, "La guerre et le féminisme," *Je Sais Tout* 13, no. 143 (Oct. 1917), 392.

126. See Gould, "Women's Military Services," 117, on antisuffragists' use of these arguments.

CHAPTER SIX

1. For women's suffrage debates in France at the war's end, see Hause, *Women's Suffrage,* esp. chs. 7–9; Paul Smith, *Feminism and the Third Republic,* ch. 3; and Bard, *Les filles de Marianne,* 144–67. For accounts of the granting of women's suffrage in Britain, see Holton, *Feminism and Democracy;* Pugh, *Women and the Women's Movement;* and Kent, *Making Peace,* ch. 4. For the effect of the war on individual suffragists, see Alberti, *Beyond Suffrage,* ch. 3. For a succinct overview of shifting arguments about women's citizenship in England from the early nineteenth century, see Clark, "Gender, Class, and the Nation"; for a historical perspective on France, see Offen, "Exploring the Sexual Politics," and Viennot, *La démocratie 'à la française';* and for a comparative perspective on women's suffrage internationally, see Pateman, "Three Questions about Womanhood Suffrage."

2. For French debates about qualifications for voting before and after the war, see Huard, *Le suffrage universel,* and Rosanvallon, *Le sacre du citoyen.* For more general discussions of changes in the franchise in Britain in 1918, see Pugh, *Electoral Reform,* and Tanner, *Political Change,* chs. 12 and 13.

3. Of course, some of this discourse has older roots, particularly in Britain, as Anne Summers points out in her discussion of prewar military service by women nurses; see Summers, *Angels and Citizens,* 287–88. The war did, however, shift some of this debate, if only because of the scale of civilian mobilization.

4. The Representation of the People Bill recognized the significance of service by disenfranchising conscientious objectors who had not performed national service, by allowing military men younger than twenty-one but older than nineteen to vote, and by including women for the first time. See Pugh, *Electoral Reform.*

5. For the rejection of French proposals to lower the voting age, see *Journal Officiel: Sénat Legislature Débats Session Ordinaire,* 22 Nov. 1918, 789.

6. For a thorough analysis of the ways in which women were used to mobilize men, see Gullace, "Women and the Ideology of War."

7. "The Call to Arms" and "Women Urge Khaki Campaign," *Evening Standard,* 26 Aug. 1914.

8. Letter to the editor, *Evening Standard,* 26 Aug. 1914. The letter is signed "Ashamed of Her Country."

9. "Women Who Want to Fight: Enthusiastic Amazon Who Tried to Enlist As a Man," *Daily Graphic,* 13 Jan. 1915. See also Wheelwright, *Amazons and Military Maids,* and Garber, *Vested Interests,* for more on female military cross-dressers. Even later in the war, after the example of the Russian Women's Battalion and the introduction of conscription, women continued to propose that they be allowed to enter the fighting line. A woman in Oxford suggested that there must be "thousands of women, like me, [who] are ungifted with either brains or beauty. Having

no particular ties, they would gladly give their lives to save a few of our much more needed men" (quoted in "Cherchez les femmes," *John Bull*, 8 Sept. 1917). The article went on to dismiss this call: "We should be ashamed of our country if, while a fit man lived, he allowed a woman to defend, with weapons in hands, the hearth of the home from which he slunk away."

10. For more on the white feather campaign, see Gullace, "White Feathers and Wounded Men."

11. "Le loyalisme des suffragettes," *Le Figaro*, 25 Feb. 1915. This article was then cited in "Suffragettes at the Front," *Daily Graphic*, 26 Feb. 1915.

12. "Women for the Front Eager to Go But in the Dark How to Get There," *Daily Mail*, 26 Feb. 1915. See also "Mystery of 1,000 Amazons. Regiment of Women Whom Nobody Knows," *Daily Express*, 26 Feb. 1915. The organizations the *Express* supposedly contacted included the Women's Social and Political Union, National Union of Women's Suffrage Societies, Women's Freedom League, International Women's Suffrage Alliance, the London Society for Woman's Suffrage, and the Actresses Franchise League. The *Express* cited *Le Temps* as its source of information. Toward the end of 1915, an article in *The Times* recorded the approval in France of the "khaki-clad, slim, young English girl" who carried stretchers and drove ambulances: "The admiration of the French trooper for the amazon-like achievements of the Englishwomen knows no bounds." The article went on to celebrate the accomplishments of women in Britain as well as in the battle zones of France. See "Behind the War: The English Girls' Part" *The Times*, 27 Dec. 1915.

13. Gould, "Women's Military Services," 118–19. More recent interpretations of women's patriotic wartime action can be found in Watson, "Khaki Girls, VADs and Tommy's Sisters," and Krisztina Roberts, "Gender, Class, and Patriotism," which deals explicitly with paramilitary and military groups.

14. "Playing at Soldiers," *Newcastle Chronicle*, 19 Mar. 1915. The letter is signed "Don't Show Off." Gould cites similar letters to the editor of the *Morning Post* from slightly later in 1915 ("Women's Military Service," 119–20). See also Violet Markham, "Woman and the War," *Sheffield Independent*, 30 June 1915.

15. Harold Ffoulkes, "Women and War Service," *North Mail*, 9 June 1915.

16. *Ladies' Pictorial*, 21 Aug. 1915.

17. "Women in Khaki," *War Budget*, 4 Nov. 1915.

18. *Globe*, 19 Sept. 1917.

19. Midland Branch WVR, WWC, [1915?], IWM VOL 2/27. Drilling was also defended as providing discipline; see "Women and War: Work of the New Volunteer Reserve," *Globe*, 2 Feb. 1915.

20. B. Hopkins, WVR Midland, "Uniform: Its Meaning and How It Should Be Worn," WWC, [1915?], IWM VOL 2/33. A depiction of the WVR officer's uniform can be found in WWC, IWM VOL 2/34.

21. *Brixton Free Press*, 15 Oct. 1915. A later defense noted that "none will ever estimate what was the lure of the khaki that the innumerable leagues and battalions and corps and platoons and squadrons of women assumed in the first six months of the war. There was no more real reason for assuming this very nondescript hue than apple green or rose pink, but it savoured of active service, and its wearers

had a faith that it showed as nothing else could that they were 'out to do their bit' " (see "Women and Khaki," *Newcastle Daily Journal,* 1 Nov. 1917).

22. The other obvious sacrifice for women—a sacrifice also involving an initial risk of life—was a maternal one. Women risked their lives in childbirth and, during the war, sacrificed the sons "produced" by that "life-threatening" experience to the war effort. See the discussions in Chapters 3 and 5.

23. *Gentlewoman,* 30 Dec. 1916.

24. "Tempora Mutantur!" *The Bystander,* 17 Feb. 1915.

25. "Amazons to the Fore," *Ladies' Pictorial,* 20 Feb. 1915, and D. D. Smithett, letter to the editor, *Bournemouth Echo,* 22 Apr. 1915. See also the *Daily Mail,* 7 Aug. 1915. Other articles emphasized the idea of women's service as consisting of not only what they actually did but also what "their capacity for service" was, predicting a time when "all hands will be called up, men and women, soldiers all for the country." See Austin Harrison, "Every Girl Is Wanted," *Sunday Pictorial,* 7 Nov. 1915.

26. "Women in Khaki," *Daily Telegraph,* 25 Oct. 1915.

27. See Pugh, *Electoral Reform,* ch. 3–4.

28. There were numerous articles debating or acknowledging women's inclusion in the register. See, for example, "War Service for Women," *The Times,* 18 Mar. 1915, "On 'Women and the National Register,'" *The Gentlewoman,* 14 Apr. 1915, and "General Anxiety to Help the Country," *Daily Express,* 10 July 1915.

29. For an overview of the National Register and the Military Service Act, see Trevor Wilson, *Myriad Faces of War,* 166–69, 396.

30. May Bateman, "Compulsory Service for Women," *Pall Mall Gazette,* 4 Mar. 1916, and letters to the editor, *Pall Mall Gazette,* 7 and 8 Mar. 1916; quotes are from Louis Vincent, letter, 7 Mar. 1916, and C. Cowdroy, letter, 8 Mar. 1917.

31. All quotes are from "Medals for Women," *Pall Mall Gazette,* 28 June 1916.

32. For more information about the creation of the WAAC/QMAAC, see files labeled "Army," in WWC, IWM; Ewing, *Women in Uniform;* Terry, *Women in Khaki;* and Gould "Women's Military Services."

33. "Women's Army Auxiliary Corps: Uniform of Officers, Proposal by Mrs. Gwynne Vaughan," WO 32/5252. Chalmers Watson, the original chief controller, was the sister of Sir Auckland Geddes, and Gwynne Vaughan served as the overseas head. Terry, in *Women in Khaki,* 44, claims that in selecting the jacket pattern, they decided to avoid breast pockets for fear these would emphasize the breast.

34. "Request to reconsider proposals 9 and 10," 12 Apr. 1917, WO 32/5252.

35. "Extract from D.P.S. Minute," 19 Apr. 1917, WO 32/52520. Emphasis in the original.

36. For contemporaneous defenses of the WAAC against the immorality charges, see Elizabeth Sloan Chesser, "The Women's Army in France," *The Contemporary Review* 113 (June 1918), 682–84; Jesse, *Sword of Deborah,* 37–39; and letters to the editor of the *Manchester Dispatch,* 26 Feb. 1918, and the *Daily News and Leader,* 4 Mar. 1918.

37. Gould, "Women's Military Services," 121. She is drawing upon the work of Lillian Faderman.

38. For an analysis of depictions of the "mannish" suffragette, see Tickner, *Spec-*

tacle of Women, 166–67, 205–13. Tickner notes that the image—notably that of Joan of Arc—from which militant women drew "claimed her 'womanliness' from another source, that of female heroism in history, allegory and myth" (207).

39. See Terry, *Women in Khaki,* 69–74. It was shortly after this, on the 9 April 1918, that "as a mark of Her Majesty's appreciation of the good services rendered by the Women's Army Auxiliary Corps" she assumed the position and title of commander-in-chief and the WAAC was renamed the Queen Mary's Army Auxiliary Corps (quote from Terry, *Women in Khaki,* 77). For contemporaneous discussions of the creation of the QMAAC, see "The Queen and the W.A.A.C.s," *Evening News,* 9 Apr. 1918, and "The W.A.A.C.," *Morning Post,* 18 Apr. 1918. To add to the confusion, even after the official name change, many continued to refer to the QMAAC as the WAAC.

40. "Khaki Friendship," *Daily Sketch,* 24 Jan. 1918. See also "Lies About The W.A.A.C.," *Bath Herald,* 21 Feb. 1918.

41. "W.A.A.C. Slandered," *The Vigilance Record* (Mar. 1918), 22–23. For a different perspective on the WAAC scandal and on WAAC recruitment, see Lamm, "Emily Goes to War."

42. Ella Hepworth Dixon, "A Glimpse of The W.A.A.C.S at Work," *Ladies' Pictorial,* 22 June 1918.

43. Hilda M. Love, "When the Khaki Girls Come Home," *Sunday Pictorial,* 17 Feb. 1918. See also Barton and Cody, *Eve in Khaki,* 65, 91, 140, 162–63, 43–44.

44. "Is the Khaki Girl A 'Snob'? Influence of a Uniform," *Sunday Herald,* 27 Jan. 1918.

45. This term is drawn from the article "Slackers in Petticoats" in *Bystander,* 21 June 1916.

46. "Single Girls First," *Daily Mail,* 12 June 1916. The question "Daddy, What Did You Do in the Great War" appeared on a Parliamentary Recruiting Poster designed by Saville Lumley that depicted a little boy playing with toy soldiers while a little girl sitting on her father's lap asked the infamous question.

47. See, for example, "Slothful Suburbia: Women Who Do Not Work," *Daily Mail,* 16 Oct. 1917; "Round-Up Women Slackers! Why Not Tribunals of Matrons to Deal with Them?" *Daily Sketch,* 19 Oct. 1917; and "The Women Are Splendid, But—," *Sunday Pictorial,* 21 Oct. 1917.

48. "Conscript Women!" *Manchester Dispatch,* 7 Dec. 1917.

49. Lady Askwith, "Should Women Be Conscripted?" *Answers,* 23 Mar. 1918. See also her "The Conscription of Women," *Pall Mall Gazette,* 29 June 1918; and for another article in favor of women's conscription, see Mrs. Flora Annie Steel, "Women Who Are Hindering Instead of Helping," *Sunday Herald,* 10 May 1918.

50. "Conscription for Women," *Evening Gazette,* 8 May 1918.

51. *Bystander,* 6 Feb. 1918.

52. Notice that the adjective "khaki" can be applied directly to the man, while the girl is merely "khaki-clad." See Hilda M. Love, "'WAACS' and Weddings," *Daily Mail,* 21 Dec. 1917.

53. See Susan Pedersen's argument about women's relationship to the state being indirect in her "Gender, Welfare, and Citizenship." The idea of women's in-

direct participation in the war was perhaps exemplified in the slogan on a WAAC recruiting poster: "The girl behind the man behind the gun" (see IWM: POS 212).

54. See the discussion of women in the factories in Chapter 3 and Downs, *Manufacturing Inequality*. For discussions of French women's service as nurses, see Thébaud, *La femme au temps,* and Darrow, "French Volunteer Nursing."

55. All references in this paragraph to Jane Misme, "Les femmes dans l'armée," *La Française,* 6 Mar. 1915. Praise of British women's military efforts can also be found in "Les Anglaises Militaires," *Le Figaro,* 28 Apr. 1915.

56. Donnay, *La parisienne et la guerre,* 52–53.

57. Amélie Hammer, "Le féminisme et la patrie," *La Vie* (Feb. 1916), in DOS 396 CON, BMD.

58. Thérèse Casevitz-Rouff, "Les femmes aux services de l'armée," *La Française,* 4 Mar. 1916.

59. See "Les femmes dans l'armée: Elles font le ménage de la France," *Le Petit Journal,* 7 Nov. 1916. See also "Le service militaire des femmes," *La Vie Féminine,* 28 Jan. 1917, and "Les femmes à la caserne," *Le Matin,* 7 Apr. 1917, all in DOS 940.3 GUE, BMD.

60. "La mobilisation civile des femmes," *République de l'Isère,* 20 Nov. 1916, and "L'armée des femmes," *L'Information,* 15 Dec. 1916, both in DOS 396 CON, BMD.

61. Donnay, *La parisienne et la guerre,* 52–53. Emmanuel Reynaud notes that the French army made use of women during the war "without giving them a military status" (see Reynaud, *Les femmes, la violence,* 15).

62. "Rapport sur la réunion d'Action des Femmes," 17 Dec. 1916, in AN F7 13266.

63. Émile Bergerat, "La femme française," *Le Figaro,* 11 May 1915.

64. Régis Gignoux, "Les nouvelles amazones," *Le Figaro,* 22 June 1917.

65. Pitrois, *Femmes de 1914–1915,* 2, 19, 193, 183–84. For further discussions of women's patriotic labor, see 26–35 (on teachers and women in the occupied territories) and 190–92. Note how closely this rhetoric resembles that of feminist pacifists such as Capy discussed in Chapter 5. There are echoes of such anecdotes about mothers in Britain, such as this response by a mother who was pitied for having five sons fighting: "I do not need pity; I am proud to have them to give. Pity is more needed by those mothers whose sons won't go" (Lyall "Our Duty in War-Time," 1).

66. "Frivolités," *Le Figaro,* 22 May 1917.

67. Jacques Flach, introduction to Combarieu, *Les jeunes filles françaises,* xi.

68. Combarieu, *Les jeunes filles françaises,* 124. For other works on French women and the war not discussed here, see Barthou, *L'effort de la femme française;* De Courson, *La femme française pendant la guerre;* De la Hire, *La femme française,* Masson, *Les femmes et la guerre de 1914;* Spont, *La femme et la guerre;* and Vincent, *Parisiennes de guerre.*

69. Descaves, *La maison anxieuse,* 35, 56, 73.

70. DuBois, *Feminism and Suffrage;* Kent, *Sex and Suffrage,* ch. 7.

71. For the first discussion of this division, see Vellacott Newberry, "Anti-War Suffragists." See also Alberti, *Beyond Suffrage;* Liddington, "Women's Peace Crusade" and *Long Road to Greenham;* Wiltsher, *Most Dangerous Women;* and Kent, *Making Peace,* 77–82. The often moving letters of resignation from the NUWSS from anti-

war women can be found in the papers of the Women's International League for Peace and Freedom—British Section, held at the British Library of Political and Economic Science, London.

72. Davin, "Imperialism and Motherhood." Antoinette Burton also argues that British suffragists claimed certain kinds of moral and even maternal authority as imperial citizens before the war. See Burton, *Burdens of History.*

73. E. Sylvia Pankhurst, "Going to War," *The Woman's Dreadnought,* 8 Aug. 1914. One can find echoes of this message in some of the fiction discussed in Chapter 1; see also Stern, *Le baptême du courage.*

74. *Daily Chronicle,* 2 Jan. 1915. For more detailed information about the activities of various women's suffrage organizations during the war, see Holton, *Feminism and Democracy;* Kent, *Making Peace;* and Pugh, *Women and the Women's Movement.*

75. Ella Hepworth Dixon, "The Suffragists in War Time," *Ladies' Pictorial,* 14 Nov. 1914. She also contrasted the loyalty of suffragists with the unwilling service of the Irish, who she deemed rebels.

76. See Pugh, *Women and the Women's Movement,* ch. 2, for evidence of the insincerity of some of these converts.

77. "The War and Woman Suffrage," *Nation,* 13 Feb. 1915.

78. Holford Knight, "Letter," *Nation,* 20 Feb. 1915.

79. "Two Opinions on Woman's Suffrage," *Sheffield Daily Telegraph,* 9 June 1915.

80. Proposals for electoral reform along these lines also coincided with the imposition of conscription and the end of the volunteer army. These "rumors of an adult suffrage bill" were discussed by the Executive Committee of the NUWSS in March 1916. See Minutes of the Executive Committee of the NUWSS, 16 Mar. 1916, Box 84, A1/8, NUWSSC.

81. Fawcett's letter was discussed in Minutes of the Executive Committee of the NUWSS, 6 Apr. 1916, Box 84, A1/8, NUWSSC, and the final version, dated 4 May 1916, was subsequently published in *The Englishwoman,* no. 90 (June 1916).

82. See Asquith's reply presented in Minutes of the Executive Committee of the NUWSS, 18 May 1916, Box 84, A1/8, NUWSSC; this reply was also reprinted in *The Englishwoman,* no. 90 (June 1916).

83. Statement for the Prime Minister, Minutes of the Executive Committee of the Consultative Committee of Women's Suffrage Societies, 4 Aug. 1916, 2, Box 249, CCWSSC.

84. John Galsworthy, "And—After?" *Observer,* 2 July 1916; "The Future Basis of the Franchise," *Observer,* 13 Aug. 1916; Cicely Hamilton, "Mr. Asquith Converted!" *Weekly Dispatch,* 20 Aug. 1916.

85. Hamilton, "Mr. Asquith Converted!"

86. Betty Balfour, "Franchise for Service," *The Englishwoman,* no. 95 (Nov. 1916).

87. Henry Asquith, *Parliamentary Debates,* Commons, 5th ser., vol. 92 (28 Mar. 1917), col. 469.

88. Walter Long, *Parliamentary Debates,* Commons, 5th ser., vol. 92 (28 Mar. 1917), cols. 517–18.

89. See discussion in *Parliamentary Debates,* Commons, 5th series, vol. 93 (1917), esp. 22–24 May, and vol. 94 (1917) and *Parliamentary Debates,* Lords, 5th ser., vol. 27 (1917–18).

90. Margaret Heitland, "The Triumph of Women's Suffrage," *Queen*, 30 June 1917.

91. For an example of this type of objection, see Miss Garland, letter to the editor, *Dundee Advertiser*, 25 June 1917, and "Women and the War," *Morning Post*, 2 Jan. 1918.

92. Eleanor Rathbone, "The Remuneration of Women's Services," in Gollancz, *Making of Women*, 100.

93. A. Maude Royden, "The Woman's Movement of the Future," in Gollancz, *Making of Women*, 128, 145.

94. Ralph Rooper, "Women Enfranchised," in Gollancz, *Making of Women*, 94–95.

95. *Yorkshire Post*, 11 Jan. 1918.

96. Interview with Mrs Fawcett, *Observer*, 13 Jan. 1918. Some critics, like Rooper, would suggest that this idea had internationalist, explicitly antimilitarist implications; others would focus literally on the domestic concerns, such as child welfare, health, and education, which were deemed the issues of most obvious interest.

97. Viscount Bryce, *Parliamentary Debates*, Lords, 5th ser., vol. 27 (17 Dec. 1917), cols. 178–79.

98. Lord Sydenham, *Parliamentary Debates*, Lords, 5th ser., vol. 27 (17 Dec. 1917), col. 213.

99. Lord Buckmaster, *Parliamentary Debates*, Lords, 5th ser., vol. 27 (19 Dec. 1917), col. 274.

100. Lord Buckmaster, *Parliamentary Debates*, Lords, 5th ser., vol. 27 (9 Jan. 1918), col. 436.

101. This included the tiny number of women over thirty who had participated in one of the auxiliary branches of the military, who were thus excused from the requirements of possessing the local government franchise. See Pugh, *Electoral Reform*.

102. R. M. Wilson, *Wife: Mother: Voter*, ix–x.

103. Ibid., xi.

104. Ibid., 32–33, 39, 41–42, 59.

105. "New Women Voters," *Daily News*, 15 Apr. 1918. Fawcett often referred to the newly enfranchised women as mothers; see *Observer*, 13 Jan. 1918, and *The Times*, 26 Mar. 1918.

106. "The Emancipation of Women," *Labour Woman* 7, no. 3 (Mar. 1919). My thanks to Angela Woollacott for this reference.

107. Julie Siegfried and Ghénia Avril de Sainte Croix, letter, 25 Aug. 1914, Conseil National des Femmes Françaises, DOS 396 CON, BMD. The conseil was "a broad coalition of women's organizations" and among the largest feminist groups in France; see Hause, *Women's Suffrage*, 28, 213.

108. Benoit, *L'énergie féminine pendant la guerre*, 5, 8.

109. "Les femmes pendant et après la guerre," *Le Petit Journal*, 17 Apr. 1916.

110. "Rapport sur la réunion d'Union Française pour le Suffrage des Femmes," 22 Apr. 1916, AN F7 13266.

111. Barrès devoted some of his daily articles to the bravery and dedication of French women. Mostly these pieces were highly sentimental, filled with anecdotes

about letters written to sons at the front and patriotic hymns to Joan of Arc, an inspiring representation of French womanhood; he even advocated the creation of a national fête of patriotism in honor of Joan of Arc. See Barrès's articles reprinted as *Chronique de la Grande Guerre*. For the issue of "suffrage for the dead," see "Le suffrage des morts," 1 Feb. 1916, in *Chronique*, 309–12, and "La nécessité du suffrage des morts," 21 Nov. 1916, in *Chronique*, 378–81. The quote is from "Le suffrage des morts," 311. For a wartime translation of some of his essays into English, see Barrès, *The Undying Spirit of France*. For more on Barrès's output as prowar intellectual, see Hanna, *Mobilization of Intellect*, 17.

112. Barrès, "La nécessité du suffrage des morts," 21 Nov. 1916, in *Chronique*, 380.

113. See the previous discussion in this chapter.

114. Jane Misme, "La volonté des morts," *La Française*, 19 Feb. 1916.

115. G. De Jaer, letter to editor, *La Française*, 4 Mar. 1916.

116. Nelly Roussel in *L'Équité*, Mar. 1916, quoted in Hause, *Woman's Suffrage*, 207.

117. "Rapport sur la réunion d'Union Française pour Le Suffrage des Femmes," 16 Feb. 1916, AN F7 13266. Hause, *Woman's Suffrage*, 207, notes that the plan was praised in *L'Action Féminine* as well.

118. "Rapport sur la réunion d'Action des Femmes," 6 Mar. 1917, AN F7 13266.

119. Hause, *Woman's Suffrage*, 206.

120. Abensour, *Les vaillantes*, 307, 309, 19–21. For a succinct discussion of the "loi Violette," see De la Hire, *Le femme française*, 205–6, and Bard, *Filles de Marianne*, 63–64. This law was originally passed by the Chamber in 1910 but not ratified by the Senate until 1917.

121. "Rapport sur la réunion d'Action des Femmes," 22 July 1917, AN F7 13266.

122. "Rapport sur la réunion du Comité d'Action Suffragiste," 2 Jan., 7 Jan., 4 Feb., and 8 Mar. 1918, AN F7 13266; copies of these reports can also be found in APP Ba 1651. The quotes are from the 4 Feb. meeting.

123. "Rapport sur congrès annuel de l'Union Française pour le Suffrage des Femmes," 6 Apr. 1917, APP Ba 1651.

124. "Rapport sur la réunion du Comité d'Action Suffragiste," 26 Dec. 1917, APP Ba 1651.

125. Marie Grimmer, "Les femmes sont splendides," Apr. 1917, in DOS 396 FEM, BMD.

126. Monette Thomas, "L'ère nouvelle," *La Voix des Femmes*, 12 Sept. 1918, DOS 396 FEM, BMD.

127. Barthélemy, *Le vote des femmes*, v–vii. The significance of this work is noted in Paul Smith, *Feminism and the Third Republic*, 112.

128. Barthélemy, *Le vote des femmes*, 39, 42.

129. Ibid., 99–106; quote is from 105.

130. For the older interpretation, see Zeldin, *France, 1848–1945*, ch. 13. For the interpretations discussed here, see Hause, *Woman's Suffrage*, chs. 8–9, and Paul Smith, *Feminism and the Third Republic*, ch. 3. For works that place these debates in a broader perspective of the meaning of "universal suffrage," see Huard, *Le suffrage universel*; Rosanvallon, *Le sacre du citoyen*; and, for women in particular, Reynolds, "Marianne's Citizens?"

131. Feminist reaction to this idea can be found in "Vers la victoire féministe," *La Française*, 24 Feb. 1917.

132. Hause, *Woman's Suffrage*, 209, 221–30. See also Paul Smith, *Feminism and the Third Republic*, 106–7, and Bard, *Les filles de Marianne*, 145.

133. Dominique Delahaye, *Journal Officiel: Sénat, Débats*, 22 May 1919, 779.

134. *Journal Officiel: Sénat, Débats*, 9 August 1919, 1306. Hause, *Woman's Suffrage*, 236–39, notes that five different proposals for varying degrees of women's suffrage, including the Chamber's, Delahaye's, and the Comte de Las Cazes's familial vote appeared before the Senate in 1919. None was debated fully.

135. *Journal Officiel: Sénat, Documents*, 3 Oct. 1919, no. 564. See Hause, *Women's Suffrage*, 236–39, for a discussion of Bérard's report and the reaction in the feminist press.

136. *Journal Officiel: Sénat, Débats*, 17 Oct. 1919, 1733–35.

137. The Marquis de Condorcet was a late-eighteenth-century advocate for women having the same civic rights as men, including the right to vote, because of the natural equality of men and women. This did not mean that he did not distinguish between the natural capacities of women for some occupations and men for others. By referring to Condorcet at the outset, the senator is linking his arguments with those advocated in the First Republic of the French Revolution.

138. Louis Martin, *Journal Officiel: Sénat*, 7 Nov. 1922, 1297, 1299–1300.

139. Antonin Gourju, *Journal Officiel: Sénat*, 7 Nov. 1922, 1304, 1306, and 14 Nov. 1922, 1339. Other senators, like Senator Hugues Le Roux, would attack Nancy Astor.

140. See "Communication d'une Pétition," *Journal Officiel: Sénat*, 14 Nov. 1922, 1335. Those opposed to women's suffrage made much of the fact that so few signatures were obtained and that, moreover, these represented a substantial decrease from prewar polls. See the discussion in Hause, *Women's Suffrage*, 232–33.

141. François Labrousse, *Journal Officiel: Sénat*, 16 Nov. 1922, 1342, 1346–47.

142. Alexandre Bérard, rapporteur, *Journal Officiel: Sénat*, 16 Nov. 1922, 1355. His claim would certainly have surprised British political commentators.

143. Senators Merlin, d'Estrounelles de Constant, and Massabuau, *Journal Officiel: Sénat*, 16 Nov. 1922, 1358–59, 1363, and 21 Nov. 1922, 1373–75.

144. For more on the reasons for this outcome and particularly for the feminist reaction, see Hause, *Women's Suffrage*; Bard, *Les filles de Marianne*; and Paul Smith, *Feminism and the Third Republic*. See also the accounts of feminist meetings in 1919, 1920, and 1921, in AN F7 13266.

CHAPTER SEVEN

1. Winter, *Sites of Memory*, 1. David Cannadine has previously pointed out the importance of death in the aftermath of the First World War; see his "War and Death." Thébaud also highlights, at least for the French, the substantial number of civilian deaths during the war. See Thébaud, "La guerre et le deuil," 105.

2. Both British men and women were buried in national cemeteries; for an account of the burial of a V.A.D. (member of the Voluntary Aid Detachment) in

France, see Dent, *A V.A.D. in France,* 202–4. Dent also wrote an article in response to a letter to the editor of the *Daily Mail* that had ask that the bereaved be allowed to tend their graves, illustrating how well tended they were by WAACs, among others. See Olive Dent, "The Beauty of Our Soldiers' Graves," the *Daily Mail,* 10 Dec. 1917.

3. See, for Britain, Moriarty, "Absent Dead," and, for France, Sherman, "Les inaugurations et la politique" and "Art, Commerce, and the Production of Memory."

4. Lloyd, "Tourism, Pilgrimage," 15.

5. A recent interpretation highlighting the differences between local and national commemoration can be found in Sherman, "Bodies and Names." For my analysis, such distinctions are less relevant.

6. "Mothers of Heroes," *The Morning Post,* 10 June 1915.

7. "War Mourning," *The Times,* 2 Sept. 1914; this also notes the appearance of even a previous article on the subject.

8. Quoted from a letter from Miss Henderson to the Queen Mary's Needlework Guild in *The Times,* 4 Sept. 1914. See also Ethel M. Wood, letter to the editor, *Westminster Gazette,* 7 June 1915. For a further discussion of the wearing of wartime mourning, see Gregory, "Lost Generations," 88–89.

9. "Anglo-Saxon," letter to the editor, *The Times,* 13 July 1915. For an account of the creation of a medal to be given by the state to bereaved relatives, see Dutton, " 'Dead Man's Penny' "; and for more on mourning mothers wearing their sons' medals and their postwar significance, see Gregory, *Silence of Memory,* 39–41.

10. See Mosse, *Fallen Soldiers,* 94–98; Laqueur, "Memory and Naming in the Great War," 156–59; Bourke, *Dismembering the Male,* ch. 5; and Lloyd, "Tourism, Pilgrimage," ch. 4.

11. Both the French and British buried their unknown soldiers on the same day, exactly two years from the signing of the armistice on 11 Nov. 1920.

12. WORK 20 1/3, [58], [216].

13. All references in this paragraph to letter from L. Storr (Secretary of Memorial Services Committee) to J. T. Davies, 28 Oct. 1920, Document F/24/3/20, David Lloyd George Papers, HLRO. An anecdote about a charwoman gaining entrance to the Abbey while the lady of the house did not was recounted in an article about the eventual ceremony in the *Daily Telegraph,* 12 Nov. 1920, cited in Lloyd, "Tourism, Pilgrimage," 91 n. 162.

14. Minutes of Meeting of Cabinet Memorial Services Committee, 3 Nov. 1920, WORK 20 1/3, [226].

15. Memoranda, Unveiling of the Cenotaph and Funeral Service in Westminster Abbey, WORK 20/1/13, [361]. Given the previous estimates, of course, the demand for seats was relatively low. Also included were 4,042 widows in category "c" and 13 relatives of VCs killed or missing. A total of 6,640 tickets were issued. In this context, a VC is one who received the Victoria Cross medal.

16. The reception to the unveiling ceremony, to the unknown warrior, and to the cenotaph are discussed in Lloyd, "Tourism, Pilgrimage," ch. 3; the significance of mourning mothers is discussed on 103–4 and in Cannadine, "War and Death," 226.

17. Program for unveiling of Lytham War Memorial, no. K8318, IWM.

18. Program for unveiling of War Memorial at Leicester—Arch of Remembrance, no. K3819, IWM.

19. See, for example, no. K3894, "Earby Urban district unveiled by Mrs. Williamson" (four Williamsons listed on roll of honour); no. K3850, "Letcliffe Park, Barnoldswick, unveiled by Mrs. Elizabethe Ann Sutcliffe" (roll of honour lists A., E., F., and J. Sutcliffe); no. K4063, where Mrs Viola Hamlin gets to place town's wreath on Newton Abbot War Memorial with two Hamlin men listed on the roll of honour; and no. K4110, Penzance, where Mrs. W. E. T. Bolitho unveils the memorial that lists both W. E. T. and W. T. M. Bolitho as dead; all at IWM.

20. "Order of Proceedings, Manchester, city of, unveiling," no. K3764, IWM. There was presumably no need to explain why the Earl of Derby was involved.

21. General information about war memorials in Britain was conveyed to me in conversations with Catherine Moriarty, formerly of the National Inventory of War Memorials at the IWM, and can be found in her doctoral thesis, "Narrative and the Absent Body," and in her article "Absent Dead."

22. "Description of Memorial," City of Manchester, no. K3764, IWM.

23. Rochdale War Memorial Unveiling, 26 Nov. 1922, no. K3861, IWM.

24. Image available at the National Inventory of War Memorials, IWM.

25. Program for unveiling of Renfrew War Memorial, 5 Aug. 1922, no. K3789, IWM.

26. St. Saviour, Southwark War Memorial and Tablet unveiling, 16 Nov. 1922, no. K3780, IWM.

27. The sculpture was the combined work of Walter Gilbert and Louis Weingartner. Image available at the National Inventory of War Memorials, IWM.

28. Program for the unveiling of the memorial at St. Annes-on-the-Sea, no. K3817, IWM.

29. *Aux veuves de la guerre,* 31, 35.

30. Sherman, "Monuments, Mourning and Masculinity," 83–84. See also Thébaud, "La guerre et le deuil."

31. For the uses of female allegory in monuments, see Warner, *Monuments and Maidens.*

32. See Agulhon, *Marianne into Battle, Marianne au pouvoir,* 345–49, and, more particularly, "Marianne en 14–18," 373–84.

33. For insight into the political uses of Jeanne d'Arc, see Krumeich, "Joan of Arc."

34. For a thorough discussion of French First World War memorials, see Annette Becker, *Les monuments aux morts.* See also Rivé et al., *Monuments de mémoire,* and Winter, *Sites of Memory.*

35. Annette Becker, *Monuments aux morts,* 59.

36. See also the discussion in Sherman, "Monuments, Mourning and Masculinity," 100. This article also discusses the ceremonies that inaugurated monuments.

37. Rivé et al., *Monuments de mémoire,* 218.

38. See photographs of these memorials in Rivé et al., *Monuments de mémoire,* 195, 186, 184 and 187.

39. A photograph of this monument is in Annette Becker, *Monuments aux morts,* 89.

40. Annette Becker, *Monuments aux morts,* 75–76.

41. See photographs of these memorials in Rivé et al., *Monuments de mémoire,* 183, 184, and 185.

42. "Rapport sur l'état d'esprit de la population parisienne: 9ème District," 11 Nov. 1918, APP Ba 1614.

43. The reasons for this in France ranged from military necessity, to hygiene, to the idea that these men were the emblem of the "equality of families of officers and soldiers fallen in an equal sacrifice of their life for the defense of the country." See the "Instruction générale sur les exhumations et les transports de corps de militaires ou de civils pendant la durée de la guerre," 2 Oct. 1917, in AN F2 2125, and, for the quotation above, the "Projet de loi concernant les sépultres militaires," Chambre des Deputés, 23 June 1919, in AN F2 2124.

44. Due to intense public pressure, this law would be adjusted. The government then allowed families to exhume and re-bury corpses locally and offered to care for its dead soldiers at the front and provide family members with travel allowances so that they could visit their loved ones' graves. See the discussion of these changes in Sherman, "Bodies and Names," 453–54, Winter, *Sites of Memory,* 26–27, where he emphasizes that parents won the right to claim bodies over widows; and articles 105 and 106 of the "Loi de 31 Juillet 1920," in *Bulletin des Lois.* Clandestine exhumations are also briefly discussed in Pourcher, *Les jours de guerre,* 471–79.

45. "Un groupe des mères et des veuves de l'Alliés," letter to the minister of the interior, [25 Feb. 1919], AN F2 2125.

46. J. Bonnafoux, Commissioner of Police, Montmorency, Seine et Oise, letter to the minister of the interior, [1919], AN F2 2124.

47. Letter from mayor of Courpalay to the prefect of Seine-et-Marne, 21 July 1919, AN F2 2125. See also the article entitled "Un Macabre Chantage," from *Le Petit Parisien,* 9 Aug. 1919, that found its way to the minister of interior. The article recounts the ordeal of Mme. Denise Lévêque of Berry-au-Bac, who exhumed the body of her son to bring it home in a car for reburial, only to be caught, extorted of 300 francs, and then allowed to continue (see AN F2 2124).

48. The most significant of the few such memorials in Britain was probably the "Five Sisters Window" in York Minster, which listed the "1,400 women of the Empire who gave their lives" in the war. See "Five Sisters Window: Names of the Women Commemorated," *Yorkshire Herald,* 24 June 1925. There is more information on this monument at the National Inventory of War Memorials, IWM.

49. Ministère des Travaux Publics, *Official Guide to the War Zone,* 3–4.

50. Lloyd, "Tourism, Pilgrimage," ch. 3, and especially ch. 4. See also Annette Becker, *La guerre et la foi,* ch. 3, for the role of religion in postwar pilgrimages, and Prost, *In the Wake of War,* for veterans' roles in postwar commemoration.

CONCLUSION

1. See Mary Louise Roberts, *Civilization without Sexes,* and Kent, *Making Peace.*

2. See Davin, "Imperialism and Motherhood"; Dwork, *War Is Good for Babies;*

Lewis, *Politics of Motherhood* and "Working-Class Wife and Mother"; Ross, *Love and Toil;* Cova, "Les droits des femmes"; and various essays in Bock and Thane, *Maternity and Gender Policies.*

3. For examples of the work on maternalism, see Koven and Michel, "Mother Worlds" in their *Mothers of a New World,* and "Womanly Duties"; and the forum on "Maternalism as a Paradigm," with an introduction by Lynn Y. Weiner and contributions by Ann Taylor Allen, Eileen Boris, Molly Ladd-Taylor, Adele Lindenmeyr, and Kathleen S. Uno in *The Journal of Women's History* 5, no. 2 (1993). For a recent quibble with the term "maternalism," see Anne Summers, "Public Functions, Private Premises," 371, 376 n. 60.

SELECTED BIBLIOGRAPHY

PRIMARY SOURCES

British Archival Sources

London
  The Fawcett Library, London Guildhall University
    Association for Moral and Social Hygiene Collection
    Consultative Committee of Women's Suffrage Societies Collection
    National Union of Women's Suffrage Societies Collection
  House of Lords Record Office
    David Lloyd George Papers
  Imperial War Museum
    Department of Art, Catalogs, and Posters, 1914–18
    Department of Documents
    National Inventory of War Memorials–Misc. Records
    Programs for Unveiling Ceremonies of War Memorials
    Women's Work Collection Press Cuttings, 1914–19, on Foreign Women,
      Women's Army Auxiliary Corps, Women's Enfranchisement, Women in
      Agriculture, Women's Volunteer Reserve
  Public Record Office
    Director of Public Prosecution (DPP)
    Home Office Records (HO 45, HO 139)
    London Central Criminal Court (CRIM 1)
    Public Works Records (WORK 20)
    Royal Air Force Records (AIR 1)
    War Office Records (WO 32, WO 95)

French Archival Sources

Paris
  Archives Nationales
    Series F2 (Ministère de l'Intérieur: départemental)
    Series F7 (Police générale)
    Series F18 (Imprimerie, librairie, presse, censure)
    Series F22 (Travail et sécurité sociale)
    Series F23 (Services extraordinaires des temps de guerre)
  Archives de la Préfecture de Police

Ba 1560–1562 (Pacifisme-surveillances hebdomadaires)
Ba 1614 (État d'esprit de la population parisienne)
Ba 1639 (Situation morale de la France)
Ba 1651 (Féminisme)
Ba 1660 (Séverine)
Ba 1689 (Prostitution)
Ba 1712 (Presse)
Bibliothèque de l'Arsenal
Fonds Rondel
Bibliothèque de Documentation Internationale Contemporaine
Bibliothèque Historique de la Ville de Paris
Fonds Marie-Louise Bouglé
Assorted Dossiers
Bibliothèque Marguerite Durand
Assorted Dossiers
Institut Français d'Histoire Sociale
Fonds Brion

Newspapers and Periodicals

L'Action Féminine
L'Action Française
Athenaeum
Bulletin de l'Academie de Médecine
Bulletin des Lois
The Common Cause
The Contemporary Review
L'Écho de Paris
L'Éclair
The English Review
The Englishwoman
La Femme Socialiste
Le Figaro
La Française
Gazette des Hôpitaux
La Guerre Sociale
L'Homme Libre
L'Humanité
Je Sais Tout
Le Journal
Journal du Droit Internationale
Journal Officiel
The Lancet
La Lutte Féministe
The Manchester Guardian
Le Matin

Mercure de France
Nineteenth Century and After
Le Petit Journal
Le Petit Parisien
The Quiver
Review of Reviews
Revue Bleue
La Revue des Cause Célèbres Criminelles et Politiques: Les Procès de Trahison
Revue des Deux Mondes
Revue Hebdomadaire
Revue d'Hygiène et de Police Sanitaire
Revue Philanthropique
Revue Pratique d'Hygiène Municipale Urbaine et Rurale
Socialist Review
The Times
The Times Literary Supplement
La Vie Parisienne
The Vigilance Record
The Vote
Weekly Dispatch
The Woman's (later *Worker's*) *Dreadnought*
The Woman Worker
Women's Industrial News
World's Work

Published Primary Sources

Abensour, Léon. *Les Vaillantes: Héroines, martyres et remplaçantes.* Paris: Librairie
    Chapelot, 1917.
Addams, Jane. *Newer Ideals of Peace.* New York: Macmillan, 1907.
Aguétant, Pierre. *Pour ceux qui pleurent: Impressions et pensées de guerre.* Paris:
    Plon-Nourrit, 1918.
Albert, François. *Le procès Malvy: Examen critique.* [Paris]: Ligue des droits de
    l'homme et du citoyen, 1919.
Allatini, Rose. [A. T. Fitzroy, pseud.]. *Despised and Rejected.* 1918. Reprint,
    London: GMP Publishers, 1988.
———. *Payment.* London: Andrew Melrose, [1915].
———. *Requiem.* London: Martin Secker, 1919.
Association Nationale Française pour la Protection Légale des Travailleurs.
    [Mme. Paul Gemanhling]. *La maternité ouvrière et sa protection légale en France.*
    Paris: Félix Alcan, 1915.
Aux veuves de la guerre: Dieu, la France, nos enfants. Paris: Gabriel Beauchesne, 1916.
Avril de Sainte-Croix, [Ghénia]. *L'éducation sexuelle.* Paris: Félix Alcan, [1918].
Ayres, Ruby M. *The Long Lane to Happiness.* London: Hodder and Stoughton, 1915.
———. *Richard Chatterton, V.C.* London: Hodder and Stoughton, 1915.
Barbusse, Henri. *Le feu (Journal d'une escouade).* Paris: Flammarion, 1916.

———. *Under Fire.* Translated by W. Fitzwater Wray. 1918. Reprint, London: Everyman, 1926.

Barrès, Maurice. *Chronique de la Grande Guerre, 1914–1920.* 1914–20. Reprint, Paris: Plon, 1968.

———. *The Undying Spirit of France.* Translated by Margaret W. B. Corwin. New Haven: Yale University Press, 1917.

[Barreville, Jean]. *Marraines de Paris: Scènes de guerre par un zouave.* Paris: Jouve, 1917.

Barthélemy, Joseph. *Le vote des femmes.* Paris: Félix Alcan, 1920.

Barthou, Louis. *L'effort de la femme Française.* Paris: Bloud and Gay, 1917.

Barton, Ethel M., and Marguerite Cody. *Eve in Khaki.* London: Thomas Nelson & Sons, [1918].

Bédier, Joseph. *Les crimes allemands: D'après des témoignages allemands.* Paris: Armand Colin, 1915.

Benoit, Marcel. *L'énergie féminine pendant la guerre.* Paris: Nilsson, [1917?].

Bizard, Dr. Léon. *Les maisons des prostitution de Paris pendant la guerre.* Poitiers: Société Française de l'Imprimerie, 1922.

———. *Les maladies vénériennes: Conference faite aux jeunes soldats appartenant aux corps de troupes du gouvernement militaire de Paris.* Paris: A. Maloine et Fils, 1917.

Blanc-Peridier, Adrienne. *Le cantique de la patrie.* Paris: Plon, 1918.

Blondel, Georges. *La guerre et le problème de la population.* Paris: Lethielleux, [1916].

Blouet, Jules. *Deux ennemis de l'intérieur.* Coigny: Grand Seminaire, 1915.

Briand, Charles. "Pour que la France vive." Paris: Bossard, 1919.

Brieux, Eugène. *Les avariés.* 1901. Reprint, 8th edition. Paris: Stock, 1902.

———. *Damaged Goods.* Translation of *Les Avariés* by John Pollock. In *Three Plays by Brieux.* 1911. Reprint, New York: Brentano's, 1914.

Brion, Hélène. *Déclaration lue au premier conseil de guerre.* Epône: L'Avenir Social, 1918.

———. *La voie féministe.* 1917. Reprint, Paris: Syros, 1978.

Cachard, Henry. *The French Civil Code.* Rev. ed. Translation. New York: Baker, Voorhis & Co., 1930.

Capy, Marcelle. *Une voix de femme dans la mêlée.* Paris: P. Ollendorff, 1916.

Celarié, Henriette. *En esclavage: Journal de deux déportées.* Paris: Bloud & Gay, 1917.

———. *Slaves of the Huns: The Experience of Two Girls of Lille.* Translated by Maude M. C. Ffoulkes. London: Cassell and Co., 1918.

Chartres, Annie Vivanti. *The Outrage.* New York: Knopf, 1918.

———. *Vae Victis.* London: Edward Arnold, 1917.

Clermont, Camille, ed. *Souvenirs de parisiennes en temps de guerre.* Paris: Berger-Levrault, 1918.

Combarieu, Jules. *Les jeunes filles françaises et la guerre.* Paris: A. Colin, 1916.

Committee on Alleged German Outrages. *Appendix to the Report of the Committee on Alleged German Outrages.* London: HMSO, 1915.

———. *Report of the Committee on Alleged German Outrages.* London: HMSO, 1915.

Cross, Victoria [Victoria Cory, pseud.]. *Evelyn Hastings.* London: T. Werner Laurie, 1917.

Davies, Margaret Llewelyn, ed. *Maternity: Letters from Working Women.* 1915. Reprint, London: Virago, 1978.

————. "Motherhood and the State." London: n.p., [1914].

Debran, Isabelle. *Monsieur Romain Rolland, initiateur du défaitisme*. Geneva: H. Jarrys, 1918.

De Courson, Comtesse. *La femme française pendant la guerre*. Paris: P. Lethielleux, [1916].

Dejean, Georges. *[Les complices:] Casque à pointe & Bonnet Rouge*. Lausanne: L. Martinet, [1917].

Delafield, E. M. *The War Workers*. London: Heinemann, 1918.

De la Hire, Marie Weyrich. *La femme française: Son activité pendant la guerre*. Paris: J. Tallandier, 1917.

Delarue-Mardrus, Lucie. *Un roman civil en 1914*. Paris: E. Faquelle, 1916.

De Meuron, Alfred. *La natalité après la guerre*. Paris: Librairie Fischbacher, 1916.

Dent, Olive. *A V.A.D. in France*. London: Grant Richards, 1917.

De Roux, Marie. *L'état et la natalité*. Paris: Nouvelle librarie nationale, 1918.

Descaves, Lucien. *La maison anxieuse*. Paris: Georges Crès, 1916.

Despard, Charlotte. *Woman in the New Era*. [London]: The Suffrage Shop, 1910.

De Torina, Martin. *Mère sans être épouse: Pour la France et pour soi-même*. Paris: chez l'auteur, 1917.

Docquois, Georges. *La chair innocente: L'enfant du viol boche*. Paris: Albin Michel, [1918].

Documents relatifs à la guerre 1914, 1915, 1916, 1917, 1918, Commission Insituée en Vue de Constater les Actes Commis par L'Ennemi en Violation du Droit des Gens: Rapport et Procès-Verbaux d'Enquete. Paris: Imprimerie Nationale, 1915–19.

Doléris, Jacques-Amédée. *Néo-Malthusianisme, maternité et féminisme*. Paris: Masson, 1918.

Donnay, Maurice. *La parisienne et la guerre*. Paris: Georges Crès, 1916.

Duhamelet, Geneviève. *Ces dames de l'hôpital 336*. Paris: Albin Michel, 1917.

Dulac, Odette. *La Houille Rouge*. Paris: Éditions Figuière, 1916.

Dulom, François. *La prostitution dans les débits*. [Paris]: n.p., [1915].

Ellis, Havelock. *Essays in War-time*. London: Constable, 1916.

Fiaux, Louis. *L'armée et la police des moeurs. Biologie sexuelle du soldat*. Paris: Félix Alcan, 1917.

Floran, Mary [Mary Leclerq, pseud.]. *L'ennemi*. Paris: Calmann-Lévy, 1916.

Fourner, Suzanne. *Amour et guerre*. Paris: E. Figuière, 1918.

Gell, the Hon. Mrs. *The War & the Objects of the Mother's Union*. London: Wells, Gardner, Darnton & Co., 1916.

Géraldy, Paul. *La guerre, madame*. 1916. Reprint, Paris: René Helleu, 1918.

Giuliani, Albert. *Les berceaux tragiques*. 6th ed. Paris: G. Beauchesne, 1917.

Gollancz, Victor, ed. *The Making of Women: Oxford Essays in Feminism*. London: Allen and Unwin, 1917.

Hallowes, Frances S. *An Address to the Mothers of Men and Militarism*. London: Headley Bros., [1915].

————. *Women and War: An Appeal to the Women of All Nations*. London: Headley Bros., 1914.

Hamilton, Cicely. *William: An Englishman*. London: Skeffington & Son, 1919.

Hamilton, Mary Agnes. *Dead Yesterday*. London: Duckworths, 1916.

Hardie, Martin, and Arthur K. Sabin, eds. *War Posters: Issued by Belligerent and Neutral Nations, 1914–1919*. London: A. & C. Black, 1920.

Hartley, C[atherine] Gasquoine. *Motherhood and the Relationship of the Sexes*. London: Eveleigh Nash Co., 1917.

———. *Women's Wild Oats: Essays on the Re-Fixing of Moral Standards*. London: T. Werner Laurie, Ltd., 1919.

Hennequin, Maurice, Pierre Veber, and Henry de Gorse. *Madame et son filleul*. 1917. Reprint, Paris: Eschig, 1950.

H. M. Government. *Catalogue of War Literature*. London: HMSO, 1921.

———. *Defence of the Realm Manual*. London: HMSO, 1915–19.

———. *Defence of the Realm Regulations: Acts and Regulations*. London: HMSO, 1915–19.

———. *Defence of the Realm Regulations Consolidated*. London: HMSO, 1920.

Hope, Lillith. *Behold and See*. London: Hurst & Blackett, 1917.

Hutchins, B[arbara] L. *Conflicting Ideals of Women's Work*. London: T. Murby & Co., 1916.

Jesse, F. Tennyson. *The Sword of Deborah: First-Hand Impressions of the British Women's Army in France*. London: Richard Clay & Sons, 1918.

Kaye-Smith, Sheila. *Little England*. London: Nisbet, 1918.

Key, Ellen. *War, Peace and the Future: A Consideration of Nationalism and Internationalism, and of the Relation of Women to War*. Translated by Hidegard Norberg. London: G. P. Putnam, 1916.

Krug, Alfred. *Pour la repopulation*. Paris: Berger-Levrault, 1918.

La Mazière, Alice. *Sauvons les bébés: Extrait du bulletin de l'Union Française pour le Suffrage des Femmes*. Niort: A. Chiron, 1920.

Landre, Jeanne. *L'école des marraines*. Paris: Albin Michel, 1917.

———. *. . . Puis il mourut*. Paris: Éditions Mignot, 1916.

Lepage, M. G. "La lutte contre l'avortement criminel." Paris: Academie de Médecine, 1917.

Le Queux, William. *German Atrocities: A Record of Shameless Deeds*. London: N.p., [1914].

Loewel, M. "Plaidoire, Cour d'Assises de la Seine, 23 Jan. 1917." Reprinted in "Les horreurs de l'occupation allemande." *Revue des Grands Procès Contemporains* 34 (1916–17).

Lyall, Beatrix. "Our Duty in War-Time: Appeal to Women and Girls." London: Central Committee of Patriotic Organizations, [1914].

Lytton, Constance. *Prisons and Prisoners: Some Personal Experiences*. 1914. Reprint, London: Virago, 1988.

Macaulay, Rose. *Non-Combatants and Others*. 1916. Reprint, London: Methuen, 1986.

Marbo, Camille. *Le Survivant*. Paris: Fayard, 1918.

Marc, Sebastien. *Contre la depopulation*. Paris: Le Mans, 1918.

Marchant, James. *Birth-Rate and Empire*. London: Williams and Norgate, 1917.

Masson, Frédéric. *Les femmes et la guerre de 1914*. Paris: Bloud & Gay, 1914.

Mayoux, Marie, and François Mayoux. *Les instituteurs syndicalistes et la guerre*.

Dignac: Fédération Nationale des Syndicats d'Institutrices et d'Instituteurs publics, Section de la Charente, 1917.

———. *Notre affaire.* Epône: L'Avenir Social, 1918.

Memorandum on the Steps Taken for the Prevention and Relief of Distress Due to the War. London: HMSO, 1914.

Ministère de l'Instruction Publique et des Beaux Arts. "Circulaire du 10 Septembre 1915." In *Receuil des lois . . . Sept. 1915.* Paris: Imprimerie Nationale, 1915.

[Ministère des Affaires Étrangères]. *The Deportation of Women and Girls from Lille.* London: Hodder & Stoughton, 1916.

Ministère des Travaux Publics. *Official Guide to the War Zone: The Sacred Way.* Paris: Mellottée, 1920.

Mr. Punch's History of the Great War. London: Cassell and Co., 1919.

National Council of Public Morals. *The Cinema: Its Present Position and Future Possibilities, Being the Report of and Chief Evidence Taken by the Cinema Commission of Inquiry, Instituted by the National Council of Public Morals.* London: Williams and Norgate, 1917.

———. *The Declining Birth-Rate, Its Causes and Effects, Being the Report of and Chief Evidence Taken by the National Birth-Rate Commission, Instituted, with Official Recognition, by the National Council of Public Morals—for the Promotion of Race Regeneration—Spiritual, Moral, and Physical.* Edited by James Marchant. London: Chapman and Hall, 1916.

———. *Problems of Population and Parenthood, Being the Second Report of and the Chief Evidence Taken by the National Birth-Rate Commission, 1918–1920.* London: Chapman and Hall, 1920.

[Ogden, C. K., with Mary Sargent Florence]. *Militarism versus Feminism.* London: Allen and Unwin, 1915.

Paget, Elma K. "Papers for War Time No. 3: The Woman's Part." Oxford: Oxford University Press, 1914.

Parliamentary Debates, Commons, 5th series (1914–19).

Parliamentary Debates, Lords, 5th series (1914–19).

Payne, Charlotte E. *Women—After the War and Now.* London: Unwin Bros., 1915.

Pitrois, Yvonne. *Femmes de 1914–1915: Les héroines les martyres.* Geneva: Jeheber, [1915].

Rabier, Paul. *La loi du mâle: A propos de l'enfant du barbare.* Paris: Vigot Frères, 1915.

Rageot, Gaston. *La Française dans la guerre.* Paris: Attinger Frères, 1918.

Rolland, Romain. *Au-dessus de la mêlée.* 1914. Reprint, 52d edition. Paris: Ollendorff, 1915.

Royal Commission on Venereal Diseases. *Report of the Royal Commission on Venereal Diseases.* 1916. Reprint, London: National Council for Combatting Venereal Diseases, 1921.

Roux, Marie de. *L'état et la natalité.* Paris: Nouvelle Librairie Nationale, 1918.

Royden, A. Maude. *The Duty of Knowledge: A Consideration of the Report of the Royal Commission on Venereal Disease, Specially for the Use of Social Workers.* London: National Council for Combatting Venereal Diseases, 1917.

Ruck, Berta. *The Courtship of Rosamond Fayre*. London: Hutchinson, 1915.

———. *Khaki and Kisses*. London: Hutchinson, 1915.

———. *The Land Girl's Love Story*. London: Hodder and Stoughton, 1918.

Sassoon, Siegfried. *Counter-Attack and Other Poems*. London: William Heinemann, 1918.

———. *The Old Huntsman and Other Poems*. London: William Heinemann, 1917.

Scharlieb, Mary. *The Hidden Scourge*. London: C. Arthur Pearson, 1916.

Schreiner, Olive. *Women and Labour*. 1911. Reprint, London: Virago, 1978.

"Sensational Charges against Soldiers." *The Batley Reporter*, 14 January 1919.

Sinclair, May. *The Tree of Heaven*. 1917. Reprint, New York: Macmillan, 1918.

Smith, G. Elliot, and T. H. Pear. *Shell Shock and Its Lessons*. 2d ed. Manchester: University Press, 1917.

The Soldiers' and Sailors' Families Association. *The Thirtieth Annual Report, 1914–1915*. London: Eyre and Spottiswoode, 1915.

Spont, Henri. *La femme et la guerre*. Paris: Perrin, 1916.

Spurgeon, Caroline F. E. *The Privilege of Living in War-Time*. London: University of London Press, 1914.

Stern, Ernesta (Maria Star). *Le baptême du courage: Manuscrit de la guerre*. Paris: Éditions de "La Nouvelle Revue," 1916.

Stopes, Marie Carmichael. *Married Love*. 1918. Reprint, Garden City, N.Y.: Sun Dial Press, 1943.

———. *The Race: A New Play of Life in Three Acts*. London: A. C. Fifield, 1918.

Suttner, Bertha von. *Lay Down Your Arms*. 1889. Reprint. Translated by T. Homes. New York: Longmans, 1914.

Swan, Annie S. *Letters to a War Bride*. London: Hodder and Stoughton, 1915.

———. *The Woman's Part*. London: Hodder and Stoughton, 1916.

Swanwick, Helena. *The Future of the Women's Movement*. London: G. Bell, 1913.

———. *The War in Its Effect upon Women*. 1915. Reprint, New York: Garland, 1971.

———. *Women and War*. 1916. Reprint, New York: Garland, 1971.

Syrett, Netta. *The Wife of a Hero*. London: Skeffington & Sons, 1918.

Tinayre, Mme. Louis. *Françaises il faut agir*. Paris: L'Union des Femmes de France, 1916.

Tinayre, Marcelle. *La veillée des armes: Le départ, Août 1914*. Paris: Calmann Lévy, 1915.

Toulouse, Docteur [Edouard]. *La question sexuelle et la femme*. Paris: Bibliothèque Charpentier, 1918.

Tweedie, Mrs. Alec [Ethel]. *Women and Soldiers*. London: John Lane, 1918.

Verdier, J. *Le problème de la natalité et la morale chrétienne*. Paris: G. Beauchesne, 1917.

Vernet, Madeleine. *Hélène Brion: Une belle conscience et une sombre affaire*. Epône: L'Avenir Social, 1917.

Villeminot-Lapoulot, Esther. *Aux femmes de France: De la lutte au triomphe*. Sens: J. Chapron, 1915.

Vincent, J. [Bory d'Arnex, Angèle Dussaud, pseud.]. *Parisiennes de guerre, 1915–1917*. Paris: Édition de la France, 1918.

Vismes, Henriette. *L'histoire authentique et touchante des marraines et des filleuls de guerre*. Paris: Perrin, 1918.

Vuillermet, F. A. *La mobilisation des berceaux*. Paris: Lethielleux, [1917].

Wells, H. G. *Mr. Britling Sees It Through*. 1916. Reprint, London: Hogarth Press, 1985.

West, Rebecca. *The Return of the Soldier*. 1918. Reprint, New York: Dial, 1980.

Weston, Jessie L. *Germany's Crime against France*. London: David Nutt, 1915.

Wilson, R. M. *Wife: Mother: Voter: Her Vote. What Will She Do With It?* London: Hodder and Stoughton, 1918.

Winnington-Ingram, Arthur F., the lord bishop of London. *Cleansing London*. London: C. Arthur Pearson, 1916.

Women's Co-operative Guild, "Memorandum on the National Care of Maternity." London: Women's Co-operative Guild, 1917.

Yerta, Gabrielle, and Marguerite Yerta. *Six Women and the Invasion*. With a preface by Mrs. Humphry Ward. London: Macmillan, 1917.

Yerta, Marguerite. *Les six femmes et l'invasion*. Paris: Plon & Nourrit, 1917.

Yver, Colette. *Mirabelle de Pampelune*. Paris: Calmann Levy, 1917.

Yvignac, Henry. *J'avais une marraine: Petit roman de la Grande Guerre*. Paris: Gémaux, 1918.

SECONDARY SOURCES

Abensour, Léon. *Histoire générale du féminisme des origines à nos jours*. Paris: Delagrave, 1921.

Adam, George. *Treason and Tragedy: An Account of French War Trials*. London: J. Cape, 1929.

Agulhon, Maurice. *Marianne au pouvoir: L'imagerie et la symbolique républicaines de 1880 à 1914*. Paris: Flammarion, 1989.

———. "Marianne en 14–18." In *Guerre et cultures 1914–1918*. Edited by Jean-Jacques Becker et al. Paris: A. Colin, 1994.

———. *Marianne into Battle: Republican Imagery and Symbolism in France, 1789–1880*. Translated by Janet Lloyd. Cambridge: Cambridge University Press, 1981.

Alberti, Johanna. *Beyond Suffrage: Feminists in War and Peace, 1914–1928*. London: Macmillan, 1989.

Albistur, Maité, and Daniel Armogathe. *Histoire du féminisme français*. Paris: Des Femmes, 1977.

Alcoff, Linda. "Cultural Feminism versus Post-Structuralism: The Identity Crisis in Feminist Theory." *Signs* 13, no. 3 (1988). Reprinted in *Culture/Power/History: A Reader in Contemporary Social Theory*. Edited by Nicholas B. Dirks, Geoff Eley, and Sherry B. Ortner. Princeton: Princeton University Press, 1994.

Allen, James Smith. *In the Public Eye: A History of Reading in Modern France, 1800–1940*. Princeton: Princeton University Press, 1991.

Armogathe, Daniel. "Historique." In *Féminisme et pacifisme: Même combat*. Edited by Danielle Le Bricquir and Odette Thibault. Paris: Les Lettres Libres, 1985.

Audoin-Rouzeau, Stéphane. *1870 la France dans la guerre*. Paris: Armand Colin, 1989.

———. *L'enfant de l'ennemi, 1914–1918*. Paris: Aubier, 1995.

———. *14–18, les combattants des tranchées*. Paris: Armand Colin, 1986.

————. *La guerre des enfants, 1914–1918*. Paris: Armand Colin, 1993.

Auslander, Leora. "Feminist Theory and Social History: Explorations in the Politics of Identity." *Radical History Review* 54 (1992).

Badinter, Elisabeth. *Mother Love Myth and Reality: Motherhood in Modern History*. Translated by Roger DeGaris. New York: Macmillan, 1981.

Bard, Christine. *Les filles de Marianne: Histoire des féminismes, 1914–1940*. Paris: Fayard, 1995.

————, ed. *Madeleine Pelletier (1874–1939): Logique et infortunes d'un combat pour l'égalité*. Paris: côté-femmes, 1992.

Béal, Jacques, ed. *Les poètes de la Grande Guerre: Anthologie*. Paris: Le Cherche Midi, 1992.

Becker, Annette. *La guerre et la foi*. Paris: A. Colin, 1994.

————. *Les monuments aux morts: Mémoire de la Grande Guerre*. Paris: Errance, 1990.

————. *Oubliés de la Grande Guerre: Humanitaire et culture de guerre*. Paris: Noêsis, 1998.

Becker, Jean-Jacques. *Le carnet B: Les pouvoirs publics et l'antimilitarisme avant la guerre de 1914*. Paris: Klincksieck, 1973.

————. *La France en guerre (1914–1918): La grande mutation*. Brussels: Éditions Complexe, 1988.

————. *The Great War and the French People*. Translated by Arnold Pomerans. Leamington Spa: Berg, 1985.

Becker, Jean-Jacques, et al., eds. *Guerre et cultures 1914–1918*. Paris: A. Colin, 1994.

Beauman, Nicola. " 'It Is Not the Place of Women to Talk of Mud': Some Responses by British Women Novelists to World War 1." In *Women and World War 1: The Written Response*. Edited by Dorothy Goldman. Houndsmills, Hampshire: Macmillan, 1993.

Berenson, Edward. *The Trial of Madame Caillaux*. Berkeley: University of California Press, 1992.

Berger, Marcel, and Paul Allard. *Les secrets de la censure pendant la guerre*. Paris: Ed. des Portiques, 1932.

Bernard, Philippe, and Henri Dubief. *The Decline of the Third Republic, 1914–1938*. Translated by Anthony Forster. Cambridge: Cambridge University Press, 1985.

Bland, Lucy. *Banishing the Beast: English Feminism and Sexual Morality, 1885–1914*. London: Penquin, 1995.

————. "In the Name of Protection: The Policing of Women in the First World War." In *Women in Law: Explorations in Law, Family and Sexuality*. Edited by Julia Brophy and Carol Smart. London: Routledge and Kegan Paul, 1985.

Bock, Gisela, and Pat Thane, eds. *Maternity and Gender Policies: Women and the Rise of the European Welfare States, 1880s–1950s*. London: Routledge, 1991.

Bonneau, Monique. "Les ouvrières et l'industrie de guerre." *Le Peuple Français* 7 (Juil.–Sept. 1979).

Boorman, Derek. *At the Going Down of the Sun: British First World War Memorials*. York: William Sessions Ltd., 1988.

Bourke, Joanna. *Dismembering the Male: Men's Bodies, Britain and the Great War*. London: Reaktion, 1996.

Boxer, Marilyn J. *Socialism Faces Feminism in France, 1879–1913.* Ph.D. diss., University of California, Riverside, 1975. Ann Arbor, Mich: University Microfilms, 1975.

Boxer, Marilyn J., and Jean H. Quataert, eds. *Socialist Women: European Socialist Feminism in the Nineteenth and Early Twentieth Centuries.* New York: Elsevier, 1978.

Braybon, Gail. "Women and the War." In *The First World War in British History.* Edited by Stephen Constantine, Maurice Kirby, and Mary Rose. London: E. Arnold, 1995.

————. *Women Workers in the First World War.* London: Croom Helm, 1981.

Brittain, Vera. *Testament of Youth.* 1933. Reprint, London: Virago, 1978.

Brownmiller, Susan. *Against Our Will: Men, Women and Rape.* New York: Simon & Schuster, 1975.

Brubaker, Rogers. *Citizenship and Nationhood in France and Germany.* Cambridge: Harvard University Press, 1992.

Buckley, Suzann. "The Failure to Resolve the Problem of Venereal Disease among the Troops in Britain during World War I." In *War and Society: A Yearbook of Military History.* Vol. 2. Edited by Brian Bond and Ian Hay. New York: Holmes & Meier, 1977.

Burton, Antoinette. *Burdens of History: British Feminists, Indian Women, and Imperial Culture, 1865–1915.* Chapel Hill: University of North Carolina Press, 1994.

Bussey, Gertrude, and Margaret Tims. *Pioneers for Peace: Women's International League for Peace and Freedom, 1915–1965.* 1965. Reprint, London: WILPF British Section, 1980.

Butler, Judith. *Gender Trouble: Feminism and the Subversion of Identity.* New York: Routledge, 1990.

Butler, Judith, and Joan W. Scott, eds. *Feminists Theorize the Political.* New York: Routledge, 1992.

Cannadine, David. "War and Death, Grief and Mourning in Modern Britain." In *Mirrors of Mortality: Studies in the Social History of Death.* Edited by Joachim Whaley. London: Europa, 1981.

Canning, Kathleen. "Feminist History after the Linguistic Turn: Historicizing Discourse and Experience." *Signs* 19, no. 2 (1994).

Cardinal, Agnès. "Women and the Language of War in France." In *Women and World War I: The Written Response.* Edited by Dorothy Goldman. Houndsmills, Hampshire: Macmillan, 1993.

Ceadel, Martin. *Pacifism in Britain, 1914–1945: The Defining of a Faith.* Oxford: Oxford University Press, 1980.

Clark, Anna. "Gender, Class, and the Nation: Franchise Reform in England, 1832–1928." In *Re-reading the Constitution: New Narratives in the Political History of England's Long Nineteenth Century.* Edited by James Vernon. Cambridge: Cambridge University Press, 1996.

Coffin, Judith G. *The Politics of Women's Work: The Paris Garment Trades, 1750–1915.* Princeton: Princeton University Press, 1996.

Cole, Joshua. "'There Are Only Good Mothers': The Ideological Work of Women's Fertility before World War I." *French Historical Studies* 19, no. 3 (Spring 1996).

Colin, Madeleine. *Ce n'est pas d'aujourd'hui . . . femmes, syndicats, luttes de classe*. Paris: Éditions Sociales, 1975.

Condell, Diana, and Jean Liddiard. *Working for Victory? Images of Women in the First World War, 1914–1918*. London: Routledge and Kegan Paul, 1987.

Cooke, Miriam, and Angela Woollacott, eds. *Gendering War Talk*. Princeton: Princeton University Press, 1993.

Cooper, Helen M., Adrienne Auslander Munich, and Susan Merrill Squier, eds. *Arms and the Woman: War, Gender, and Literary Representation*. Chapel Hill: University of North Carolina Press, 1989.

Corbin, Alain. "Commercial Sexuality in Nineteenth-Century France: A System of Images and Regulations." In *The Making of the Modern Body: Sexuality and Society in the Nineteenth Century*. Edited by Catherine Gallagher and Thomas Laqueur. Berkeley: University of California Press, 1987.

———. *Women for Hire: Prostitution and Sexuality in France after 1850*. Translated by Alan Sheridan. Cambridge: Harvard University Press, 1990.

Cott, Nancy F. *The Grounding of Modern Feminism*. New Haven: Yale University Press, 1987.

Cova, Anne. "Les droits des femmes et la protection de la maternité en France, 1892–1939." Doctoral thesis, European University Institute, 1994.

———. "French Feminism and Maternity: Theories and Policies, 1890–1918." In *Maternity and Gender Policies: Women and the Rise of the European Welfare States, 1880s–1950s*. Edited by Gisela Bock and Pat Thane. London: Routledge, 1991.

Cruickshank, John. *Variations on Catastrophe: Some French Responses to the Great War*. Oxford: Clarendon Press, 1982.

Curtis, Barry. "Posters As Visual Propaganda in the Great War." *Block* 2 (1980).

Daley, Caroline, and Melanie Nolan, eds. *Suffrage and Beyond: International Feminist Perspectives*. New York: New York University Press, 1994.

Dangerfield, George. *The Strange Death of Liberal England, 1910–1914*. 1935. Reprint, New York: Perigee, 1980.

Darracott, Joseph, ed. *The First World War in Posters*. New York: Dover, 1974.

Darrow, Margaret H. "French Volunteer Nursing and the Myth of War Experience in World War I." *American Historical Review* 101, no. 1 (February 1996).

Davin, Anna. "Imperialism and Motherhood." *History Workshop Journal* 5 (1978).

De Grazia, Victoria. *How Fascism Ruled Women: Italy, 1922–1945*. Berkeley: University of California Press, 1992.

de Vilaine, A.-M., L. Gavarini, and M. Le Coadic, eds. *Maternité en mouvement.: Les femmes, la re/production et les hommes de science*. Grenoble: Presses Universitaires de Grenoble, 1986.

Downs, Laura Lee. *Manufacturing Inequality: Gender Division in the French and British Metalworking Industries, 1914–1939*. Ithaca: Cornell University Press, 1995.

———. "Women's Strikes and the Politics of Popular Egalitarianism in France, 1916–1918." In *Rethinking Labor History: Essays on Discourse and Class Analysis*. Edited by Leonard Berlanstein. Urbana: University of Illinois Press, 1993.

Dreher, Nan H. " 'Courting Couples' or Courting Disaster? Conflict over Public

Indecency in Nineteenth-Century London." Unpublished paper presented to Midwest Conference on British Studies, Ann Arbor, Mich., November 1995.

Dubesset, Mathilde, Françoise Thébaud, and Catherine Vincent. "Les munitionettes de la Seine." In *1914–1918: L'autre front.* Edited by Patrick Fridenson. Paris: Ed. Ouvrières, 1978.

Ducasse, André, Jacques Meyer, and Gabriel Perreux. *Vie et mort des français, 1914–1918.* Paris: Hachette, 1962.

Dubief, H. "Brion, Hélène, Rose, Louise." *Dictionnaire biographique du mouvement ouvrier français 4è. Partie, 1914–1939.* Paris: Éditions Ouvrières, 1983.

DuBois, Ellen Carol. *Feminism and Suffrage: The Emergence of an Independent Women's Movement in America, 1848–1869.* Ithaca: Cornell University Press, 1978.

———. "Woman Suffrage Around the World: Three Phases of Suffragist Internationalism." In *Suffrage and Beyond: International Feminist Perspectives.* Edited by Caroline Daley and Melanie Nolan. New York: New York University Press, 1994.

Dutton, Philip. " 'The Dead Man's Penny': A History of the Next of Kin Memorial Plaque." *Imperial War Museum Review,* no. 3 (1988).

———. "Moving Images? The Parliamentary Recruiting Committee's Poster Campaign, 1914–1916." *Imperial War Museum Review,* no. 4 (1989).

Dyer, Colin. *Population and Society in Twentieth-Century France.* London: Hodder and Stoughton, 1978.

Dyhouse, Carol. *Feminism and the Family in England, 1880–1939.* Oxford: Basil Blackwell, 1989.

Dwork, Deborah. *War Is Good for Babies and Other Young Children: A History of the Infant and Child Welfare Movement in England, 1898–1918.* London: Tavistock, 1987.

Eksteins, Modris. *Rites of Spring: The Great War and the Birth of the Modern Age.* Boston: Houghton Mifflin, 1989.

Elshtain, Jean Bethke. *Women and War.* New York: Basic Books, 1987.

Elshtain, Jean Bethke, and Sheila Tobias, eds. *Women, Militarism, and War: Essays in History, Politics, and Social Theory.* Savage, Md.: Rowman and Littlefield, 1990.

Enloe, Cynthia, *Does Khaki Become You? The Militarisation of Women's Lives.* London: Pluto, 1983.

———. "Feminists Thinking about War, Militarism and Peace." In *Analyzing Gender: A Handbook of Social Science Research.* Edited by Beth B. Hess and Myra Marx Ferree. London: Sage, 1987.

Evans, Richard. *The Feminists.* London: Croom Helm, 1977.

Ewing, Elizabeth. *Women in Uniform through the Centuries.* London: B. T. Batsford, 1975.

Ferguson, John. *The Arts in Britain in World War I.* London: Stainer and Bell, 1980.

Ferré, Max. *Histoire du mouvement syndicaliste révolutionaire chez les instituteurs.* Paris: Société Universitaire d'Éditions et de Librairie, 1955.

Field, Frank. *British and French Writers of the First World War.* Cambridge: Cambridge University Press, 1991.

———. *Three French Writers and the Great War.* Cambridge: Cambridge University Press, 1975.

First, Ruth, and Ann Scott. *Olive Schreiner: A Biography.* New York: Schocken, 1980.

Fisher, H. C., and Dr. E. X. Dubois. *Sexual Life during the World War.* London: Francis Aldor, 1937.

Flammant, Thierry. *L'école emancipée: Une contre-culture de la belle époque.* Treignac: Les Monedieres, 1982.

Fridenson, Patrick, ed. *The French Home Front, 1914–1918.* 1978. Translated by Bruce Little and Helen McPhail. Providence: Berg, 1992.

———. *1914–1918: L'autre front.* Paris: Éditions Ouvrières, 1978.

Fuller, J. G. *Troop Morale and Popular Culture in the British and Dominion Armies, 1914–1918.* Oxford: Clarendon Press, 1991.

Fussell, Paul. *The Great War and Modern Memory.* Oxford: Oxford University Press, 1975.

Garber, Marjorie. *Vested Interests: Cross-Dressing and Cultural Anxiety.* 1992. Reprint, New York: Harper, 1993.

Garfield, John. *The Fallen: A Photographic Journey through the War Cemeteries and Memorials of the Great War, 1914–1918.* London: Leo Cooper, 1990.

Gervereau, Laurent, and Christophe Prochasson, eds. *Images de 1917.* Paris: Musée d'Histoire Contemporain and Bibliothèque de Documentation Internationale Contemporaine, 1987.

Gilbert, Sandra. "Soldier's Heart: Literary Men, Literary Women and the Great War." *Signs: Journal of Women in Culture and Society* 8, no. 3 (Spring 1983). Also reprinted in *Behind the Lines: Gender and the Two World Wars.* Edited by Margaret Higonnet et al. New Haven: Yale University Press, 1987.

Glenn, Evelyn Nakano, Grace Chang, and Linda Rennie Forcey, eds. *Mothering: Ideology, Experience, and Agency.* New York: Routledge, 1994.

Goldman, Dorothy, ed. *Women and World War 1: The Written Response.* Houndsmills, Hampshire: Macmillan, 1993.

Gordon, Felicia. *The Integral Feminist: Madeleine Pelletier, 1874–1939.* Minneapolis: University of Minnesota Press, 1990.

Gould, Jenny. "Women's Military Services in First World War Britain." In *Behind the Lines: Gender and the Two World Wars.* Edited by Margaret Higonnet et al. New Haven: Yale University Press, 1987.

Grayzel, Susan R. "Mothers, Marraines, and Prostitutes: Morale and Morality in First World War France." *International History Review* 19, no. 1 (February 1997).

———. " 'The Mothers of Our Soldiers' Children': Motherhood, Immorality, and the War Baby Scandal, 1914–1918." In *Maternal Instincts: Motherhood and Sexuality in Britain, 1875–1925.* Edited by Claudia Nelson and Ann Sumner Holmes. Houndsmills, Hampshire: Macmillan, 1997.

———. " 'The Outward and Visible Sign of Her Patriotism': Women, Uniforms, and National Service during the First World War." *Twentieth Century British History* 8, no. 2 (1997).

———. "Writers of La Grande Guerre: Gender and the Boundaries between the Fronts." *Proceedings, Western Society for French History* 21 (1994).

Gregory, Adrian. "Lost Generations: The Impact of Military Casualties on Paris, London and Berlin." In *Capital Cities at War: London, Paris, Berlin, 1914–1919.*

Edited by Jay Winter and Jean-Louis Robert. Cambridge: Cambridge University Press, 1997.

—————. *The Silence of Memory: Armistice Day, 1919–1946*. Providence, R.I.: Berg, 1994.

Gromaire, George. *L'occupation allemande en France, 1914–1918*. Paris: Payot, 1925.

Grossmann, Atina. "A Question of Silence: The Rape of German Women by Occupation Soldiers." *October* 72 (Spring 1995).

Gullace, Nicoletta F. "Sexual Violence and Family Honor: British Propaganda and International Law during the First World War." *American Historical Review* 102, no. 3 (June 1997).

—————. "White Feathers and Wounded Men: Female Patriotism and the Memory of the Great War." *Journal of British Studies* 36, no. 2 (April 1997).

—————. "Women and the Ideology of War: Recruitment, Propaganda, and the Mobilization of Public Opinion in Britain, 1914–1918." Ph.D. diss., University of California at Berkeley, 1993.

Hanna, Martha. *The Mobilization of Intellect: French Scholars and Writers during the Great War*. Cambridge: Harvard University Press, 1996.

Harris, Ruth. "The 'Child of the Barbarian': Rape, Race and Nationalism in France during the First World War." *Past and Present* 141 (October 1993).

Harrison, Brian. *Separate Spheres: The Opposition to Women's Suffrage in Britain*. New York: Holmes & Meier, 1978.

Haste, Cate. *Keep the Home Fires Burning: Propaganda in the First World War*. London: Allen Lane, 1977.

Hause, Stephen. "More Minerva Than Mars." In *Behind the Lines: Gender and the Two World Wars*. Edited by Margaret Higonnet et al. New Haven: Yale University Press, 1987.

Hause, Stephen, with Anne Kenney. *Women's Suffrage and Social Politics in the French Third Republic*. Princeton: Princeton University Press, 1984.

Higonnet, Margaret R. "Cassandra's Question: Do Women Write War Novels." In *Borderwork: Feminist Engagements with Comparative Literature*. Edited by Margaret R. Higonnet. Ithaca: Cornell University Press, 1994.

—————. "Not So Quiet in No-Woman's Land." In *Gendering War Talk*. Edited by Miriam Cooke and Angela Woollacott. Princeton: Princeton University Press, 1993.

Higonnet, Margaret R., and Patrice L-R. Higonnet. "The Double Helix." In *Behind the Lines: Gender and the Two World Wars*. Edited by Margaret Higonnet et al. New Haven: Yale University Press, 1987.

Higonnet, Margaret R., Jane Jenson, Sonya Michel, and Margaret C. Weitz, eds. *Behind the Lines: Gender and the Two World Wars*. New Haven: Yale University Press, 1987.

Hirschfeld, Dr. Magnus. *The Sexual History of the World War*. Translation. New York: Panurge Press, 1934.

Hochschild, Arlie Russell. *The Managed Heart: Commercialization of Human Feeling*. Berkeley: University of California Press, 1983.

Holton, Sandra Stanley. *Feminism and Democracy: Women's Suffrage and Reform Politics in Britain, 1900–1918*. Cambridge: Cambridge University Press, 1986.

Horne, John N. *Labour at War: France and Britain, 1914–1918.* Oxford: Clarendon Press, 1991.

Horne, John N., and Alan Kramer. "German 'Atrocities' and Franco-German Opinion, 1914: The Evidence of German Soldiers' Diaries." *Journal of Modern History* 66 (March 1994).

Huard, Raymond. *Le suffrage universel en France, 1848–1946.* Paris: Aubier, 1991.

Hurwitz, Edith. "The International Sisterhood." In *Becoming Visible.* Edited by Renate Bridenthal and Claudia Koonz. Boston: Houghton Mifflin, 1977.

Huss, Marie-Monique. "Pronatalism and the Popular Ideology of the Child in Wartime France: The Evidence of the Picture Postcard." In *The Upheaval of War: Family, Work, and Welfare in Europe, 1914–1918.* Edited by Richard Wall and Jay Winter. Cambridge: Cambridge University Press, 1988.

Huston, Nancy. "The Matrix of War: Mothers and Heroes." In *The Female Body in Western Culture.* Edited by Susan Rubin Suleiman. Cambridge: Harvard University Press, 1986.

Huston, Nancy, and Sam Kinser. *À l'amour comme à la guerre.* Paris: Seuil, 1984.

Hynes, Samuel. *A War Imagined: The First World War and English Culture.* 1990. Reprint, New York: Collier, 1992.

Ingram, Angela, "Un/Reproductions: Estates of Banishment in English Fiction after the Great War." In *Women's Writing in Exile.* Edited by Mary Lynn Broe and Angela Ingram. Chapel Hill: University of North Carolina Press, 1989.

Ingram, Norman. *The Politics of Dissent: Pacifism in France, 1919–1939.* Oxford: Clarendon Press, 1991.

Kamester, Margaret, and Jo Vellacott. Introduction to *Militarism versus Feminism: Writings on Women and War,* by [C. K. Ogden with Mary Sargent Forence]. 1915. Reprint, London: Virago, 1987.

Kennedy, Thomas C. *The Hound of Conscience: A History of the No-Conscription Fellowship, 1914–1919.* Fayetteville: University of Arkansas Press, 1981.

Kent, Susan Kingsley. "Gender Reconstruction after the Great War." In *British Feminism in the Twentieth Century.* Edited by Harold L. Smith. Aldershot: Edward Elgar, 1990.

———. *Making Peace: The Reconstruction of Gender in Interwar Britain.* Princeton: Princeton University Press, 1993.

———. "The Politics of Sexual Difference: World War I and the Demise of British Feminism." *Journal of British Studies* 27 (July 1988).

———. *Sex and Suffrage in Britain, 1860–1914.* Princeton: Princeton University Press, 1987.

Klejman, Laurence, and Florence Rochefort. *L'égalité en marche: Le féminisme sous la Troisième République.* Paris: Presses de la Fondation Nationale Des Sciences Politiques, 1989.

Klug, Francesca. " 'Oh to Be in England': The British Case Study." In *Woman Nation State.* Edited by Nira Yuval-Davis and Floya Anthias. Basingstoke: Macmillan, 1989.

Koonz, Claudia. *Mothers in the Fatherland: Women, the Family, and Nazi Politics.* New York: St. Martin's, 1987.

Koven, Seth, and Sonya Michel. "Introduction: Mother Worlds." In *Mothers of a New World: Maternalist Politics and the Origins of Welfare States*. Edited by Seth Koven and Sonya Michel. New York: Routledge, 1993.

———. "Womanly Duties: Maternalist Politics and the Origins of Welfare States in France, Germany, Great Britain, and the United States, 1880–1920." *American Historical Review* 95 (1990).

———, eds. *Mothers of a New World: Maternalist Politics and the Origins of Welfare States*. New York: Routledge, 1993.

Krumeich, Gerd. "Joan of Arc between Right and Left." In *Nationhood and Nationalism in France: From Boulangism to the Great War, 1889–1918*. Edited by Robert Tombs. London: HarperCollins, 1991.

Kuhn, Annette. *Cinema, Censorship, and Sexuality, 1909–1925*. London: Routledge, 1988.

Lamm, Doron. "Emily Goes to War: Explaining the Recruitment to the Women's Army Auxiliary Corps in World War I." In *Borderlines: Genders and Identities in War and Peace, 1870–1930*. Edited by Billie Melman. New York: Routledge, 1998.

Landry, Donna, and Gerald MacLean. *Materialist Feminisms*. Cambridge, Mass.: Blackwell, 1993.

Laqueur, Thomas W. *Making Sex: Body and Gender from the Greeks to Freud*. Cambridge: Harvard University Press, 1990.

———. "Memory and Naming in the Great War." In *Commemorations: The Politics of National Identity*. Edited by John R. Gillis. Princeton: Princeton University Press, 1994.

Le Bricquir, Danielle, and Odette Thibault, eds. *Féminisme et pacifisme: Même combat*. Paris: Les Lettres Libres, 1985.

Leeds, Eric J. *No Man's Land: Combat and Identity in World War I*. Cambridge: Cambridge University Press, 1979.

Levine, Philippa. "'Walking the Streets in a Way No Decent Woman Should': Women Police in World War I." *Journal of Modern History* 66 (March 1994).

Lewis, Jane. "Models of Equality for Women: The Case of State Support for Children in Twentieth-Century Britain." In *Maternity and Gender Policies: Women and the Rise of the European Welfare States, 1880s–1950s*. Edited by Gisela Bock and Pat Thane. London: Routledge, 1991.

———. *The Politics of Motherhood: Child and Maternal Welfare in England, 1900–1939*. London: Croom Helm, 1982.

———. *Women in England, 1870–1950: Sexual Divisions and Social Change*. Sussex: Wheatsheaf, 1984.

———. "The Working-Class Wife and Mother and State Intervention, 1870–1918." In *Labour and Love: Women's Experience of Home and Family, 1850–1940*. Edited by Jane Lewis. Oxford: Basil Blackwell, 1986.

———, ed. *Labour and Love: Women's Experience of Home and Family, 1850–1940*. Oxford: Basil Blackwell, 1986.

Liddington, Jill. *The Long Road to Greenham: Feminism and Anti-Militarism in Britain since 1820*. London: Virago, 1989.

———. "The Women's Peace Crusade," In *Over Our Dead Bodies*. Edited by Dorothy Thompson. London: Virago, 1983.

Light, Alison. *Forever England: Femininity, Literature and Conservatism between the Wars*. London: Routledge, 1991.

Liu, Tessie. "Teaching the Differences among Women from a Historical Perspective: Rethinking Race and Gender as Social Categories." *Women's Studies International Forum* 14, no. 4 (1991).

Lloyd, David. "Tourism, Pilgrimage and the Commemoration of the Great War in Great Britain, Australia and Canada, 1919–1939." Ph.D. diss., University of Cambridge, 1994.

Longenbach, James. "The Men and Women of 1914." In *Arms and the Woman: War, Gender, and Literary Representation*. Edited by Helen M. Cooper, Adrienne Auslander Munich, and Susan Merrill Squier. Chapel Hill: University of North Carolina Press, 1989.

McAleer, Joseph. *Popular Reading and Publishing in Britain 1914–1950*. Oxford: Clarendon Press, 1992.

McLaren, Angus. *Sexuality and Social Order: The Debate over the Fertility of Women and Workers in France, 1770–1920*. New York: Holmes & Meier, 1983.

McMillan, James F. *Housewife or Harlot? The Place of Women in French Society, 1870–1940*. New York: St. Martin's Press, 1981.

————. *Twentieth-Century France: Politics and Society, 1898–1991*. London: Edward Arnold, 1992.

Magraw, Roger. *France, 1815–1914*. 1983. Reprint, New York: Oxford University Press, 1986.

Maitron, Jean, ed. *Dictionaire biographique du mouvement ouvrier français. 4e partie, 1914–1939*. Paris: Éditions Ouvriers, [1964–]1993.

Marcus, Jane. "The Asylums of Antaeus: Women, War, and Madness — Is There a Feminist Fetishism?" In *The New Historicism*. Edited by H. Aram Veeser. New York: Routledge, 1989.

————. "Corpus/Corps/Corpse: Writing the Body in/at War." Afterword to *Not So Quiet . . . : Stepdaughters of War*, by Helen Zenna Smith. 1930. Reprint, New York: The Feminist Press, 1989.

Margadant, Jo Burr. *Madame le Professeur: Women Educators in the Third Republic*. Princeton: Princeton University Press, 1990.

Martin-Fugier, Anne. *La Bourgeoise: Femme au Temps de Paul Bourget*. Paris: Grasset & Fasquelle, 1983.

Marwick, Arthur. *Women at War, 1914–1918*. London: Croom Helm, 1977.

Maugue, Annelise. *L'identité masculine en crise au tournant du siècle, 1871–1914*. Paris: Éditions Rivages, 1987.

Mayhall, Laura E. Nym. "Creating the 'Suffragette Spirit': British Feminists and the Historical Imagination." *Women's History Review* 4, no. 3 (1995).

Melman, Billie, ed. *Borderlines: Genders and Identities in War and Peace, 1870–1930*. New York: Routledge, 1998.

Melzer, Annabelle. "Spectacles and Sexualities: The 'Mise-en-Scène' of the 'Tirailleur Sénégalais' on the Western Front, 1914–1920." In *Borderlines: Genders and Identities in War and Peace 1870–1930*. Edited by Billie Melman. New York: Routledge, 1998.

Messinger, Gary S. *British Propaganda and the State in the First World War.*
   Manchester: Manchester University Press, 1992.
Mitchell, David. *Monstrous Regiment: The Story of the Women of the First World War.*
   New York: Macmillan, 1965.
Moeller, Robert G. *Protecting Motherhood: Women and the Family in the Politics of
   Postwar West Germany.* Berkeley: University of California Press, 1993.
Morey, Anne. "Sexuality, Maternity, and Femininity in Films Exhibited in
   Britain, 1914–1919." In *Maternal Instincts: Visions of Motherhood and Sexuality in
   Britain, 1875–1925.* Edited by Claudia Nelson and Ann Sumner Holmes.
   Houndsmills, Hampshire: Macmillan, 1997.
Moriarty, Catherine. "The Absent Dead and Figurative First World War
   Memorials." *Transactions of the Ancient Monuments Society* 39 (1995).
———. "Narrative and the Absent Body: Mechanisms of Meaning in First
   World War Memorials." Ph.D. diss., University of Sussex, 1994.
Moses, Claire Goldberg. *French Feminism in the Nineteenth Century.* Albany: State
   University of New York Press, 1984.
Mosse, George L. *Fallen Soldiers: Reshaping the Memory of the World Wars.* New York:
   Oxford University Press, 1990.
Naimark, Norman M. *The Russians in Germany: A History of the Soviet Zone of
   Occupation, 1945–1949.* Cambridge: Harvard University Press, 1995.
Nicholson, Linda. "Interpreting Gender." *Signs* 20, no. 1 (1994).
O'Brien, Catherine. "Beyond the Can[n]on: French Women's Responses to the
   First World War." *French Cultural Studies* 7 (1996).
Offen, Karen. "Body Politics: Women, Work and the Politics of Motherhood in
   France, 1920–1950." In *Maternity and Gender Policies: Women and the Rise of the
   European Welfare States, 1880s–1950s.* Edited by Gisela Bock and Pat Thane.
   London: Routledge, 1991.
———. "Depopulation, Nationalism and Feminism in Fin-de-Siècle France."
   American Historical Review 89 (1984).
———. "Exploring the Sexual Politics of Republican Nationalism." In
   Nationhood and Nationalism in France: From Boulangism to the Great War, 1889–1918.
   Edited by Robert Tombs. New York: HarperCollins, 1991.
Oldfield, Sybil. *Spinsters of This Parish: The Life and Times of F. M. Mayor and Mary
   Sheepshanks.* London: Virago, 1984.
———. *Women against the Iron Fist: Alternatives to Militarism, 1900–1989.* Oxford:
   Basil Blackwell, 1989.
Ouditt, Sharon. *Fighting Forces, Writing Women: Identity and Ideology in the First World
   War.* London: Routledge, 1994.
Ozouf, Jacques, and Mona Ozouf. "Le thème du patriotisme dans les manuels
   primaires." *Le mouvement social* 44 (Oct./Dec. 1964).
Paillard, Rémy. *Affiches 14–18.* Reims: Matot Braine, 1986.
Pankhurst, E. Sylvia. *The Home Front: A Mirror to Life in England during the First
   World War.* 1932. Reprint, London: The Cresset Library, 1987.
Parsons, I. M., ed. *Men Who March Away: Poems of the First World War.* London:
   Chatto & Windus, 1965.

Pateman, Carole. *The Disorder of Women*. Stanford: Stanford University Press, 1989.

—————. *The Sexual Contract*. Stanford: Stanford University Press, 1988.

—————. "Three Questions About Womanhood Suffrage." In *Suffrage and Beyond: International Feminist Perspectives*. Edited by Caroline Daley and Melanie Nolan. New York: New York University Press, 1994.

Paxton, Robert O. *Europe in the Twentieth Century*. 3d ed. New York: Harcourt Brace, 1997.

Pedersen, Susan. "Catholicism, Feminism and the Politics of the Family during the Late Third Republic." In *Mothers of a New World: Maternalist Politics and the Origins of Welfare States*. Edited by Seth Koven and Sonya Michel. New York: Routledge, 1993.

—————. "The Failure of Feminism in the Making of the British Welfare State." *Radical History Review* 43 (Winter 1989).

—————. *Family, Dependence, and the Origins of the Welfare State: Britain and France, 1914–1945*. Cambridge: Cambridge University Press, 1993.

—————. "Gender, Welfare and Citizenship in Britain during the Great War." *American Historical Review* 95, no. 4 (1990).

Pedroncini, Guy. *Les mutineries de 1917*. Paris: Presses Universitaires de France, 1967.

Perreux, Gabriel. *La vie quotidienne des civils en France pendant la Grande Guerre*. Paris: Hachette, 1966.

Perrot, Michelle, ed. *A History of Private Life: From the Fires of Revolution to the Great War*. Translated by Arthur Goldhammer. Cambridge: Harvard University Press, 1990.

—————. "The New Eve and the Old Adam." In *Behind the Lines: Gender and the Two World Wars*. Edited by Margaret R. Higonnet et al. New Haven: Yale University Press, 1987.

Pierson, Ruth Roach, ed. *Women and Peace: Theoretical, Historical and Practical Perspectives*. London: Croom Helm, 1987.

Plat, Hélène. *Lucie Delarue-Mardrus: Une femme de lettres des années folles*. Paris: Grasset, 1994.

Poovey, Mary. *Uneven Developments: The Ideological Work of Gender in Mid-Victorian England*. Chicago: University of Chicago Press, 1988.

Porter, Roy. "Rape—Does It Have a Historical Meaning?" In *Rape: An Historical and Social Enquiry*. Edited by Sylvana Tomaselli and Roy Porter. Oxford: Basil Blackwell, 1986.

Posonby, Arthur. *Falsehood in War-Time*. London: Allen & Unwin, 1928.

Potter, Jane. " 'A Great Purifier': The Great War in Women's Romances and Memoirs, 1914–1918." In *Women's Fiction and the Great War*. Edited by Suzanne Raitt and Trudi Tate. Oxford: Oxford University Press, 1997.

Pourcher, Yves. *Les jours de guerre: La vie des Français au jour le jour 1914–1918*. Paris: Plon, 1994.

Prost, Antoine. *In the Wake of War: "Les Anciens Combattants" and French Society, 1914–1939*. Translated by Helen McPhail. Providence, R.I.: Berg, 1992.

Pugh, Martin. *Electoral Reform in War and Peace, 1906–1918*. London: Routledge and Kegan Paul, 1978.

————. *Women and the Women's Movement in Britain, 1914–1959*. Houndsmills, Hampshire: Macmillan, 1992.

Rabaut, Jean. *L'anti-militarisme en France, 1810–1975: Faits and documents*. Paris: Hachette, 1975.

Raitt, Suzanne, and Trudi Tate, eds. *Women's Fiction and the Great War*. New York: Oxford University Press, 1997.

Rathbone, Irene. *We That Were Young*. 1932. Reprint, London: Virago, 1988.

Rawls, Walton. *Wake Up, America! World War I and the American Poster*. New York: Abbeville, 1988.

Reilly, Catherine, ed. *Scars Upon My Heart: Women's Poetry and Verse of the First World War*. London: Virago, 1981.

Relinger, Jean. "Le feu d'Henri Barbusse: Grandeur et permanence d'un témoignage." In *Mémoire de la Grande Guerre: Témoins et témoignages*. Edited by Gérard Canini. Nancy: Presses Universitaires de Nancy, 1989.

Remarque, Erich Maria. *All Quiet on the Western Front*. 1928. Reprint, New York: Fawcett, 1967.

Reshef, Ouriel. *Guerre, mythes et caricature: Au berceau d'une mentalité française*. Paris: Presses de la Fondation Nationale des Sciences Politiques, 1984.

Reynaud, Emmanuel. *Les femmes, la violence et l'armée*. Paris: FEDN, 1988.

Reynolds, Siân. "Marianne's Citizens? Women, the Republic and Universal Suffrage in France." In *Women, State and Revolution*. Edited by Siân Reynolds. Amherst: University of Massachusetts Press, 1987.

Rich, Adrienne. *Of Woman Born: Motherhood as Experience and Institution*. New York: Norton, 1976.

Rickards, Maurice, and Michael Moody. *The First World War: Ephemera, Mementoes, Documents*. London: Jupiter, 1975.

Riley, Denise. *"Am I That Name?" Feminism and the Category of 'Women' in History*. Minneapolis: University of Minnesota Press, 1988.

————. *War in the Nursery: Theories of the Child and the Mother*. London: Virago, 1983.

Rivé, Philippe, et al., eds. *Monuments de mémoire: Les monuments aux morts de la Grande Guerre*. Paris: MPCIH, 1991.

Robert, Jean-Louis. "Women and Work in France during the First World War." In *The Upheaval of War: Family, Work, and Welfare in Europe, 1914–1918*. Edited by Richard Wall and Jay Winter, Cambridge: Cambridge University Press, 1988.

Roberts, Krisztina. "Gender, Class, and Patriotism: Women's Paramilitary Units in First World War Britain." *International History Review* 19, no. 1 (February 1997).

Roberts, Mary Louise. *Civilization without Sexes: Reconstructing Gender in Postwar France, 1917–1927*. Chicago: Chicago University Press, 1994.

————. "Samson and Delilah Revisited: The Politics of Women's Fashion in 1920s France." *American Historical Review* 98, no. 3 (1993).

Ronsin, Francis. *La grève des ventres: Propagande néo-Malthusienne et baisse de la natalité en France 19e–20e siècles*. Paris: Aubier Montaigne, 1980.

Rosanvallon, Pierre. *Le sacre du citoyen: Histoire du suffrage universel en France*. Paris: Gallimard, 1992.

Rose, Lionel. *The Massacre of the Innocents: Infanticide in Britain, 1800–1939*. London: Routledge and Kegan Paul, 1986.

Rose, Sonya. "Sex, Citizenship, and the Nation in World War II Britain." *American Historical Review* 103, no. 4 (October 1998).

Ross, Ellen. *Love and Toil: Motherhood in Outcast London, 1870–1918*. Oxford: Oxford University Press, 1993.

Rowbotham, Sheila. *Friends of Alice Wheeldon*. New York: Monthly Review Press, 1987.

Rubinstein, David. *A Different World for Women: The Life of Millicent Garrett Fawcett*. New York: Harvester, 1991.

Ruddick, Sara. *Maternal Thinking: Toward a Politics of Peace*. Boston: Beacon, 1989.

Sanders, Michael, and Philip M. Taylor. *British Propaganda during the First World War, 1914–1918*. London: Macmillan, 1982.

Scarry, Elaine. *The Body in Pain: The Making and Unmaking of the World*. Oxford: Oxford University Press, 1985.

Schweik, Susan. *A Gulf So Deeply Cut: American Women Poets and the Second World War*. Madison: University of Wisconsin Press, 1991.

Scott, Joan Wallach. *Gender and the Politics of History*. New York: Columbia University Press, 1988.

———. *Only Paradoxes to Offer: French Feminists and the Rights of Man*. Cambridge: Harvard University Press, 1996.

Sherman, Daniel J. "Art, Commerce, and the Production of Memory in France after World War I." In *Commemorations: The Politics of National Identity*. Edited by John R. Gillis. Princeton: Princeton University Press, 1994.

———. "Bodies and Names: The Emergence of Commemoration in Interwar France." *American Historical Review* 103, no. 2 (April 1998).

———. "Les inaugurations et la politique." In *Monuments de mémoire: Les monuments aux morts de la Grande Guerre*. Edited by Philipe Rivé et al. Paris: MPCIH, 1991.

———. "Monuments, Mourning and Masculinity in France after World War I." *Gender and History* 8, no. 1 (April 1996).

Showalter, Elaine. *The Female Malady: Women, Madness, and English Culture, 1830–1980*. 1985. Reprint, New York: Penquin, 1987.

Silver, Kenneth E. *Esprit de Corps: The Art of the Parisian Avant-Garde and the First World War, 1914–1925*. Princeton: Princeton University Press, 1989.

Skocpol, Theda. *Protecting Mothers and Soldiers: The Political Origins of Social Policy in the United States*. Cambridge: Harvard University Press, 1992.

Slater, Catherine. *Defeatists and Their Enemies: Political Invective in France, 1914–1918*. Oxford: Oxford University Press, 1981.

Slaughter, Jane, and Robert Kern, eds. *European Women on the Left: Socialism, Feminism, and the Problems Faced by Political Women, 1880 to the Present*. Wesport, Conn.: Greenwood, 1981.

Smith, Harold L., ed. *British Feminism in the Twentieth Century*. Aldershot: Edward Elgar, 1990.

Smith, Helen Zenna [pseud]. *Not So Quiet: Stepdaughters of War*. 1930. Reprint, New York: Feminist Press, 1989.

Smith, Leonard V. *Between Mutiny and Obedience: The Case of the French Fifth Infantry Division during World War I.* Princeton: Princeton University Press, 1994.

———. "Masculinity, Memory, and the French First World War Novel: Henri Barbusse and Roland Dorgelès." In *Authority, Identity and the Social History of the Great War.* Edited by Marilyn Shevin-Coetzee and Frans Coetzee. Providence, R.I.: Berghahn Books, 1995.

Smith, Paul. *Feminism and the Third Republic: Women's Political and Civil Rights in France, 1918–1945.* Oxford: Clarendon, 1996.

Soloway, Richard Allen. *Birth Control and the Population Question in England, 1877–1930.* Chapel Hill: University of North Carolina Press, 1982.

———. "Eugenics and Pronatalism in Wartime Britain." In *The Upheaval of War: Family, Work, and Welfare in Europe, 1914–1918.* Edited by Richard Wall and Jay Winter. Cambridge: Cambridge University Press, 1988.

Sowerwine, Aude, and Charles Sowerwine, eds. *Le mouvement ouvrier français contre la guerre, 1914–1918: Textes et documents.* Vols. 1–2 and 7. Paris: EDHIS, 1985.

Sowerwine, Charles. *Sisters or Citizens?: Women and Socialism in France Since 1876.* Cambridge: Cambridge University Press, 1982.

Sternhell, Ze'ev. "Paul Déroulède and the Origins of Modern French Nationalism." In *Contemporary France: Illusion, Conflict and Regeneration.* Edited by John C. Cairns. New York: Franklin Watts, 1978.

Stewart, Mary Lynn. *Women, Work, and the French State: Labour Protection and Social Patriarchy, 1879–1919.* Kingston: McGill-Queen's University Press, 1989.

Stiglmayer, Alexandra, ed. *Mass Rape: The War against Women in Bosnia-Herzegovina.* Lincoln: University of Nebraska Press, 1994.

Summers, Anne. *Angels and Citizens: British Women as Military Nurses, 1854–1914.* London: Routledge and Kegan Paul, 1987.

———. "Public Functions, Private Premises: Female Professional Identity in Britain and the Domestic Service Paradigm in Britain, c. 1850–1930." In *Borderlines: Genders and Identities in War and Peace, 1870–1930.* Edited by Billie Melman. New York: Routledge, 1998.

Sweeney, Regina Marie. "Harmony and Disharmony: French Singing and Musical Entertainment during the Great War." Ph.D. diss., University of California at Berkeley, 1992.

Tanner, Duncan. *Political Change and the Labour Party, 1900–1918.* Cambridge: Cambridge University Press, 1990.

Tate, Trudi. "HD's War Neurotics." In *Women's Fiction and the Great War.* Edited by Suzanne Raitt and Trudi Tate. Oxford: Oxford University Press, 1997.

———. *Modernism, History, and the First World War.* Manchester: Manchester University Press, 1998.

Taylor, Richard, and Nigel Young, eds. *Campaigns for Peace: British Peace Movements in the Twentieth Century.* Manchester: Manchester University Press, 1987.

Temeron, H. "Dulac (Jeanne-Marie-Claire Latrilhe, dite Odette)." *Dictionnaire de biographie française.* Vol. 12. Paris: Letouzey and Ané, 1970.

"Témoignages: Les femmes et la guerre de 14–18." *Le Peuple Français* 7 (1978).

Terry, Roy. *Women in Khaki: The Story of the British Woman Soldier.* London: Columbus Books, 1988.

Thane, Pat. "Visions of Gender in the Making of the British Welfare State: The Case of Women in the British Labour Party and Social Policy, 1906–1945." In *Maternity and Gender Policies: Women and the Rise of the European Welfare States, 1880s–1950s.* Edited by Gisela Bock and Pat Thane. London: Routledge, 1991.

Thébaud, Françoise. "Le féminisme à l'épreuve de la guerre." In *La tentation nationaliste, 1914–1945.* Edited by Rita Thalmann. Paris: Deux Temps Fiere, 1990.

———. *La femme au temps de la guerre de 14.* Paris: Stock, 1986.

———. "La Grande Guerre: Le triomphe de la division sexuelle." In *Histoire des femmes: Le XXe siècle.* Edited by Françoise Thébaud. Paris: Plon, 1992.

———. "La guerre et le deuil chez les femmes françaises." In *Guerre et cultures, 1914–1918.* Edited by Jean-Jacques Becker et al. Paris: A. Colin, 1994.

———., ed. *Histoire des femmes: Le XXe siècle.* Paris: Plon, 1992.

Thibault, Odette. *Non à la guerre disent elles.* Lyon: Chronique Sociale, 1982.

Thom, Deborah. "Tommy's Sister: Women at Woolwich in World War I." In *Minorities and Outsiders.* Vol. 2 of *Patriotism: The Making and Unmaking of British National Identity.* Edited by Raphael Samuel. London: Routledge, 1989.

———. "Women and Work in Wartime Britain." In *The Upheaval of War: Family, Work, and Welfare in Europe, 1914–1918.* Edited by Richard Wall and Jay Winter. Cambridge: Cambridge University Press, 1988.

Tickner, Lisa. *The Spectacle of Women: Imagery of the Suffrage Campaign, 1907–1914.* London: Chatto & Windus, 1987.

Tomaselli, Sylvana, and Roy Porter, eds. *Rape: An Historical and Social Enquiry.* Oxford: Basil Blackwell, 1986.

Tranter, N. L. *Population and Society, 1750–1940: Contrasts in Population Growth.* London: Longman, 1985.

Trebilcot, Joyce. *Mothering: Essays in Feminist Theory.* Totowa, N.J.: Rowman and Allanheld, 1984.

Tröger, Annemarie. "Between Rape and Prostitution: Survival Strategies and Chances for Emancipation for Berlin Women after World War II." In *Women in Culture and Politics: A Century of Change.* Edited by Judith Friedlander, Blanche Wiesen Cook, Alice Kessler Harris, and Carroll Smith-Rosenberg. Bloomington: Indiana University Press, 1986.

Tylee, Claire M. *The Great War and Women's Consciousness: Images of Militarism and Womanhood in Women's Writings, 1914–1964.* Iowa City: University of Iowa Press, 1990.

Valverde, Mariana. "Poststructuralist Gender Historians: Are We Those Names?" *Labour/Le Travail* 25 (Spring 1990).

Vardi, Liana. "Construing the Harvest: Gleaners, Farmers, and Officials in Early Modern France." *American Historical Review* 98, no. 5 (December 1993).

Vellacott Newberry, Jo. "Anti-War Suffragists," *History* 63, no. 2 (October 1977).

Vellacott, Jo. "Feminist Consciousness and the First World War." In *Women and Peace: Theoretical, Historical, and Practical Perspectives.* Edited by Ruth Roach Pierson. London: Croom Helm, 1987.

Viennot, Éliane, ed. *La démocratie 'à la française' ou les femmes indésirables.* Paris: Cahiers du CEDREF, 1996.

Waelti-Walters, Jennifer. *Feminist Novelists of the Belle Epoque: Love as a Lifestyle.* Bloomington: Indiana University Press, 1990.

Walkowitz, Judith R. *City of Dreadful Delight: Narratives of Sexual Danger in Late-Victorian London.* Chicago: University of Chicago Press, 1992.

———. *Prostitution and Victorian Society: Women, Class, and the State.* Cambridge: Cambridge University Press, 1980.

Wall, Richard, and Jay Winter, eds. *The Upheaval of War: Family, Work, and Welfare in Europe, 1914–1918.* Cambridge: Cambridge University Press, 1988.

Warner, Marina. *Monuments and Maidens: The Allegory of the Female Form.* London: Weidenfeld and Nicolson, 1985.

Watson, Janet S. K. "Khaki Girls, VADs and Tommy's Sisters: Gender and Class in First World War Britain." *International History Review* 19, no. 1 (February 1997).

Weber, Eugen. *Peasants into Frenchmen.* Stanford: Stanford University Press, 1976.

Wheelwright, Julie. *Amazons and Military Maids: Women Who Dressed As Men in Pursuit of Life, Liberty and Happiness.* London: Pandora, 1989.

———. *The Fatal Lover: Mata Hari and the Myth of Women in Espionage.* London: Collins & Brown, 1992.

Wilkinson, Mary. "Patriotism and Duty: The Women's Work Collection at the Imperial War Museum." *Imperial War Museum Review* 6 (1991).

Wilson, Trevor. *The Myriad Faces of War: Britain and the Great War, 1914–1918.* Cambridge: Polity Press, 1986.

Wiltsher, Anne. *Most Dangerous Women: Feminist Peace Campaigners of the Great War.* London: Pandora, 1985.

Winter, J[ay]. M. *The Experience of World War I.* New York: Oxford University Press, 1989.

———. *The Great War and the British People.* Houndsmills, Hampshire, Hampshire: Macmillan, 1986.

———. *Sites of Memory, Sites of Mourning: The Great War in European Cultural History.* Cambridge: Cambridge University Press, 1995.

Winter, Jay, and Blaine Baggett, *The Great War and the Shaping of the Twentieth Century.* New York: Penquin, 1996.

Winter, Jay, and Jean-Louis Robert. *Capital Cities at War: London, Paris, Berlin, 1914–1919.* Cambridge: Cambridge University Press, 1997.

Wishnia, Judith. "Feminism and Pacifism: The French Connection." In *Women and Peace: Theoretical, Historical, and Practical Perspectives.* Edited by Ruth Roach Pierson. London: Croom Helm, 1987.

———. "Natalisme et nationalisme pendant la Première Guerre Mondiale." *Vingtième siècle,* no. 45 (1995).

Wohl, Robert. *The Generation of 1914.* Cambridge: Harvard University Press, 1979.

Woolf, Virginia. *Three Guineas.* London: Hogarth Press, 1938.

Woollacott, Angela. " 'Khaki Fever' and Its Control: Gender, Class, Age and Sexual Morality on the British Homefront in the First World War." *Journal of Contemporary History* 29 (1994).

———. *On Her Their Lives Depend: Munitions Workers in the Great War.* Berkeley: University of California Press, 1994.

————. "Sisters and Brothers in Arms: Family, Class, and Gendering in World War I Britain." In *Gendering War Talk*. Edited by Miriam Cooke and Angela Woollacott. Princeton: Princeton University Press, 1993.

Wright, Gordon. *France in Modern Times*. 3d ed. New York: Norton, 1981.

Zeldin, Theodore. *France, 1848–1945: Love and Ambition*. Oxford: Oxford University Press, 1979.

INDEX

Bereavement. *See* Mourning

Bergerat, Émile, 204

Berne: 1915 meeting of socialist women at, 162–64

Berthet, Alice, 26

Bicycling, 172, 175

Birth control: devices as protection against venereal disease, 141; French reaction to, 164–65

Birthrate: anxiety over, 4, 87–89, 101–2, 103–20 passim, 125–26, 222, 243, 261 (n. 3); in Britain, 4, 89, 101–2, 111–19, 146, 243; in France, 4, 50–63, 73–77, 84–85, 89–90, 103–10, 125–26, 222, 243. *See also* Population; Pronatalism

Bizard, Léon, 141, 143

Bloch, Oscar, 171, 183

Body: and experience of pain, 7–8, 236; female, 6, 8–9, 120–23, 215; maternal, 8, 51–89, 91, 119–20, 236, 259 (n. 63), 266 (n. 91)

Boer War, 91–92, 274 (n. 5)

Bok, Edward, 136–38

Bolo. *See* Treason: trials for

Bonnet Rouge. *See* Treason: trials for

Bouet, Jules, 103–4

Bouvier, Jeanne, 110

Boyle, Nina, 130

Breast-feeding, 105–10, 117–18, 264 (n. 67)

Brieux, Eugène, 152–56, 273 (n. 113)

Brion, Hélène, 9, 158, 162, 165–86, 188, 244; witnesses at trial of, 178–80. *See also* Treason: trials for

British Empire. *See* Imperialism

Britishness. *See* Nationality

Brittain, Vera, 95

Brothels: and British soldiers, 144–45, 271 (n. 85). See also *Maisons Tolerées*

Brunschvicg, Cécile, 42, 254 (n. 74)

Bryce, James, Lord, 65, 211–12, 220

Bryce Committee of Inquiry into Alleged German Atrocities in Belgium, 39, 65–66, 99

Bully: war memorial at, 237

Burials, 239–40, 242, 291 (n. 2), 292 (n. 11). *See also* Corpses: exhumation of soldiers'; Interment

Burnet, James, 136

Burton, Antoinette, 288 (n. 72)

Buzançais: war memorial at, 239

Cabinet Memorial Services Committee, 229–39

Caillaux, Henriette: trial of, 26, 277 (n. 44)

Caillaux, Joseph: trial of, 166, 277 (n. 42). *See also* Treason: trials for

Canterbury, archbishop of, 97–100, 129, 199

Capy, Marcelle, 162–63

Cardiff: behavior of women in, 129–30

Cartier, Denise, 203

Casevitz-Rouff, Thérèse, 203

Catholicism: in Britain, 66, 69–72, 82–83; depicted in war literature, 67–72, 80–83; in France, 4, 66–69, 169, 185, 219–20, 237, 257 (n. 28)

Celarié, Henriette, 43–45

Cenotaph, 229

Censorship: first-person accounts of civilian experiences with, 39–42; lifted from theaters, 152; wartime, 12, 166, 169, 275 (n. 17), 277 (n. 39), 278 (n. 62)

Chamber of Deputies, French, 90, 218–20; Commission du Suffrage Universel, 218

Charity: for unwed mothers, 94–95, 100; women soliciting for, 128–29; and women's organizations, 30, 202

Charity Organisation Society, 100

Chartres, Annie Vivanti, 67, 77–83

Chéron, Henry, 221

Childbirth. *See* Body: maternal; Motherhood

Childs, B. E. W., 187

Church of England, 98, 132–33

Cinema. *See* Culture: popular forms of

Citizenship: and First World War, 5, 9, 180–81, 190–225 passim, 283 (n. 4),

151–52, 273 (n. 111); used to control sexual behavior, 129–30, 150–52, 155, 243, 269 (n. 30)
Defense loans, 105, 107
Delahaye, Dominique, 220, 291 (n. 134)
Delarue-Mardrus, Lucie, 27–30, 35, 49, 57, 63, 222
Deportations: of French civilians in occupied territory, 42–45, 254 (n. 73)
Descaves, Lucien, 206
Despard, Charlotte, 133, 148
Dixon, Ella Hepworth, 199, 207
Docquois, Georges, 53–57, 76
Doléris, Jacques-Amédée, 108
Downs, Laura Lee, 6, 170, 202
Dreyfus affair, 175–76, 280 (n. 88)
Drouineau, Gustave, 62
Dubesset, Mathilde, 170
Dubois, Ellen Carol, 206
Duchêne, Gabrielle, 163
Dufour, Suzanne, 171
Dulac, Odette, 66, 73–77, 82–83, 244, 260 (nn. 73, 74)
Dulom, François, 125
Durand, Marguerite, 53, 165, 180–81

East London Federation of Suffragettes, 207
Education: in France, 57, 158, 168–70; for girls, 57, 168, 178, 218, 278 (n. 55); regarding public health, 141–43, 146–49; and women, 188. *See also* Teachers
Electoral reform. *See* Franchise reform
Endowment of motherhood. *See* Motherhood: endowment of
Englishness. *See* Nationality
Equeurdreville: war memorial at, 238
Espionage: accusations of, 175, 280 (n. 89); in war literature, 73–74, 259 (n. 67), 260 (n. 74)
Eugenics: and motherhood, 101, 113; and rape, 57–59

Faivre, Paul, 142–43
Family: arrangements in war literature,

36–38; importance of preserving, 188, 205–6; life under occupation in France, 39–43, 67–69; and voting rights, 216–22
Fashion: changes in women's, during war, 136, 172–75, 192–202 passim, 246, 280 (n. 83); as marker of status, 177; in war literature, 74. *See also* Uniforms
Fatherhood, 18, 22, 51, 60, 68–69, 256 (n. 6), 261 (n. 48)
Fawcett, Millicent Garrett, 110, 149, 211, 213, 244, 289 (nn. 96, 105)
Federation of Trade Union Teachers (France), 168–70
Federation of Women Workers, 114
Fell, Eleanor, 173, 279 (n. 80)
Femininity, 2, 18, 20, 36–37, 139, 164–65, 167, 174–75, 180–81, 188, 199–202, 205–6, 213, 244, 280 (nn. 81, 83), 285 (n. 38). *See also* Body: female; Identity: and gender
Feminism: archival collections regarding, 4; in Britain, 3–4, 9, 110–11, 147–48, 150–51, 158–61, 186–87, 190–91, 207–13, 243; and First World War, 6, 9, 190–225 passim; in France, 3–4, 9, 56–57, 59–63, 109–10, 143–44, 163–67, 173–86 passim, 188–90, 203–4, 215–18, 223–25, 243, 280 (n. 92); as moral force, 158, 182, 186, 189, 274 (n. 1), 282 (nn. 125, 126); and pacifism, 9, 157–90 passim, 206–7, 238, 244; theoretical differences within, 57, 158, 186, 247 (n. 1), 274 (n. 2)
Fiaux, Louis, 143
Film. *See* Culture: popular forms of
Finot, Jean, 58–59, 63
Fisher, W. Hayes, 92–93
Flach, Jacques, 205
Flammant, Thierry, 169
Flappers, 122–23, 134, 147
Fotenay-sous-Bois: war memorial at, 239
Franchise reform: in Britain, 190–91,

Ireland: people of, 287 (n. 75)
Irishness. *See* Nationality

Janvion, Émile, 165
Jaurès, Jean: assassination of, 26
Jeanne d'Arc, 237, 285 (n. 38), 289
(n. 111), 293 (n. 33)

Kenney, Rowland, 91
Kent, Susan, 5, 206, 244, 268 (n. 26)
Khaki: symbolism of, during war, 192–
202 passim, 224, 243, 284 (n. 21),
286 (n. 52)
Kitchener, Horatio Herbert, Lord:
warning about "women and wine,"
131, 145, 269 (n. 38)
Knight, Elizabeth, 150
Knight, Holford, 208
Krug, Alfred, 105

Labrousse, François, 222
La Marzière, Alice, 218
Land Girl, 136
Landre, Jeanne, 30–35, 252 (n. 47)
Lansbury, George, 130
Léal, Anne, 216
Legislation: debates over, 8–9, 55, 87,
90, 94, 144, 209–12, 219–25, 294
(nn. 43, 44); enacted during the war,
90, 102, 110, 124–25, 129–30, 145–
152, 169, 190–91, 196–97, 209–12,
239, 283 (n. 4), 294 (nn. 43, 44)
Legrelle de Ferrer, Mme. (Alliance
Féministe pour l'Union Sacrée de
Mères), 109–10
Leicester Arch of Remembrance, 231
Lenin, Vladimir Ilyich, 174
Lesbianism. *See* Homosexuality; Sexual-
ity: gay and lesbian, in wartime
Letters: between fronts, 12, 14, 22, 30,
32–33, 245, 289 (n. 111)
Lévy, Raphael-Georges, 104
Ligue des Droits de L'Homme, 214,
254 (n. 74)
Ligue Patriotique des Françaises, 276
(n. 33)

Lille: under occupation, 42–44, 48,
67–68
Literacy, 7, 12, 244
Literature. *See* War literature
Liverpool war memorials: Eccleston
Park, 233; Port Sunlight, 232–33
Lloyd, David, 227, 241
Lloyd, Francis, 134
Lloyd George, David, 229, 282 (n. 119)
Local Government Board, 100, 110
Loewel, Maître (lawyer), 60–61
Loi Strauss, 110
Loi Violette, 217, 289 (n. 120)
London: American soldiers in, 136–39;
behavior of women in, 128–39 pas-
sim; criminal court cases in, 102–3;
and moral campaigns during war,
128, 132–33
London, bishop of. *See* Winnington-
Ingram, Arthur
London Council for the Promotion of
Public Morality, 128
Long, Walter, 210
Longman, Mary, 96
Love, Hilda, 202
Lytham War Memorial, 231

McAleer, Joseph, 12
Macaulay, Rose, 1, 19–21
McKenna, Reginald, 94
Macmillan, Margaret, 147
McNeill, Ronald, 94–96
Macready, Nevil, 136
"Maiden Tribute" incident, 44
Maisons tolerées, 123, 140–44, 151, 155
Malthusianism, 108, 172–75, 280
(n. 83). *See also* Birth control
Malvy, Louis, 54, 166, 176, 277 (n. 42)
Manchester: war memorial at, 231
Marianne: as mother emblem of the
French nation, 237
Marin, Louis, 218
Marne, battle of, 95, 104
Marraine de guerre, 30–33, 124
Marriage: encouragement of, 93; by
proxy, 89–90

Martin, Louis, 55, 221–22

Masculinity, 36–37, 51, 200–202, 224

Mason, M. H., 135–36

Maternalism, 245, 257 (n. 28), 274 (n. 3)

Mayoux, François, 169, 171, 185

Mayoux, Marie, 169–71, 185, 279 (n. 65)

Medical treatment: forced gynecological exams of women, 44–45, 151–52, 156; for venereal diseases, 141–43, 146–55

Medicine, French Academy of, 107–9, 141–42

Mélin, Jeanne, 217, 244, 275 (n. 23), 281 (n. 106)

Memory. *See* Commemoration

Merlin, Fernand, 222

Michel, Louise, 180, 183

Midwives, 56, 73–74

Militancy, 195–96, 207

Militarism versus Feminism, 161

Military medals, 198, 228

Military service. *See* Women: and military service

Military Service Act, 197

Military structure: in Britain, 2, 7, 189–91, 203, 223, 243; in France, 2, 7, 189–91, 243

Millet, Jean-François, 105

Misme, Jane, 56–57, 125–26, 202–3, 226, 279 (n. 80)

Mons, battle of, 95

Montorgueil, Georges, 54

Monuments. *See* War memorials

Morale: civilian, 166, 169, 185; military, 166; women's maintenance of, 23, 26, 28, 49, 86, 129–33, 165, 185, 188–89, 203–4, 245

Morality: concern over women's, 86–103 passim, 119–20, 121–55 passim, 198–99, 202; and patriotism, 148–49; women's influence on men's, 128, 132–33, 136–39

Moriarty, Catherine, 227, 231, 293 (n. 21)

Motherhood: as basis for political rights, 213–19, 289 (n. 105); endowment of, 112–16, 210–11, 213, 266 (n. 105); as equivalent of soldiering, 2, 107, 115, 213, 219, 222, 227–29, 239, 241, 245, 266 (n. 87); and legal rights, 217, 289 (n. 120); and mourning, 10, 204–5, 212–13, 215–16, 226–46 passim; and pacifism, 38, 157–62, 164–65, 176, 206–7, 229, 232, 238, 245, 287 (n. 65); and patriotism, 2–3, 26–27, 37–38, 59, 62–63, 84–85, 96–97, 101–3, 111–12, 157–58, 164–65, 176, 182, 207, 213, 215–19, 245–46, 287 (n. 65); and sons, 37–38, 66–83, 86–87, 101, 147–48, 158–60, 205–7, 215–17, 219, 227–42, 245–46, 253 (n. 56), 285 (n. 22); unwed, 87–103 passim, 125–26, 205–6, 213, 244; and war, 2–3, 6–8, 264 (n. 60); and war work, 107–19 passim, 213, 244, 267 (n. 107); and women, 1, 5, 7, 17–18, 37–38, 125, 146–47, 182, 264 (n. 55), 269 (n. 38). *See also* Body: maternal; Rape: and motherhood

Mother's Union, 227

Mouflard, Gaston, 165, 171, 176, 178, 183

Mourning: communal, 226–27, 228–39; emblems of, 228, 292 (n. 9); and men, 22, 226–27, 228, 230, 241; and women, 10, 18, 33–34, 185, 204–5, 213, 215–17, 220, 223–42 passim, 245, 294 (n. 44)

Municipal vote: for French women, 216–18

Munitions work: and women, 102, 108–10, 114–19, 166, 170, 184, 213, 245, 267 (n. 107)

Mutinies, 166, 184

National Birth-Rate Commission, 116–17

National Council for Combating Venereal Diseases (NCCVD), 146, 148–49

Second International, 163

Senate, French, 90, 218–23; and participants in debate over women's suffrage, 219–23

Separation allowances, 87, 90–103 passim, 119, 261 (n. 2)

Service: of women during war, 5, 9, 19–20, 28–30, 111–19, 190–225 passim, 285 (n. 25)

Séverine (Caroline Guebhard), 165, 180–81, 222, 281 (n. 103)

Sexual education, 126, 145, 273 (n. 113)

Sexuality: double standard for, 98–99, 122, 125–28, 149; during First World War, 7, 30, 120–56 passim, 198–99; gay and lesbian, in wartime, 36–37, 199; and men, 259 (n. 59); and women, 9, 86–103 passim, 121–56 passim, 198–202, 257 (n. 34), 267 (nn. 6, 7, 9), 269 (n. 35). See also Prostitution; Soldiers: and sexual relationships

Sexual violence, 281 (n. 107); and British women, 98–99; and threats to women under occupation, 40–45, 84–85, 183. See also Rape

Shell shock: and air raids, 47–48, 255 (nn. 90, 91); and soldiers, 21, 33, 251 (n. 24), 252 (n. 52)

Sherman, Daniel, 227, 236, 292 (n. 5)

Siegfried, Julie, 144

Sinclair, May, 19–21, 49, 136

Smith, Lees, 144

Smith, Paul, 219

Smoking: during the war, 95, 121–22; and women, 121–22, 136, 155

Socialism, 158, 163, 166–69, 184; and feminism, 161–63, 168, 185–86, 188, 276 (nn. 24, 26)

Social Welfare Association, 128

Soldiers: American, and women, 127, 136–38; as audience for wartime media, 154; colonial and commonwealth, 124, 147, 257 (n. 34), 267 (n. 9); criticism of, 98–99, 186–87; and fatherhood, 89–105 passim, 261

(n. 7); and motherhood, 2, 14, 34, 107, 213, 227–33, 237, 239–42; and political rights, 190–91, 208–9, 224, 283 (n. 4); portrayed in literature, 13–18, 20–26, 34; portrayed on war memorials, 231–38; and sexual relationships, 91–103 passim, 123, 127–56 passim, 257 (n. 34), 267 (nn. 8, 9). See also Combatants; German military

Soldiers' and Sailors' Family Association (SSFA), 91–94

Somme, battle of the, 104

Stern, Ernesta, 34–35

Stewart, Mary Lynn, 107–8

Stopes, Marie, 101

Strauss, Paul, 109

Streatfeild, Lucy Dean, 95

Strikes, 166, 170, 184

"Suffrage for the Dead," 215–16

Suffragettes, 192–96, 203, 207, 253 (n. 55)

Sûreté, 164, 184

Swan, Annie S., 23, 25

Swanwick, Helena, 159–60, 162, 273 (n. 108), 274 (n. 8)

Syndicalism, 158, 167–68, 188

Syphilis. See Venereal diseases

Tchaikovsky, Barbara, 97, 100

Teachers: in France, 158, 167–70, 174, 178–79, 188, 278 (nn. 54, 55, 58, 64)

Theater, 132, 152–54; reception of, 153–54

Thébaud, Françoise, 52, 170, 202

Thomas, Monette, 218

Tinayre, Marcelle, 26–27, 49, 222

Tomb of the Unknown Warrior, 229–30, 242

"Tommy." See Soldiers

Torina, Martin de, 126

Toulouse, Edouard, 128

Trade unionism. See Syndicalism

Training camps, 129–30

Treason: trials for, 157–58, 165–89 passim, 277 (nn. 42, 43), 278 (n. 64), 280 (n. 85). *See also* Defeatism

Trials: criminal. *See* Abortion; Infanticide; Treason: trials for

Trotsky, Leon, 174

Tylee, Claire, 36

Underwood, Florence, 150

Uniforms: women and, 192–202, 207, 224, 241, 243, 284 (n. 21), 285 (n. 33)

Union Française pour le Suffrage des Femmes (UFSF), 42, 61, 144, 163, 215–17, 254 (nn. 74, 79)

Union sacrée, 165–66, 168, 202, 259 (n. 69), 276 (n. 33)

United States: troops in London, 136–37. *See also* Soldiers: American, and women

Vaughan, Helen Gwynne, 198, 285 (n. 33)

Venereal diseases, 122, 130, 137, 140–56 passim, 264 (n. 52), 272 (nn. 87, 97)

Verdun, battle of, 104, 205

Vernet, Madeleine, 175–76, 281 (n. 103)

Veterans, 241, 294 (n. 50)

Vincent, Catherine, 170

Vismes, Henriette, 124

Voluntary Aid Detachment, 291 (n. 2). *See also* Women: and war work

Voting rights. *See* Women's suffrage

Vuillermet, F. A., 104–5

Wade, George A., 147

Wainwright, L. (minister), 92–93

"War babies," 91–103 passim, 263 (nn. 48, 49)

Ward, Mrs. Humphry, 39

War literature, 7, 9, 12–38 passim; comparison of French and British, 35, 49, 82–83; English and French translations of, 13, 16 22, 39, 252 (n. 40); portrayal of atrocities in, 9, 66–85; and readers, 12; reception of, 13, 16,

21, 22, 24, 26, 30, 69–70, 72, 76–77, 81–82, 250 (n. 9); reviews of, 13, 16–17, 21–24, 26–27, 30, 69–70, 72, 76–77, 81–82, 250 (n. 9); romance in, 23–36 passim, 49; by soldiers, 5, 8, 13–18; and women writers, 8, 19–21, 23–38, 69–77, 82–83

War memorials: in Britain, 226–36, 241–42; and feminine images, 10, 227, 231–40, 293 (n. 31); in France, 226–27, 236–39, 241–42; unveiling ceremonies for, 227, 229–31, 242, 292 (n. 16), 293 (nn. 19, 36)

War work. *See* Women: and war work

Watson, Mona Chalmers, 198, 285 (n. 33)

Welfare: provisions for mothers and pregnant women, 55–56, 103–19 passim. *See also* Separation allowances

Welfare state, 6, 265 (n. 83)

Wells, H. G., 19, 21–23, 49

Wheeldon, Alice, 282 (n. 119)

White, Douglas, 145

White, Dundas, 94

Whitting, Harriet, 95

Widows. *See* Mourning: and women

Wilson, R. M., 212–13

Winnington-Ingram, Arthur, 99, 132–33

Winter, Jay, 226, 294 (n. 44)

Witt-Schlumberger, Marguerite de, 61, 104, 125–26, 144, 163, 215–16

Women: behavior criticized during wartime, 44, 124–39 passim; and citizenship, 5, 181–82, 190–225 passim, 283 (nn. 4, 9), 289 (n. 96); class relations among, 28–29, 87, 92, 184, 195, 204, 228–30, 292 (n. 13); and health during war, 89, 113–19; and identity, 1–10, 243–46; and military service, 192–204 passim, 283 (n. 9), 284 (nn. 12, 13), 287 (nn. 55, 61); and relations with men during war, 137–39, 155–56, 204, 214, 241, 257 (n. 34), 267 (n. 9), 270 (n. 61); and

CPSIA information can be obtained
at www.ICGtesting.com
Printed in the USA
LVHW03s1115190618
580835LV00002B/6/P

9 780807 848104